HISTORY OF THE UNITED STATES RUBBER COMPANY

HISTORY OF THE UNITED STATES RUBBER COMPANY

A CASE STUDY IN CORPORATION MANAGEMENT

GLENN D. BABCOCK

INDIANA BUSINESS REPORT NO. 39

BUREAU OF BUSINESS RESEARCH

GRADUATE SCHOOL OF BUSINESS / INDIANA UNIVERSITY

Price: $9.50

COVER DESIGN BY GARY C. SPRINGER

Preface

THERE HAS long been a need for a book such as this—a readable, reasonably concise history of a large corporation, focused primarily on the philosophy of management and corporate objectives during its early years of growth and development. Mr. Babcock's book is a rewarding look at the first fifty of almost seventy-five years in the life of United States Rubber Company.

This dynamic corporation, in business in scores of countries, is scarcely recognizable as the small company that started in 1892 when there were far more rubber-tired buggies than rubber-tired autos. In the half-century that followed, there was consolidation, diversification, regression, and reorganization. While the volume by Mr. Babcock records a half-century of change, there is *no* change, as he points out, in the basic principles that should guide management. This book is the story of how management policies were applied, and how they shaped the destiny of United States Rubber Company.

While many future generations of students of business will be indebted to the author of the present volume, the Indiana University Graduate School of Business is particularly privileged to have had the efforts and energy of the author. Mr. Babcock joined the School after a long and rewarding career in the rubber industry, which culminated in the presidency of the Mishawaka Rubber Company. At an age when many people seek the solace and comfort of gentler climates and less demanding schedules, Mr. Babcock started a new career for which his business experience provided a particularly sound infrastructure—the preparation and analysis of business cases for classroom use. His interest in finding cases uniquely applicable to sound principles of management led naturally into the lengthy and difficult work that produced this book. It has been a particular pleasure to have had Mr. Babcock working here in our midst during the preparation of the manuscript, and we feel his continued scholarly productivity is a source of inspiration to all of us.

We hope this book will serve to sharpen the memories of those who lived through these eventful years and will provide (for generations of students yet to come) a true picture of the environmental forces that influenced the decision of the period.

—W. George Pinnell
Dean, Graduate School of Business

Acknowledgements

OBVIOUSLY, this history could not have been compiled without the generous assistance of many individuals. The names of some appear in footnotes throughout the book. But many others in the company, either active or retired, have lent valuable assistance in many ways. I am deeply indebted to each who has helped, but am refraining from a lengthy listing of names at this point lest some be inadvertently omitted. Special mention, however, should be made of G. T. Pownall, secretary of United States Rubber Company, who first obtained approval for me to undertake the compilation of the history; I also wish to thank expressly H. E. Humphreys, Jr., a former president and chairman of the board, and George R. Vila, the present president and chairman of the board of United States Rubber Company, the two officers who gave that approval. Without their friendly interest and encouragement, much of the information in the history could not have been obtained.

I much appreciate the time taken by T. V. Horrigan and T. W. Nisius to make the necessary adjustments so that the financial data for some of the earlier years, particularly with respect to net income, would conform, as far as possible, to current accounting practice.

Reliance has been placed on the company archives and publications for considerable material; for example, all photographs have come from this source, unless otherwise credited.

Help also has been received from members of the faculty, graduate students, and staff of the School of Business, Indiana University, particularly from the editorial staff of the Bureau of Business Research. Finally, I would be very remiss if due acknowledgment were not made of the steadfast support given by Arthur W. Weimer, former dean, and W. George Pinnell, present dean of the School of Business.

GLENN D. BABCOCK

June, 1966

vii

Contents

ERRATA: *Page 121, line 22, for $10,441,000 read $9,459,000.*

Page 158, line 24, for Lawrence *read* Millville. *The Lawrence plant of the Lawrence Felting Company burned in 1877, and operations were moved to Millville.*

Illustrations

Tables

Introduction

THIS IS not an "official" history of the United States Rubber Company during the first fifty years of its corporate existence. It was not compiled at the request of that company or of any of its officials, nor was the undertaking financed by United States Rubber Company, directly or indirectly. The dean of the School of Business, Indiana University, reognized the desirability of a series of case studies dealing with a multiproduct, multiplant corporation with international operations that would be suitable for use in a graduate course in business administration. The present work stems from discussions he had with the author. The officers and other employees of the United States Rubber Company have cooperated freely in supplying information and material, but have not dictated the author's selection or omission of material. He has had complete freedom in, and assumes complete responsibility for, the choice of material and the presentation and interpretation of facts.

The corporation has undergone great changes during its existence. Its present physical plant and products little resemble those that comprised its tangible assets at the turn of the century. Even more noteworthy changes have occurred in its organization, its philosophy of management, and its corporate objectives. (Even its name has been changed; on April 19, 1966, the stockholders voted to change the name of the company to UniRoyal, Inc.) What then is the value of a history dealing primarily with management policies that have been altered to those better suited to current conditions?

The answer lies in the fact that while situations change, the principles of management do not; only the manner changes in which these principles are applied. The respective merits of various theories of management practice or of differing responses to new challenges may be more intelligently evaluated on some occasions through knowledge of former policy decisions and the effects flowing from such decisions. So although this history, confined as it is to the years 1892 to 1942, does not provide a picture of United States Rubber as constituted and functioning in 1966, it does discuss many of the forces, both internal and external, that have helped to mold the corporate image which the company has today.

The history is divided into four parts. The first covers the period prior to 1901; the other three cover the administrations of each of three presidents of the company: Colonel Samuel P. Colt, Charles B. Seger, and Francis B. Davis, Jr. Within each chapter, the subject matter is presented in much the same manner as it would be for a series of case studies, each dealing with a specific phase of the business during the given period. This arrangement precludes a strictly chronological recital of events, but enables the reader who is primarily interested in a particular aspect of the company's activities to quickly review the record pertaining to that activity. At the same time, the interrelation of the various operations is indicated. Except in a few instances, critical comment, either favorable or otherwise, has been avoided to permit the reader to form his own independent appraisal of the merits of the decisions, policies, and procedures that have been responsible for the growth of the company and have helped to determine its composition and character.

The history of United States Rubber is intensely interesting for the student of business administration. It affords many examples of astute management; it also provides instances of mistakes in weighing the relative importance of pertinent factors in certain situations. It has comprised distinct and successive periods of consolidation, expansion, and diversification, then regression, reorganization, rehabilitation, and strong recovery. Financially prosperous in its early years, the company dangerously skirted the brink of receivership for a few years, then successfully emerged from that critical condition.

Although the corporation's activities prior to World War II were confined almost exclusively to rubber and rubber-related items, its production was more diversified than that of any other member of the rubber industry, and in many fields its production exceeded that of any other manufacturer in the industry. Finally, though the importance of research and development may not have been fully recognized during the earlier periods, the company's development programs in more recent times have placed it in the forefront of rubber manufacturers.

The author's discussion of various matters is more detailed than would be customary in a volume designed for the general public, since the principal interests of individual students as well as of other readers will be quite diverse. They will embrace such varied subjects as accounting and finance, marketing, personnel and organization, production management, industrial engineering, product development, public relations, business law, international operations, and so on. To serve properly the purposes of such readers, an attempt has been made to present a reasonably comprehensive narrative.

Certain facts and observations will be of interest primarily to employees of the company who may not have had an opportunity to become familiar with the past records of departments or divisions of the company other than the ones in which they have been employed. The recital of circumstances connected with some events may help such readers to gain more benefit from the company's past experience. For this reason, some past mistakes and errors in judgment have been recorded.

In order to include sufficient information relating to a particular situation or development and still keep within the limitations of one convenient volume, it has been necessary for the author to make a rather arbitrary selection of subject matter and to devote relatively little or no space to other matters connected with the company's history. At the same time, the present work includes a limited amount of relevant background information pertaining to events that significantly influenced the affairs of the company. The half-century following the incorporation of the United States Rubber Company was importantly influenced by the invention of the internal combustion engine and the motorization of the American economy. The Spanish-American War was followed by years of deceptive international peace. It was an expansive period. World War I brought dislocations and stresses in the world economy that eventually contributed to the causes of the Great Depression of the early 1930's. Efforts by the British government to limit the exportation of crude rubber, independently during the 1920's and jointly with the Dutch and other governments in the 1930's, exacted tribute from consumers, principally from American rubber manufacturers. With the election of Franklin D. Roosevelt in 1932 came new policies and legislation affecting every type of business and almost every employer. The history of United States Rubber cannot be properly comprehended without some understanding of the effects of these and other controlling forces.

The company's history during its first fifty years emphasizes the necessity for well-informed, qualified personnel at all levels of management; the imperative need of efficient organization, operating with well-defined lines and areas of authority and responsibility; and the importance of clear, free communication of ideas as well as of information and directives. It illustrates the imponderable worth of *esprit de corps*, but also the inertial resistance, often inherent in corporate continuity, to marked or sudden shifts in over-all policy or objectives. It accentuates the value of adequate research and development programs. Above all, it underlines the paramount requisite, in such a highly diversified and complex corporation, of strong leadership, capable of realizing the full potential of strengths acquired through adherence to sound business principles, and the need of timely, effective, and profitable direction and coordination of its far-flung operations.

For over forty years prior to his retirement, the author was employed by the Mishawaka Rubber Company, Inc. (originally the Mishawaka Woolen Mfg. Co.), a subsidiary of the United States Rubber Company. The subsidiary, in its sale and distribution of BALL-BAND (Red Ball) footwear, actively competed with the parent company. Consequently, the author's background has given him a somewhat more detached viewpoint of the operations of United States Rubber than would have been possible under other circumstances. He has earnestly and conscientiously endeavored to present a factual, reliable, and impartial record of its growth and progress from 1892 through 1942.

In addition to bringing to a close the first half-century of the corporate existence of United States Rubber Company, 1942 was the first full year of our country's active military involvement in World War II. It also marked the end of the term of office of F. B. Davis, Jr. as president of the company. An important period of the corporate history had been completed; a new and exciting era was commencing. The record of the subsequent years could not be treated adequately within the present volume and therefore has not been included.

GLENN D. BABCOCK

I

Before 1901

First plant, Goodyear Metallic Rubber Shoe Co., Naugatuck, Conn., 1843.

Out of the Jungle

Prior to the white man's arrival in the Western hemisphere, natives of the South American jungles had learned to make use of the milky fluid, now known as rubber latex, found beneath the outer bark in a layer of soft bark (or cortex) of certain trees scattered through the jungle. The most important of these trees was the one they called the "weeping tree," which has since been named *Hevea brasiliensis.*

In some areas the *Hevea* trees, averaging from 30 to 60 feet in height, were abundant, rarely standing more than thirty paces apart. Two native *seringueiros* (rubber collectors), working as a team, would open a path connecting 100 to 120 *Heveas* in a rough loop. Starting before sunrise, the *seringueiro* would tap each tree by making an oblique incision in the bark with a hatchet having a blade about one inch long. On large old trees, as many as six slashes would be made. A clay cup to collect the rubber latex would be attached at the lower end of each incision. Since latex flows freely only in the early morning hours, the tapping had to be completed before the heat of the day.

Working his way back along the path to the camp, the native would rest for lunch and then start collecting the latex, emptying into a hollowed-out gourd or a bucket the very small amount of fluid that had collected in each cup. The quantity collected daily would vary. In Charles Goodyear's time the route was said to cover up to about 80 *Hevea* trees, from which the native would collect 1 to 2 gallons of latex a day; in 1940, from 2 to 3 gallons a day were reported to represent the average daily yield from 100 to 120 trees. In the Brazilian territory of

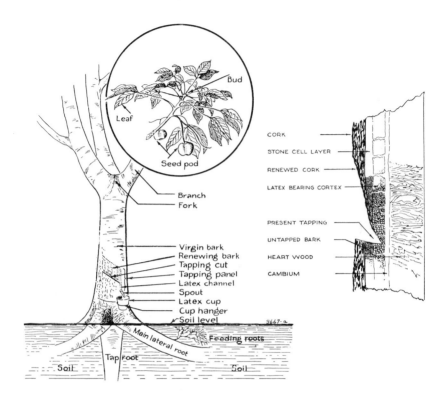

1.   Diagram of a rubber tree (Hevea brasiliensis). A full-grown rubber
tree averages 30-60 feet in height; its useful life is about 25 years.
Leaves grow to 8 inches in length and three to a stem. Rubber latex,
unlike sap, comes from the bark. The method of tapping illustrated is
commonly used on modern plantations.

SOURCE: P. W. Barker, *Rubber: History, Production, and Manufacture*, U.S. Dept. of
Commerce (Washington: U.S. Gov't Printing Office, 1940), p. 5.

Acre, collections have been said to average more than 5 gallons a day.
In 1922 the average annual yield from each tree on the United States
Rubber Company's plantations was said to be from 3 to 4 pounds of
rubber (dry weight).[1] Yield per tree has been increased materially
since then.

The tapping season began in May and lasted until January, but best
yields were obtained in the dry season from May to August, when rain
did not interfere with tapping and collecting. The rubber gathered then
usually commanded a higher price, since the rainy season adversely
affected latex stability. According to the Brazilian Ministry of Foreign

Affairs, the tapping season's yield of latex from a "path" of 100 to 120 trees in 1940 was about 1,700 to 1,800 pounds, from which the native *seringueiro* obtained 800 to 900 pounds of rubber.[2] Since a better daily yield was obtained when the trees were allowed to rest for a period, it was customary for at least two paths to be opened, each returning to the native's camp. Sometimes the native would work one path for about ninety days and then tap the trees along another path for the next ninety days.

Back at camp the *seringueiro* would empty the latex into a basin, cleaning it of foreign matter as he poured. He would then build a fire of palm nuts and place a funnel-shaped chimney over it to concentrate the smoke. The nuts used were generally those of the uricuri palm, and their smoke contained certain acidic ingredients such as acetic acid and the phenols. In the early nineteenth century it was customary for the native's wife or children to hold a clay form in the thick smoke and to turn it slowly while pouring latex over it. From twenty to twenty-five coats of latex would thus be deposited on the form, and a crude rubber bottle or rubber shoe would be fashioned. The smoking process had to be completed quickly or the latex would coagulate and then could not be deposited on the forms.[3]

As the demand for rubber increased, the crude forms for making rubber shoes were replaced by poles over which were built up large "biscuits" of rubber. In the early years of the rubber industry, these usually weighed 5 to 6 pounds, but later the weight ranged from 35 to 50 pounds each. Except for these biscuits and an improved hatchet and a tapping knife similar to the knives used on rubber plantations in the Far East, no significant change in the native *seringueiros'* methods has been observed during the five hundred years of recorded history on this subject.

The rubber shoes remained on the clay form for about four or five days, after which the clay was washed out and the shoes stuffed with grass or hay. During the next several months, the rubber would gradually harden enough to make the shoes serviceable.

The first white man believed to have had some realization of the potential commercial importance of rubber was a French scientist, Francois Fresnau, who, through his friend Charles Marie de la Condamine, made a comprehensive report on rubber to the French Academy in 1751. Condamine and Fresnau spent several years in scientific travel in northern South America. These two men are credited with giving rubber its French name *caoutchouc* (pronounced "kowchook"), which is a variation of the Indian word meaning "weeping tree."

COMMERCIAL BEGINNINGS

The commercial use of rubber began in 1791 when an Englishman, Samuel Peal, obtained a patent on a process for waterproofing fabric or leather by treating it with a solution of rubber in turpentine. The first U.S. patent involving rubber was granted in 1813 to Jacob F. Hummel for a gum elastic varnish made by a similar process. In 1811, J. N. Reithoffer established a factory in Vienna for the manufacture of elastics, the first factory in the world for manufacturing rubber articles. Thomas Hancock opened the first English rubber factory in 1820 in London, and, in 1823, Charles Macintosh opened the first in Scotland.[4]

About 1820, it is said, a pair of rubber shoes was brought to this country. About 500 pairs are believed to have been brought to Boston in 1825 by Thomas Crane Wales, the first Boston rubber footwear merchant.

One of the first dealers—perhaps the first dealer—in rubber shoes in New York City is said to have been S. C. Smith and Son, who held back their stock of rubber shoes until they were well seasoned and thus established for themselves a high reputation for the superior quality of their goods. The product was further improved by well-shaped wooden lasts, which were sent to Brazil by T. C. Wales to replace the crude clay forms. A large trade was rapidly built up for these rubber shoes, which could be purchased from the South American Indian for 15¢ to 20¢ a pair and retailed in Boston at prices ranging all the way from 50¢ to $5.00 a pair.

However, before these rubber shoes could be offered to the public in Boston, clay and dirt that had adhered to the inside had to be washed out, the upper edges trimmed, the shoes stretched over a last (sometimes heating was necessary), and the outside blackened. Next, the shoes were graded according to the evenness of texture, shapeliness, and the elaborateness of the design stamped on the upper by the natives. The most highly decorated shoes brought the best prices. Even the best of such rubber shoes were soft at moderate temperatures, tore readily, and were easily penetrated by stones and sticks underfoot.[5]

Charles Goodyear, writing in 1851, stated that the export of rubber shoes to the United States from Para, Brazil, had averaged 500,000 pairs annually since 1820, and that the "export of India rubber from Para in the form of shoes will no doubt continue for a long time to come." Apparently Goodyear's information regarding imports of rubber shoes was inaccurate. Official statistics are not available, but total

2. Primitive collecting and processing methods. The Brazilian *seringueiro* (right) is tapping a tree. Below, a native dips a paddle into the milky juice and turns it rapidly in the smoke until the rubber bakes. The operation was repeated until 5-6 pounds of rubber collected on the paddle. The "biscuit" was then cut off with a wet knife.

pairs of rubber shoes exported annually from Brazil, the bulk of which were imported into the United States during the period from 1837 to 1844 inclusive, have been estimated to range from a low of 128,000 pairs in 1839 to a high of 478,000 in 1842. U.S. imports of rubber shoes were recorded in long tons, and it is impossible to reconcile the two sets of figures.[6]

As early as 1819, Charles Macintosh, the Scottish manufacturer, had found that naphtha was a good solvent for rubber and that it did not have the objectionable odor of turpentine. By spreading a thin layer of the dissolved gum over a piece of fabric and laying another piece of cloth over the rubberized surface, he obtained a double texture material suitable for the raincoats that have since borne his name (spelled "mackintoshes"). He took out a patent on his process in 1823. Also about 1819, Thomas Hancock had begun cutting rubber into thin strips to make elastic thread for glove wristbands. Hancock, who possessed both an inventive mind and mechanical aptitude, took out several patents in England and Scotland connected with rubber manufacture. One of his inventions was a masticator; by calling it the "pickle," he was able for about twelve years to prevent disclosure of the real process. His machine, the first specially designed for processing rubber, consisted of a spike-covered cylinder turning in a chamber, into which Hancock put the scraps of rubber remaining after thread-like strips had been cut from a bottle or other rubber articles imported from South America.

Hancock had expected to find the rubber scrap ground into particles, but was pleasantly surprised to discover the process had compacted the material into a solid mass. Within a couple of years, Hancock had enlarged the masticator until it would handle 15 pounds of rubber at a time, and before long had one capable of turning out masticated blocks of rubber about 6 feet in length, 12 to 13 inches wide, and approximately 7 inches thick.[7] In 1826, Hancock and Macintosh entered into a working agreement concerning their respective patents, and built a new factory at Manchester, England to manufacture waterproof clothing.

Fortunately for the British manufacturers, the more humid, milder climate of the British Isles did not subject their products to the extremes of heat and cold characteristic of the northeastern section of the United States. Therefore, goods made of unvulcanized rubber gave reasonably satisfactory service in England and Scotland, and the industry prospered.

On Feb. 11, 1833, Edwin M. Chaffee, Roxbury, Mass., and some other residents of Roxbury and Boston incorporated the Roxbury India

3. Collecting and shipping biscuits of Para rubber.

Rubber Factory. The original capitalization of $30,000 was increased in 1834 to $240,000, to $300,000 in 1835, and to $400,000 in 1836. Great financial success was anticipated, and the ready sale of the early production seemed to justify these hopes. Other rubber companies were rapidly formed on Staten Island and in New York City; New Brunswick, N.J.; Woburn, Northampton, Springfield, Lynn, Salem, and Easton, Mass.; Providence, R.I.; Hamden and New Haven, Conn.; and Philadelphia. Investors purchased stock worth about $2 million in the rubber manufacturing concerns and looked for handsome profits.

The Roxbury company dissolved rubber in turpentine to which lampblack had been added, and applied the solution to fabrics to make them waterproof. These fabrics then were made into a wide variety of goods, including raincoats and life preservers as well as shoes, carriage curtains, and robes. Various solvents were used by the different companies. Some sent their fabric shoes to Brazil to be coated with fresh rubber latex. But whatever the method used, all these articles became sticky and foul smelling in summer when temperatures rose near 90° F., and were stiff and brittle when the temperature fell to about 40°.

In 1835, the Roxbury company's customers returned goods worth about $20,000, and returns in 1836 reached $30,000 at wholesale prices. Such returns, coming just when the country was entering the depression of 1837, not only forced the Roxbury company to discontinue operations, but brought about the failure of the other rubber companies that had been organized in this country. Usually there was a total loss of the capital invested. Consequently, when the panic of 1837 ended very few were willing to invest more money in such a profitless industry. By 1839, the total number of persons employed in all the rubber factories probably did not exceed one hundred, and the total value of their production was perhaps only $20,000. Such was the condition of the rubber industry immediately before Goodyear made his great discovery.

EXPERIMENTS BY CHARLES GOODYEAR

In 1834, Charles Goodyear (1800-60) saw at the store of the Roxbury India Rubber Company in New York City a life preserver made in the Roxbury factory. He returned to the store some months later to suggest an improvement in the construction of the inflating apparatus, but was informed that the company had received so many complaints and had had so much of its production returned that it was being forced to go out of business. He was told that fame and fortune awaited the man who could discover a way to render rubber suitable for use in all kinds of weather.

Goodyear was not a chemist, but he felt that he had been given a mission to perform. For the next five years, despite repeated failures and the most discouraging circumstances, he persisted in his efforts to find a method of treating rubber in order to make it tough and firm in extremes of heat and cold.

Goodyear's father, Amasa Goodyear, had a small factory in New Haven, Conn., where for many years he made various items of hardware, including a hayfork of spring steel that he had invented in 1810 and that was superior to the heavy iron forks then in common use. Amasa also made the first pearl buttons manufactured in the United States. Charles had gone to Philadelphia when he was seventeen and served an apprenticeship with a firm of hardware importers and merchants for four years, after which he returned to New Haven and became a partner with his father in Amasa Goodyear and Son. After marrying in 1824, he again went to Philadelphia in 1826 and opened the first store for the sale of domestic hardware in the United States. Unwise extension of credit forced him to suspend payments to his creditors in 1830, but he refused to consider bankruptcy, partly because this state would divest him of title to unfinished inventions. This decision led to his imprisonment for debt on several occasions, the first time being in 1830. While in jail, he continued to work on his inventions.

When he examined the life preserver in 1834 he was insolvent, subject to arrest for debt, and, on his return home to Philadelphia, he was again thrown into the debtor's prison. For some time Goodyear had been experimenting with rubber and now he began devoting all his energies and resources to seeking a way to make rubber suitable for general use. So began years of almost unbelievable privation and hardship, during which he was repeatedly imprisoned for debt. His wife and children loyally endured direst poverty, while he used every dollar he could obtain to carry on unceasing experiments. Furniture, his wife's jewelry, and even his children's textbooks were sacrificed. He prevailed upon a succession of men with some financial means to advance funds for his experiments—repeatedly unsuccessful. He borrowed from friends until they lost all faith in his ability to discover a satisfactory method of treating rubber and refused to lend any more money.

At times it seemed he had found the answer. He would enjoy respite from poverty, but on each occasion the success proved illusory, and

again he would be forced to beg assistance from friends. Between 1835
and 1836, he worked out a method of treating sheets of rubber by what
he referred to as the "nitric acid gas process." With it he made deco-
rative draperies that attracted considerable favorable attention. A patent
on this process was issued to Goodyear in 1837, and he soon received
an order from the government for 150 mail bags. However, he was
doomed to disappointment once more, for the mail bags and other articles treated by the acid gas process soon deteriorated. The gas had
hardened only the surface of the rubber; the remainder had not been
affected.

In 1838, Goodyear employed as an assistant Nathaniel M. Hayward,
who formerly had been in charge of the factory of the Eagle Rubber
Company, Woburn, Mass., until it had been forced to discontinue operation. Hayward disclosed to Goodyear that when rubber which had
been combined with a small amount of sulfur was exposed to sunlight,
the surface—but the surface only—was tougher and not sticky. He did
not appear to have recognized the full significance of his findings; furthermore, the strong odor of sulfur was unendurable. On Oct. 18, 1838,
Hayward appointed Goodyear as his agent to apply for a patent that
covered the use of sulfur, but not a heating or vulcanizing process,
agreeing to assign the patent to Goodyear for $100 cash, a six-month
note for $900, and a license to manufacture 300 yards of cloth a day
under the patent. The license was to be relinquished on payment of
$2,000 additional by Goodyear.[8] Goodyear now felt he was on the
brink of the discovery and made countless experiments using varying
amounts of sulfur and rubber, and varying degrees of heat, but never
intentionally subjecting the rubber compound to heat of more than
100° F. since sad experiences had shown that rubber would melt at
about 200° F. and, in sunlight, at about 100° or less.

The Great Discovery, 1839

In the winter of 1838-39, while standing near a hot stove in a room at
Woburn, a town then about ten miles from the limits of Boston, Goodyear happened to have in his hand a sample of fabric coated with a
compound containing rubber, sulfur, and white lead. While talking to
his brother and some friends who were in the room, Goodyear, in his
own words, "was surprised to find that the specimen, being carelessly
brought in contact with a hot stove, charred like leather."[9] About to
throw the material away in disgust at his own carelessness, he noticed
that a remarkable change had occurred. (The white lead in the "triple

compound," as he later referred to it, acted as an accelerator to speed the process of vulcanization. A compound including only rubber and sulfur would have cured so slowly that Goodyear might not have immediately realized what was taking place. Commercial manufacture of rubber products would not have been economically feasible without the use of such an accelerator.[10]) Goodyear was excited by the phenomenon but was unable to convince his brother or any of the others present that the changed nature of the material was "worthy of notice" or that he was any closer to ultimate success. They had been disappointed on too many previous occasions.

Not until 1844, after five more years of endless trials and careful observation of the results of each experiment, did he succeed in developing an economical process with certain outcome. The severest hardships encountered by the experimenter and his family were still ahead of him. Fortunately, his brother-in-law, William DeForest, came to his support. DeForest, who was a prominent woolen manufacturer, supplied Goodyear with funds that totaled, over a period of years, about $45,000, and that enabled Goodyear to conduct the necessary numerous experiments and to care for his family. Only after the death of the inventor in 1860 did DeForest obtain partial repayment, when his claim against the estate was settled for $30,000.

Goodyear filed with the U.S. Patent Office on Nov. 6, 1841 a caveat or "claim for record" claiming invention of a compound consisting of one pound of gum elastic, $\frac{1}{4}$-$\frac{1}{2}$ pound of sulfur, and $\frac{1}{2}$-1 pound of white lead.

The dissolved gum and the white lead and sulfur, ground with spirits of turpentine, could be applied to fabrics and subjected to a temperature of 270° F. He did not make formal application for a patent until July 5, 1843, receiving patent No. 3633 on June 15, 1844. He also filed for patents in England and France and received the French patent on April 11, 1844.

Goodyear's Patents Abroad

Goodyear was not granted an English patent. In 1836, through the kind services of Dr. Joseph Bradshaw, who had been treating him for a fever contracted during the course of his experiments, Goodyear had sent to England samples of rubber drapery treated by the "acid gas process" in an effort to interest a manufacturer in aiding him financially. These are said to have come to the attention of Thomas Hancock, then a partner with Charles Macintosh.[11]

Hancock, in his "Personal Narrative of the Origin and Progress of the Caoutchouc or India-Rubber Manufacture in England," related that he had seen a sample of cambric coated with rubber about 1840 but did nothing about it. In August, 1842, he was shown some samples of "improved rubber," which had been taken to England by Stephen Moulton to whom they had been entrusted by Goodyear for the purpose of negotiating sale of his vulcanizing process to British manufacturers.

Since Moulton was unable to describe to the principals of Charles Macintosh and Company the method by which the samples had been produced, they declined to invest in the process, according to Hancock's narrative. He said he then began to experiment with sulfur to try to duplicate Goodyear's results. On Nov. 21, 1843, he filed an application for a patent on vulcanization in England, eight weeks before Goodyear, on Jan. 30, 1844, applied for an English patent. The existing British law required Hancock to swear, not that he was the inventor, but only that he was the introducer of the invention into England. The law allowed him six months in which to file detailed specifications of his claims. Before the expiration date, he worked out the essential steps in the process and was granted a patent on May 30, 1844. Meanwhile, the French patent granted Goodyear had been published on April 16, 1844, and may or may not have come into Hancock's hands in time to have provided him with useful data. At any rate, Hancock at a later date made statements under oath indicating that he was indebted to Goodyear for practically the entire substance of the patent he had obtained.[12]

The first important shipments of rubber footwear made in America under Goodyear's patent arrived in England in 1847. The rights of the American Goodyear licensees to sell their products in the United Kingdom were contested, and shortly afterwards the Hayward Rubber Company of Colchester, Conn., in consideration of a royalty to be paid to Charles Macintosh and Company, was granted the sole right to sell its rubber footwear in the British market.

Between 1847 and 1856, the validity of the Hancock patent on vulcanization was repeatedly attacked in the British courts by the group of American manufacturers licensed under the Goodyear patents and known as Goodyear Associates and Licensees. The courts upheld the Hancock English patent, but Goodyear meanwhile had obtained a Scotch patent. An application on Goodyear's behalf had been filed in Scotland on March 12, 1844, more than three months before Hancock applied for a Scotch patent, and Goodyear's specifications were filed Sept. 11, 1844, while Hancock's were not filed until Oct. 19 of that year.

Goodyear obtained full rights over the Scottish patent in November, 1852, and in August, 1856, they were transferred to the directors of the North British Rubber Company, Edinburgh, Scotland (originally organized as Norris and Company). The original partners in that firm were five Americans who had put a little over $100,000 into the venture. They were James Bishop (25%), John R. Ford (25%), Christopher Meyer (25%), B. F. Breeden (15%), and Spencer T. Parmalee (10%). On Oct. 30, 1855, 205 cases of rubber factory machinery and fixtures not currently needed by Ford & Company at their New Brunswick, N.J. plant were shipped to Scotland. The shipment included everything needed for initial operation of a rubber footwear factory except a vulcanizing heater, a steam engine for power, and some shoe lasts, which were purchased in Glasgow. The shipment of machinery was valued at more than $13,000 and represented a little more than one-half of Ford's share in the venture.

Henry Lee Norris, a partner of James Bishop and Company, arrived in Glasgow in the winter of 1855 and succeeded in making all preliminary arrangements for establishment of the firm, including lease of a factory building. Since an alien, unless naturalized, could not hold land in Scotland, the firm of Norris and Company was reorganized in 1856 as North British Rubber Company, Ltd., and in that year it began the first manufacture of rubber footwear outside the United States.

Meyer is believed to have been the one who first thought of establishing branch manufacturing operations in Scotland, but he needed the cooperation of Bishop and Ford. Bishop was a prosperous shipping and commission agent, and is considered to have been the most influential member of the group. His New York firm conducted all the initial transactions involving the transference of funds, recruitment of workers, and shipment of crude rubber, machinery, and supplies. The operation was very profitable during the early years, but in 1864 the principal American stockholders began to extend their commitments at New Brunswick and to withdraw from Scotland. Eventually, the North British Rubber Company passed into British hands.[13] In the 1850's American branches of the rubber industry were also founded at Hamburg and Harburg, Germany, and at St. Petersburg, Russia.[14]

The Inventor's Philosophy

Charles Goodyear took out several more patents pertaining to rubber manufacture, and received many thousands of dollars from royalties, sale of licenses, and court judgments, but his unflagging efforts to discover additional uses for rubber "so as to form a connected system of inventions,"[15] his unwise and even lavish expenditures whenever he had funds at his disposal, coupled with extended litigation and poor health, combined to keep him in financial difficulties until his death in 1860. At the time of his death he owed over $200,000, but the royalties and other returns from licenses granted for the rights to manufacture and sell goods embodying one or more of his patents are believed to have provided sufficient funds to pay all his creditors and leave a small balance for his heirs in the few years before the patents expired.

Goodyear's account of his years of pioneer work is entitled "Gum Elastic and Its Varieties, with a detailed account of its applications and uses, and of The Discovery of Vulcanization." Copies of the first edition were bound with hard India rubber, and the plates and maps were printed on India rubber fabric. A few copies intended for use in public libraries were printed on thin sheets of rubber tissue, and were also bound with hard rubber. One statement in this work helps to explain the author's indomitable courage and persistence as well as his ultimate success:

> "The inventor was, however, encouraged in his efforts by the reflection, that that which is hidden and unknown, and cannot be discovered by scientific research, will most likely be discovered by accident, if at all, and by the man who applies himself most perseveringly to the subject, and is most observing of everything relating thereto."[16]

Others before Goodyear, in Europe and in America, had experimented with combinations of rubber and sulfur. The important difference between their work and that of Goodyear lies in (1) his "triple compound" of rubber, sulfur, and white lead; (2) his discovery of the effect of a higher degree of heat than had previously been considered practical for working with a rubber compound; (3) his thoroughness in seeking to determine the most advantageous degree of heat and the timing of its application; (4) his equal thoroughness in observing the effect of variations in the proportions of the ingredients; and (5) his recognition of the practical applications of his discoveries.

To dramatize as well as demonstrate its many possible uses, Goodyear had a great variety of articles made of rubber. These included a desk, styled in the manner of Louis XV, embodying highly polished hard rubber, and specially made for exhibition at the Crystal Palace in Hyde Park, London in 1851. About 1850 he had his portrait painted on hard rubber by G. P. A. Healey, one of the celebrated artists of the period. These articles, together with a walking cane of hard rubber and other memorabilia of Goodyear, were displayed for years in the

CHARLES GOODYEAR

Library of Congress

4. Charles Goodyear and Goodyear memorabilia. The portrait of Goodyear in the photograph at right (painted on hard rubber), the table utilizing hard rubber, and Goodyear's canes were displayed in C. B. Seger's reception room.

reception room of the office of the president of United States Rubber, and in 1915 were exhibited in one of the large display windows of the headquarters building at 1790 Broadway.[17]

By 1851, Goodyear considered rubber a possible substitute for a number of other materials, among which he listed the following (obviously, he did not foresee the role of rubber tires in the development of either the bicycle or motor vehicle) :

Steel or iron—Car springs
Lead, copper, zinc—Roofing, tubes, kitchenware
Stone—Gritted goods
Wood or leather—Boxes, trunks, and the like; boots, shoes, carriage cloths, belting
Cordage—Twine, tape
Cloth—Carpeting, umbrellas, sails, furniture covering
Oil silk or oil cloth—Surgical articles, medical uses, floor cloth
Paper, parchment—Maps, charts, globes
Crockery, glassware—Pitchers, ewers
Wickerwork—Baskets
Sponge and curled hair—Mattresses, pillows
Bristles—Brushes, scrubs.[18]

A curious circumstance connected with the discovery of the vulcanization process is that, although Goodyear was given some assistance by Professor L. D. Gale of New York College of Pharmacy, New York University, and Professor Benjamin Silliman of Yale, chiefly through their endorsement of some of his experimental methods and of the results of some of these experiments, Goodyear's discovery was admittedly and in fact empirical. After more than a century of research and development, the actual nature of the vulcanization process still remained to be determined scientifically.[19]

[1] *Between US,* house organ of United States Rubber Company (February, 1922), p. 18.

[2] Other sources give conflicting reports of rubber yields obtained from *Hevea* trees growing wild in the Brazilian jungle. Percy H. Walker, Bureau of Standards, U.S. Dept. of Commerce, said in 1916 the average yield per tree was about 6 or 7 pounds of latex, equal to 3 to 5 pounds of dry rubber. See *Proceedings of the Second Pan-American Scientific Congress, Washington, D.C., 1915-1916* (Washington: U.S. Gov't Printing Office, 1917), p. 376.

[3] Charles Goodyear, *Gum Elastic and Its Varieties,* I, 1853, privately published, New Haven, pp. 43-46; W. A. Gibbons, "The Rubber Industry, 1839-1939," *Industrial and Engineering Chemistry,* XXXI (October, 1939), 1,199 ff.; and *Brazil, 1939-40, An Economic, Social and Geographic Survey* (Rio de Janiero: Ministry of Foreign Affairs).

[4] P. W. Barker, *Rubber: History, Production, and Manufacture,* U.S. Dept. of Commerce (Washington: U.S. Gov't Printing Office, 1940), pp. 2-3.

[5] Nancy Paine Norton, "Industrial Pioneer: The Goodyear Metallic Rubber Shoe Company," I, 1950, unpublished dissertation, Radcliffe College, pp. 12, 13; *Between US* (May, 1918), pp. 12-13.

[6] See P. W. Barker, *Rubber Industry of the United States,* U.S. Dept. of Commerce (Washington: U.S. Gov't Printing Office, 1939), p. 3.

[7] "Annals of Rubber," reprinted from *India Rubber World* (New York. 1936), p. 2.

[8] *Between US* (November, 1923), pp. 7, 8.

[9] *Gum Elastic and Its Varieties,* p. 118.

[10] "Industrial Pioneer: The Goodyear Metallic Rubber Shoe Company," p. 27.

[11] Howard and Ralph Wolf, *Rubber, A Story of Glory and Greed* (New York: Covici-Friede, 1936), pp. 304-5.

[12] "Annals of Rubber," p. 7.

[13] William Woodruff, "The American Origins of a Scottish Industry," *Scottish Journal of Political Economy,* II (February, 1955), pp. 17-31. Also see "Annals of Rubber," p. 12.

[14] William Woodruff, "An Inquiry into the Origins of Invention and the Intercontinental Diffusion of Techniques of Production in the Rubber Industry," *The Economic Record* (Melbourne: December, 1962), p. 483; also William Woodruff, *The Rise of the British Rubber Industry During the Nineteenth Century* (Liverpool: Liverpool University Press, 1958), pp. 210-17.

[15] *Gum Elastic and Its Varieties,* p. 226.

[16] *Gum Elastic and Its Varieties,* p. 101. Known copies of this book are in the possession of Yale and Harvard Universities, New York Public and Los Angeles Public Libraries, North British Rubber Company, Goodyear Tire and Rubber Company, Boston Public Library, and the Library of Congress.

In 1936, the *India Rubber Journal* quoted a letter from the curator of the Rare Book Collection, Library of Congress, which said, "Some years ago a representative of the Goodyear Company brought to the Rare Book Room one of the copies printed on india rubber. It had been affected by the heat to such an extent that the rubber had melted so that the pages stuck together. The book had actually become merely a block of rubber." *India Rubber Journal,* XCI (April 11, 1936), p. 430.

The copy in the possession of Goodyear Tire and Rubber Company was on display at the Smithsonian Institution until the latter part of 1963. However, that copy was not printed on rubber; it has an elaborately engraved hard rubber cover, and Paul Campbell, historian in charge of the collection of memorabilia of Charles Goodyear for the Goodyear Tire and Rubber Company, has reported the copy to be in good condition.

[17] *Between US* (January, 1916), p. 7. Also see *"U.S." Rubber News,* house organ of United States Rubber Company (Nov. 15, 1925), pp. 10-11.

[18] *Gum Elastic and Its Varieties,* p. 179. Goodyear listed more than six hundred items that could be made out of rubber, including a "Wheel-barrow tire . . . an English invention."

[19] "An Inquiry into the Origins of Invention and the Intercontinental Diffusion of Techniques of Production in the Rubber Industry," p. 482.

2

Consolidations Effected

Prior to 1840, the largest annual production of uncured rubber footwear, made mostly by natives in the countries where crude rubber was gathered, was estimated to be 400,000 to 500,000 pairs. Within about eight years after the manufacture of vulcanized rubber footwear began in 1843, about 15,000 pairs per day were produced in the United States under Charles Goodyear's patent.[1] From Goodyear's basic discoveries developed the modern rubber industry, in which the United States Rubber Company was the third largest corporation in 1965.[2]

The corporation formed by the 1892 consolidation of nine domestic manufacturers of rubber boots and shoes developed into the exceedingly complex structure that now ranks among the fifty largest manufacturing corporations in our country. The application for listing the stock of the company on the New York Stock Exchange, dated Dec. 1, 1892, claimed total assets of slightly less than $13 million. In contrast, the annual report for 1964 showed net sales of $1,086,588,000, working capital of $305 million, and net worth of $364,549,000.

The company in 1965 had 62,000 employees. They were engaged in the manufacture and marketing of approximately 33,000 items, produced in 89 plants (located in 20 states and 22 foreign countries),[3] and sold in about 180 countries. The international business of the company represented about 25% of its total sales in 1964. In 1964, the company's rubber plantations had over 83,000 acres in cultivation, with an annual yield of approximately 39 million pounds of rubber in dry forms or as latex (dry content). However, products using rubber (natural or synthetic) were responsible for only 80% of total sales dollars in recent years. In 1961, for example, natural rubber accounted for only about 9% of the total value of all materials consumed by the company. In 1964, United States Rubber ranked as one of the 20 largest chemical manufacturers, annually producing about 50 million pounds of chemicals with annual sales in excess of $130 million. It also was among the 15 largest textile producers in the nation, and an important manufacturer of vinyl fabric and other plastic products.

The corporation was also a major supplier of the 500 parts that the rubber industry made for motor vehicles in 1964. Among the more important items were tires, foam cushions, upholstery fabrics, shock-resistant padding, rigid plastic parts, door seals, and floor mats. About 20% of the company's total output went into new cars. United States Rubber continued to be the leading manufacturer of rubber footwear and rubber-soled fabric footwear, made more bicycle tires than any other company in the United States, and made more firehose, more golf balls, and more bathing caps than any other manufacturer in the world.[4]

Such tremendous growth and diversification was not accomplished without strains and stresses, often more acute because of the wide and erratic fluctuations in the price of crude rubber, which plagued manufacturers of rubber products prior to the development of the synthetic rubber industry during World War II. However, no attempt is made in this review of the historical background of the United States Rubber Company to treat in full detail the events that occurred during the first fifty years of its corporate existence, but rather to show how various policies and actions influenced its subsequent history.

ATTEMPTS AT ORGANIZATION TO 1890

To comprehend the factors bearing upon decisions affecting policies and objectives that must be made by the top management of the company today, it is helpful to know something of the circumstances surrounding the formation and development of the company. On April 3, 1841, Nathaniel Hayward was granted a license to manufacture or to authorize any other persons to manufacture under his inspection "boots and shoes of felt or woolen cloth and India rubber . . . under all the patents heretofore taken out by said Goodyear or that may hereafter be taken out by him . . . and to sell the said boots and shoes so manufactured. . . ." The agreement provided that if Goodyear should pay to Hayward $1,000 in six months, the license should be considered null and void. Goodyear failed to pay the $1,000, and Hayward transferred the license to Leverett Candee of New Haven, Conn., on Aug. 22, 1843. The previous year, Candee had entered into a partnership with Henry and Lucius Hotchkiss under the firm name of Leverett Candee for the manufacture of rubber shoes. (An advertisement for this company appears in Figure 5.) Candee has been said to be the first Goodyear licensee, but this cannot be stated definitely since some of the early records have been lost.

In his work *Gum Elastic and Its Varieties* Goodyear stated that "the Naugatuck Company . . . was the first company licensed." Probably he referred to Samuel J. Lewis and Company, Naugatuck, which started manufacture of vulcanized rubber overshoes in 1843, and was reorganized in 1845 as the Goodyear Metallic Rubber Shoe Company. (This was the official corporate name, although "Goodyear's Metallic Rubber Shoe Company" was used in printed matter for many years.) The United States Rubber Company possesses an unsigned, undated, handwritten copy of a partnership agreement between the four Lewis brothers, Milo, Thomas, Samuel J., and William B. of Naugatuck. This document has been described as the "oldest relic in existence having to do with beginnings of the rubber industry."[5] It referred to "the India rubber shoe business in which he Samuel J. is now engaged . . .," and in a later section stated: "The business . . . at the shoe shop . . . shall be done in the name of S. J. Lewis & Co. . . ." Since the firm of Samuel J. Lewis & Co. is known to have started in 1843, it is believed that the agreement between the brothers was executed previously, and that therefore Samuel was engaged on his own account before the firm of Samuel J. Lewis & Co. was formed. (Appendix B includes an exact copy of the agreement.)

Both Candee and G.M.R. were later among the companies consolidated in 1892 to form the United States Rubber Company. By 1848, four additional firms were licensed to make rubber boots and shoes under the Goodyear patent: Newark India Rubber Company, Newark, N.J.; Ford and Company, Milltown, N.J.; Hayward Rubber Company, Colchester, Conn.; and Onderdonk and Letson, New Brunswick, N.J.

These six firms entered into a voluntary association known as Goodyear Associates and Licensees, and agreed to pay into a common fund —to be used for prosecution of infringers of the patent—a royalty of 3¢ a pair on all salable footwear manufactured under the Goodyear license. This sum was in addition to the royalty of one-half cent a pair paid to Goodyear. They also agreed on minimum prices and maximum discounts, and further agreed to meet annually to decide on prices.

5.   Advertisement for Candee tennis shoes.

By 1851, according to Charles Goodyear's record, some twenty manufacturing establishments were operating under licenses granted by him. These included manufacturers not only of rubber footwear but also of other articles vulcanized under his patents.[6] For the purpose of the present study, the discussion of the events of the period during the remainder of the century is largely confined to those affecting the rubber footwear industry.

From 1852 until the Goodyear patents expired in 1865, a tight control over production of rubber footwear as well as prices was maintained, with severe cash fines for noncompliance with the terms of the agreements. To ensure payment of fines that might be levied, each firm was required to give to Candee three $2,500 notes. In 1852, the firms then included in the group of associates and licensees assigned the following production quotas, taking into consideration both plant capacity and inventory as of April 1, 1852:

	Inventory, April 1, 1852 (in pairs)	Production Quota (in pairs)
Candee	150,000	300,000
Ford	180,000	280.000
G.M.R.	73,000	310,000
Hartshorn	70,000	320,000
Hayward	275,000	400,000
New Brunswick	60,000	320,000
Newark	60,000	320,000
	868,000	2,250,000

The quotas were revised each year and by 1857 were divided into quantities permitted for the domestic and foreign markets.[7]

By 1853[8] eight companies with total capitalization of $1,200,000 were in the group of associates and licensees; five were to become subsidiaries of United States Rubber. In June of that year, a committee representing the eight firms recommended formation of a company to be capitalized at $1,800,000. Provision was made for acquiring the constituent companies by purchase of the capital stock or of the assets at the book or appraised value; provision was made also for purchase of the Goodyear patent rights and for eliminating duplication of similar products in various plants.

If these provisions were carried out, said the committee, "We should then have in reality what we now have but in name, one interest and no competition." The committee estimated that savings in selling expenses, salaries of officers, purchases of crude rubber, and in manufacturing costs would total $472,000 a year. Profits of the eight companies averaged annually about $480,000 or 40% on the current capitalization; if the profits were only $420,000, the added savings would make $892,000 available for dividends, according to the committee.

Apparently no agreement on the proposed consolidation was reached, but the eight companies continued to join in issuing to the trade an annual letter containing the agreed prices and terms. Between 1865 and the formation of the United States Rubber Company in 1892, a series of agreements and attempted agreements was aimed at improving profits by maintaining prices, limiting production, or consolidating the several companies. An agreement for fixing prices was made by the Associated Rubber Shoe Companies and maintained until 1886; in 1876, six of the nine companies then in the association bought and closed the factory of the Newark India Rubber Company. In 1886, the Rubber Boot and Shoe Selling Company, having exclusive charge of sales for five constituent companies, was incorporated in Massachusetts with a capital of $300,000. This "selling company" was dissolved in 1887, but the several companies continued to agree on prices.

In 1882, Dr. B. F. Goodrich sent a letter to various rubber companies proposing a "central company" with capitalization of $25 million, which would absorb the sixty-two companies he said were then making mechanical rubber goods, clothing, or boots and shoes. Such a company, he said, would also "control the crude rubber product of the world." Goodrich added that the rubber "business is unstable, liable to great fluctuations, and does not yield a reasonable return on the investment; all are constantly tempted to disregard cost of production while endeavoring to hold customers . . ." (see Figure 6). Evidently not enough rubber footwear companies were interested in the project. In 1886, the Central Rubber Company, a Rhode Island corporation, was formed to control the mechanical rubber goods market. Except for the Erie Rubber Company, Erie, Pa., and the B. F. Goodrich Company, Akron, Ohio, all the companies brought together in this corporation were located in Trenton, N.J. Dissension among the stockholders resulted in court actions, and the corporation was dissolved in 1892.

Between 1886 and 1888, another attempt was made to form a new corporation to buy the stock of ten boot and shoe companies. The plan was carefully considered but never materialized. In 1889, ten out of fourteen active companies making rubber boots and shoes formed the Rubber Boot and Shoe Manufacturers' Association. Apparently their principal objective was to secure higher prices for their products, for the prices of crude rubber had increased rapidly following the popularity of bicycles, which had begun to use pneumatic rubber tires.[9]

6. Average annual prices, Para rubber and all commodities, 1856-90 (see Table A-1; 1860=100).

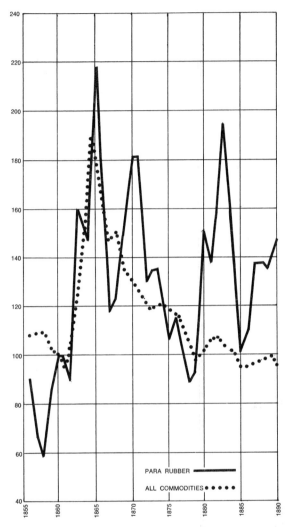

The list of all the companies manufacturing rubber footwear in 1890 (Table 1) is arranged in order of their probable net sales for that year as estimated by one described as a "leading rubber manufacturer." All of these companies except the last two (Goodyear and Lambertville) became part of the United States Rubber "system."[10]

The Census of Manufactures for the fiscal year ended May 31, 1890 reported total value of all rubber manufactures as $42,854,000. There-

TABLE 1.   Rubber footwear manufacturers, 1890.

Incor- porated		Estimated Net Sales in 1890
1853	Boston Rubber Shoe Company*	$ 5,000,000
1867	Woonsocket Rubber Company	3,500,000
1852	The L. Candee and Company†	2,500,000
1845	Goodyear Metallic Rubber Shoe Company‡	1,500,000
1878	American Rubber Company	1,500,000
1881	Para Rubber Shoe Company	1,500,000
1888	Colchester Rubber Company§	1,250,000
1877	New Jersey Rubber Shoe Company‖	1,000,000
1847	Goodyear's India Rubber Glove Manufacturing Company#	1,000,000
1861	Meyer Rubber Company**	750,000
1850	New Brunswick Rubber Company	750,000
1888	Brookhaven Rubber Company	750,000
1864	National India Rubber Company ††	500,000
1890	Lycoming Rubber Company‡‡	500,000
1878	Boston Rubber Company	250,000
1872	Goodyear Rubber Company	250,000
1860	Lambertville Rubber Company	200,000
		$22,700,000

*Originally incorporated as Malden Manufacturing Company; name changed, May 17, 1855.
† The firm of Leverett Candee was first organized in 1842 for manufacture of rubber footwear.
‡ Succeeded partnership of Samuel J. Lewis and Company, organized in 1843.
§ Plant formerly owned by Hayward Rubber Company.
‖ Succeeded New Jersey Rubber Company formed in 1870.
Probably succeeded Litchfield India Rubber Company formed in 1844 "for the purpose of manufacturing and selling India Rubber Gloves and other India Rubber Goods"; Litchfield is the only company in which Charles Goodyear is known to have been a stockholder.
**Christopher Meyer started in the rubber business in 1844 or before.
††About 1840, George O. Bourn started manufacture of rubber shoes with leather soles and heels.
‡‡ A limited partnership, "Lycoming Rubber Company, Limited," was organized Sept. 15, 1882.

SOURCE: Walter Emery, "First Section of History of United States Rubber Company," unpublished, United States Rubber Company, company archives, 1946.

fore, if the foregoing estimate of sales of rubber footwear in 1890 was approximately correct, footwear then represented about half of the rubber industry.

CONSOLIDATION ACTIVITIES OF CHARLES R. FLINT

The obvious advantages that would result from an effective consolidation of the principal manufacturers of rubber boots and shoes aroused the active interest of Charles R. Flint. Born in 1850 into a family that at one time owned the second largest fleet of sailing vessels under the American flag, Flint had operated as an international merchant, financier, and negotiator. Among other items, he dealt in munitions (including naval war vessels), and at different times he outfitted and sold ships to various nations, including Brazil, Japan, and Russia. At the request of Brazil, he even provided officers and crews for war vessels furnished by him when the Brazilian navy tried to start a revolution. As one of the original partners in W. R. Grace & Co., he was intimately acquainted with South America, and became a dealer in crude rubber in 1878.[11] Instrumental in forming a successful and profitable combination of the principal importers and dealers in crude rubber, Flint was also an organizer of consolidations in the wool, chewing gum, electric, and several other industries.

In his autobiography, he wrote, "I have consistently advocated such [industrial] consolidations as a most essential factor in economic development." In a talk given in Boston in 1899, he listed the following benefits that he claimed could result from consolidated management:

Purchase of raw material at more favorable prices
Use of specialized machinery and processes, resulting in lower costs
Improved quality of the product
Fewer styles
Higher standards
Production channelled to most efficient or best located plants
Prevention of loss by moving production to other plants in case of local work stoppage for any reason
Fewer but better salesmen; fewer but better branches
More uniform terms and conditions of sale
Credits more safely granted
Less inventory; less cost for storage
Less interest paid; less cost for insurance
Greater skill in management applied to whole organization rather than to part only
Benefits of comparative accounting and comparative administration, resulting in a much lower market price benefiting consumers.[12]

It was Flint's belief that industrial consolidations were best accomplished by "a disinterested intermediary, who as a neutral would have commanded the confidence of the manufacturers, and who would have secured all the facts necessary to formulate a plan."

In 1889, New Jersey enacted an amendment to its general incorporation law that cleared the way for formation of a holding company empowered to acquire the majority of the voting capital stock of subsidiaries, locally chartered in New Jersey or other states. This legislation made it possible to avoid the restrictions enjoined by some states on out-of-state corporations, which often were prohibited from owning real estate in the state or were subjected to special taxes. Evidently Flint quickly recognized the opportunities opened by this legislation. He related that he told several of the rubber manufacturers who interviewed him in 1892 that he could bring about a consolidation within sixty days if he were left free to handle the negotiations, and if the manufacturers would agree not to discuss consolidation with one another. To this offer, he said, they consented.

Flint could scarcely describe himself as an entirely "disinterested intermediary" in the formation of the United States Rubber Company, for in 1891 the Lycoming Rubber Company, Williamsport, Pa. had sold him $50,000 of its capital stock and had given him two separate options to buy additional stock. Apparently he exercised these options, since his interest represented 3,300 shares at Lycoming's annual meeting on May 16, 1892. In September and October, 1892, United States Rubber acquired from the Flint syndicate 3,990 of the 4,000 shares then outstanding of Lycoming's capital stock.

Flint related in his autobiography that the participating manufacturers supplied him with detailed financial statements, which he treated confidentially. He then formulated the plan of consolidation. His negotiations were conducted with each company separately, in accordance with the observation stated in his autobiography that "in organizing, it is well not to bring the interested parties together until all have been brought into agreement; for otherwise some kind of argument is bound to start, and once an argument gets under way so many ancient grudges pop out that the real purpose of the meeting is soon lost in a general disagreement."[13]

On Jan. 27, 1892, an agreement was signed by the banking firm of H. B. Hollins and Company and the "subscribers," providing for formation of a company to be known as The United States Rubber Corporation or some other appropriate title (see Appendix C). The company was to have the right to issue $25 million of 8% noncumulative preferred stock, and $25 million of common stock. The preferred stock was to be issued in payment for "various plants or interests now engaged in the manufacture of rubber boots and shoes within the United States," which might be acquired by the company; value of the plants, equipment, and all other assets were to be subject to appraisal, and the net worth of the receivables to be guaranteed by the sellers. The common stock would "represent the increased earning capacity by reason of the consolidation" and would be issued to an amount equal to the issue of preferred. In payment for all expenses incurred in organizing the company, Hollins would be paid 5% of the total capital stock of the company, payment to be made in common stock only as the stock of the company should be issued.

A separate agreement, dated Feb. 1, 1892, by H. B. Hollins and Company with Charles R. Flint, Joseph P. Earle, and Richard C. Sibley (see Appendix C), shows Flint to have been the principal promoter of the project; the commission received under the first agreement was to be divided—$200,000 to Flint, $100,000 to Hollins, $100,000 to Earle, and the remaining commission to be divided in four equal parts between Flint, H. B. Hollins and Company, Earle, and Sibley.

Next, Flint enlisted the support of men of recognized importance outside the rubber industry. According to testimony given by Flint to the Industrial Commission on Trusts and Industrial Combinations, $1.5 million was subscribed to a fund to be used by him to acquire interests in rubber boot and shoe companies.

Stock purchase options were taken covering a majority of the stock of each company. These options did not mention the names of other companies that were expected to form part of the new consolidation; instead, it was specified that, unless the new corporation possessed $15 million in tangible assets, the options would not become operative. Those giving the options knew that initial tangible assets of this amount would necessitate the inclusion of some of the important manufacturers of rubber boots and shoes.

Questions regarding the fairness of settlements with the shareholders were resolved to their satisfaction by a clause which stated that the net assets of each company, including accounts and bills receivable, would be appraised by three men prominent in the financial community or by experts whom they might employ.[14] Payment for the physical assets was to be made in preferred stock of the new company. As previously stated, an equal amount of common stock would be issued "to represent the increased earning capacity by reason of the consolidation of the interests acquired" (see Appendix C). (When the stock purchase contracts were executed, United States Rubber covenanted to purchase at the agreed price all or any part of the remainder of the outstanding stock of the acquired company.) It was also stipulated that 15% of the pledged stock was to be deposited with a bank and not released until United States Rubber Company had received the full value of the receivables.

INCORPORATION OF UNITED STATES RUBBER COMPANY

The original certificate of organization specified that the capital stock with which the company was to commence business on March 30. 1892 was $100,000, divided between 500 shares of preferred and 500 shares of "general" stock, each of $100 par value. The five incorporators each subscribed for 100 shares of preferred and 100 shares of general stock.

None of the five men who signed the certificate of organization of the United States Rubber Company on March 29, 1892 under the laws of New Jersey were actively connected with the rubber industry. They were:

William Barbour, Barbour Brothers, Paterson, N. J., linen thread manufacturer

J. Edward Simmons, president, Fourth National Bank, New York City, and former president, New York Stock Exchange

John P. Townsend, president, Knickerbocker Trust Company, New York City

William L. Trenholm, president, American Surety Company, New York City, and a director in two banks

John I. Waterbury, vice-president, Manhattan Trust Company, New York City.

Flint's name did not appear in the list of incorporators, but in September, 1892 he was elected a director and appointed director of finance and accounts. On Oct. 15, 1892, he became treasurer of the corporation, serving until 1901.

A press release by the new company stated that the objectives for which the company was being formed were improved quality at no increase in price, lower manufacturing costs, production of certain of its requirements (principally buckles, fabrics, litharge, whiting, and so on), ample cash resources, and the achievement of savings by "classifying" its manufacturing operations.

Organization

At the organization meeting on March 30, 1892 nine directors, including the incorporators, were elected. Misstatements appeared in later years regarding the names of members of that first board. In addition to the five incorporators, the other four members were:

Robert M. Gallaway, president, Merchants National Bank, New York City

Thomas F. Patterson of the firm of Sawyer, Manning and Company, Boston, woolen manufacturers

Henry Steers, president, Eleventh Ward Bank, New York City

Charles E. Thayer, Boston, dealer in dyewoods.[15]

On April 4, 1892 William L. Trenholm became the first president of United States Rubber, and served until he was succeeded on Oct. 15, 1892 by Robert D. Evans. The other officers elected April 4, 1892 were John I. Waterbury as secretary, and John P. Townsend as treasurer.

Three of the original board resigned before the end of 1892, and

CHARLES R. FLINT
Library of Congress

7. Charles R. Flint and first four presidents of United States Rubber Company. Trenholm was in office April 4-Oct. 15, 1892; Evans, Oct. 15, 1892-May 12, 1893 and March 4, 1896-May 26, 1897; Banigan, May 12, 1893-March 4, 1896; and Shepard, May 26, 1897-May 23, 1901.

WILLIAM L. TRENHOLM

FREDERICK M. SHEPARD

JOSEPH BANIGAN

ROBERT D. EVANS

four others resigned during 1893 and 1894. The number of directors was increased three times in 1892, first to fifteen, then to twenty, and in October to twenty-five. With only minor exceptions, as the different companies were acquired, one or more of the officials of each would be elected to the board of United States Rubber. Application No. A-1333 dated Dec. 1, 1892 for listing 129,425 shares of preferred and 134,811 shares of the common stock of the company on the New York Stock Exchange showed that thirteen of the twenty-five men then on the board of directors were officers of the acquired companies. They continued to exercise a considerable degree of independence and were reluctant to abandon their individual brands or to agree to other action that they did not consider beneficial to their respective companies.

In September, 1892, the directors, then numbering twenty, had elected an executive committee comprised of the following men:

Samuel P. Colt, National India Rubber Company
Robert D. Evans, American Rubber Company
Charles R. Flint, New York Commercial Company
Henry L. Hotchkiss, The L. Candee and Company
Charles L. Johnson, The L. Candee and Company
George A. Lewis, Goodyear Metallic Rubber Shoe Company
Mahlon C. Martin, New Jersey Rubber Shoe Company.

Areas of responsibility were divided among the seven men as follows:

Production, Lewis, director of manufacturing.

Purchases (other than crude rubber), Evans, director of purchases. Evans also was to control any plants that might manufacture material to be used in the finished product.

Purchase of crude rubber, Hotchkiss, director of purchasing crude rubber. Among his other duties he was to carry out plans for the best methods of operation in the world rubber markets.

Sales of footwear, Johnson, director of sales. He was to employ selling agents, direct sales methods, employ a traffic manager, report on market conditions. Later he was placed in charge of advertising.

Finance, Flint, director of finance and accounts. Martin, second director of finance and accounts.

Legal, Colt, director of contracts and litigation. He would engage and consult with counsel, and keep informed of all patent, trademark, and other litigation.

Apparently these "directors" operated independently until the following committees were appointed in 1894: sales; crude rubber; classification of product; lasts, weights, heights, and styles of goods; audit and accounts; and legal. Meanwhile, the Woonsocket Rubber Company was acquired, and its president, Joseph Banigan, was immediately elected president of United States Rubber on May 12, 1893. Four days later, he was made executive head of the company to "have general charge of the direction of the affairs of the Company in all of its Departments, subject only to control of the Executive Committee and the Board of Directors." When re-elected president in 1894, he was also made general manager.

Banigan resigned from the office on March 4, 1896, and Evans was again elected president. In June, 1896 Evans was also elected general manager, and served in both capacities until May 26, 1897 when he was succeeded by Frederick M. Shepard. On May 23, 1901, Shepard, then in his seventy-fourth year, declined reelection, and Colonel Samuel P. Colt became president.

On May 19, 1896, the stockholders had voted unanimously to reduce the number of directors from twenty-five to fifteen, and the number on the board varied from fourteen to sixteen until 1906. The size of the executive committee varied from six to eight directors from 1892 until 1902 when it was reduced to four.

First Factory

On April 5, 1892, the company purchased the property, plant, equipment, and all other assets of New Jersey Rubber Shoe Company, New Brunswick, N.J. (incorporated 1877), valuation to be fixed by appraisal and payment to be in "general" and preferred stock of United States Rubber Company. Payment of $1 million in stock was made for the plant on April 5, and at the same time possession of all personal property was given to United States Rubber. In September, 1892, the appraisers set the total value at $2,310,000 for which a total of 23,100 shares of United States Rubber stock (half in common, half in preferred) was delivered. At the time of purchase by United States Rubber, the factory had daily capacity of 15,000 pairs of boots and shoes. Manufacturing operations were continued until 1929; in 1930 the land and buildings were sold.

Contracts

Evidently, negotiations with other manufacturers had been started even before the company had been incorporated, for on April 5 the directors also approved a contract with The L. Candee and Company, under which Candee agreed to manufacture boots and shoes for United States Rubber Company for five years at cost plus 5%, with the stipulation that annual volume was not to exceed $500,000 at gross list prices.

Candee also contracted to purchase from United States Rubber all its crude rubber and other raw materials as soon as the new company was able to supply them. If the materials were *manufactured* by United States Rubber, Candee would pay 5% over actual cost; if *purchased* by United States Rubber, actual cost would be charged to Candee.

By October, 1892, almost identical contracts with each of the following companies had been approved:

American Rubber Company, Cambridge, Mass.
Boston Rubber Company, Chelsea and Franklin, Mass.
Goodyear Metallic Rubber Shoe Company, Naugatuck, Conn.
Lycoming Rubber Company, Williamsport, Pa.
Meyer Rubber Company, Milltown, N.J.
National India Rubber Company, Bristol, R.I.
New Brunswick Rubber Company, New Brunswick, N.J.

Also, "service contracts" were entered into with the key officials of the purchased subsidiaries to prevent their starting another company in competition with United States Rubber. As will be noted later, these contracts were not sufficient to prevent the formation of competing companies, even though the letter of the contracts was observed.

Immediately following execution of the cost-plus manufacturing contract with Candee, the directors of United States Rubber contracted to purchase all of its crude rubber from New York Commercial Company, Ltd., with which Flint was associated. Under that contract, United States Rubber would pay cost plus 1% for all rubber purchased in the United States, and cost plus 2¾% for all rubber purchased abroad. Apparently, it was expected that centralized buying of all the crude rubber requirements of the several factories acquired by United States Rubber would reduce competitive buying and at least partially offset speculative price advances (Figure 8). The contract also provided that the foreign organization of New York Commercial Company would keep United States Rubber informed regarding stocks of crude rubber and present and prospective output of crude rubber in all producing countries.

The First Nine Years

In the application to the New York Stock Exchange dated Dec. 1, 1892 for listing preferred stock and common stock of United States Rubber, it was stated that the company then either owned absolutely or permanently controlled each of the original nine companies out of "the fifteen manufacturing companies in which is centered the entire rubber boot and shoe business of the country." The application also stated that the

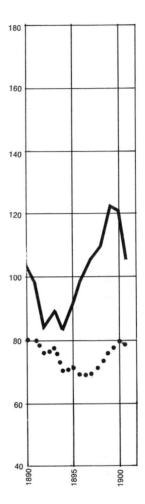

8. Average annual prices, Para rubber and all commodities, 1890-1901 (see Table A-2; 1913=100).

PARA RUBBER ▬▬▬▬▬

ALL COMMODITIES ● ● ● ● ● ●

property of the Para Rubber Shoe Company, South Framingham, Mass., had been acquired and that United States Rubber had contracted for control of two other boot and shoe properties.

Attached to the application was a statement of an appraisal of the value of all real estate, plants, machinery, tools, fixtures, and lasts, with claimed value of $5,055,000 (exclusive of the plant of the Para Company). Value of other assets, including accounts receivable and inventories of manufactured goods, was given as $6,491,000. Total assets of the corporation, which evidently included the Para plant, other investments, and perhaps cash, were said to be "equal to the par of the total issue of Preferred Stock," or $12,942,500. Average earnings of the nine companies for the past ten years were said to be $959,499, and, for the fiscal year 1891, $1,181,186, "more than sufficient to pay the dividend on the present issue of Preferred Stock."

The Para Rubber Shoe Company, which had had a peak daily production of 14,000 pairs, did not have an efficient factory layout and had been closed in 1891. United States Rubber acquired the plant and goodwill in 1892 but sold the plant in 1893. The second annual report stated that the sale had been made "with the provision that it should not be used for the manufacture of any article in competition with the product of any mill in which the United States Rubber Company is a large stockholder." It was used later for the manufacture of bicycles.

One of the other two boot and shoe properties mentioned in the application for listing was the Brookhaven Rubber Company, which manufactured third-grade rubber footwear. United States Rubber's second annual report said it had bought Brookhaven's stock (actually 1,251 out of 2,500 shares had then been purchased) and real estate "at a sacrifice of more than $200,000 for the sole purpose of stopping such low grade production, and to protect the public from such a deception." In 1894, it was reported United States Rubber had destroyed the shoe lasts and had turned the remaining property over to the Brookhaven stockholders.

Other Acquisitions

In 1893, United States Rubber Company gained control of Goodyear's India Rubber Glove Manufacturing Company, Naugatuck, Conn. Incorporated in 1847, it began making rubber footwear in 1876. The total outstanding stock of Woonsocket Rubber Company (the second largest company in the industry) was also purchased in 1893, with payment in preferred and common stock of United States Rubber having par value of $9,227,800. Woonsocket had a plant in Woonsocket, R.I., with a daily capacity of 30,000 pairs of rubbers, and a plant at Millville, Mass., with a daily capacity of 9,000 pairs of boots. Woonsocket also owned the Marvel Rubber Company in Woonsocket and the Lawrence Felting Plant in Millville, both included in the purchase of Woonsocket Rubber Company. Wool felt boots as well as felt linings for rubber boots were made in the Lawrence Felting Plant. Although the name "Lawrence Felting Company" was used on letterheads and although, by decisions of the executive committee, the Lawrence plant was managed and controlled as if it were a corporation, there was no actual company. Control of the Colchester Rubber Company, Colchester, Conn., was also acquired in 1893.

In 1893, the common stock of United States Rubber rose from a 42-45 range in March to a high of 60⅝ in April. This rise was said to have been "attributable to the shrewd manipulation of a few speculative favorites about this time." Possibly word of the approaching acquisitions of Goodyear's India Rubber Glove Manufacturing Company (April) and of the Woonsocket Rubber Company (May) influenced buyers of the company's common stock. But the price dropped back to less than 33 in May and, by the end of August, was down to 16; it recovered to about 45 in October. It should be remembered that the summer of 1893 was marked by a severe depression, brought on largely by the fear of capitalists that a change in the money standard might be made.[16]

Supply Plants Acquired

Some of the factories acquired in 1893 had facilities for reclaiming scrap rubber by use of acids, chiefly sulfuric. These included an acid reclaiming plant built in 1883 at Naugatuck by the Goodyear Metallic Rubber Shoe Company. That plant, which produced about 1,000 pounds of reclaimed rubber per day, was destroyed by fire in January, 1894, was rebuilt and again destroyed by fire, after which it was not rebuilt.[17] It had been decided in 1893, however, to erect a new reclaiming plant at Naugatuck, with daily capacity of 40,000 pounds of reclaimed. The new plant started operations in April, 1894. At first, it supplied only the plants located in Connecticut, but by September, 1895, it was decided to concentrate all reclaiming in Naugatuck, resulting in a saving of about 20% of the previous cost.

Until May, 1902, each manufacturing plant was credited with a proportionate share of the profits of the reclaiming plant. Beginning in May, 1902, this policy was changed, and thereafter the reclaiming plant retained its entire profit.

In 1894 further integration was accomplished when a majority stock interest was acquired in the Hammond Buckle Company, Rockville, Conn., thus providing a dependable supply of buckles for arctics and "lumbermen's overs" at actual cost of production. United States Rubber dissolved the Hammond Buckle Company in 1902; meanwhile, the Shoe Hardware Company, Waterbury, Conn., had been organized to supply the system's requirements in buckles and lasts.

Excess Capacity

In his report dated April 17, 1894, Banigan told of steps taken (1) to have each company make a weekly report of details of its purchases, (2) to exchange information between superintendents of the plants regarding more efficient methods and equipment, and (3) to reduce costs in other ways. In addition to closing the inefficient Para Rubber Shoe Company plant and the Brookhaven plant, he recommended consolidation of production in the most efficient factories of the system. He concluded by noting, "There are too many factories for the production of rubber boots and shoes, and this will be particularly true when the improved methods are fully adopted."

The next year he repeated his recommendation for consolidation of production in the plants of the larger companies, saying an annual saving of $1 million could be effected by operating the two large mills at Woonsocket three hundred days a year. The advantages of such a policy were again discussed in his successor's report for the year ended March 31, 1896. It is evident that the officers of plants that would be adversely affected by such a program had not acquired a wholly corporate viewpoint and were resisting its implementation.

Boston Rubber Shoe Company Acquired

On Aug. 1, 1898, the largest rubber footwear company, Boston Rubber Shoe Company, was purchased for a cash payment of $1 million, plus 41,250 shares of preferred and 35,000 shares of common stock of United States Rubber, with total par value of $7,625,000. Based on the lowest stock market prices for that day, the value of these shares was not less than $5,355,937. However, this amount did not represent the total cost of the acquisition by United States Rubber; prior to the sale of its properties and assets, the Boston company had issued to its stockholders $5 million of 5% ten-year gold debenture bonds, due Aug. 1, 1908, which later were guaranteed by United States Rubber. Boston Rubber Shoe's efficient sales organization, backed by emphasis on the superior quality of its products, had won for the company leadership in the rubber footwear industry. The company had a plant at Malden, Mass., with a daily capacity of 32,000 pairs of rubber boots and shoes, and a plant at Melrose, Mass., with a daily capacity of 23,000 pairs. Approximately 3,600 were employed in 1898, and the average weekly payroll was between $30-$35,000. Net quick assets were stated to be over $5,000,000.[18] For the last three years ended May 1, 1898, annual net sales had averaged over $7,700,000, and reported annual net earnings had averaged $1,523,333. With this purchase, factories for the manufacture of lasts and cartons also were acquired by United States Rubber.[19]

The annual report for fiscal year ended March 31, 1902 stated that by the acquisition in 1892 of majority interest in the original nine companies United States Rubber accounted for about one-third of the total output of rubber footwear in the United States, and that the 1893 acquisitions had raised the percentage of the industry's production to about one-half. Boston Rubber Shoe Company's daily capacity of 55,000 pairs of boots and shoes raised United States Rubber's share of the industry to three-fourths, according to the annual report for 1902. With purchase of the Boston Rubber Shoe Company, all but two of the rubber footwear companies operating in 1890 had been absorbed by United States Rubber. The two not absorbed were the Goodyear Rubber Company in Massachusetts and the Lambertville Rubber Company in New Jersey.

New Competing Companies Organized

George H. Hood, president of the Boston Rubber Company, had signed the usual "service contract" when that company was acquired by United States Rubber in 1892. He became a director of the latter and was reputed to be its fourth largest stockholder. On April 25, 1896, he and his son Frederick resigned as officers of Boston Rubber, and on May 19, 1896 he ceased to be a director of United States Rubber. On Oct. 12, 1896, the Hood Rubber Company was organized with $50,000 capital. Apparently, he complied with the letter of his contract and did not own any stock in the new company or hold an office, but his two sons were officers in it.[20]

The service contract with Joseph Banigan ended March 22, 1896; after this date, he purchased a woolen mill at Olneyville, R.I., organized Joseph Banigan Sons Rubber Company of Providence on Dec. 1, 1896, and in January, 1897 started the manufacture of rubber boots and shoes. For the remainder of his life, he was said to be "an implacable foe of the company." The year following his death in 1898, United States Rubber acquired control of the Banigan company.

The winter of 1895-96 had been marked by "an unusual amount of open, fine weather," resulting in poor sales of rubber footwear. This fact, together with reports that Banigan and his sons were about to withdraw from United States Rubber and set up a rival concern, brought a decline in the market quotations of United States Rubber common.

From a high of 48 at the end of May, 1895, it slid to a low of 14½ by August, 1896. In July, 1898, rumors that a dividend would be paid on the common were said to have been used by a group of operators in the market who reportedly "energetically manipulated the stock for a rise and caused tremendous activity for a time." After the death of Banigan on July 28, 1898, United States Rubber common sold as high as 48½ in August of that year, and in April, 1899 it touched $57 a share.

On Dec. 1, 1895, United States Rubber accepted the surrender of the service contract of George Watkinson, former president of Colchester Rubber Company, which was acquired by the company in 1893 and closed in 1894. In 1896, he organized George Watkinson & Company, Philadelphia, which was adjudged bankrupt Dec. 31, 1901. In 1904, United States Rubber purchased the business and liquidated the company.

George A. Lewis, former president of Goodyear Metallic Rubber Shoe Company and for several years a director of United States Rubber, severed his connection in October, 1898 and with his sons incorporated Beacon Falls Rubber Shoe Company, Beacon Falls, Conn., in March, 1899. Lewis, however, did not hold any office in the new company.

On July 1, 1897, Emmet A. Saunders, who was then assistant general manager of United States Rubber, resigned with the intention of going into business for himself. In September, 1897, he became associated with Mishawaka Woolen Manufacturing Company, Mishawaka, Ind., as a director and superintendent of the newly created rubber footwear department of that company.

Earnings and Dividends

No reference to earnings appeared in the first annual report, which showed only the balance sheet as of March 31, 1893. The next report, in 1894, said "our investments in other Manufacturing Companies have earned during the past year sufficient to pay the 8% dividend on the preferred stock of $19,400,500, and leave in the Treasuries of the several Companies a substantial surplus."

An article in the Boston News Bureau reporting the second annual meeting of United States Rubber said the company had earned 7% ($1,411,620) on the common stock in addition to the 8% dividend paid on the preferred stock. In February, 1895, the first dividend on the common stock ($2.50 per share) was declared, and dividends of $2 per common share were paid in 1897, 1899, and 1900, after which they were discontinued until October, 1911, when $1 was paid in the last quarter. Such information as is now available regarding income during the years up to and including 1901 is shown in Figure 9.

In 1895, United States Rubber became the selling agent for the entire product of each of the subsidiaries. Each sales contract prescribed a commission of 5% of net sales for "services," plus 7½% to cover such expenses as freight, storage, insurance, advertising, and price lists. During the next few years, these commissions provided less than one-third of total income of the parent company. Not until the annual report for fiscal year ended March 31, 1902 was a report made of sales.

The adverse effect of increased competition from the formation of new companies on the income of United States Rubber was reflected in shrinkage of income from $2,716,000 in 1894-95 to $1,579,819 for the year ended March 31, 1898.

The increase of approximately $1 million in earnings of $2,596,649 reported for the year ended March 31, 1899 appears to have been due largely to the acquisition of Boston Rubber Shoe Company on Aug. 1, 1898. Net earnings of that one company for its fiscal year ended May 1 had been $1,500,000 in 1897 and $1,270,000 in 1898.

Earnings for the fiscal year ended March 31, 1900, were $2,837,861, but two mild winters in succession and the competition from other footwear manufacturers cut sales sharply in 1900-01, as shown by the decline in "commission on sales" from $987,743 for the year 1899-1900 to $34,266 the following year.

Operations for 1900-01 resulted in net loss of $101,926, down by more than $2,900,000 from the previous year's earnings. Whereas the directors had declared dividends of $1,882,040 on the preferred and $946,640 on the common stock out of earnings for the year ended March 31, 1900, dividends on the common stock were omitted in fiscal 1900-01.

In sympathy with the general trend of the stock market, the company's common stock declined in 1900 from a high of 44 in January to 21 in July. In November, rumors of possible acquisitions of competing companies brought heavy trading in the stock, and it touched 39. After the announcement on Jan. 3, 1901, of a 25% reduction in its prices of rubber footwear, United States Rubber common declined to 12½ by October, 1901. Meanwhile, the 8% preferred, which had sold as high as 121 in January, 1899 and had remained above 110 until early in December of that year, had fallen to 74½ by the end of 1900. After the company's announcement of the cut in its prices on Jan. 3, 1901, the preferred declined until it reached 47 by October, 1901.

9. Financial trends, 1893-1901 (see Table A-5).

9a. Net income.

9b. Earnings per common share outstanding at end of fiscal year.

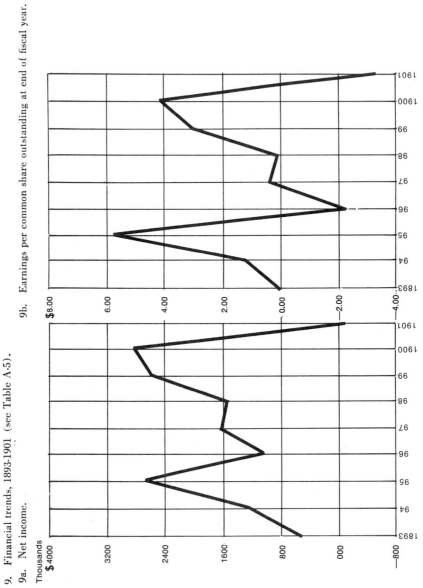

42

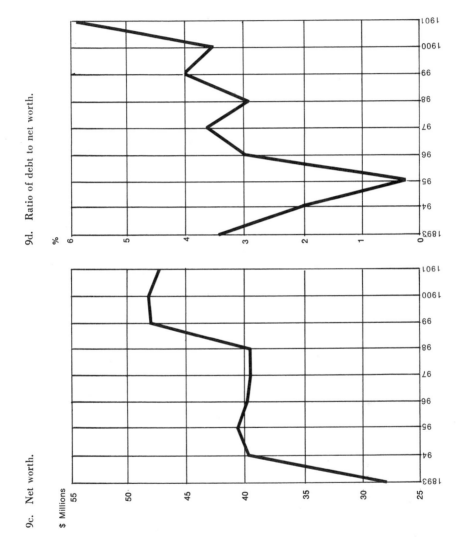

9c. Net worth.

9d. Ratio of debt to net worth.

43

Payment of a 2% dividend on the preferred on Oct. 31, 1900 was followed by declaration of only a 1% dividend on Jan. 31, 1901, giving preferred shareholders a total of 3% instead of the normal 8% for the year. After payment of these reduced dividends, the surplus of the parent company as of March 31, 1901 was only $25,013.

Obviously, the directors faced a serious problem.

FORMATION OF RUBBER GOODS MANUFACTURING COMPANY

After his success in forming the United States Rubber Company, Charles R. Flint said he was engaged by August H. Belmont to bring about a consolidation of manufacturers of mechanical rubber goods, which would include the New York Belting and Packing Company. Belmont was the "paternal banker" of that company, the principal owners of which at that time were said to be British nationals.[21] For a period the corporation had been known as New York Belting and Packing Company, Ltd.

The company appears to have been founded in 1846 and to have been incorporated in 1856 in Connecticut for $200,000[22] by John H. Cheever and Henry F. Durant. (In 1871 Durant was to become the founder of Wellesley College.) The factory was first located at Sandy Hook, Conn. (When interviewed by the author, Willard H. Cobb said he had been told that as one of the founders was driving past the future site of the factory, he noted that that was where they would build the plant. Cobb added that this site was chosen solely for the available water power, without any study of other advantages or disadvantages pertaining to the location selected.) Operations were licensed under Charles Goodyear's original patents. The initial production consisted of transmission belting, rubber packings, and sheet rubber goods. Hose was manufactured using long flat boards as mandrels, and belting was cured in roll form in open heaters. During the Civil War the New York Belting and Packing Company's sales increased substantially. Among its products were waterproof rubber blankets. In 1865, New York Belting and Packing Company was the first in this country to produce solid grinding wheels commercially, made by embedding Turkish emery in a hard rubber (vulcanite) bond.[23]

The supply of water power at Sandy Hook was insufficient, especially in the summer months, for operation of a rubber mill, and some of the operations were transferred to Passaic, N.J., in 1869; Passaic became the main manufacturing plant about 1886. Not only did the new site have a dependable and adequate supply of water power, but it was much better located with respect to rail and water transportation, availability of labor, and room for future expansion. (After all the production of N.Y.B. and P. was transferred to Passaic, the portion of the Sandy Hook property known as "the lower mill" was occupied by the Fabric Fire Hose Company. The supply of water power was always adequate to operate this company's looms.) In order of their relative importance, the chief products of N.Y.B. and P. were: hose (about 40%), belting (about 25%), packings, grinding wheels, molded products, and miscellaneous (about 35%).

The first rubber-surfaced conveyor belt, for use in the Edison mine in Morris County, N.J., was produced in the 1890's by N.Y.B. and P. working with the Robins Conveyor Company.[24] Prior to that time, conveyor belts had been made of heavy duck which had been "frictioned" with rubber; that is, rubber had been pressed into the duck fabric as it passed between two cylinders of a calender, one of which revolved at a faster speed than the other, thus rubbing or "frictioning" the rubber into the meshes of the fabric. The hematite iron ore in the Edison mine was very hard, heavy, and sharp-edged, and Thomas Edison conceived the idea that a conveyor belt with a rubber surface of sufficient thickness would last much longer than the conventional frictioned belt. He discussed his idea with Mr. Robins of the Robins Conveyor Company, who referred the suggestion to N.Y.B. and P., and the belt made with a rubber cover of approximately $\frac{1}{8}$ inch thickness proved to be very satisfactory.[25]

Flint relates that the same night after his conversation with Belmont, he went to Cleveland where he inspected the plant of the Cleveland Rubber Company; he then inspected the plant of the Chicago Rubber Works. The following two days and nights, which he spent in almost continuous negotiations with all interested parties, resulted in the formation of the Mechanical Rubber Company with headquarters at Passaic, N.J. According to Flint's account of the transaction, no cash was involved, each company being compensated by the transfer of preferred and common stock of the new corporation. Included in the Mechanical Rubber Company in 1892 were:

	Year Incorporated
New York Belting and Packing Company, Ltd., Passaic, N.J.	1856
Stoughton Rubber Company, Stoughton, Mass.	1889
Fabric Fire Hose Company, Sandy Hook, Conn.	1880
Cleveland Rubber Company, Cleveland, Ohio	1872
Chicago Rubber Works, Chicago	1882

In 1898, Flint was again active in the formation of the Rubber Goods
Manufacturing Company, incorporated Jan. 26, 1899 under the laws
of New Jersey. Members of a syndicate subscribed $5 million, of which
$3 million in cash was allotted to Flint to be invested by him in prop-
erties of manufacturers of rubber goods and allied products other than
boots and shoes. The consolidation was to become operative when it
comprised at least eight plants, with annual sales of at least $5 million
and net tangible assets of at least $4 million.

The authorized capital stock of the Rubber Goods Manufacturing
Company was $25 million of 7% cumulative preferred shares and $25
million of common stock. It differed in two important aspects, however,
from that of the United States Rubber Company. The 8% preferred
stock of the latter was noncumulative, while the Rubber Goods Manufacturing Company issued 7% cumulative preferred stock, limited in
amount to the appraised value of the tangible assets of the companies
consolidated. Also, the issue of common stock of the Rubber Goods
Manufacturing Company was limited to 14 2/7 times the earnings of the
previous year, thus presumably placing it on an earnings basis of 7%.
The original issue was about $6 million of preferred and $13 million of
common stock. In April, 1901 Flint testified that the company, during
the two years of its existence, had earned the 7% dividend on the preferred and had earned about 7% on the common, on which dividends
of 4% per annum had been paid.[26]

An article in the *Financial Review* for February, 1903 stated that
the Rubber Goods Manufacturing Company had acquired 99¾% of the
capital stock of the Mechanical Rubber Company, 75% of the stock
of Morgan and Wright, Chicago, and the entire stock of the following:

Peerless Rubber Manufacturing Company, New Durham, N. J.
Akron India Rubber Company, Akron, Ohio
Sawyer Belting Company, Cleveland, Ohio
Hartford Rubber Works Company, Hartford, Conn.
Indianapolis Rubber Company, Indianapolis, Ind.
Peoria Rubber and Manufacturing Company, Peoria, Ill.

(The Indianapolis Rubber Company made G & J tires for Gormully
& Jeffery, Chicago manufacturers of the famous Rambler bicycle. On
Nov. 17, 1899, G & J Tire Company was incorporated in New Jersey
to act as a holding company for G & J patents, and to make and sell
tires under its name. On June 16, 1910, the name of Indianapolis Rubber Company was changed to G & J Tire Company [of Indiana]).[27]

Also included in the consolidation forming the Rubber Goods Manufacturing Company, although not mentioned in the article, were Sandy

Hook Reclaiming Works, Sandy Hook, Conn.; Mechanical Fabric Company, E. Providence, R.I.; American Dunlop Tire Company, Belleville, N.J.; and Single Tube A and B Company (location not known). After formation of the Rubber Goods Manufacturing Company, the designation of Mechanical Rubber Company was retained by the plants in Cleveland and Chicago only.

Flint became the first chairman of the executive committee, and his brother Wallace was the first treasurer. The steps by which United States Rubber in 1905 acquired the controlling interest in the Rubber Goods Manufacturing Company are related in Chapter IV.

INVENTION AND PRODUCTION OF PNEUMATIC RUBBER TIRE

The pneumatic rubber tire was patented in England in 1845 and in America in 1847 by Robert William Thomson, a twenty-three year old Scotch civil engineer. At first he encased the inflated rubberized tube with circular segments of leather and, to prevent creeping, fastened the latter to the wheel's metal tire with seventy security bolts. Later he replaced the leather case with canvas. Thomson carefully tested his pneumatic tire to determine the saving of energy needed to pull a carriage on different types of road surfaces; he found a saving of 60% on a smooth hard macadamized road, and of 310% over new broken rock.[28] While he clearly visualized the advantages of pneumatic tires, the market at that time would not support profitable commercial production.

After a few years, his patent was so completely forgotten that another Scotsman, John Boyd Dunlop (a veterinary surgeon in Belfast, Ireland), was granted a patent in 1888 when he made pneumatic tires for his small son's tricycle. Dunlop's first tire was a rubber tube inside a canvas casing, which was cemented to the wheel. Unlike Thomson, Dunlop did not recognize the importance of his patent and sold his patent rights to William Bowden. The invention came to the attention of an Irish industrialist, W. H. duCros, who, because of his active interest in bicycle racing, quickly grasped the opportunity for profitable development of a large market for pneumatic tires. He acquired the patent rights from Bowden and together with him and J. M. Gillies founded the Pneumatic Tyre Company, Ltd., later known as Dunlop Pneumatic Tyre Company, Ltd. It has been aptly said that "Thomson had the patent and no business, while Dunlop had the business and no patent."[29]

Although Thomson had taken out a patent in the United States in 1847, it was not until 1895 that pneumatic tires for automobiles were made in this country. The Hartford Rubber Works, which later became

10. The pneumatic tire. The Duryea Motor Wagon (above), with J. Frank Duryea at the tiller, won America's first automobile race (Chicago to Evanston) while equipped with pneumatic rubber tires. The first known advertisement for pneumatic tires (below) appeared in *Motocycle* (January, 1896).

one of the companies consolidated in the Rubber Goods Manufacturing Company, began making solid bicycle tires in 1885, and is believed to have made the first tires cured in a circular shape. Previously, solid tiring was produced in an extruded strip. In 1891, Hartford began production of pneumatic tires that were first used in 1892 on trotting sulkies. Early in 1895, Hartford made a set of 2-inch, single-tube tires for the Duryea Motor Wagon Company, Springfield, Mass., which put them on one of its "motor wagons" in March. Still in good condition, these tires were used by Charles E. Duryea when, with an average speed of 5.05 miles per hour, he won a road race sponsored by the Chicago *Times-Herald,* and run in deep snow in Chicago on Thanksgiving Day, 1895 (Figure 10). (The day before the race, a bystander stuck a knife into one of the tires to see if it was solid, but the hole was quickly patched.) [30]

Most skeptics were now convinced of the merits of pneumatic tires for passenger cars. With care, the pneumatic tires made at the turn of the century might last 1,500 miles before they failed completely, and motorists considered themselves lucky if able to drive a few hundred miles without a blowout or tire failure.

In 1896, United States Rubber started manufacturing solid rubber bicycle tires in the plant of the New Brunswick Rubber Company, which was no longer being used for footwear production. It was hoped, according to the annual report for the year ended March 31, 1897, that this move would "help pay running expenses" and prove profitable. Solid rubber bicycle tires were also made for a time at the Bristol plant of the National India Rubber Company. However, the volume of business done by United States Rubber on bicycle tires was small and unprofitable. In 1901, the stockholders were informed that the New Brunswick plant had been sold, and that the United States Rubber Company had discontinued its tire business, which had been sold to the Rubber Goods Manufacturing Company. Until the acquisition of the latter in 1905, United States Rubber remained essentially a rubber footwear manufacturing company.

[1] W. A. Gibbons, "The Rubber Industry, 1839-1939," *Industrial and Engineering Chemistry,* XXXI (October, 1939), p. 1199 ff.

[2] Net sales reported by General Tire and Rubber Company for 1963 exceeded those reported by United States Rubber Company, but about 65% of General's sales were contributed by its subsidiary, Aerojet-General Corporation, engaged principally in the development and production of rocket engines and other hardware connected with defense and space projects.

Total net sales by the rubber industry in the United States in 1963 were $10,406 million. See *Quarterly Financial Report for Manufacturing Corporations, Fourth Quarter,* Securities and Exchange Commission (Washington: U.S. Gov't Printing Office, 1963), p. 48.

[3] As of Dec. 31, 1963, United States Rubber had a controlling interest in plants operating in eighteen foreign countries (letter from E. J. Higgins, 1964).

[4] *Royal Dealer*, house organ of United States Rubber Company (June, 1963), p. 3.

[5] *Between US*, house organ of United States Rubber Company (January, 1916), p. 7.

[6] The principal rubber products in 1850 were boots and shoes, elastic fabrics or "shirred goods," rubberized cloth and clothing, rubberized tents, rubber pontons, mail bags, blankets and ponchos for the Army and Navy, druggist's rubber sundries, and rubber toys. The Civil War brought a heavy demand from the Union Army for many types of rubber goods. See P. W. Barker, *Rubber Industry of the United States*, U.S. Dept. of Commerce (Washington: U.S. Gov't Printing Office, 1939), pp. 14-15.

[7] Nancy Paine Norton, "Industrial Pioneer: The Goodyear Metallic Rubber Shoe Company," I, 1950, unpublished dissertation, Radcliffe College, pp. 517-20.

[8] In the remainder of this section, the author has drawn freely on "First Section of History of United States Rubber Company" by Walter Emery, former manager, Commercial Research Department, United States Rubber Company, company archives, 1946.

[9] "First Section of History of United States Rubber Company," pp. 16-17.

[10] "First Section of History of United States Rubber Company," p. 3 ff.

[11] Charles R. Flint, *Memories of an Active Life* (New York: G. P. Putnam's Sons, 1923), p. 287. Also "Testimony of Charles R. Flint, Merchant," April 8, 1901, *Report to the 57th Congress, 1901, of the Industrial Commission on Trusts and Industrial Combinations*, XIII (Washington: U.S. Gov't Printing Office, 1901), p. 34 ff.

[12] Charles R. Flint, James J. Hill, and others in James H. Bridge, ed., *The Trust: Its Book* (New York: Doubleday, Page and Company, 1902), pp. 87, 88. Also Alfred D. Chandler, Jr., *Strategy and Structure* (Cambridge: Massachusetts Institute of Technology Press, 1962), pp. 33-34, p. 403.

[13] *Memories of an Active Life*, pp. 299-303.

[14] The three men named as appraisers were "Charles S. Smith, a prominent manufacturer, ex-Comptroller Henry W. Cannon, and Charles H. Dalton, a prominent manufacturer." See "Testimony of Charles R. Flint, Merchant," p. 48.

[15] "First Section of History of United States Rubber Company," pp. 21-22. Also "Annals of Rubber," reprinted from *India Rubber World* (1936), p. 14.

[16] *Report to the 57th Congress, 1901, of the Industrial Commission on Trusts and Industrial Combinations*, pp. 915, 930.

[17] John E. Caskey, unpublished paper, 1940, company archives.

[18] The terms of the debentures of Boston Rubber Shoe Company required that net quick assets be equal at all times to the full amount of the debentures outstanding. *Annual Report*, United States Rubber Company (May 19, 1903), p. 6.

[19] Homer E. Sawyer, "Histories of the United States Rubber Company and Some of the Subsidiary Companies," 1915, privately printed, p. 14.

[20] "First Section of History of United States Rubber Company," pp. 29-30.

[21] H. W. Willard, interview, 1963.

[22] Nancy Paine Norton, letter to author, Feb. 8, 1963.

[23] Muriel F. Collie, *The Saga of the Abrasives Industry* (Greendale, Mass.: The Grinding Wheel Institute and The Abrasive Grain Association, 1951), pp. 54-56.

[24] Willard H. Cobb, interview, 1962.

[25] A. W. Moyer, interview, 1963.

[26] "Testimony of Charles R. Flint, Merchant," pp. 37-38.

[27] United States Rubber Company, "Some Historical Facts about the Tire Division," c. 1950, unpublished, company archives.

[28] *Mechanics Magazine*, No. 1233 (London, 1849) as quoted by Sir Arthur duCros in *Wheels of Fortune* (London: Chapman and Hall, Ltd., 1938), pp. 296-97.

[29] *Wheels of Fortune*, p 4 ff.

[30] George E. Hewitt, letter Dec. 31, 1895, reprinted in *Motocycle* (June, 1896), pp. 10-11; also "Some Historical Facts about the Tire Division"; also United States Rubber Company, "History of the Automobile Tire," c. 1963, unpublished, company archives.

II

1901 to 1918

3

Expansion and Diversification

SAMUEL P. COLT

COLONEL Samuel P. Colt, president of United States Rubber from May
24, 1901 until Dec. 5, 1918, served in that capacity longer than any
other president of the company. During his tenure of office, the company became truly international in scope, acquiring the Canadian Consolidated Rubber Company in 1907, operating rubber plantations in
Sumatra by 1910, and expanding numerous overseas branches, principally in Europe and Latin America. His presidency also saw the changeover from a group of factories devoted almost entirely to the manufacture of rubber footwear and rubber clothing to factories making rubber
tires, rubber "mechanical goods," and fabrics and chemicals, in addition
to rubber footwear. With this changeover came a growth in investments
from $47,323,000 shown on the balance sheet of March 31, 1901,
to $134,887,000 as of Dec. 31, 1918. On March 31, 1901, just prior
to Colt's election as president, total capital stock and surplus stood
at $47,217,000, and undivided net earnings of its subsidiaries were
$1,175,000. When, in December, 1918, he was succeeded as president
by Charles B. Seger and became chairman of the board, capital stock
and surplus had increased to $146,967,000.

Samuel Pomeroy Colt (1852-1921) graduated with honors from the
Massachusetts Institute of Technology in 1873; he enrolled in the Columbia Law School in 1874, receiving the degree of LL.D. in 1876.
Entering the practice of law in Providence, R.I., he became a member
of the state legislature in 1876 and in 1879 was appointed assistant
attorney general of Rhode Island. During his first term he was appointed
aide-de-camp to the governor, with the honorary title of "colonel" and
afterwards was known as Colonel Colt. He became attorney general of

11.   Samuel P. Colt.

the state in 1882. In 1886, he founded the Industrial Trust Company
of Providence, of which he remained president until 1908. His introduction to the rubber industry came when in 1887, he was appointed
assignee of the bankrupt National Rubber Company, Bristol, R.I., which
he reorganized and incorporated in November, 1887 as the National
India Rubber Company. To the surprise of his friends and competitors,
it was said, the company was soon paying dividends. He was to be eventually a director in forty corporations, many of which were subsidiaries
of United States Rubber Company.

The National India Rubber Company was one of the companies
brought together in 1892 to form the United States Rubber Company.
On its acquisition Colt was made a director and member of the executive
committee of the new company, with specific responsibility for contracts and legal matters. In 1896, he was elected secretary of the company and served in that capacity until his election as president.

Possessed of great vitality and a wide range of interests, he was prominent in social, civic, and political affairs, and was a generous contribu-
tor to many charitable and educational institutions. A writer of an
article that appeared in the Providence *Tribune* for Aug. 14, 1921, after
mentioning that Colt had started his career with only modest resources,
paid tribute to his "close and minute attention to details," and to his

"hard, unremitting, personal work" kept up until the end of his life. Indicative of his close attention to detail was the fact that the annual reports issued during his presidency contained much more information than those of either his immediate predecessor or his successor.

Colt, the writer continued, was "preeminently a man of vision," and was able to foresee the opportunities for profitable growth and expansion that awaited the United States Rubber Company. He was said to have unusual ability to win cooperation of other businessmen and financiers as well as the employees of United States Rubber. This faculty, it was asserted, was the result of his "studious maintenance of friendly relations" even with those who might be in opposition to him at the moment, and to his "naturally genial and unfailing courteous manner" in his efforts to effect a compromise resulting in an amicable settlement.[1]

The resolution adopted by the board of directors, following the death of Colt on Aug. 13, 1921, bears out this evaluation:

> "To the affairs of the Company he gave the benefit of a keen legal mind, of a broad grasp of finance, of sound business judgment, of skill in handling both of men and of problems, of untiring attention and of a rare personality. His constant aim was to build up a sound and loyal organization, and in this we feel he was successful. . . . "

However, the truly remarkable growth and transformation of United States Rubber under Colt's administration was accompanied by an indebtedness that later jeopardized the financial position of the company. A remark said to have been made by Colt, when the issue of $60 million of 5% first and refunding mortgage bonds was negotiated in 1917, may have been indicative of his confidence that the future growth and continued earnings of the company justified heavy borrowings. The negotiations with the underwriters, Kuhn, Loeb and Company, were spearheaded by Edgar B. Davis, then a vice-president of United States Rubber. Accompanying him was Lucius D. Tompkins, who recalled in 1963 that when Colt was told that Kuhn, Loeb would underwrite the bond issue, he said, with evident satisfaction, "Now that's taken care of." It may be questioned whether the president felt much, if any, concern at that time regarding the ability of the company to meet the obligation by the maturity date.

FINANCIAL PROBLEMS FACED BY COLT

Competitive Situation

Reference has been made to the adverse effect that the steps taken by United States Rubber to meet the increased competition of newly formed rubber footwear companies had on its earnings in the year ended March 31, 1901 (Figure 9). In his report of May 20, 1902 to the stockholders, Colt commented on the increased competition and the formation of new companies manufacturing footwear. He reported that, in January and February, 1901, prices had been reduced to "about the cost of manufacture." The severity of the competition may be judged by the statement he made in May, 1903. After commenting that prices for the past season had been about the same as during the previous year and were the lowest—costs considered—"ever known in the history of the trade," he mentioned that five companies manufacturing boots and shoes had failed or gone out of business.

Gross sales for the year ended March 31, 1902 increased 42.5%, but the fact that net sales increased only 22% in the same year indicates that orders were taken at much greater discounts than before. The report for fiscal 1903-04 contained a statement that only the stronger companies survived, and that United States Rubber had regained its full share of the market. Discounts from "list" prices were shortened in fiscal year 1902-03, and net sales increased by $2,840,000, with only $570,000 added to manufacturing costs, so that gross profit of the parent and subsidiary companies rose by $2,270,000 and net income from $119,000 to $1,342,000. For the year ended March 31, 1904, net profits, before provision of $500,000 for depreciation of securities, were approximately $1,576,000 and Colt said they would have been about doubled except for the extraordinary and unanticipated advance in prices of crude rubber and other materials (see Figure 12).

Temporary reversals occurred in 1908, 1909 (after reserves established during that year), and 1911, due chiefly to depressed general business conditions or to weather unfavorable to the sale of rubber footwear; the general trend of profits, however, was steadily upward until 1920.

The various steps taken during Colt's administration to strengthen the company's financial position, to provide additional working capital, or furnish funds for acquisition of land for rubber plantations in the Far East, as well as acquiring several other companies in this country and in Canada, will be discussed later. However, a somewhat different problem confronted the newly elected officers in 1901.

Settlement with Crude Rubber Company

At the meeting of the executive committee held June 28, 1901, the president reported that the Crude Rubber Company was indebted to United States Rubber for about $2,750,000. This indebtedness was unconditionally guaranteed by Flint and Company. The minutes did not disclose the details of the debt, but it may have arisen through advances made by United States Rubber for purchase of rubber that had not been delivered by the Crude Rubber Company. In December, 1900, Charles R. Flint, with the backing of prominent financiers, had incorporated the International Crude Rubber Company, capitalized at $30 million. The board of directors included Flint and representatives of Standard Oil, Amalgamated Copper, and United States Rubber. However, early in 1901, some backers withdrew from the International Crude Rubber Company and the latter collapsed.[2] The indebtedness of Crude Rubber Company to United States Rubber undoubtedly was connected with this unsuccessful venture.

Crude Rubber Company proposed to sell to United States Rubber $650,000 of rubber on the basis of up-river fine Para at 85¢ a pound, and to give a sixty-day option to purchase a like amount at the same price; United States Rubber would pay ten-thirteenths of the purchase price with its five- or six-month notes, and credit the Crude Rubber Company's account with the remaining three-thirteenths. Disregarding the option, the proposed $650,000 purchase would result in a credit of $150,000. For the remaining debt of about $2,600,000, Crude Rubber offered to give its notes, $500,000 due Nov. 8, 1902, $500,000 due March 8, 1903, and the balance due Oct. 8, 1903, all at 6% interest payable quarterly. The notes were to be secured by collateral valued at about $2,770,450. Punctual payment of principal and interest would be guaranteed by Flint and Company.

This proposal was accepted, but, before the transactions could be completed, Crude Rubber Company was found to be bankrupt. United States Rubber received a letter from the officers of Crude Rubber stating that it could not pay 5% of its liabilities. Flint and Company offered, in settlement of Crude Rubber Company's obligations, $50,000 in funds and securities of nominal value of about $400,000. This offer was declined. Several meetings between the executive committee and Flint and his legal counsel followed, and in the end the United States Rubber Company agreed to release International Crude Rubber Company from its indebtedness upon the payment of $25,000 cash plus certain securities, in addition to the previous offer, and the realization of at least $500,000 on previous collateral furnished by Flint and Company. It was felt that United States Rubber would receive by this plan more than would have been realized if it had tried to enforce its claim against the Crude Rubber Company.

United States Rubber then assigned to its subsidiary, the Meyer Rub-

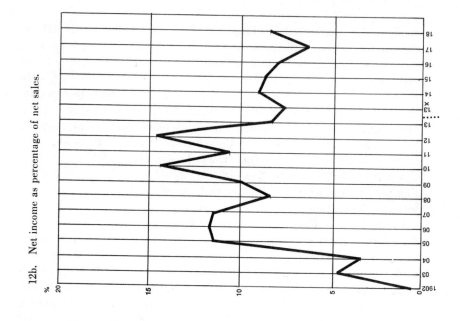

12. Financial trends, 1902-18 (see Table A-7).

12a. Net sales and net income.

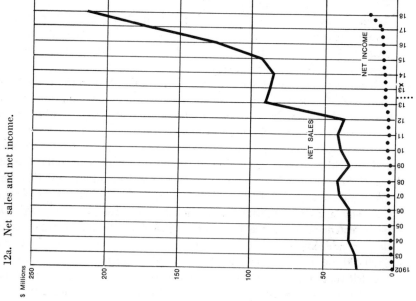

12b. Net income as percentage of net sales.

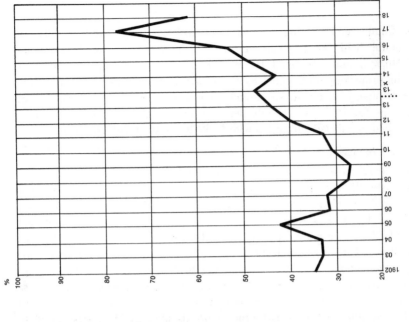

12c. Earnings per common share outstanding at end of fiscal year.   12d. Ratio of debt to net worth.

*Nine-month period ended Dec. 31, 1913; fiscal year changed to calendar year.

ber Company, its claims against Flint and Company, together with all collateral held for the balance due on those claims for the sum of $2,746,935, and appointed H. M. Sadler, Jr., to give special attention to the properties represented by the securities transferred to Meyer Rubber Company. Later it was found advisable to reserve $500,000 out of earnings for 1903 for possible depreciation in value of these securities.[3] Flint had no official connection with United States Rubber after 1901.

Federal Income Tax Enacted

The federal income tax was first levied in 1913, following ratification of the Sixteenth Amendment to the Constitution. The 1913 rate was only 1%, and the charge against the United States Rubber's net profit was only $171,103. The rate was raised to 2% in 1916 with an additional tax of 12½% on annual profits realized from production and sale of war munitions. United States Rubber paid $447,882 in income tax that year. Then came the entry of this country into World War I, and the combined taxes assessed against the company for federal income tax, excess profits tax, and Canadian business profits tax rose to $3,465,530. In 1918, the normal tax on corporation profits above $2,000 was raised to 12%, with provision for additional taxes on profits due to the war. The total charge for these taxes was $3,992,000.

Even the larger sums assessed against 1917 and 1918 earnings seem very small, however, in comparison with 1964's total of $29,461.000 paid by United States Rubber for federal and foreign income taxes.

Funded Indebtedness Increased

In addition to $4,800,000 of debentures of the Boston Shoe Company outstanding when Samuel P. Colt was elected president of United States Rubber in May, 1901, the latter company had a large floating indebtedness. To strengthen its financial position, arrangements were made to fund the floating indebtedness, and on April 1, 1902, $12 million of 5% three-year funding notes were sold, secured by an equal amount of notes of the subsidiary companies.

Of these notes, $4 million had been paid and canceled by the maturity date in 1905, and the balance was refunded for another three years. In 1907. both the remaining $8 million of funding notes and $4,500,000 of the $4,800,000 outstanding of Boston Rubber Shoe Company debentures were refunded, with maturity dates of Sept. 15, 1909 and Sept. 15. 1910, respectively.

"To simplify its debt structure," United States Rubber created in 1908 an issue of $20 million of 6% ten-year collateral trust bonds, of which $15 million were sold; out of the proceeds, the entire issue of 5% funding notes and the $4,500,000 of Boston Rubber Shoe debentures were called and paid. The balance was used for working capital. The unsold portion of the issue, $5 million, was reserved for the company's future requirements, and before the end of 1909 became a source of funds for purchase of the Revere Rubber Company.

The General Rubber Company (a subsidiary incorporated March 29, 1904 under the laws of New Jersey to handle transactions in crude rubber) executed in 1905 an indenture covering an issue of $9 million of 4½% ten-year gold debentures. Of these, $6 million were sold and were guaranteed both as to principal and interest by United States Rubber and the Rubber Goods Manufacturing Company. The remaining $3 million were issued prior to Dec. 31, 1913, when a consolidated statement of United States Rubber Company and all of its subsidiaries was published for the first time. When the $9 million came due in 1915, payment was made by the issue of $9 million of 5% debenture bonds of the General Rubber Company, maturing Dec. 1, 1918. Two other issues of 5% debenture bonds of subsidiaries of United States Rubber, with maturity date of Dec. 1, 1918, were also sold at the same time— $2,500,000 by Canadian Consolidated Rubber Company, Ltd. and $3 million of a $5 million issue by Morgan and Wright. Proceeds of these two issues were used for reduction of floating debts and for extensions of the plants of the two companies. The Dec. 1, 1918 maturity date of each of the three issues coincided with that of the 6% ten-year collateral trust bonds of United States Rubber, which, through the sinking fund, would be reduced to $15 million by the maturity date. The directors then planned to issue one class of security for the retirement of all these obligations.

In addition to the obligations just mentioned, the balance sheet as of Dec. 31, 1915 showed:

Ten-year 5% debentures, Eureka Hose Mfg. Co.	$ 970,000
Forty-year 6% collateral trust gold bonds, Canadian Consolidated Rubber Co., Ltd.	2,597,000
Mechanical Rubber Co. and New York Belting and Packing Company bonds	791,000

Working capital as of Dec. 31, 1915 was $47,570,000. Net sales rose from $83,679,000 in 1914 to $92,861,000 in 1915, to $126,759,000 in 1916, and to $176,160,000 in 1917. To provide additional working capital for the rapidly increasing business, as well as to simplify the funded indebtedness of United States Rubber and its subsidiaries, the stockholders of United States Rubber authorized the issue on Feb. 14,

1917, of 5% thirty-year first and refunding mortgage gold bonds, limited to an aggregate principal amount of $97,252,900 (this being the par value of the company's fully paid preferred and common stocks outstanding on Jan. 15, 1917). Kuhn, Loeb and Co. agreed to underwrite an issue of $60 million of these bonds, secured by an indenture of mortgage, dated Feb. 15, 1917, with provision for possible later issue of $11,600,000 additional for retirement of the bonded indebtedness of the General Rubber Company and of Canadian Consolidated Rubber. Including discount and expense, it cost the company $5,363,000 to float the $60 million issue, an indication that United States Rubber did not then enjoy the best credit rating.[4]

Under the mortgage indenture, the company pledged all its property, real and otherwise, except its holdings of securities or obligations of companies in which it owned less than a majority of the capital stock, cash, receivables, and inventories of finished products.

Prior to Feb. 1, 1917, United States Rubber operated largely as a holding company. To provide the company with sufficient real property that could be pledged as security for payment of the principal and interest of the bonds, the following subsidiary corporations deeded to United States Rubber on Feb. 1, 1917, their lands and interests in lands:

American Rubber Company*
Joseph Banigan Rubber Company*
Boston Rubber Shoe Company*
The L. Candee and Company*
Eureka Fire Hose Manufacturing Company
Goodyear's India Rubber Glove Manufacturing Company*
Goodyear Metallic Rubber Shoe Company*
Hastings Wool Boot Company*
National India Rubber Company*
Naugatuck Chemical Company
Revere Rubber Company
Rubber Regenerating Company
Shoe Hardware Company*
Woonsocket Rubber Company*

(The Mishawaka Woolen Manufacturing Company did not deed its lands to United States Rubber at that time.)

*Subject to prior lien of collateral indenture dated Dec. 1, 1908 securing $16 million of 6% collateral trust sinking fund gold bonds, due Dec. 1, 1918.

Among other provisions, the indenture stipulated that no additional bonds (except for refunding) were to be issued (1) unless the unencumbered quick assets of the company and of the subsidiary companies (other than General Rubber Company and its subsidiaries) whose assets were pledged as security should exceed the aggregate debt of the company and of its subsidiaries, including the outstanding bonds and any increased indebtedness resulting from the issue; and (2) unless the annual net income for three years next prior to such issue were at least twice the annual interest upon the entire debt of the company and of its subsidiaries. No dividends (except dividends payable in January and April, 1917 on the preferred stock) were to be paid except from earnings after Dec. 31, 1916 and, other than stock dividends, none were to be paid on its common stock unless the total of unencumbered quick assets after such payment exceeded the aggregate debt.

Another provision was that the net unencumbered quick assets of the wholly owned subsidiaries, excluding the General Rubber Company and its subsidiaries, should at all times equal at least $30 million, of which at least $20 million should be in companies whose stock was directly pledged under the mortgage. This stipulation would cause much concern to the management of the company in later years.[5]

Proceeds of the issue were used to retire all the outstanding obligations of the company and its subsidiaries, with the exception of $2,600,000 of 6% gold bonds of the Canadian Consolidated Rubber Company, Ltd., due Oct. 1, 1946, and $9 million of 5% debentures of the General Rubber Company, due Dec. 1, 1918. For the purpose of retiring these two issues, the 1917 indenture provided for subsequent issue, from time to time, of $11,600,000 of first and refunding mortgage bonds, so long as the total bonds outstanding at any one time would not exceed $97,252,000.

As of Dec. 31, 1917, notes and loans payable were down from $26,704,000 to $19,431,000, and working capital was up to $85,168,000.

The $9 million of General Rubber Company debentures were paid at maturity Dec. 1, 1918, through an issue of $6 million of temporary 7% five-year gold notes, secured by deposit of an additional issue of $9 million of 5% first and refunding mortgage gold bonds series A. (Holders of the debentures who took the new notes received for each $1,000 debenture a $1,000 gold note plus $15 in cash.) The balance of $3 million was obtained from the company's general funds. It is interesting to note that the new offering was delayed until completion of a Liberty Loan campaign.[6]

As noted in Chapter II, payment for the net assets of the several rubber boot and shoe manufacturing companies consolidated to form the United States Rubber Company in 1892 was made with 8% noncumulative preferred stock of United States Rubber. An equal amount of com-

mon stock of the new firm was issued, representing its "increased earning capacity by reason of the consolidation." Thus the original capitalization was virtually twice the appraised value of the assets of the subsidiary companies. The terms of subsequent acquisitions modified the
ratio of capitalization to net worth, but the relatively low book value of
the common stock persisted throughout Colt's administration. Since the
organization of the company in 1892, total dividends declared on preferred and common stock amounted to $69,955,000, as of Dec. 31,
1916. During the same period, the company had financed its expansion in
large measure with a succession of issues of bonds, notes, and debentures.

As of March 31, 1904, the company's total debt had been a little less
than $20 million, and Colt had expressed the directors' belief that it
could be gradually reduced until it was entirely wiped out. However,
the following year the total debt had increased to more than $25 mil-
lion; held to less than $30 million until 1911, it climbed steadily in the
next few years, and the ratio of debt to net worth (which then included
intangible assets) rose to approximately 53% by Dec. 31, 1916. Total indebtedness, including current liabilities, stood at $73,115,000 at the
beginning of 1917 when the decision was made to float the new $60
million bond issue.

This excessive debt load levied a heavy toll on operating profit. Interest charges paid in 1917 amounted to $3,117,857. In 1918, $4,119,-
055 was paid for interest. When the period of expansion came to an
abrupt end in 1920, the financial policies followed in the company's
early years were a heavy burden in the face of reduced earnings.

Organization and Employee Relations

New Plan of Organization

According to Homer E. Sawyer, little had been done, prior to the administration of Colt, toward concentration of authority, proper organization of the various departments, or definition of duties of department
heads. Upon becoming president in May, 1901, Colt had a "plan of organization" prepared by Lester Leland, treasurer of the Boston Rubber
Shoe Company. It was approved "in principle" by the executive committee on June 13, 1901. A revision of the plan, dated Sept. 1, 1902, is
shown in Appendix E. The essential difference of the latter plan from
the one approved in June, 1901 was the creation of the position of "manager of branch stores." Previous to that time they had been under the
general supervision of the manager of sales. In both plans, Leland, the
general manager and treasurer of the Boston Rubber Shoe Company,

reported directly to the president of United States Rubber, and Boston Rubber Shoe was not included with the other rubber companies that were under the supervision of C. L. Johnson.[7]

In 1906, following the acquisition of the Rubber Goods Manufacturing Company, the number of directors was increased to nineteen, and in 1918 to twenty-four. The executive committee was reduced to four members in 1902, but the following year it was enlarged to five, two years later to six, and in 1907 to seven; this number was reduced to five on Dec. 31, 1915. At that time, three additional vice-presidents were named to be in charge of the development, footwear, and tire and mechanical departments.

The manner in which the various companies comprising United States Rubber Company had been brought together created a serious human problem that confronted Colt throughout most of his administration. There were the employees of the several rubber footwear companies from which the United States Rubber Company was formed originally, together with employees of footwear companies acquired later. The employees of the several tire and mechanical goods companies brought into the organization with the acquisition of the Rubber Goods Manufacturing Company in 1905 formed a second large group. Neither of these two major groups was homogeneous in itself. Employees of the companies so consolidated did not readily relinquish their loyalties to their own firms and immediate associates. The later purchases of Canadian Consolidated Rubber Company, Ltd., Revere Rubber Company, and the Rubber Regenerating Company, and the organization of the development department only magnified the problem.[8]

In May, 1914, the company began monthly publication of *House Organ*, which shortly became known as *Between US*. It was devoted to the interests of the branches, and over the next ten years endeavored to foster a community of interest among salesmen for the different elements in the United States Rubber System. This goal also was one of the principal objectives of the conventions of salesmen that were held in the late months of 1915. Even though Colt was not entirely successful in his efforts to weld the many units and their executives into a fully harmonious, cooperative organization, the degree to which harmony was effected is evidence of his skill, tact, and perseverance.

To strengthen the management of the company, the by-laws were amended in March, 1918 to provide for creation of the offices of chairman and vice-chairman of the board of directors, and to recognize formally the operating council, composed of heads of the operating departments. The president presided over the meetings of the operating council and presented its recommendations to the executive committee, of which he was also a member.

Profit Sharing and Stock Subscription Plans

United States Rubber was one of the first of the larger corporations to make it possible for key employees to acquire a financial interest in the company on favorable terms.

Early in 1904, the company distributed among about 150 of its principal employees a certain number of shares of its preferred and common stock. The stock was immediately transferred to the name of the employee, and thereafter he received all dividends paid on the shares in his name. The certificates were endorsed by him in blank and were held by the Meyer Rubber Company. If the employee continued in the service of the United States Rubber Company until Jan. 1, 1908, he could take possession of the stock upon payment of $45 a share (and interest from April 1, 1904 at 6% per annum) for the preferred and $10 a share and interest for the common stock. Payments on account could be made from time to time for purchase of the stock, and, if the employee did not exercise his option in January, 1908, any money paid by him would be refunded with interest at 6% per annum. In no event would interest charged be in excess of dividends paid on the stock. Under certain conditions the option would be extended to Feb. 1, 1910.

Comments in the annual reports in 1905 and 1906 indicate that the effect on the interest, zeal, and loyalty of the participating employees had been all that was desired.

Under a profit sharing and stock subscription plan adopted in 1912, all officials and salaried men receiving $1,300 and more per annum were given options to subscribe for common stock of the company at $45 a share. The number of shares allotted ranged from one share for an employee receiving a salary of $1,300 a year to twenty shares for those with annual salaries of $10,000 or more. As an inducement to purchase stock under this plan, the employee was awarded a share in the company's profits in accordance with the following schedule:

Salary Ranges*	Percentage as Basis for Share of Profits
$ 1,300-4,500, inclusive	3
5,000-7,000, inclusive	5
7,500-9,500, inclusive	8
10,000 and up	15

*Apparently, salary increments above $4,500 were in $500 units.

The shares of common stock were purchased in the market by the Meyer Rubber Company and repurchased from Meyer by United States Rubber, which then sold them to the employees at a price decided each year by the company. This price in 1912 was $45 a share; by 1919, it had risen to $70, and in 1920 was $100 a share. None was issued after 1920.

Payments were made at the rate of not less than $4 a month per share. The employee subscribing for stock would receive all dividends declared on the stock and, in addition, the company would give the subscriber a cash payment of $3 per share each year for five years, provided the subscriber retained his stock for five years and obtained at the end of each year a certificate of satisfactory service during the year. The employee could cancel his stock subscription at any time and have his money refunded with 5% interest. If he should die within the five-year period, his family would be entitled to the credits he would have had under the plan had he lived.

In an effort to broaden the interest of employees in the company and to enable them "to share in the values which they were helping to create," a value sharing plan was set up in 1916. Under this plan, the company carried, for certain employees, common stock of the company bought in the open market and sold to them at cost. This plan provided that the shares sold to an employee should be carried for ten years. However, at the end of two years a worker could withdraw one-fifth of his stock, paying one-fifth of the amount owed to the company. At the end of four years, he could withdraw another fifth, paying one-fourth of the amount owed; at the end of six years, another fifth, paying one-third of the amount owed; at the end of eight years, another fifth, paying one-half of the amount owed; at the end of the tenth year, the residue was to be withdrawn on payment of the full amount due.[9] By 1920 over 4,500 employees were reported to be included in the several stock option, profit sharing, and value sharing plans, and the balance sheet of Dec. 31, 1920 showed over $7 million in notes receivable of employees given for stock purchased and carried for them by the company. In addition, common stock of the company with book value of $2,427,705 was being carried by the company under service contracts and agreements with certain of the principal officers. As previously indicated, it had been Colt's judgment that ownership of the stock of the company increased the employee's interest in the prosperity of the company and was therefore of advantage both to it and the employee.

The contributions by the company under the profit sharing and stock subscription plans for the first and final two years of operation were:

Year	Price Established for Common Stock of Company	Company Contributions For Profit Sharing	For $3 a Share Payments
1912	$ 45	$188,000	$ 27,266
1919	70	293,937	126,756
1920	100	391,619	144,918

The payments of $3 on each share purchased by employees under the stock subscription plan were continued until 1925, in accordance with the original offer.[10] (The sharp decline in the market price of United States Rubber common, which would occur in the 1920's and the steps the company would take to protect the interests of employees who had signed five-year notes covering cost of stock subscriptions will be discussed in Chapter V.)

In 1917, United States Rubber inaugurated a pension plan for "aged and infirm employees." This was one of the first pension plans to be adopted by a major business firm in the United States. Compared to the company's pension plan of recent years, the provisions of the 1917 plan were very modest. Even though the plan was not funded, it marked an important advance in corporate concern for employees with long service.

The comments regarding the foregoing plans that were made in the president's annual reports from time to time make it appear obvious that Colt was personally responsible for much of the thinking which was accountable for their adoption. Edgar B. Davis was another officer who held strong views regarding the importance of profit sharing plans as well as of other means that would assist employees to obtain a larger financial interest in the company.

In a letter dated Feb. 7, 1917, Davis wrote that the "Value Sharing Plan of the United States Rubber Company . . . represents one of our first moves to increase the earning power of the Company."[11] However, the beneficial effects anticipated by both him and Colt would not be realized because of the sharp decline in the value of the company's stock due to the break of commodity prices in 1920. In the judgment of a later writer, neither the value sharing plan nor a plan inaugurated in 1919 to assist employees in purchasing additional stock in United States Rubber were successful either as morale builders or as incentives for increasing the company's profits.[12]

DIVERSIFICATION

Mention has been made of United States Rubber's sales of nonrubber products, which formed 20% of the company's total net sales in 1963. The company's earliest ventures into these fields and into the production of such items as reclaimed rubber, buckles, felt linings, and lasts for boots and shoes were prompted by the advantages of having materials used in the manufacture of rubber footwear supplied by the company's own plants. During the presidency of Colt, the first major steps were taken toward the manufacture of items not related to footwear.

Formation of Naugatuck Chemical Company

Large quantities of dilute sulfuric acid were required for the process then used for reclaiming old rubber. Prior to 1904, United States Rubber had bought sulfuric acid from the General Chemical Company, which was a member of an association of manufacturers of acids. It was suspected that the members had an informal understanding regarding allocation of territories, for when General Chemical raised the price of sulfuric acid in 1903, United States Rubber was unable to obtain its requirements from any other source.

On May 12, 1904, the board of directors appointed Commodore Elias C. Benedict (who was one of its members), Homer E. Sawyer, and William T. Rodenbach (manager of the company's reclaiming works at Naugatuck) as a committee to consider the advisability of manufacturing sulfuric acid. The committee approved a proposal submitted by Charles E. Sholes for incorporation of a company that would manufacture and deal in chemicals; the company would contract to supply the entire acid requirements of the United States Rubber Reclaiming Works at Naugatuck at cost plus 10%, but not in excess of 60¢ per 100 pounds, for 66 degree acid. Naugatuck Chemical Company was incorporated under the laws of New York, June 1, 1904, and Sholes was hired to supervise construction and to manage the plant.

The company was capitalized at $100,000, of which the Meyer Rubber Company, a wholly owned subsidiary of United States Rubber, subscribed $85,000. Benedict subscribed $10,000 and Sholes, $5,000, both men having first agreed to assign their stock to Meyer Rubber Company. At the first directors' meeting, Benedict was elected president and Sholes, secretary-treasurer. In addition to these two officers, the first board of directors included Colt, Sawyer, James B. Ford, Samuel Norris, and John J. Watson, all officially connected with United States Rubber Company.[13]

13.   Naugatuck Chemical Company plant, Naugatuck, Conn., 1905.

Sholes' most recent employment had been with the General Chemical Company, apparently as a commission salesman. In one capacity or another, he had been in the chemical business for more than twenty years. At his suggestion, Matthew Adgate, who at the time was superintendent of the General Chemical Company's plant at Syracuse, was employed as superintendent of the Naugatuck acid plant (Figure 13). Ground for the new plant was broken on July 12, 1904. Although Sholes' first proposal had been for a plant with annual capacity of 4,000-4,500 tons of 60 degree acid (almost twice the requirements of the Naugatuck Reclaiming Works), Benedict is said to have encouraged him to build a 9,000-ton plant, and construction actually was begun on a plant with a capacity of 10,000 tons of sulfuric acid a year. Before it was completed, Sholes recommended that it be enlarged one-third, and that units for manufacturing muriatic, nitric, and acetic acids be added. He said he needed $83,000 more than the original capital of $100,000, and on Nov. 10, 1904 he was given authority to borrow $85,000 for these purposes.

Meanwhile, in August, 1904, Naugatuck Chemical Company had contracted for 16,200 tons of iron pyrites (pyrite is a relatively common iron disulfide) to be delivered over the next three years. This mineral would be burned or roasted to form gaseous sulfur dioxide. By using gaseous nitrogen oxide as a catalyst and by injecting water, either as steam or spray, into the lead chamber through which the gases were circulated, sulfuric acid of about 50 degree Baume purity, suitable for the acid process of reclaiming rubber, was formed and could be drawn off.

Sholes' conception of the proper function of the Chemical Company appears to have been far different from that of the directors of United States Rubber. While they were probably chiefly interested in obtaining sulfuric acid at a lower cost, he, supported by Benedict, set about to build a plant that would make a line of acids and derivatives. Since it would be necessary to sell the surplus sulfuric acid in direct competition with General Chemical Company and others, Sholes thought it essential to have a line that included other acids. Lead acetate and Glauber's salt were also among other items produced prior to 1915.

Colonial Tank Line, Inc.

In keeping with his ambitious plans, the Colonial Tank Line Company, Inc. was incorporated Nov. 21, 1904 under the laws of Connecticut, with authorized capital stock of $10,000, $5,000 of which was issued and, except for directors' qualifying shares, was entirely taken by Naugatuck Chemical Company. In 1906, Naugatuck Chemical subscribed another $5,000 issue. Five tank cars were purchased by the Tank Line Company, two of which were sold in 1906, but in March, 1909 the reported assets included eight tank cars valued at $6,263 after depreciation. Earnings of the Tank Line Company averaged only $315 for each of the last five years of its operation, and the corporation was dissolved in 1914.

Charles E. Sholes Company

A five-year contract, effective June 1, 1904, had granted Sholes 5% commission on sales to purchasers other than United States Rubber or any of its subsidiaries. He assigned this contract to the Charles E. Sholes Company, which later was appointed selling agent of the Naugatuck Chemical Company.

Between 1904 and 1910, under Sholes' management, Naugatuck Chemical Company incurred indebtedness of a little over $400,000. A price war with the General Chemical Company was largely responsible for this indebtedness. However, Sholes' overambitious efforts to extend the activities of the company far beyond the intention or authorization of the board of directors of United States Rubber as well as, to a small extent, an alleged diversion of funds collected for the account of Naugatuck Chemical Company were also contributing factors.

Since Benedict was highly regarded at that time by the other directors of United States Rubber, there seems to have been an inclination to concur in his judgment or that of his protégé, Sholes, but as early as 1905, some questions may have been raised regarding the obligations that Naugatuck Chemical was incurring. Benedict offered to guarantee United States Rubber's investment in Naugatuck Chemical, but his offer was declined. In 1906, there was some talk of selling Naugatuck Chemical, and an offer from Benedict to take over United States Rubber's investment in the company at cost and interest was accepted by the executive committee; but for some reason no action was taken.

In June, 1908, a committee of its members, appointed by the board of directors of the rubber company, charged that Benedict had been lax in protecting the interests of Naugatuck Chemical and United States Rubber. It was alleged that he had permitted funds collected for the account of United States Rubber and others to be used by the Sholes company in acquiring the capital stock of the Binns Chemical Works and in enlarging that plant. Eleven creditors, including Naugatuck Chemical, accepted 4½% debenture notes of the Sholes company, due June 1, 1910. Naugatuck Chemical's claim was $39,199. In September, 1908, Sholes resigned as vice-president of Naugatuck Chemical, but remained a director for another year. Meanwhile, the charges against Benedict had not been pressed. In 1910, the creditors' committee accepted, in full settlement of claims against the Sholes company, 10% cash and a one-year note for an additional 5% plus accrued interest on the 4½% notes. The sales contract with the Sholes company expired in 1910, and H. Stuart Hotchkiss was appointed manager of sales of Naugatuck Chemical Company.

Dissolution of the New York Corporation

A new company was incorporated in Connecticut on Jan. 18, 1911 under the name of The Naugatuck Chemical Company, with authorized capital stock of $500,000. The new company, which was a wholly-owned subsidiary of the United States Rubber Company, purchased all the assets of the old (New York) corporation for an amount equal to the liabilities of that corporation, totaling $402,000, and the New York corporation was dissolved on Oct. 19, 1911.

Acquisition of Rubber Goods Manufacturing Company

At a special meeting on May 25, 1905, United States Rubber stockholders unanimously approved a contract with A. N. Brady (a director of the company and manager of a syndicate including certain other directors), which authorized the syndicate to acquire capital stock of the Rubber Goods Manufacturing Company, New Brunswick.

At the same meeting the certificate of organization of United States Rubber was amended. First, the 8% preferred stock was changed to 8% first preferred and increased to 400,000 shares; of these, 235,255 shares would be issuable share for share of the outstanding preferred stock of United States Rubber Company, and 90,514 shares of first preferred would be issuable share for share of the preferred stock of Rubber Goods Manufacturing Company. The remainder would be reserved for future requirements. Second, the amendment also authorized the issue of 100,000 shares of 6% second preferred, all issuable to the syndicate.

The contract with Brady stipulated that, if the syndicate should deliver to United States Rubber Company all of the capital stock of the Rubber Goods Company by Nov. 30, 1905, United States Rubber would issue in exchange 90,514 shares of its own 8% first preferred and 100,000 shares of 6% second preferred stock. If not all but at least 67% of the capital stock of Rubber Goods Company were delivered by Nov. 30, 1905, United States Rubber Company would deduct from the above totals $100 of 8% first preferred for each share of preferred not delivered, and $50 of 6% second preferred for each share of common stock of Rubber Goods Manufacturing Company not delivered. If 67% of the capital stock of Rubber Goods Manufacturing Company should be delivered by Nov. 30, 1905, the offer would be extended to holders of the remaining shares until May 1, 1906. Later this provision was extended to Nov. 1, 1906, and 3,000 shares of first preferred stock of United States Rubber were authorized to be issued from time to time until Nov. 1, 1906.

In the listing statement to the New York Stock Exchange, dated Oct. 5, 1905, it was said that United States Rubber had issued 51,148 shares of its 8% first preferred in exchange for an equal number of shares of the preferred stock of Rubber Goods Manufacturing Company, and had issued 83,873 shares of 6% second preferred stock to the syndicate for 137,163 shares of the common stock of Rubber Goods Manufacturing Company.

After its incorporation in January, 1899 (see Chapter II) the Rubber Goods Company, as it was frequently called, had prospered. It had net income of $1,267,000 for 1901 and paid dividends of $563,598 on its preferred stock and $338,834 on its common stock.

Among its subsidiaries were four of the larger tire companies of that period, with large and profitable sales of bicycle tires and a growing market for automobile tires. The company's strategic position in the tire market, as well as the firmly established market for its hose, belting, packing, grinding wheels, and other mechanical rubber goods, attracted the attention of a young financier, Bernard Baruch, who related that in the brief panic of 1903 he purchased some shares of Rubber Goods Company. He then tried to interest Daniel Guggenheim in joining him in buying control of the company, but when he did not receive any immediate response, Baruch sold his holdings.[14]

In 1900, Rubber Goods Company, through one of its subsidiaries, had acquired the capital stock of American Dunlop Tire Company. This acquisition was particularly important since it gained for the company the American patent rights on the Dunlop straightside tire. However, the importance of this tire construction was not properly recognized at the time.

In 1905, when United States Rubber had acquired more than a controlling interest in the Rubber Goods Company, the latter was about the same size as United States Rubber and was said to control about 60% of the business on mechanical rubber goods.[15] In the president's annual report, dated May 15, 1906, Colt said over 80% of the capital stock of Rubber Goods Manufacturing Company had been thus acquired, to the benefit of both companies. No footwear was manufactured by Rubber Goods Company, and the sales of the miscellaneous rubber goods it made (belting, packing, hose, automobile tires, bicycle and carriage tires, flooring, clothing, druggist's sundries) were affected more by general business conditions than by weather. On the contrary, the United States Rubber Company's production had been confined almost exclusively to rubber footwear; its sales volume therefore depended largely upon the severity of the winter. Since both companies used much the same materials and distributed their products through agencies located in the same centers, it was anticipated that substantial economies could be effected. The annual report of the president added that the volume of both business and profits should tend to equalize in years of varying conditions.

It will be noted that in many respects the product mix of the United States Rubber Company through the years has steadily tended to make the company more nearly an outgrowth of the Rubber Goods Manufacturing Company than of the group of factories that were brought together to form the original United States Rubber Company in 1892. The extent of the contribution which the acquisition of the Rubber Goods Manufacturing Company made to the over-all sturdiness of United States Rubber is indicated by an analysis of the balance sheet and operating statement of the latter as of March 31, 1913, which was the first time the operations of the Rubber Goods Company were included in the consolidated statements of United States Rubber. The statement reveals that the surplus of the Rubber Goods Company as of Jan. 1, 1912 had been $8,260,877, almost as much as United States Rubber's $9,175,730 surplus as of April 1, 1912.[16] Net sales were almost $50 million more than the previous high, established in fiscal 1907-08, and net worth as of March 31, 1913 had been increased by more than $29 million over the previous year's figure. A substantial portion of these gains had been contributed by the Rubber Goods Company.

Mishawaka Woolen Mfg. Co.

Control of the Mishawaka Woolen Mfg. Co., a manufacturer of rubber and woolen footwear, located in Mishawaka, Ind., was acquired in 1905 by Colt as manager of a syndicate including about thirty men. The Mishawaka company later became a wholly owned subsidiary of United States Rubber.

Canadian Consolidated Rubber Company, Ltd.

Early in 1907, United States Rubber had acquired "much more than a controlling interest" in the Canadian Consolidated Rubber Company, Ltd. (now known as Dominion Rubber Company, Limited), which had been formed through a consolidation of the principal rubber companies in Canada. This company manufactured "practically all lines of rubber goods, including tires," according to the United States Rubber Company's annual report for the year ended March 31, 1911. The Canadian operations will be discussed further in connection with other international undertakings of United States Rubber.

Revere Rubber Company

The next important acquisition of United States Rubber was the purchase in late December, 1909 of "virtually all" the stock of the Revere Rubber Company for $4 million. Revere was purchased, according to Colt's statement in the annual report for the fiscal 1909-10 year, in order to obtain the services of Elisha S. Williams, Revere's general

14. Elisha S. Williams

manager. The president of the Rubber Goods Manufacturing Company, Charles H. Dale, died in July, 1908, and Williams was found to be the most qualified person to succeed him. When negotiations were opened with Williams in December, 1909, he agreed to accept the presidency of the Rubber Goods Company only on condition that all shareholders of Revere should receive an offer for all their shares at the market price.

To provide the necessary funds for this purchase and $1 million for the purchase of outstanding shares of the Canadian Consolidated Rubber Company, Ltd., as well as to supply United States Rubber Company with the additional working capital needed for its expanding business, Colt and some of the other directors formed a Revere-Canadian syndicate. An agreement was made to buy at $110 a share all of the as yet unissued 35,614 shares of first preferred stock which would remain unsold after being offered to stockholders. The syndicate also offered to purchase at par $2,500,000 of the $5 million of 6% collateral trust sinking fund bonds remaining unsold from an issue of $20 million created Dec. 1, 1908, and to purchase the remaining $2,500,000 at the option of the company any time prior to Dec. 20, 1910, meanwhile lending the full amount at 6% interest.

In a circular dated Dec. 23, 1909, the new issue of first preferred was offered to shareholders for pro rata subscription on the basis of 5%

of their holdings of record Jan. 15, 1910, whereupon they took 27,997 shares of first preferred and the syndicate took the remaining 7,617 shares. The syndicate also carried out the other parts of its agreement. By these transactions, the company was provided with about $9 million cash, leaving about $4 million to be added to working capital after the purchase of the capital stock of Revere and additional shares of the Canadian Consolidated Rubber Company, Ltd.

Williams became president of Rubber Goods Manufacturing Company on Jan. 5, 1910 and was later elected a director of United States Rubber. While the major reason for acquiring the Revere Rubber Company was undoubtedly as stated by Colt, this acquisition also gave United States Rubber an important position in the manufacture and sale of rubber soles and heels.

The contract provided that the syndicate, as compensation for its services in financing the acquisition of the Revere Rubber Company, should receive the net profits of Revere during the twenty-five month period ending Dec. 31, 1911, but that any profits in excess of $700,000 would be divided equally between the syndicate and company. After Dec. 31, 1911, United States Rubber would receive all the profits. (Revere's earnings during the twenty-five month period were $762,578, and the syndicate was paid $731,289.) In the annual report to the stockholders issued in May, 1911, Colt stated that the volume of business done during the fiscal year just closed by companies acquired prior to April 1, 1905, was $31,869,000; the year's volume done by companies acquired since April 1, 1905 was $52,143,000, and the percentage of profit on the latter, based on the cost of acquisition of those properties, was more than twice the profit on the business of the properties purchased prior to April 1, 1905, estimated on a like basis.

Other Acquisitions

A relatively minor acquisition in 1913 was the purchase of the controlling interest of the Wellman Company, manufacturers of shoe machinery, including Wellman sole cutters. Practically all rubber boot and shoe manufacturers paid royalties, based on the number of soles cut, for the use of the Wellman machines. Also acquired during Colt's presidency were Eureka Fire Hose (1906), Hastings Wool Boot Company (1906), Rubber Regenerating Company (1912), and McCord-Norton Shoe Company, manufacturers of leather shoes (1917).[17]

The policy of retaining the corporate identity of most of the companies acquired led to the maintenance of most of the manufacturing plants operated by the subsidiaries. United States Rubber Company proudly advertised in 1916 that it owned "forty-seven great factories,"[18] with combined floor space of over 8,300,000 square feet, equivalent to 191 acres, and employed about 35,000 persons (Figure 15). From our present viewpoint, the excessive cost incurred in operating many inefficient plants is obvious, but apparently it was not so clear to top management in 1916 or in 1919 when it boasted it was "the largest rubber company in the world, largest in value of output, largest in control of sources of raw materials, largest in number of employees, largest in number of manufacturing plants, and largest in extent of its activities."[19] When F. B. Davis, Jr. became president in 1929, he acted quickly to close many of these plants and to consolidate production in the most efficient and best located factories.

TYPES OF MECHANICAL RUBBER GOODS

The various subsidiary companies in the United States Rubber System offered a wide variety of hose, including water, fire, steam and air hose, oil suction hose, air drill and steam drill hose for rock blasting operations, suction hose and sleeves for dredging, and hose for oil well drilling capable of withstanding pressure of 200 pounds per square inch (as much as 2,000 p.s.i. is required now).

In the early days, manufacture of rubber hose began by wrapping a sheet of rubber around a mandrel. Next, multiple plies of cotton duck impregnated with rubber were wound spirally around the rubber tube; finally a covering sheet of rubber was applied. This structure was tightly wrapped with fabric strips and vulcanized. After the mandrel was removed, the hose was ready for service. Hose made in this manner was subject to failure because of thin spots in the tube or rubber cover caused by the bias laps of fabric or failure of the bias laps.

Over the years many improvements were made in the art of making rubber hose. In 1910 the New York Belting and Packing Company, Passaic, N.J., started working toward elimination of the most common defects. Vertical braiding machines were available for producing a reinforcing ply, but these would not produce hose uniform in size and strength. Development of horizontal braiding equipment was undertaken in the period before World War I, and N.Y.B. and P. introduced a new line of hose for water, steam, or air, in which a braided ply of yarn replaced the bias fabric directly underneath the rubber cover. Eventually, all the bias fabric plies were replaced with braided plies. Accurate size was maintained by the use of mandrels; a highly uniform prod-

The Fruits of the Rubber Tree

RUBBER TREES first gave shade and a harborage to the birds of the forest. That was all they gave for many ages. Then a beetle bored into the bark and a liquid oozed out which barbaric man discovered could be dried into crude balls to play with. Then civilized man found how these balls could be transformed into things to serve all mankind.

The birth of the rubber tree is lost in the shadowy past. The birth of the rubber industry is comparatively recent. Seventy-four years ago the first factory was licensed to make rubber goods. This pioneer plant—the great-great-grandfather of the entire rubber industry of the world—is now an important unit of the United States Rubber Company.

Pictured here are thirty-four of the forty-seven great factories owned by the United States Rubber Company, the world's largest producer of rubber goods, including Footwear, Clothing, Automobile and Bicycle Tires, Druggists' Sundries, Insulated Wire, Soles and Heels, Belting, Hose, Packing, Mechanical and Moulded Rubber Goods of all kinds.

If all of these factories were grouped in one locality, if the army of workers and their families were housed around the mammoth plant so formed, there would arise a mighty city—larger than Rochester, larger than Louisville, St. Paul or Denver.

It is only by such an imaginative comparison that one can sense the tremendous size and activities of this giant organization, which manufactures and distributes throughout the world every article into which rubber is made.

That the United States Rubber Company is the leader in this great field is a distinction won simply by merit. It has responded most satisfactorily to the rubber requirements of the people. It has, through persistent and exhaustive research, been constantly active in finding new ways to turn rubber to the benefit of mankind. It has consistently maintained the quality of its products under all conditions. It has been enabled through its size, through the variety and quantity balance of its output, and through the age and organized experience of its associated companies to combine, in all its products, quality and economy in the maximum.

United States Rubber Company

15.   Advertisement. "The Fruits of the Rubber Tree" (*Life*, Aug. 3, 1916).

uct was obtained by extruding the tube and rubber cover, and by curing with a lead jacket, which resulted in a smooth outer surface and exact exterior measurements. These developments eventually led to the introduction of wire-braided hose in the 1920's (see Chapter VI).

Among the mechanical rubber goods manufacturers who were part of the Rubber Goods Manufacturing Company, the N.Y.B. and P. was the largest. In 1909 the total production of the Revere Rubber Company, acquired by United States Rubber in late December of that year, was approximately $6 million, but this production included its manufacture of Continental tires as well as mechanical rubber goods. A general line of belting, hose, packings (both sheet and rod), molded specialties, tubing, and sundries was offered by N.Y.B. and P. Rubber soles and Spring-Step heels were important products of the Providence plant of Revere; Revere also made insulated wire, flooring, and roll covering.

However, most of the mechanical rubber goods companies that were consolidated in the Rubber Goods Manufacturing Company, or otherwise acquired by United States Rubber, were relatively small and tended to specialize in certain products. For example, the Peerless Rubber Company, New Durham, N.J., which made rubber belting and other mechanical goods, was best known for its Rainbow packing. Peerless for many years made all the flooring for Pullman cars, as well as the safety treads for the car steps.

Sawyer Belting Company, Cleveland, Ohio, specialized in canvas belts. Mechanical Rubber Company, also of Cleveland, was one of the largest producers of jar rings, tape, and molded specialties. Mechanical Rubber Company of Chicago made roll covering and flooring in addition to belting. Fabric Fire Hose Manufacturing Company, Sandy Hook, Conn., and the Eureka Fire Hose Company, Jersey City, N.J. (acquired by United States Rubber in 1906) made fire hose only. A principal product of the Mechanical Fabric Company, Providence, R.I., was rubber thread, which also was manufactured by N.Y.B. and P. and by Revere. Mechanical Fabric also made printers' blankets. Hard rubber goods were made by the India Rubber Company, New Brunswick, Conn.

The specialized equipment and know-how possessed by these companies did much to assure quality products. Continued development of new products to keep abreast of changing demands contributed materially to the over-all success of United States Rubber. Perhaps even more important, the inclusion in the System of such a broad range of products, in addition to rubber footwear and tires, enabled management in future years to avail itself of an exceptionally wide variety of skills when new conditions called for further diversification.[20]

Packings

Belting

Hose

16. Products and uses, 1919. Above are some types of mechanical rubber goods made by United Rubber Company. Below, a "U.S." transmission belt is installed on the bleachers at a Spanish Fork factory.

Insulated Wire and Cable

Railroads and mining operations offered large markets for mechanical rubber goods. Also, until most machinery was operated by motors directly connected with or incorporated in each machine, most factories had a central power plant and engine room using either waterpower or steam. The power thus developed was transmitted to some parts of the factory directly by line shafts, and to other sections by belts or rope transmissions that turned other line shafts. If the equipment in a given room did not require gear drives, the machines were often connected by belts to an overhead line shaft. This practice created a large market for many sizes and types of transmission belting. From the early days of the rubber industry, rubber conveyors and elevator belting were in common use in grain elevators and mining operations, and it so happened that by 1910, when direct motor drives were decreasing the demand for transmission belting, the use of rubber belts for conveying or elevating bulk materials was increasing rapidly.

Successful salesmen for the System's mechanical goods had to have some knowledge of engineering principles and their practical application in order to render satisfactory service to their accounts. In 1915 their combined sales accounted for approximately 60 million pounds of mechanical rubber goods, a creditable performance.[21]

RUBBER PLANTATIONS ESTABLISHED

Formation of General Rubber Company

Prior to 1914, most of the crude rubber used in the United States came from Brazil where the wild rubber trees grew in the Amazon jungle. Of the many types and qualities of native rubber, the best known was "up-river fine Para," which took its name from the port from which much of it was shipped. By the latter part of the nineteenth century, Para was ordinarily formed into large "biscuits" somewhat in the shape of a large ham. With the advent of the high prices for rubber that prevailed during much of the time prior to World War I, it became customary to saw each biscuit in half to detect rocks or other foreign material, often deliberately inserted by the natives between successive layers of rubber to increase the weight.

The prices of crude rubber fluctuated widely, and began to mount as more uses were found for rubber—first in footwear, raincoats, blankets, and robes, then in tires for bicycles and, by the end of the century, in automobile tires. Sharp and sudden price increases often resulted from efforts of speculators to corner the crude rubber market, from unfavorable gathering conditions, or from threatened interference with shipping, such as the threat of blockade of shipments of rubber from South America prior to and during the Spanish-American War.

The original formation of United States Rubber had as one of its stated objectives the purchase of its requirements of crude rubber at more favorable prices as the result of centralized buying. The first important step toward this goal was taken in 1894, when each company was asked to report details connected with its purchases and, by 1896, a central buying agency was established. As early as 1895, the company and its subsidiaries consumed from 7 to 10 million pounds of crude rubber annually. In 1901 their purchases of crude rubber amounted to $9,068,379. Earnings were significantly affected by the erratic changes in the price of the company's principal raw material, which at that time represented almost 50% of the total cost of manufacture. (Prices for crude rubber are shown in Figure 17.) By 1902, United States Rubber had arranged to import most of its rubber under its own letters of credit, saving commissions formerly paid to importing firms.

In 1903, the company obtained an interest in concessions, granted by the Bolivian government to British principals, covering 30 million acres on the upper Amazon. Evidently part of the acreage lay in territory claimed by Brazil, and the undertaking had to be abandoned "owing to complications with Brazil, Brazil paying an indemnity."[22] Brazil did not pay the indemnity, for a revolution occurred soon after, and the new government repudiated the debt. Numerous attempts to collect it were unsuccessful.[23] In 1904, the General Rubber Company, a subsidiary, was established to give United States Rubber advantages in price and a "guarantee as to supply, not at the present time enjoyed by any other consumer in the world."[24]

The General Rubber Company established agencies for the purpose of acquiring and trading in crude rubber at Para and Manaos on the Amazon River in Brazil, and also in London and Liverpool. Before World War I, as plantation rubber became important, other offices were opened in Singapore, Straits Settlements, and in Colombo, Ceylon.

Guayule Promoted by Intercontinental

The rapid advance in the price of crude rubber (fine Para rose from an annual average price of 72.7¢ a pound in 1902 to an average of $1.088 a pound, landed New York, for the year 1904) aroused great interest in the possibility of profitable extraction of rubber from the guayule shrub, which grew wild on semiarid lands in northern Mexico. The rubber se-

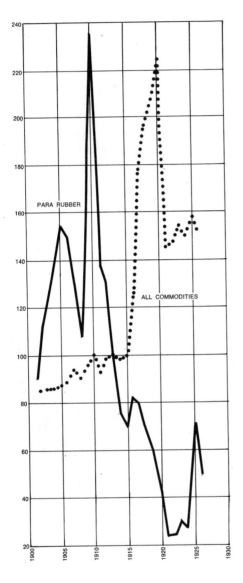

17. Average annual prices, Para rubber and all commodities, 1902-26 (see Table A-2; 1913= 100).

creted in its fibers was extracted by pulverizing the dried shrub and separating the rubber from the fiber by a flotation process.

In November, 1904, Bernard Baruch formed the Intercontinental Rubber Company to cultivate guayule. Associated with Baruch in this undertaking were Senator Nelson E. Aldrich, Thomas Fortune Ryan, Daniel Guggenheim, John D. Rockefeller, Jr., H. P. Whitney, and others. The

Intercontinental Rubber Company purchased more than 3 million acres of land and erected an extraction plant at Torreon in the state of Coahuila, Mexico. In 1905, 10,656 tons of guayule rubber were imported by the United States, but by 1908, imports had fallen to 2,756 tons.[25]

In his autobiography, Baruch stated that the Rubber Goods Manufacturing Company contracted for practically the entire output for two years, but later claimed that the product did not meet specifications and canceled the contract. Baruch said he was dissuaded from suing United States Rubber, which by that time had acquired Rubber Goods Manufacturing Company.[26]

Baruch then proposed to some of his associates that they should buy the United States Rubber Company in order to have a manufacturing outlet for guayule, but the proposal did not materialize and Baruch sold his holdings in Intercontinental. It was probably to this proposal that reference was made by Colt in the annual report for 1906 when he said, "A suggested consolidation with the Continental [sic] Rubber Company] was deemed by Your Directors to be non-advisable," and he added "that the Company and the General Rubber Company have now agreed upon terms of an arrangement which insures complete harmony and cooperation hereafter between the United States Rubber Company and the Continental Rubber Company. . . ."

Guayule had a high resin content and lost an estimated 15% of its weight on the removal of this resin.[27] This fact, together with other properties of the guayule gum, rendered it unsatisfactory for general use, but it was employed successfully in combination with other rubbers, particularly to soften a compound or to give it extra tackiness. During World War II, after natural rubber was no longer available for the purpose, guayule was used with buna-S synthetic rubber in a "sealant" compound in self-sealing fuel cells for military aircraft.[28] During the revolutionary fighting which started in Mexico in 1910, following the overthrow of Diaz by Madero, various armies overran the properties of the Intercontinental Rubber Company, and the plant at Torreon was closed.

Land Leased for Plantations

In 1905 and 1906, the activities of Brazilian and European speculators forced the spot price of Para rubber to above $1.30 a pound. A similar pool drove the price of fine Para rubber to an unprecedented high in July, 1910. During a period of about fifteen months in 1909-10, the price remained above $1.50 a pound, and much of that time it ranged above

18. Tapping of rubber tree on United States Rubber Company plantation, Malaya.

$2.00. The New York price of fine Para rubber rose from $2.73 a pound on April 1, 1910 to $3.00, then fell to a low of $1.13, and at the end of March, 1911 was quoted at $1.43 a pound.

Several companies had been formed in London and Holland to operate rubber plantations in Ceylon, Sumatra, Java, Borneo, and the Malay Peninsula, where tropical temperatures, abundant and regular rainfall, moderate winds, and an abundant supply of suitable labor provided favorable conditions for rubber plantations. (As late as 1946, it was stated that on a well-run estate about 235 men were required for each 1,000 acres being tapped.[29]) On May 17, 1910, in the annual report for the 1909-10 fiscal year, Colt commented that the current price of about $3 a pound was about eight to ten times the cost of producing a pound of rubber on these plantations.

While on a trip through the Far East in 1908, Edgar B. Davis, then a vice-president of the Crawford Shoe Company, had been impressed by the growing importance of rubber cultivation and was imbued with the idea that United States Rubber could profitably operate a rubber plantation in Sumatra. Returning to America, he sold this idea to the directors who appropriated $1.5 million in 1909 to cover the initial expense connected with acquiring rubber plantations in the Far East. Davis was sent to investigate the most promising sites and was aided by W. J. Gallagher, then director of agriculture for the Malay States, and by Huibreght Ketner, a veteran tobacco planter. The problems of adequate rainfall, drainage, soil, quantity and quality of available labor, transportation, and many other matters bearing upon the profitable operation of a rubber plantation were carefully surveyed.

Titles to the plantations in Sumatra were agricultural concessions made for a period of years subject to payment of annual charges and with right of renewal under certain conditions, which were granted by the local governments subject to approval by the Netherlands East Indies government. Davis and his associates recommended against leasing previously planted rubber plantations (probably to avoid starting with diseased trees). Acting on their recommendation, Colt went to Holland in 1910 and purchased from the Nieuwe Asahan Tabac Maatschappij (a tobacco company) for 1,750,000 guilders (then about $700,000) a fifty-two year lease on the Soengei Sikassim concession for cultivation of some 88,000 acres, partially cleared and cultivated for raising tobacco, about 100 miles south of the port of Belawan on the northeast coast of Sumatra. Much of the property was still jungle. This was to become the first rubber plantation owned by an American rubber manufacturer. (The first year's tobacco crop sold for $300,000, thereby reducing net cost of the lease to $400,000.[30])

Ketner was placed in charge of operations, and Gallagher was retained for his expert knowledge of rubber cultivation. Davis became the managing director of plantations (succeeded by Gallagher), and was made a director of United States Rubber in 1916. He resigned from the board in January, 1919.

Additional investments were made in the Far East in 1911. Between 1911 and 1915 the Hollandsch-Amerikaansche Plantage Mij. (H.A.P.M.), the Nederland Langkat Rubber Mij., and later the Si Pare Pare Rubber Mij. (all operating in Sumatra) were incorporated under the laws of Holland. These operated as subsidiaries of the General Rubber Company until 1917 when another subsidiary of General Rubber, United States Rubber Plantations, Inc., was formed with capitalization of $10 million preferred and $20 million common stock, and took over the management of the plantations and the operating subsidiaries.

Planting Started

Planting started in July, 1910; about 14,000 acres, or about 22 square miles, were planted with 1,320,000 trees in 1911. Planting continued in 1912 at the rate of almost 6,000 trees per working day, and on May 5, 1913 the president was able to report that more than 32,500 acres had been planted with over 3,900,000 trees of the type then available in the East, ordinary unselected seedlings of *Hevea brasiliensis*. This was a major accomplishment, especially when it is realized that all of this land had to be cleared and that commissary and medical departments had to be set up. In 1915, 14,200 acres were planted under Ketner's direction, a record that ten years later was believed unbroken.[31] The first shipments of rubber from the company's plantations were received in this country in 1914. By September, 1915, 1,300,000 trees were reported tappable; 1,157,520 trees were actually tapped on Sept. 1. The plantations were then employing approximately 14,000 Chinese and Javanese workers under a staff of about 90 Europeans and Americans. About 200,000 pounds of dry rubber were being produced per month, mostly in the form of ribbed smoked sheet. As most of the trees were less than five years old, it was still too soon to determine how profitable the plantations would be.

Shipments of rubber received from the plantations in 1916 were greater than had been estimated previously, and as more and more of the young trees reached the age when they could be tapped, production continued to expand in 1917 and 1918. But United States Rubber Company's management was considerably disappointed that the yield in 1918, the third full year of tapping, was only about 250 pounds per acre, not enough to provide an adequate return on the investment ($9 million by 1915) at the generally prevailing prices for crude rubber.[32] But as a result of experiments started in 1919 using nitrogenous fertilizers, a regular program of manuring was adopted, and yield improved substantially over the years that followed.

As Brazilian rubber declined in importance, the General Rubber Company, in order to make the greatest possible use of its facilities and organization in Brazil, became the principal exporter of cedar logs from the Amazon basin. It also exported Brazil nuts, cocoa, deerskins, and other products of the region.

TEXTILE MANUFACTURE BEGUN

United States Rubber Company required great quantities of fabrics for production of rubber footwear, clothing, tires, and much of its mechanical rubber goods. Annual consumption had reached 55 million yards by 1916. In 1917, J. N. Gunn, president of the United States Tire Company, negotiated acquisition of the controlling interest in the Winnsboro Mills, Winnsboro, S.C.; United States Rubber thus became the first rubber tire manufacturer to have its own mills for the production of cord for tires. There were two chief reasons for this acquisition. The management of United States Rubber was convinced that the "waste factor" used by textile manufacturers was excessive and that the company's needs in tire fabrics could be filled at a lower cost. The company also felt that the textile manufacturers had shown insufficient interest in developing better fabrics specially designed to meet the specifications of the tire manufacturers. United States Rubber therefore decided to operate its own textile mills in order to obtain the highly specialized cords and fabrics then being designed in its development department.

United States Rubber completely reequipped the Winnsboro mill so that it could supply suitable tire fabrics and quadrupled production in three years. Management of operations of the 77,000-spindle mills was left in the hands of Lockwood, Greene and Company, a Boston engineering firm that specialized in the management and operation of textile mills and held the minority interest. Liaison was maintained chiefly through a young man in the United States Tire Company, H. Gordon Smith, who dealt principally with the company's requirements of tire cord and with the relations between United States Rubber and Lockwood, Greene and Company. Even after Winnsboro Mills became a fully owned subsidiary of United States Rubber in 1925, Lockwood, Greene and Company continued to operate the mills for a management fee until June, 1928.[33]

Although the acquisition of Winnsboro Mills marked the first direct participation of United States Rubber in textile manufacture, a subsidiary—Mishawaka Woolen Manufacturing Company—had from its very early days produced its own requirements of knitted cotton and wool jerseys and knitted fleece linings for rubber footwear. Years later those facilities would play an important part in the development of elastic coated fabrics marketed by United States Rubber after World War II.

INTERNATIONAL OPERATIONS

Expansion of Export Business

A selling agent in London was included in the nine selling agents reporting to Homer E. Sawyer under the "plan of organization" approved by the executive committee in June, 1901. In his annual report dated May 20, 1902, Colt noted with satisfaction that the company's exports of rubber footwear had increased from $122,000 in 1899 to almost $742,000 in the fiscal year ended March 31, 1902. Each comment regarding exports that was made in the annual reports for the next few years told of an increase over the previous year, and by 1910 several foreign agencies for the sale of United States Rubber Company's footwear had been "established on a substantial basis."

The United States Rubber Export Company, Ltd. was organized on Dec. 15, 1914 "for the purpose of more systematically and efficiently pushing this department of the business." Since it was thought that this effort would produce greater sales at a lower ratio of sales expense, the company began taking over the export business formerly transacted by the subsidiary companies.

Until about 1917, United States Rubber Export Company, Ltd., made the larger part of its sales in Great Britain and South Africa. Sales in Great Britain prior to World War I, and for several years thereafter, were made through a London subsidiary, India Rubber Products, Ltd. A branch of the export company, opened in Johannesburg, South Africa in October, 1916, did a good business on Rainbow conveyor belting with practically every gold mine on the "reef" (the area where the mines were located). The sugar mills in that section were also good users of the company's belting. However, because of lower prices offered by British and French tire manufacturers, the Johannesburg branch did not enjoy large volume on United States Rubber Company's tires. Keds and other rubber-soled canvas shoes found a ready sale.

In 1914, Fred H. Hauser went as a salesman to Buenos Aires with authority to do business on an indent basis. Convinced that a stock should be carried in Buenos Aires, he returned to New York and submitted his recommendation to E. H. Huxley, president of the export company. The plans were approved, and the Buenos Aires branch opened in September,

1916. The following year a branch was opened in Italy, and in 1918 one was opened in New Zealand. Since relatively little business was done in either Belgium or Holland before 1919, sales in those countries were handled from the New York office, but in June, 1919, a sales office was opened in Brussels.[34]

Export sales, which represented 7% of the total business of United States Rubber in 1917, continued to expand during World War I, and profits were said to be satisfactory despite exchange problems. Consequently, plans were made to extend the overseas operations as soon as conditions permitted.

Operations in Canada

Manufacture of rubber products in Canada had been started in 1854 when the partnership of Brown, Hibbard, Bourn and Co. was formed. William W. Brown was associated with the New England manufacturer, Edwin M. Chaffee; Ashley Hibbard supplied £6,000, the major portion of the capital; George Bourn owned a small factory building at the corner of St. Mary and Monarque Streets (now Papineau Avenue and Notre Dame Street) in Montreal, near the banks of the St. Lawrence River (Figure 19). Rubber springs and rubber footwear were the first items produced, and a shipment of 2,016 pairs of rubber overshoes was made on Sept. 12, 1854 to Liverpool, consigned to Hamburg, Germany. Rubberized belting and rubberized fabric were soon added to the items manufactured. By 1863, other men had replaced the original partners, and the firm name had changed to Canadian Rubber Company, which was chartered in 1866 as the Canadian Rubber Company of Montreal.

By 1900, the Papineau factory was making rubber raincoats, garden and fire hose, druggists' sundries, and bicycle tires, in addition to rubber footwear. The year 1906 marked the initial manufacture of automobile rubber tires in Canada; clincher tires were made in the plant on Papineau Avenue. (At that time an entire day was required to manufacture four tires!) The same year, Barney Oldfield, the famous racing driver, drove a car equipped with "Canadian" clinchers around a track in Montreal at the "amazing" speed of forty miles an hour.

In the early summer of 1906, when the Canadian Rubber Company acquired the Granby Rubber Company, Granby, Quebec, the Canadian Consolidated Rubber Company, Ltd., was organized under the guidance of D. Lorne McGibbon as a holding company for the two corporations. Later that year the Maple Leaf Rubber Company, Port Dalhousie, On-

19.   First rubber goods factory in Canada (Dominion Rubber Company, Montreal).

tario, was acquired, together with the Commercial Rubber Company, Ltd., which operated a rubber footwear plant at St. Jerome, Quebec. In February, 1907, Canadian Consolidated Rubber acquired the Berlin Rubber Manufacturing Company and the Merchants Rubber Co., Ltd., both located in Berlin, Ontario. (The name of the city was changed to Kitchener in 1916 in honor of Earl Kitchener, British field marshal and Secretary of War from 1914 until his death in 1916.)

Thus when Colt, in April, 1907, negotiated the purchase by United States Rubber of approximately two-thirds of the outstanding capital stock of Canadian Consolidated Rubber Company, the latter owned or controlled six rubber companies. In 1910, United States Rubber's interest was increased, and McGibbon became a director of United States Rubber Company. During the same year the name of the idle Commercial Rubber Company was changed to Dominion Rubber Company, Ltd., and the St. Jerome plant was reopened for the manufacture of rubber-soled canvas footwear.

Most of United States Rubber's tire business in Canada was supplied from its plants in the United States until 1914. In 1912, a small group of workers from plants in Berlin and Port Dalhousie was sent to Detroit and Indianapolis to be trained in tiremaking. In 1913, construction of a million dollar tire plant was started in Berlin for the Dominion Tire Company, and the first tire in the new plant was made on Jan. 6, 1914. The management of the Morgan and Wright Detroit plant assisted the Canadian company in the building and equipping of the Berlin plant as well as in training workers. Dominion built 48,000 tires and 45,500 inner tubes in its first year, and the company's tire sales in Canada increased sharply.[35]

In 1900, the Granby Rubber Company had opened a reclaiming plant at Granby, and in 1916, the reclaiming operation was moved by Canadian Consolidated Rubber to Montreal. Monthly production of reclaimed rubber in Canada rose from 200,000 pounds in 1910 to as much as 700,000 pounds a month during World War I.[36]

[1] George F. Redmond, *Financial Giants of America*, II (Boston: The Stratford Co., 1922), pp. 101-09.

[2] Howard and Ralph Wolf, *Rubber, A Story of Glory and Greed* (New York: Covici-Friede, 1936), pp. 217-18.

[3] "Minutes of Executive Committee," unpublished, 1901, 1902. In 1963, H. M. Kelton said that among the securities received from Flint in 1901 was the capital stock of the Pacific and Idaho Northern Railway Company. The line served the Idaho potato and green pea country, and was 104 miles long with 125 bridges. In the early 1930's United States Rubber disposed of the rolling stock and put a specially equipped automobile on the tracks. Finally, in 1936, the company sold the railroad to the Union Pacific (H. M. Kelton, interview, May 6, 1963). The charter was forfeited in 1937.

[4] W. M. Dougherty, speech at sales managers' committee meeting, April 15, 1957, unpublished, United States Rubber Company archives.

[5] F. B. Davis, Jr., statement to P. Arthur, 1952, company archives.

[6] *New York Times* (Oct. 22, 1918), p. 17.

[7] Walter Emery, "First Section of History of United States Rubber Company," 1946, unpublished, company archives, p. 42.

[8] Homer E. Sawyer, "Histories of the United States Rubber Company and Some of the Subsidiary Companies," 1916, privately printed, pp. 9-10.

[9] C. M. Carroll, letter, Sept. 27, 1963.

[10] Memorandum, 1952, company archives.

[11] Edgar B. Davis, letter dated Feb. 7, 1917, company archives.

[12] Memorandum, 1952, company archives.

[13] Walter Emery, "History of Naugatuck Chemical Company," I, Jan. 21, 1946, unpublished, company archives, p. 4 ff.

[14] Bernard Mannes Baruch, *My Own Story* (New York: Henry Holt & Co., Inc., 1957), p. 206.

[15] Franklin Pierce, *The Tariff and the Trusts* (New York: The MacMillan Co., 1907), p. 78.

[16] *Listing Statement, A-4197*, New York Stock Exchange, July 19, 1912, showed net profit of Rubber Goods Manufacturing Company and its subsidiaries for eleven months ended Nov. 30, 1912 to be $2,307,627 on net sales of $32,808,000 and surplus as $8,638,470, in addition to fixed surplus (subsidiary companies) of $2,499,219.

[17] Leonard Smith, memorandum, 1962.

[18] Advertisement, *Life* (Aug. 3, 1916).

[19] "A Brief History of the Organization of the United States Rubber Company," company publication, 1919.

[20] Information obtained from Willard H. Cobb and from company records.

[21] Charles C. Case, address at sales meeting, branch store footwear salesmen, Dec. 30, 1915, in "Histories of the United States Rubber Company and Some of the Subsidiary Companies," p. 43. Also see *US*, house organ of United States Rubber Company (September, 1943), p. 9.

[22] *Annual Report* (May 19, 1903), p. 4.

[23] Leonard Smith, correspondence, 1964.

[24] *Annual Report* (May 16, 1905), p. 5.

[25] *Proceedings of the Second Pan-American Scientific Congress, Washington, D.C., 1915-1916* (Washington: U.S. Gov't Printing Office, 1917), p. 381.

[26] *My Own Story*. pp. 208-14.

[27] J. M. Arnold, *Rubber*, Report to the Railroad Committee for the Study of Transportation, Association of American Railroads (March 8, 1946), p. 60150-10.

[28] George B. Newitt, "History of the Fuel Cell Division, United States Rubber Company," company publication, Mishawaka, 1947, p. 69.

[29] Wallace E. Cake, pamphlet, 1946.

[30] "U.S. Rubber II, Sumatra," *Fortune*, IX (February, 1934), p. 601.

[31] *"U.S." Rubber News*, house organ of United States Rubber Company (Sept. 1, 1925), p. 16.

[32] Wallace E. Cake, interview, Aug. 15, 1962.

[33] H. Gordon Smith, company archives, 1951.

[34] *The Ribbon and Seal*, house organ of United States Rubber Export Company, Ltd. (1922, 1923).

[35] Leslie Roberts, "From Three Men," privately printed, Dominion Rubber Company, Ltd., 1954, pp. 5-28.

[36] John M. Ball, *Reclaimed Rubber, the Story of an American Raw Material* (New York: Rubber Reclaimers Association, 1947), p. 128.

4

Policies, Problems and Progress

Prior to the 1920's

THE DEVELOPMENT of the present well-organized sales and advertising departments in each division of United States Rubber was accomplished only after a prolonged period of trial and error.

SALES AND DISTRIBUTION

When the American Rubber Company was acquired in 1892, it turned over to United States Rubber three branch stores: E. G. Stearns, Chicago; George W. Perry & Company, St. Louis; and William Morse and Company, New York. Sales of these three stores in 1895 amounted to $785,000. By 1901, sales of eleven stores were $2,562,000.

The organization chart issued Sept. 1, 1902 listed six selling agents for the Boston Rubber Shoe Company, which were not under the supervision of the general manager of the United States Rubber Company, but which operated quite independently. Nine other selling agents reported to the sales manager of United States Rubber, but eighteen branch stores (located in nine cities) reported to the manager of branch stores rather than to the manager of sales. Obviously considerable overlapping of sales efforts resulted, to say nothing of vigorous and often costly competition between various units for the business of the same customer.

The appointment early in 1902 of Edward R. Rice as manager of branch stores was said to mark the beginning of branch store organization. His success in building the organization and increasing branch store sales led to his promotion in 1909 as manager of sales for the entire company. By the end of 1915, there were about 375 footwear salesmen operating through the branch stores (about 25% of the total sales force of United States Rubber), and footwear sales that year through branch stores were approximately $17 million.[1] In 1919, the number of branch stores had grown to forty and their volume in that year had reached $53 million.[2]

Multiplicity of Brands

One of the first actions taken in April, 1892, by the directors of the newly organized United States Rubber Company had been the appointment of a committee to arrange for the "production of a new and special brand of rubber goods of superior quality, to be distinguished by the brand or trademark of United States Rubber Company." Despite this decision, the great bulk of the goods produced prior to 1916 had been under the brands of the subsidiary companies rather than under the label of the United States Rubber System. For example, the price lists dated Jan. 1, 1913 included the following brands of rubber footwear:

First Quality	*Second Quality*
American	Para
Banigan	Woonasquatucket
Boston Hub	Bay State
Candee	Federal
Goodyear Glove	(no second quality line was made by Goodyear Glove)
Lycoming	Keystone
Malden	Melrose
Meyer	Jersey
Wales Goodyear	
Wales Goodyear Bear	Connecticut
Woonsocket	Rhode Island
	New Brunswick
Commonwealth	Security
Rex*	
United States Rubber*	
Old Elm*	
Unika*	
Everstick*	

Third Quality
Empire
King
*Used on certain specialties.

"Tennis" or "sporting and outing shoes" were offered under these brands:

First Quality	*Second Quality*
Goodyear Glove	(No second quality)
National India Rubber Co.	Champion
Lycoming	Keystone

The same policy of continuing the brands of subsidiary companies had been followed by the Rubber Goods Manufacturing Company. These brands included Hartford, Hartford-Dunlop, Morgan and Wright, and G & J. The Revere Rubber Company, acquired late in 1909, made Continental tires. U.S. tires have been on the market since 1911, but not until 1912, a little more than six years after the Rubber Goods Manufacturing Company had been acquired by United States Rubber, was a tire under the United States label referred to in an advertisement. Figures 20a and 20b are the first known advertisements that sought to transmit to United States tires the popularity then enjoyed by the G & J, Hartford, and Morgan and Wright brands.

Indicative of the predominant position of the United States Rubber System in the distribution of tires in 1911 was the claim that tires bearing the company's brands were "sold by more than four-fifths of all the best dealers in the United States." In April, 1912, an advertisement showed United States brand tires only, saying that United States tires were now made in plants, "each of which formerly made a brand of tires": Continental, G & J, Hartford, and Morgan and Wright.

The Morgan and Wright Company had used the slogan, "Morgan and Wright tires are good tires," since 1894. After United States tires began to be actively promoted and advertised, this slogan was adapted to read, "United States tires are good tires." The tire division thus led the way toward ultimate replacement of many brands of subsidiary companies with the seal of the United States Rubber System. For several more years, however, the brand names of Morgan and Wright, Hartford, G & J, and Continental were prominent in the United States Tire Company's advertisements. In January, 1916, the U.S. Royal trademark was adopted for tires.

The annual report for 1913 stated that "steps have been taken to connect the name 'United States Rubber Company' with the subsidiary companies" to indicate, among other things, "the integrity of the product." The advertisement shown in Figure 20c, which appeared Jan. 19, 1918 in the *Saturday Evening Post*, is evidence, however, that the seal of the United States Rubber System was only then beginning to be directly associated with the subsidiaries' brands of mechanical goods.

Wholesale Outlets Converted to Branch Stores

Since the policy for many years was to maintain the identity of each brand and thus capitalize on the good will enjoyed by the footwear manufacturing companies brought into the consolidation, each company's distribution outlets were likely to be maintained virtually intact. Some of these outlets were company owned; more frequently, the product was sold through shoe wholesalers. In the early years of this century, some Western branches bought part of their rubber footwear through jobbers, rather than directly from United States Rubber, or the jobber received a commission on certain lines shipped into the jobber's territory by the branch.[3] In a large city, in addition to the branch store, there would often be several wholesale shoe firms, each with its own sales force, competing against each other and offering the brand or brands of one or more of the factories in the newly consolidated United States Rubber System. In 1915, 350 shoe wholesalers, usually called "jobbers," were distributing 75% of the rubber footwear made by the factories of the United States Rubber System. Orders placed by these wholesalers helped to level out the production curve. Early in each year, sometimes as early as November of the previous year, the company would ask them to submit detailed orders which could be put into the manufacturing schedule, and by January, United States Rubber would have a good complement of orders to work on.

Prior to 1910, it was fairly common practice to consign stocks of rubber footwear to jobbers. Such a practice was exceedingly risky with a seasonal commodity, because sales were largely dependent on weather conditions; the practice was discontinued by United States Rubber shortly after the end of World War I.[4]

Because the principal business of these wholesalers was leather footwear, many found themselves in financial difficulty when leather shoe manufacturers began to sell directly to retailers instead of through jobbers. Some jobbers were only too glad to sell out to United States Rubber. In other instances, the company had to take over in order to salvage what it could from the jobber's indebtedness to it. In either event, the wholesale business often was operated as a subsidiary and continued to use the name of the previous firm. Even if the name was changed, it still might not have any relation to the name of the parent corporation (see organization chart, dated Sept. 1, 1902, Appendix E). For example, before 1896, the Goodyear Metallic Rubber Shoe Company had sold its Wales-Goodyear brand and Bear brand rubber boots and shoes to a jobbing firm in Des Moines, Iowa, known as B. F. Jaquith and Company. In 1896, this firm was taken over by United States Rubber and the name was changed to A. B. George & Co.; later it was changed again to Des Moines Rubber Company.[5]

20a. First known advertisement referring to United States Tires (*Saturday Evening Post*, April 8, 1911).

United States Tires
Will Mean Lower Up-Keep
Cost for Every Motorist

It has been easy for the automobile dealer to realize how much the organization of the United States Tire Company means in improved manufacturing conditions, in greater purchasing power, and in wider distribution and sales efforts for the four great tire companies which comprise this new organization.

It should be just as easy for the motorist to realize how much the United States Tire Company means to him in the production of better automobile tires.

We propose to reduce the up-keep tire cost for every motorist in America. We propose to make possible the more economical operation of every automobile in this country. We propose, through the production of superior automobile tires, to give added pleasure, added safety and added economy to motoring everywhere.

For many years Continental tires, G & J tires, Hartford tires and Morgan & Wright tires have been recognized by the motoring world as leaders in the tire field. In the five great factories of these four leading tire makers, throughout a period of time so long that these names have become household words, these four leading manufacturers have made good tires

| Continental | Hartford |
| G & J | Morgan & Wright |

Each of these tires has had its own marked points of superiority. Motorists have come to know wherein each of these tires has been better than any other tire made. It remained for the United States Tire Company to bring into one working group all the tire knowledge, all the tire skill, all the tire experience which have given to each of the four brands its own field of leadership.

Every point of superiority which in the past has identified each of these tires individually will be applied to all of them. Into each of these good tires the United States Tire Company is building every better feature of the three others. Our application of this aggregate knowledge, this aggregate of proven methods, must be and is productive of

America's Predominant Tires

United States tires embody advantages which the motorist could not and cannot secure through the use of any other tires. From no other source can he even hope to secure tires into which have been built such complete superiority. Furthermore, he can actually buy these tires

At the Same Price Asked for Other Kinds

United States tires are sold under the four well-known brand names: Continental, G. & J, Hartford and Morgan & Wright, and include eight styles of treads and three styles of fastenings—the widest range of selection ever offered the motorist.

United States Tire Company, New York
Branches, Agencies or Dealers Everywhere

Four-fifths of the Best Dealers Sell

UNITED STATES TIRES

All the way from one American coast to the other—wherever automobiles or automobile accessories are sold—there you will find a United States Tire dealer. It means much to the motorist that thousands of dealers—four-fifths of all the best dealers in America—have pinned their faith and their future to United States Tires. These dealers are not the sort that take chances with desirable patronage. They make it their business to sell the best products the market affords, building not for a day, but for the years to come. The fact that an overwhelming majority of these leading dealers, these responsible dealers, have recognized the superiority of United States Tires is conclusive corroboration of whatever we have said or might say of the better service to be had from our products.

Don't Buy Tires *Because* of Advertising but because of what is *Back of* the Advertising

There have been a lot of "talking points" on tires. Newspapers and magazines cry them out to you day after day.

As a motor-car owner you read tire advertising with interest. But *fundamentally* you are *not* interested in tire advertising. You are interested in *tires*—you are particularly interested in how they are *made* and what service you may reasonably expect from them on your car.

Let us make a suggestion. Just for a moment, if you will, shelve the "talking points," put them to one side, forget them! Then ask yourself this question:

"Why should n't the United States Tire Company be able to build *better tires* than anyone else? With four great manufacturing plants, with the very *pick* of *experts* and processes from four old, established tire companies—each of the four for many years making a tire good enough to become famous—with an aggregate of experience and facilities unapproached by any other tire manufacturer—with all these *obvious* advantages, why should n't United States Tires be *better* than other kinds for which I have to pay just as much? "

Ask yourself the question. Then *answer* it yourself. We will abide by your judgment.

United States Tires

G & J, Hartford, Morgan & Wright, and *United States*—are sold by four fifths of all the best dealers in the United States. They cost no more than you are asked to pay for other kinds.

United States Tire Company

Broadway at 58th Street - - - **New York**

Branches, Agencies or Dealers Everywhere.

20c. Advertisement associating United States Rubber System seal with trademarks of subsidiaries in Mechanical Goods Division (*Saturday Evening Post,* Jan. 19, 1918).

Specialized Service On Mechanical Rubber Goods

Every user of any kind of mechanical rubber goods will recognize many old, trustworthy friends among the brands on this page.

And from now on, every user will recognize *all* of these brands as friends to be trusted, and will find, conveniently at hand, a full supply of the mechanical rubber goods they identify.

For all of these goods are now being stamped with the seal of the United States Rubber Company—a quality-mark known to everyone—in addition to the original brand of its Subsidiary Companies, which will continue to make the goods. And all the marketing activities of these Companies have been centered in a single great organization, the United States Rubber Company Mechanical Goods Division, with branches in principal cities, and with distributors *everywhere*.

Included are Rubber Belting, Packing, Fire, Steam, Water, Garden and all other kinds of Hose, Rubber Tiling, Rubber Mats and Matting, Jar Rings, Rubber Toys, Fibre Soles, Rubber Soles and Heels, Plumbers' Supplies, Rubber Tape, and the multitude of other mechanical rubber items produced by

Revere Rubber Co.	Mechanical Rubber Co., Cleveland	Sawyer Belting Co.
Peerless Rubber Mfg. Co.	Mechanical Rubber Co., Chicago	India Rubber Co.
	Eureka Fire Hose Mfg. Co.	

—all units of the United States Rubber Company Mechanical Goods Division, which stand united "for the better service of the public."

Mechanical Goods Division
United States Rubber Company

101

Our Mr. Downs

If you had lived in New Haven, Conn., back in the early forties, you would have seen Mr. Downs quite often.

He used to go from one store to another with a basket on his arm.

If you had looked into the basket, as he argued with the skeptical storekeeper, you would have been astonished to see queer shoes, made of a strange new material. It was rubber.

Mr. Downs was the first salesman employed by the first firm ever licensed to make rubber goods—a firm founded in 1842.

Today, 6500 Mr. Downses are required to sell the enormous volume of footwear developed by the United States Rubber Company during the last 74 years.

There are 47 great companies which are the producing units of the United States Rubber Company, *the largest rubber manufacturer in the world.*

In the early days, rubber shoes were crude and few. They were an oddity, suspected by the public and only accepted by the doubting retail dealers for sale on a commission basis.

How time has changed all this!

The world has learned to look on rubber footwear as a blessing. You see it on the streets, in homes, playgrounds, industries, camps and wilderness. You find it in every shoe store.

Over sixty million pairs of rubber boots, shoes, overshoes and canvas shoes with rubber soles were produced in the factories of the United States Rubber Company in the last twelve months—enough to shoe half the people in this vast country.

Yet the production of footwear is only one of the activities of the United States Rubber Company.

On an equally tremendous scale it makes *raincoats, tires, druggist sundries, hose, belting, packing, and all rubber goods for mechanical uses.*

The output of the United States Rubber Company, though huge, is balanced. Its prosperity does not depend on any one product. And thus the full and continued degree of service rendered by this great organization to the public is assured.

United States Rubber Company

Has your Rubber Footwear a Pedigree?

These are famous trade-marks in the rubber footwear industry. Each one of these marks stands for the product of a great factory—great in reputation as well as size. If your rubber footwear bears one of these brands, it is the descendant of a long line of quality products; it has a worthy "pedigree."

20e. Advertisement, "Has Your Rubber Footwear a Pedigree?" (*Woman's Magazine*, December, 1916).

It would require an expert to determine, from appearance alone, the difference in *quality* between good and poor rubber footwear. The principal guide would be the better shaping—snappier style. And style in rubber footwear—off the foot—might baffle even keen eyes.

Only well-made, high-grade rubber footwear will *look* well, *fit* well and *wear* well. Only by securing a standardized, trade-marked, pedigreed quality product such as these brands represent can you distinguish the best from the rest and be sure of wear, fit, style and quality.

Seventy-four years of successful manufacturing and the experience of forty-seven great factories are back of every pair of rubber shoes, overshoes, arctics, boots, etc., produced by the United States Rubber Company, the largest rubber manufacturer in the world.

Rubbers that fit wear twice as long as rubbers that do not fit

United States Rubber Company

Put Your Family in

Keds

Canvas Rubber-soled Footwear for Men, Women and Children

KEDS is the name to guide you to grace, beauty and solid comfort in footwear. Keds is the new name of an old-established family of ultra-stylish, serviceable and comfortable rubber-soled shoes with uppers of a specially woven fine grade of canvas.

If you glory in a light, springy step, full of noiseless grace, ask your dealer for Keds. There are many styles and shapes. You can find your particular Keds, whether for the fashionable boulevard or afternoon tea on your own porch.

Keds are vogue—they are worn by particular dressers at all the smart places—they add a refreshing grace to the dainty feet of society women—they give substantial wear with good looks and solid comfort to business men—for children they are next to going "barefoot."

There are three grades of Keds. Choose the kind you want. You are sure of wear in every pair. Each grade carries with it the reputation of the largest rubber manufacturer in the world.

NATIONAL Keds $1.50 up	**CAMPFIRE Keds** $1.25 to $2.00	**Keds** $1.00 to $1.50

There is style in Keds. They are built on popular lasts and approved by fashion authorities.

There is comfort in Keds. The tops offer full, elastic support; the soles are durable, flexible and buoyant.

There is economy in Keds. Cost considered, Keds outwear any other footwear yet devised.

Ask your dealer to show you Keds and shoe the family in style and comfort.

United States Rubber Company

New York

104

United States Rubber Company of California

James Brendan Brady, first employed by Revere Rubber Company in 1910, went to the Pacific Coast in 1911 as sales manager of Gorham-Revere Rubber Company. This organization was a consolidation of all branches of the Gorham Rubber Company with (1) those of the Revere Rubber Company on the Pacific Coast, (2) the western interests of the Eureka Fire Hose Company, and (3) the five Pacific Coast branches formerly operated by the Pacific Coast Rubber Company (established in 1900) and the Washington Rubber Company, which had been taken over previously by United States Rubber. In 1914, the Pacific Coast branches of United States Tire Company were amalgamated with Gorham-Revere as the United States Rubber Company of California, with Brady as vice-president and general manager. Within the territory west of the Rocky Mountains, comprising the states of Washington, Oregon, California, Idaho, Utah, Nevada, Arizona, and part of Montana, Brady held full and final authority, except for setting price policy, for sales and distribution of all commodities other than chemicals made by United States Rubber. That he exercised such authority was true regardless of the fact that on the organization charts of the parent United States Rubber Company, Brady was shown as reporting to the sales manager of the General Division, George H. Mayo in the earlier years, and, after 1925, to Herbert E. Smith.

The headquarters of Brady's territory, the Pacific Coast Division, was in San Francisco, with major branches in Seattle, Spokane, Portland, Salt Lake City, Los Angeles, and San Francisco. For a few years branches were also maintained in Tacoma, Butte, Great Falls, Phoenix, Sacramento, Fresno, and San Diego. Each branch manager was responsible for coordinating all the business operations of the branch. Product managers were in charge of all matters pertaining to their respective product lines within the Pacific Coast Division; they reported directly to Brady and worked out of the headquarters in San Francisco. Brady's method of managing his territory met with considerable criticism from various executives of the United States Rubber Company, but Colt gave Brady his full support, as did his successor, C. B. Seger.

Excessive Selling Expense

Before World War I, merchants in the territory served by a United States Rubber branch might be canvassed by salesmen representing other wholesale subsidiaries of the company. If, on a trip to a large city, a dealer had called on the branch there and his name had been placed on their mailing list, he would have been likely to receive price lists and other literature from that branch, as well as from the branch in whose territory his store was located. Needham recalled that when he was president of the Des Moines Rubber Company, retail shoe stores in Iowa frequently were canvassed by salesmen from several wholesale houses in Chicago, from two or three in Minneapolis, and by others from St. Louis, Omaha, or Milwaukee, each one offering one or more of the brands made by a factory in the United States Rubber System.

The excessively high sales expense incident to maintenance of so many separate and overlapping organizations for sales and distribution is graphically illustrated in Figure 20d. The advertisement which appeared in the *Literary Digest*, Aug. 26, 1916, and also in the *Saturday Evening Post*, boasted that 6,500 salesmen were then required to sell more than 50 million pairs of rubber footwear and rubber-soled canvas shoes produced during the previous twelve months by the factories of the United States Rubber System. Obviously, the figure of 6,500 probably included all the salesmen of all the jobbers of footwear made by United States Rubber, in addition to the salesmen employed by the company.

Promotion of U.S. Brand

Another undesirable consequence of maintaining numerous brands was the perpetuation of old rivalries and jealousies. In December, 1915, a convention of branch store footwear salesmen was held in Boston. Colt and the three vice-presidents (in charge, respectively, of the Footwear, Tire, and Mechanical Departments), as well as several other top executives of the company, addressed the convention. The main purpose of the meeting was to instill in each salesman a common desire to promote the welfare of all units of the United States Rubber Company, regardless of brand or type of goods manufactured, and to generate pride in and a desire to push the sale of goods bearing the U.S. Rubber System's label. These goals were achieved to a considerable extent. Although production under the old established brands was continued, U.S. Rubber brand merchandise was worked into the stock of each branch store, and gradually this brand gained more importance. However, the persistence of the original brands may be seen in the fact that, as late as 1919, only three of the United States Rubber System's factories were commonly referred to by the name United States Rubber Company. Most of the factories were still known by their local, or original, names.

In the case of footwear, the entire production of goods with the round seal of the System was not confined to one factory. Sometimes when a

branch, after receipt of its initial shipment, placed fill-in orders for similar styles, the new shipment contained goods made in a different factory
from the one that had produced the earlier shipment. Speeds of mixing
mills and calenders were not uniform in all plants. Other kinds of manufacturing equipment, as well as specifications and standards of quality
and workmanship, also varied from factory to factory, so that frequently
the goods received by the branch on its reorder differed in quality and in
details of construction or styling, in compounds, color, fabrics, lasts, or
even in measurements of goods marked the same size. These discrep-
ancies created problems for both the branch and the retailer. As the
chemistry of rubber came to be better understood, steps were taken to
concentrate production in fewer factories, with centralized control of
specifications and standards, but several years passed before this consolidation was accomplished.

After the decision was made to push the sale of footwear under the
U.S. label, salesmen reported, as late as 1920, that this brand was not
so well known as those of some competitors, particularly BALL-BAND and
Goodrich.[6] BALL-BAND (Red Ball) rubber and woolen footwear had
been nationally advertised since 1909 by the Mishawaka Woolen Mfg.
Company. Although that company had been acquired in 1905 by a syndicate headed by Colt and later became a wholly owned subsidiary of
United States Rubber, Mishawaka continued to operate with a considerable degree of independence and in direct competition with the parent
company. Its red circular trademark was widely known, especially in
rural communities and smaller towns. In 1915, Mishawaka's full-page
advertisements claimed that over 50,000 merchants were handling BALL-
BAND footwear. B. F. Goodrich Rubber Company, Akron, Ohio, had
begun manufacturing rubber footwear under the Goodrich label about
1912, and a short time thereafter had begun extensive advertising of its
brands.

To meet such competition and obtain greater recognition of the United
States Rubber System's label, N.W. Ayer and Company, an advertising
agency located in Philadelphia, was engaged. However, the advertisement which appeared in *Woman's Magazine*, December, 1916 (Figure
20e) clearly shows why it was impossible to develop an effective campaign at that time.

Keds Brand Adopted

In the same year, adoption of a distinctive name for the rubber-soled
tennis shoes made in the factory of the National India Rubber Company,

Bristol, R.I., was suggested. In a memorandum written several years later, R. W. Ashcroft (Figure 20f), who had recently been placed in charge of United States Rubber's advertising and publicity, said that after examining about 300 names suggested by the advertising agency or by company employees, he submitted ten names to the operating council, and they chose Peds. Ashcroft proposed to have the legal department institute a search to see if there were any conflicting registrations, but was informed by the operating council that such a search was unnecessary since they would buy out any conflicting registrations. He was told to prepare advertising copy, and, at the same time, instructions were given for processing the necessary labels, dies, and so forth.

About a month later, according to Ashcroft, the legal department reported several conflicting registrations; not all the owners could be bought out, and some undoubtedly would contest any use of Peds by United States Rubber. Ashcroft was then asked to recommend an alternative name and two were submitted—Keds and Veds. Some objected that neither of these words meant anything, but Kodak was cited as an example of a coined word which had become a valuable trademark.

The operating council, according to Ashcroft's memorandum, "very reluctantly . . . decided to make the best of a bad job and adopted the name Keds." With one exception, he added, the name Keds was enthusiastically approved by the sales organization at home and abroad. The exception was the representative in Johannesburg, who informed the New York office that, in South Africa, bedbugs were called "keds."[7] However, within a comparatively short time, the same branch was reporting good sales of Keds.

The first advertisement in which the new name was used appeared in April, 1917 in the *Literary Digest* (Figure 20g). Consistent advertising coupled with the superior quality of the merchandise and skillful sales promotion at the retail level, from that date to the present, won for U.S. Keds predominant leadership in their field and has made Keds one of the most valuable trademarks owned by the company. The problems of other products were more difficult to solve, since for various reasons it was thought necessary to continue to offer many brands rather than risk loss of valuable distribution.

Changes in Footwear Distribution and Sales Policies

In 1916, for tax reasons, most wholesale subsidiaries, including the Des Moines Rubber Company, were dissolved and replaced by branches operated under the name of United States Rubber. In some cities, where the company owned more than one wholesale subsidiary, usually only one would be operated as the local branch; the others remained under their individual firm names and continued selling other brands made by the company. Privately owned wholesale firms also continued to offer certain of the company's other brands of footwear in direct competition with the company owned branch.[8] Understandably there was neither uniformity in the sales practices of the companies brought together to form United States Rubber, nor were these practices always based on sound policy.

Particularly in sales of rubber footwear was sound policy sometimes subordinated to expediency. Demand for this footwear, largely dependent as it was on the season and prevailing weather, fluctuated greatly so that various inducements to customers were offered. Long dating and anticipation discount of 1% a month for payment before the due date were regularly offered for placement of advance orders. Relatively few customers, strange as it may seem, took advantage of the opportunity to receive 12% per annum for prepayment, but merchants could, and some did, make profitable use of their capital.[9] Some were glad to borrow funds from local banks to anticipate bills with the rubber company.

Before World War I it was customary to make relatively few changes in list prices for rubber footwear. Adjustments in prices were made by applying a series of discounts to the list. Annual reports for the years 1902-11, inclusive, showed gross as well as net sales. In those years net sales were the following percentages of gross:

Year Ended March 31	Net Sales Percentage of Gross	Year Ended March 31	Net Sales Percentage of Gross
1902	46.0%	1907	66.5
1903	54.5	1908	66.8
1904	51.6	1909	68.8
1905	57.6	1910	68.9
1906	60.1	1911	74.5

The foregoing percentages reflect sales to all types of accounts, retailers and wholesalers. Some typical discounts from list prices on rubber footwear generally quoted retailers by the United States Rubber System were:

1905 List less 25, 8 and 3%
1910 List less 15 and 5%
1913 List less 15 and 5%, with an extra 5% for detailed orders placed prior to July 1 for shipment prior to October 15
1914 List less 25 and 5% with no premium for early orders
1915 List less 25 and 5% with an extra 5% for early orders (gross list was also changed on March 1, 1915)
1917 List less 15 and 5%.[10]

The larger outlets with distribution over a wide territory would have been quoted additional discounts of 8, 8 and 5%. Most jobbers of rubber footwear would receive discounts of 8 and 8% from prices paid by retailers.

After 1915, the percentage of footwear sold through jobbers gradually declined, principally because most jobbers could not be depended upon to carry on an intensive sales effort when there was unusual sales resistance. Just as the company was most in need of volume, jobbers would curtail or stop their selling efforts in order to cut expenses, and the factory they represented would get little or no business from them.

When independent footwear jobbers were succeeded by company-owned branches, the branch manager "bought" his stock of footwear on the same basis as the jobber, namely the price to retailers less 8 and 8% discount. He was responsible for sale of any surplus or obsolete merchandise, and was expected to show a profit. A well-managed branch could and did show such profit, according to Needham, who said this policy was still in effect in 1925. Sometimes the branch manager had to contend with the handicap of unrealistic valuation of fixed assets, which was most likely to occur when the property had been taken in settlement of an uncollectible account.

Tire Sales Organization

The United States Tire Company, Inc.[11] maintained its own branch stores and had a large corps of salesmen. In 1912, its midwestern district, headquartered in Chicago, had a sales force of sixty-five salesmen, "every man a college graduate." The district manager believed that sales success depended chiefly on hard work, constant calls on dealers, and helpfulness. He has related that he challenged the other districts for leadership in volume, and started a sales promotion campaign which appealed to both the salesmen and the dealers. With this stimulus, the district finished the year in first place.[12]

Before World War I a group of tire service stations or retail tire stores was acquired to provide service to owners of tires made by United States Rubber's tire factories. Some of these stores sold gasoline as well as the company's brands of tires and tire accessories, and were operated by subsidiaries under the supervision of a special department in the New York office. Among those operated prior to 1920 were:

	Established
Quick Tire Service, Inc. (Kentucky)	1915
Quick Tire Service, Inc. (New York)	1917
Newsum Tire Company of Arkansas	1912
(with tire stores in Memphis and Little Rock)	
Atlantic Tire Service, Inc.	1918

Within a few years United States Rubber had about twenty similar tire service companies that were operating about twenty-two tire stores during the 1920's.

Unfortunately, the United States Tire Company, as did the other divisions, suffered from imperfect communication between the central office and the salesmen in the field. For example, plans might be made to open a company-owned tire store in a certain city but the local salesman might not learn of the project until the new store was almost ready to start competing with the established dealers in the community. Although such lack of coordination happened only rarely and was of small consequence in comparison with the achievement of the over-all goal, it was very disturbing to the individual salesmen or customers involved.

In material prepared in 1919 for a training course used by a subsidiary of the company, the sales organization of the Tire Division was described as selling chiefly to retail tire dealers and distributors (wholesale dealers in hardware and other items, who in turn sold tires to retail hardware stores, country general stores, and the like). Apparently this statement referred only to the salesmen working out of the branch stores operated by the Tire Company, since no mention was made of sales of original equipment tires, although there were such sales at that time.

Sales Management Policies

Other divisions had salesmen who specialized in their products, but, to a certain extent, the selling departments of one division sold products of the other divisions. Thus, branch stores in the Pacific Coast Division frequently sold tires or certain mechanical rubber goods in addition to footwear and clothing. Ordinarily, the general line salesmen were expected to sell practically any of the products of United States Rubber except chemicals—footwear, clothing, soles and heels, sundries, mechanical rubber goods, and, on occasion, even tires. It was almost impossible for the average salesman to acquire a thorough knowledge of most of the products, or of the potential market for them in his territory, but the necessity of controlling sales expenses outweighed this factor in determining the number of salesmen for a given territory.

Modern ideas regarding sales supervision and management, compensation of salesmen, and control of sales expense were not generally practiced in the rubber industry in the years before World War I. There were, however, some notable exceptions. As early as 1900, the Mishawaka Woolen Mfg. Company maintained detailed records of sales by geographical divisions—town, county, and territory, as well as individual accounts. With this information, a workable, if imperfect, basis was established for measuring sales potential and evaluating the performance of salesmen. The salesmen for the Mishawaka company were paid a commission, out of which they paid their own expenses. They were not full-time employees, and worked only until each had completed the advance order canvass of his territory, usually by May or early June of each year. They did not have a drawing account and were not guaranteed a minimum income.

Most of the salesmen working out of the United States Rubber Company branches were paid by salary rather than commission, and were either reimbursed for expenses or were given an allowance established by the branch. It was not until much later that expense budgets or sales quotas were adopted generally. Where the branch sales manager was efficient, industrious, well-informed, and a good judge of sales ability, and knew how to get top performance from his sales force, the branch would normally have a profitable operation, provided weather conditions were favorable to the sale of waterproof rubber footwear.

The present network of paved highways did not crisscross the country until after the mid-twenties; therefore, merchants in many of the smaller towns were visited by the salesman only once or twice a year. Because the salesman probably would not be back for several months or even for a full year, the percentage of the dealer's expected year's volume in rubber goods, which was placed on the initial advance order, was much greater than has been customary since the early thirties. It was a period of high pressure salesmanship, and only rarely did a salesman feel he had any personal responsibility to help his customer control his inventory, or to assist the dealer in promoting the resale of the goods ordered.

Principles of successful merchandising now widely accepted were not generally recognized as practical by the great majority of men engaged in the sale of consumer goods prior to World War I. Therefore, in any judgment of sales techniques and practices, the vastly different conditions prevailing in that period should be taken into account.

Early Use of Market Analysis

A more modern approach to a marketing problem was evidenced in the assignment given on Jan. 5, 1917 to Ernest S. Bradford, marketing analyst, to make a study of the golf ball market and to present his findings within thirty days. Preliminary development work on golf balls had been carried on at the Cleveland plant of the Rubber Goods Manufacturing Company for several years but commercial production had not been undertaken.[13] Bradford was requested to submit suggestions for marketing golf balls made by United States Rubber should it decide to enter this field.

His report, dated Feb. 6, 1917, is one of the early examples of market research. In the short time allotted Bradford interviewed editors of two golf magazines, scanned other publications, talked with golf instructors, professional and amateur golfers, and called on sporting goods dealers in New York, Philadelphia, and Washington, D.C. Since it was winter he went to Pinehurst, N.C., "the center of winter golf," to visit two municipal links. He had been directed to try to ascertain: (1) the use of golf balls in this country, (2) consumers' considerations in choosing golf balls, (3) selling methods of each of the principal brands mentioned, and (4) retail selling methods.

Among his findings were these statistics: (1) 1,200 golf courses in the United States, comprising 935 private golf clubs listed in the American Annual Golf Guide, 150-65 unlisted private golf clubs, 50 municipal golf links, 50 golf courses operated by hotels; (2) total annual sales of golf balls, 500,000-600,000 dozen; (3) standard prices, 75¢, 65¢, and 50¢, but two companies had recently advanced the price from 75¢ to 85¢; (4) 250,000-300,000 players; (5) the number of players was rapidly increasing, and present manufacturers could not supply the demand; (6) to play golf, a single man should have an annual income of $3,000; a married man, an income of $4,000 to $5,000 a year. He noted that, for 1915, approximately 337,000 federal income tax returns had been filed by single persons having an income of over $3,000 or married persons with income of over $4,000. He observed that golf was passing "into the hands of the man of moderate income" resulting in "a greatly increased number of players."

Bradford also reported on the qualities consumers considered desirable in a golf ball, the channels through which golf balls were distributed, the margins allowed to golf pros and to retail dealers, percentage of the business done by golf pros, terms granted, guarantees, advertising done by manufacturers, and packaging. He included information regarding ten companies manufacturing golf balls in the United States and Great Britain. The last five pages of his report covered twenty-four recommendations regarding qualities desired in the product, quality control and field testing, packaging, channels of distribution, pricing, advertising, sales organization, sales promotion, and timing of initial production and initial marketing efforts.[14] On the basis of Bradford's report, the United States Rubber Company decided to manufacture golf balls, and produc-

tion was begun at the Providence plant in 1917; the venture proved to
be very profitable.

A commercial research department, formally organized about 1918
by United States Rubber, continued to function under one name or another most of the succeeding years. It was charged with responsibility
for making available to management a great variety of data pertaining
to the company's business, including the general economy; production,
sales, and inventory figures so far as known for the rubber industry,
broken down by major commodity classifications; United States Rubber
Company's position in the industry; existing and potential foreign and
domestic markets for the company's products or for new products being
considered; the market prices of rubber and cotton; estimated world production, consumption, and stocks on hand of rubber and cotton; world
conditions affecting the international operations of United States Rubber; competition; and trend of use of tires per motor vehicle registered.

Growing Importance of Tire Business

Introduction of Straight-Side Tires

In 1900, the Hartford Rubber Works, which had become a subsidiary
of Rubber Goods Manufacturing Company, began manufacturing straight-
side bicycle tires under a license from the Dunlop Tyre Company, Ltd.
Prior to that time all the pneumatic tires made in this country had been
clincher tires under patent #454,115, issued June 16, 1891 to Thomas
B. Jeffery, of Gormully and Jeffery, bicycle manufacturers. Extreme care
and considerable effort were required to mount a clincher tire on the
wheel. Although Hartford marketed its straight-side tires under the Hartford-Dunlop brand as early as 1903, the strong appeal that a straight-
side, easily removable tire would have for the motoring public was not
appreciated at first. Ten years elapsed before United States Rubber,
under the pressure of competition from another manufacturer, featured
Hartford's straight-side tires in national advertising.[15]

Expanding Market for Tires

When United States Rubber Company acquired a majority of the capital
stock of the Rubber Goods Manufacturing Company in 1905, the total
production of motor vehicles in this country was only 25,000 passenger
cars and trucks.[16] Fortunately, the importance of having a tire plant
located in Detroit was recognized, and in 1906, the Morgan and Wright
plant was moved from Chicago to Detroit. Including the equipment, the
new plant was valued at $15 million, had a floor area of 900,000 square

feet, and was able to produce 300 tires a day.[17] Automobile production more than doubled by 1908, and in his annual report for 1909, Samuel P. Colt told the stockholders of the United States Rubber Company that sales of its subsidiary, Rubber Goods Manufacturing Company, for the calendar year 1909 were $25,629,593, up from $18,491,897 in 1908, and explained that the larger part of the increase had been in sale of automobile tires. He added, "Judging from the past, the growth of the automobile tire business will be of momentous importance in the future. Ten years ago, rubber tires [were] not important . . . [they] now consume one-half of the raw product." In 1910, factory sales of motor vehicles in this country totaled 181,000 passenger cars and 6,000 motor trucks; the Rubber Goods Company's sales were up to $35,188,295, and again it was stated the increase had been mostly in tires.

United States Tire Company Incorporated

On Feb. 1, 1911, the United States Tire Company was incorporated to market all the brands of tires made by the Rubber Goods Company and Revere; it was claimed this move would "place the United States Rubber Company, through the United States Tire Company, in the front rank as the largest manufacturer and distributor of rubber tires in the world." Elisha S. Williams was largely instrumental in the formation of the Tire Company and was its president until 1915.

Because it was felt that the tire business of the company needed adequate facilities in the uptown section of New York City, commonly known as "automobile row," a twenty-one-year lease for a lot on the southeast corner of 58th and Broadway was executed in April, 1911. A twenty-story building was erected on it, and the new quarters at 1790 Broadway were ready for occupancy in August, 1912. The ground floor was occupied by the United States Tire Company, and the upper ten floors of "1790" became the home of the New York headquarters of United States Rubber. The remaining space was rented to outside tenants.

Coast-to-Coast Highway Promoted

In 1912, Carl Fisher, one of the brothers who founded the Fisher Body Corporation (acquired by General Motors in 1926), conceived the idea that the automobile industry should raise funds for the construction of a good highway from the East Coast to the West Coast. At a meeting of leaders of the industry in September, 1912, he estimated that such a highway could be constructed at a cost of $10 million and that the road could be completed in time for the opening on May 1, 1915 of the Panama-Pacific Exposition in San Francisco.

21. Early headquarters of United States Rubber Company. The company occupied these buildings during the first forty-eight years of its existence.

FRANKLIN BUILDING,
9-15 Murray St.,
May 1898
April 1904

42 Broadway Bldg.
April 1904
Aug. 1912

FARMERS
LOAN & TRUST CO.
BUILDING,
16 William Street,
Oct. 1892
Aug. 1893

90 Reade Street,
Aug. 1893
May 1898

UNITED STATES
RUBBER CO. BUILDING,
1790 Broadway
since August 1912

There was no federal aid for building highways prior to 1916, and Fisher actually raised $4 million in pledges by May, 1913. In this way the Lincoln Highway Association came to be formed for the purpose of laying out and constructing a highway over the shortest and most practicable route between New York City and San Francisco. Among the largest contributions was one of $130,000 from the United States Rubber Company. Other large contributors included General Motors Company, $100,000; Goodyear Tire and Rubber Company, $75,000; Carl Fisher, $25,000; and Frank Seiberling, then president of Goodyear Tire and Rubber Company, $25,000.

The Lincoln Highway Association soon gave up the idea that the road could be constructed with funds raised by the automotive industry and devoted many years of effort to getting local funds appropriated for this purpose by counties and states along the route.[18]

As its contribution to the good roads movement, United States Rubber later assisted in the building of an "ideal section" of the Lincoln Highway, extending for several miles between the towns of Dyer and Schererville in Lake County, Ind. This section was proclaimed the finest and most beautiful piece of road in America. Highway engineers from all sections of the country were invited to inspect its construction, and special attention was called to the illumination by specially designed, automatically controlled overhead lamps, recently developed by General Electric. The funds supplied by United States Rubber were augmented by appropriations from the federal government and from Indiana.[19]

Vigorous Competition

In 1912, United States Rubber represented about 25% of the rubber tire industry (which produced approximately 4,400,000 casings that year),[20] and the company remained the largest tire manufacturer for several more years. Vigorous and growing competition, however, was coming from several tire companies, chiefly those centered in Akron, Ohio.

United States Rubber's sales volume on tires was followed very closely in 1912 by B. F. Goodrich Company and the Diamond Rubber Company, with the Goodyear Tire and Rubber Company in fourth place. Shortly afterward Goodrich and Diamond merged, but Goodyear's tire sales soon surpassed those of the newly merged companies and took second place.[21] Meanwhile, the Firestone Tire and Rubber Company, incorporated in 1900, was becoming important in the tire industry and was capitalizing on the close friendship that had recently developed between Harvey S. Firestone, Sr., and Henry Ford.

In addition to these tire companies, which later became known as the Big Four, the extraordinary growth of the automotive industry just prior to World War I led to the organization of numerous smaller tire companies. At one time or another there were said to have been more than 500 concerns making rubber tires in this country,[22] of which about 200 were operating in the period from 1910 to 1920. A breakdown of United States Rubber Company's shipments of tires, between original equipment tires and replacement tires, is not available for the years prior to 1915, when the company accounted for 21.8% of the industry's shipments of original equipment tires. In 1917, the first year for which data regarding the company's shipments of replacement tires are available, it enjoyed 10% of all shipments of replacement tires.[23] United States Rubber endeavored in several ways to maintain its industry position.

Improvements in Construction

The manufacture of cord tires had been started by a subsidiary of the Rubber Goods Manufacturing Company in 1903, and its cord tires had been used in a race at Ormond Beach in 1906, where the driver did a mile in 28½ seconds.[24] Quality problems and resultant failures of cord tires were encountered in the early years of their production, but by January, 1916, the company was ready to promote and advertise the U.S. Royal Cord Tire. Testimonials reported service ranging from over 22,000 miles to as much as 41,633 miles given by U.S. Royal Cord tires; these were quoted in subsequent advertisements in 1916, indicating that the early problems had been fairly well overcome and reasonably wide distribution obtained. The significance of the introduction of the cord tire may be realized when it is recalled that the average fabric clincher tire could be expected to last only about ten months.[25]

About Jan. 1, 1910, Morgan and Wright introduced a tire with raised knobs on the tread and named it Nobby Tread to distinguish it from previous tires made by the subsidiaries of United States Rubber, which had smooth treads. At first, the "nobs" were molded in a drum and were applied individually. Soon, of course, the inner surface of the mold was engraved to produce the knobs. Strong claims were made for the effectiveness of the Nobby Tread, which was said to be "replacing tire chains."

For several years Nobby Tread and Chain Tread tires were prominently featured in United States Rubber's advertising with such assertions as: "Will stop your skidding," "Will hold the wheels secure against every possible slip or skid," "Will grip even wet, greasy asphalt with bulldog tenacity."[26] In August, 1916, they were proclaimed to be the "first successful anti-skid tires built." In judging the accuracy of such claims, it should be kept in mind that lower acceleration and inefficient brakes, common to cars of that period, did not require as much resistance to skidding as do cars today. Also, for the most part, cars were driven at slower speeds in those years, and it was customary for owners in northern states not to drive their cars at all during winter months. (In December, 1920, United States Rubber took a full page in *Life* to advertise its service to users of U.S. tires and advised owners to jack up their cars in winter or remove the tires if they were not using the car.)

As early as 1911, United States Rubber had tested the first pneumatic tires specifically designed for use on motor trucks. These were used on two 3½ ton trucks at its Detroit factory with noticeable prolongation of the service life of the trucks, which were kept in continuous service until August, 1919. They then toured the country with the original tires.[27] When the tests were being made, only about 25,000 motor trucks were registered, and most users still thought solid rubber tires were more economical and practical for use on trucks. By 1917, about 60% of the commercial cars in the country were said to be using pneumatic tires; solid tires were still used by the remaining 40%.[28] Between 1919 and 1921, the production of solid rubber tires for trucks declined by over 70%; pneumatic truck tires had proved their worth through the use of cords in the tire carcass.

Improvements had also been made in the construction of fabric tires, so that by 1913 the company could boast that by an exclusive process it had been able to increase the fabric strength practically 50%. In February, 1914, the company announced that, from the experience of the past four years, adjustments on Nobby Tread tires would be made on the basis of 5,000 miles.

Rubber manufacturers had learned that zinc oxide increased the tensile strength of rubber compounds. Therefore, as automobiles began to be produced in larger numbers, it was natural that the rubber tire companies early adopted zinc oxide as the standard filling ingredient in compounds for automobile tire treads. Due to the sizable content of zinc oxide, white was the almost universally accepted color for good tires for many years. But zinc oxide was expensive, and before World War I a few tire companies began using carbon black for tire treads. (The first use of carbon black was by an English manufacturer who chose it to get a distinctive color.) During World War I a shortage of zinc oxide forced other companies to make increased use of carbon black as a substitute filler in

22. Pneumatic tires for trucks. The first pneumatic tires specially designed for truck use were put on the vehicle above. The first fire apparatus to be equipped with pneumatic tires was the H. & L. No. 11 of the Indianapolis fire department; the tires were United States Rubber's Nobby fabric.

Photograph taken in 1911

tread compounds, but it appears that the added abrasive resistance obtained with carbon black was not generally recognized at first. In most cases its early use was one of necessity rather than of choice. Since a superintendent in those days was likely to be an experienced "hand" who had worked up from the ranks and carried his jealously guarded formulas in a small notebook in an inside coat pocket, it is remarkable that quality improved as fast as it did.

The steady lengthening of the useful life of a tire was an important factor in the creation of the industry's excess capacity, which has plagued it since the end of World War I. However, with factory sales of motor vehicles increasing from only 187,000 in 1910 to 970,000 in 1915 and 2,227,000 in 1920 (Figure 23), the growing number of passenger cars and trucks in use during each of those years more than offset the longer service given by the improved product. This is graphically illustrated by the following estimates from the *Encyclopaedia Britannica* (13th ed.) of total production in this country of pneumatic tires: 1913, 6,588,000; 1915, 12,840,000; and 1920, 32,400,000.

Production Capacity Enlarged

Under such conditions distribution did not appear to constitute a serious problem. Comments in the company's annual reports give evidence: 1909, sales of Rubber Goods Company up $7,138,000, "larger part of increase being in automobile tires"; 1910, sales of Rubber Goods Company up $10,441,000, "mostly tires"; 1913, sales of tires in first three months about 40% over same period in 1912.

Colt, in his annual report for the fiscal year ended March 31, 1912, referred to what he termed "close competition" that for some years past had kept tire profits at less than 10% of sales. But with the facts then known, it was decided in 1914 to enlarge the Morgan and Wright plant in Detroit at a cost of $870,000, and to make other additions, totaling $355,000, to tire and mechanical goods plants. One wonders what his recommendations would have been if he could have foreseen the bitter competition and unsatisfactory earnings that were to prevail in the rubber tire industry after the inflated demands resulting from World War I had been satisfied. Expansion of the company's five tire plants was authorized in the early part of 1919, with the aim of more than doubling their total capacity by early 1921. Other tire and rubber companies also enlarged their productive capacity in 1920, and that year's capital expenditures by the rubber industry for productive facilities totaled $105 million, a far larger amount than would be spent by the industry in any

23. Motor vehicle factory sales, 1900-29 (see Table A-6).

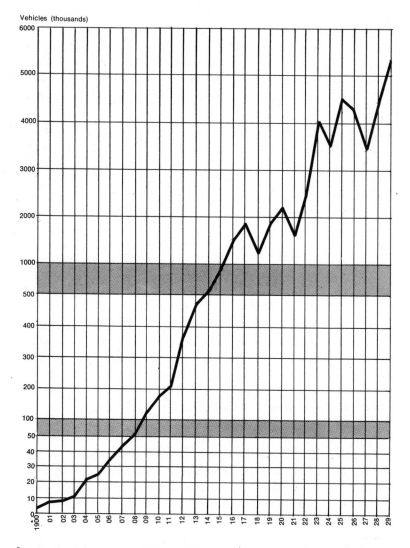

subsequent year prior to World War II.[29] Thus the stage was being set for the intense struggle for the market that would occur in the 1920's.

Before the multistoried addition to the Detroit plant was completed, United States Rubber's annual shipments of tire casings fell from 2,908,000 in 1919 to 2,217,000 in 1920, and did not exceed four million until 1925. Meanwhile, the introduction of the flat-band method of making tires had increased labor productivity by about 50%. As a con-

sequence, the Detroit addition was largely excess capacity until the Hartford plant was closed in 1929 and its production was moved to Detroit.

STEPS TO IMPROVE EQUIPMENT, METHODS, AND PRODUCT

Although formally organized departments for research and development
were unknown in the early years of the rubber industry, inventive individuals were not idle. In 1836, Edwin M. Chaffee, Roxbury, Mass., an
intimate friend of Charles Goodyear and later one of the partners in the
National India Rubber Company, had patented a rubber-mixing mill
which had two steam-heated rollers turning in opposite directions at
different speeds. In the same year, Chaffee also patented the rubber
calender, consisting of four hollow, steam-heated iron rollers, placed one
above the other, that turned at the same speed. Rubber could be forced
under pressure into a fabric passed between a pair of the rollers. These
two machines have remained among the most important types of rubber
processing machinery.[30]

Prior to 1850, L. Candee and Company had developed an elastic
varnish for rubber footwear, and Thomas Wales had invented the buckle
overshoe, or arctic, which was introduced by the Goodyear Metallic Rubber Shoe Company under the Wales-Goodyear label. The Meyer Rubber
Company was said to have been first to use a calender engraved to deliver a sheet of rubber outsole stock with three different gauges of thickness for the sole, shank, and heel sections.[31] The principle of curing
rubber products under pressure was discovered in 1901 by A. O. Bourn,
but the Naugatuck plant of United States Rubber was unable to obtain
a satisfactory surface finish on rubber footwear by his method.[32]

For many years manufacturers of rubber footwear had sought to find
a satisfactory substitute for wooden lasts and boot trees. Even though
the maple blocks had been kiln dried for as long as six months before
the lasts and boot trees were shaped, the wood would still shrink after
repeated trips through the vulcanizers. Trying to fit precut parts over
a shrunken last was such a problem that it was necessary for the pattern
makers to be continually revising the patterns. Wooden lasts also tended
to splinter after extended use; at a single plant several skilled workmen
would be employed in repairing them. The added expense was not the
only disadvantage with wooden lasts; neither the merchant nor the
consumer could ever be sure that the size or the width of the finished
item agreed with the size marked on the lining.

In April, 1894, in his annual report to the stockholders, Joseph P.
Banigan had announced that, since solid iron lasts had been found too

heavy to be practical, United States Rubber had obtained a patent on a sheet metal last that would avoid the necessity of recutting patterns and make it possible to produce footwear that would better satisfy the customer. However, sheet metal lasts did not prove to be a satisfactory answer to the problem. In 1909, the Shoe Hardware Company began making lasts of hollow aluminum at its plant in Waterbury, Conn.[33] In addition to retaining the proper size and well-defined bottom edges, aluminum conducted heat much more rapidly than wood and thus contributed to a better cure. The many advantages more than offset the added cost of aluminum whenever the same last could be used without change for several seasons.

Improved Mixing Equipment

Before the development of the Banbury mixer by the Birmingham Iron Foundries (incorporated later into the Farrell Birmingham Company), all mixing of rubber compounds was done on open mills. The Banbury was a much larger machine, which performed the mixing operation in an enclosed chamber (Figure 24). It is believed that the second Banbury in existence was installed in the Goodyear Metallic Rubber Shoe Company plant at Naugatuck in 1914.[34] According to F. E. Worley, the Banbury mixer was still in its development stage, for he recalled hearing the inventor, Fernly H. Banbury, remark on several occasions that it was only with the help of the foreman of the Naugatuck millroom that the mixer then being installed was made into a practical production machine. In December, 1962, Worley wrote the author as follows:

> "This particular machine was called size 3 as it was supposed to have the capacity of three small mixing mills in vogue at that time. [It] really was too small for volume production work in a factory of any consequence, and in a very few years was superseded by sizes 9, 11, and 27, with some variations."

The Banbury not only had far greater capacity than an open mill, but also provided more accurate control over the mixing operation, ensuring greater uniformity in the mixed batch.

Early "Making" Methods

For more than sixty-five years (1845-1910), it was customary for each article of rubber footwear to be assembled by an individual "maker" to whom the lasts and cut parts (ranging from about twenty to even more than fifty for each pair) had been delivered from other departments of the factory (Figure 24). Since the rubber outsoles, heels, and outer layers of rubber for the uppers, as well as some intermediate rubber parts, would not have been previously combined with fabric, and since rubber

24. Mixing and "making" methods.

24a. Open grinding and mixing mills, Mishawaka. In the foreground is Para rubber before and after preliminary grinding.

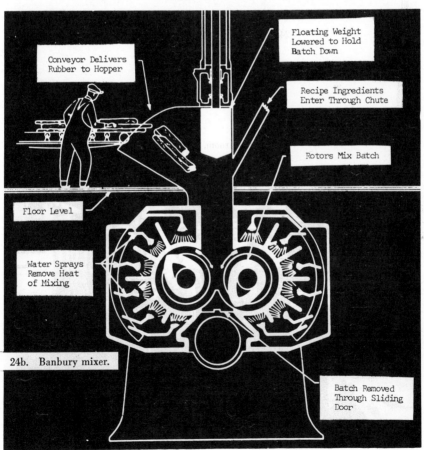

Floating Weight Lowered to Hold Batch Down

Conveyor Delivers Rubber to Hopper

Recipe Ingredients Enter Through Chute

Rotors Mix Batch

Floor Level

Water Sprays Remove Heat of Mixing

24b. Banbury mixer.

Batch Removed Through Sliding Door

24c.   Gum calender. Mishawaka.

24d.   Boot room, Mishawaka.

24e. Pressure process vulcanizer, Naugatuck.

24f. Boots ready for shipment, Woonsocket.

which had been compounded and processed in the millroom but had not
yet been vulcanized was very sticky, these rubber parts could be readily
ruined if precautions were not taken to keep them flat and free from
contact with each other. This was done by placing them in "books."
Each book consisted of a flat board to which several layers of cloth were
attached at one end, like the leaves of a book. The rubber parts could
be carefully placed between these fabric leaves, and each maker would
receive several such books containing the cut rubber parts for the particular type and sizes of footwear he was scheduled to make that day.
He or she (women were employed to make the lighter items) would also
receive linings and reinforcing parts that had been cut from rubber-
coated or "frictioned" fabrics. These were separated by layers of paper.

The cloth leaf books were stored in racks and on shelves under the
table; even so, the lasts and parts needed for the maker's daily ticket
or work quota (ranging from twelve to thirty-six pairs), crowded the space
on his table so badly that he could assemble only about one-third of his
ticket at one time. The assembly operations were divided into three
cycles: (1) assembling linings and other cut parts on the lasts, preliminary
rolling of some parts to remove trapped air and to get good adhesions;
(2) covering the previously placed parts with the rubber uppers; (3)
placing the outsoles (and heels where these were separately formed as
on boots), and rolling by hand all the surface, soles, and uppers to remove all trapped air from between the layers. Depending on the skill
and energy of the individual, the workday of the makers varied from
about eight to fourteen hours. Most of them were able to finish the day's
ticket in less than ten hours.

The assembly process required considerable dexterity and the quality
of the finished article depended to a large degree upon the skill and care
of the individual operator. Piecework rates had been used since the early
days of the industry. Each maker stamped his "maker's number" on the
finished boot or shoe, and penalties for poor workmanship were common. Skilled workers prided themselves on their almost perfect records.

Pairs of finished footwear were taken from the making rooms to the
heaters or vulcanizers. After vulcanization the footwear was placed on
tables where it was stripped from the lasts, trimmed of projecting por-
tions of the lining, and inspected. Obviously, this was a costly method of
producing rubber footwear.

Efforts to Reduce Costs

In 1903, the assistant general manager of the United States Rubber system inaugurated what was described in the annual report of May 17,

ERRATA

On page xv, the new name of the corporation is shown as UniRoyal, Inc.,
following the style of lettering adopted for the trademark and previously used
in advertisements (see pages 410 and 411). However, the letter "r" was not
capitalized in the new corporate name, Uniroyal, Inc., approved by the stockholders on April 19, 1966.

Page 92, Figure 19, _for_ "Dominion Rubber Company" _read_ "Birthplace of
Dominion Rubber Company." See pages 91 and 209 for changes in the firm name.

Page 323, line 30, _for_ "the German occupation officials" _read_ "German
officials."

Page 339, Figure 51, _add_ "Source: Ralph C. Epstein, 'Concentration and
Price Trends in the Rubber Tire Industry, 1930-47.' See Table A-11."

Page 423, Table A-13, second footnote, _for_ "1920, $39,859,000; 1925,
$5,000,000; 1926" _read_ "shown in footnote to Table A-12. On ....."

UNIROYAL, Inc.
Rockefeller Center
1230 Avenue of Americas
New York, N. Y. 10020

Office of the
Chairman and President

Dear Librarian:

    We are pleased to present to you this copy of the *History of United States Rubber Company* (now UNIROYAL, Inc.) published by the Indiana University Press.

    The author of the *History*, Glenn Babcock, is a former executive of our Company who in recent years has been associated with the University. He spent several years of painstaking research before writing this book. It is not an official history of the Company, but an academic case study of the formation and progress of a major corporation. Mr. Babcock records the early development and then the growth of our Company as an integral part of the rubber industry and the American economy up to World War II.

    Naturally, in the 25 years which have elapsed since that time, the Company has undergone widespread change in management methods, technical and marketing capability and product diversification. However, since this book deals with economic history for one segment of the American industrial revolution, we trust you will find it a worthwhile addition to your library.

Sincerely,

George R. Vila

1904 as a "complete system of comparison of costs of the different factories." It was said to have already shown large savings without detracting from the quality of the product. Since there was a wide variation in the type of equipment used in the different factories, as well as in floor plans, layouts, processes, methods, standards of quality and volume of production, any true comparison must have revealed startling differences in unit costs.

In 1903, the accounting department also began systematic comparisons of the operating profits of each mill, and these comparisons were submitted monthly to the directors. Gradually these comparisons of production costs and of net operating profits began to bear results.

Shortly after 1910, one of the rubber footwear companies not included in the United States Rubber system began to experiment with a team of five operators working around a making table. On each of two sides there were two operators, a "laster" assembling the lining and cut parts, and an "upperer" who placed the uppers on the lasted parts. Shoes for the right foot were assembled on one side, those for the left foot on the other side. An "outsole placer and roller" worked at the end of the table. Each member of the team placed from four to six pairs of lasts with his finished work on a stick that held the lasts in an upright position; there was considerable waste motion, and much time was lost in sorting the lasts out of the bin under the table and getting them into proper sequence. The team of five operators could make from 120 to 180 pairs a day, which, considering the types of shoes made by this method, was better than when the entire assembly was completed by one maker.[35]

A graduate of Massachusetts Institute of Technology, Myron H. Clark is given much of the credit for introducing better concepts of factory management, both for production methods and handling of factory personnel. Clark joined the United States Rubber Company in 1903. In 1913 and 1914, as superintendent of the Goodyear Metallic Rubber Shoe Company's Naugatuck plant, he started a comprehensive reorganization of management and production practices. He designed and built a rotary conveyor for making buckle arctics; in 1913, this unit was used at the Williamsport plant of the Lycoming Rubber Company. In 1914, he hired a group of college graduates whom he inspired with his progressive ideas.

In 1917, Clark engaged a consulting engineer, Frank Gilbrith, for two days a month, reportedly at $250 per diem, to initiate improved industrial engineering concepts. Motion picture studies of operations filmed at that time led to important changes in equipment and methods, especially in the millroom. Many of the management techniques he introduced are still employed.

In 1918, Clark was appointed general factory manager for footwear and miscellaneous products, but resigned in 1922 when he did not receive full support from top management.[36]

One of the steps taken in 1919 to reduce costs was the merger of manufacturing operations in the Naugatuck factories of Goodyear Metallic Rubber Shoe Company and Goodyear's India Rubber Glove Manufacturing Company. While the corporate indentities of the two companies were retained, they operated thereafter practically as one plant.

By 1919, the Footwear Division had a service department located in New Haven, next to the L. Candee factory. The service department included a laboratory control department, an industrial relations department, a planning department, and an engineering department. The central department acted as a clearing house for the ideas of the separate factories. It also participated in the training of new men. About this time the planning department conducted a training program concerned with work planning, job analysis, time studies, and graphic charts. Men with no factory experience were also given a thorough and intensive training in the factory department. While good in theory, a central training department had serious drawbacks psychologically, and did not prove successful because of the different conditions and organizations encountered in various factories of the system.

The central service department also contained departmental committees made up of representatives from various factories. They studied conditions in the different factories in order to bring about the best procedures for all factories. More new methods were tried during the 1920's and will be discussed in the following chapter.

Beginning of Production Control

Before 1918, United States Rubber System's footwear factories generally relied heavily on foremen and even on individual operators to determine the quantities of materials, compounds, and fabrics needed to make the footwear specified on the manufacturing order, or ticket, issued to the factory. The ticket would be issued from seven to fourteen calendar days prior to the final assembly, or making, date. The foreman of the cutting department then would have his cutters list the quantities of various stocks required for cutting the parts needed for the making ticket. Combining these estimates, the foreman would then place an order with the foreman of the millroom, who was responsible for maintaining an adequate supply of the different types of rubber compounds and rubberized fabrics. Under such procedures it was unavoidable that, on the one hand, excessive amounts of scrap would accumulate in the cutting rooms, while at the same time, there were shortages of cut parts needed by the makers. High costs and serious delays in filling orders for finished goods resulted.

The magnitude of the problem is only partially indicated by the following condensed summary[37] of rubber footwear produced by United States Rubber in 1917:

	Pairs
Rubber boots	2,486,000
Lumbermen's (rubber overs for wear over wool boots or socks)	1,197,000
Buckle arctics	5,194,000
Gum shoes	25,173,000
	34,050,000

The large number of parts for each pair has previously been mentioned. If the total number of pairs is multiplied by twenty, the minimum number of parts in a pair of gum shoes as then constructed, we have a staggering figure of 681 million parts. It must also be remembered that this production was scattered over hundreds of styles, further complicated by the wide variety of brands offered. Men who were keenly conscious of costs involved in excessive scrap losses looked for more efficient methods of operating.

In 1920, when H. S. Marlor was factory manager of the Williamsport, Pa., plant of the Lycoming Rubber Company, a program was developed at that plant in conjunction with the central planning department of United States Rubber. The program established the standard number of pairs per square yard to be obtained for each cut part from a specific type of stock. While the conversion of pairs to square yards of stock could not be accurate because the proportions of small or large sizes varied from one ticket to the next, this was a great improvement over the former method of estimating. The new system, which came to be known as production control, was steadily improved and refined over the succeeding years.[38]

Written Standard Practice (WSP) *Adopted*

By 1919, the footwear factories were using the written standard practice (WSP), which was intended as a permanent record of the best results which various departments and representatives had produced on a certain feature of their work. Details of operation, as practiced by the different factories, were considered by the departmental committees in the central service department in New Haven. The departmental committee then drew up a proposed WSP, which was submitted by the committee to the superintendents of the several factories. If the superintendents accepted the plan, it then became the WSP for the entire Footwear Division.

A talk delivered in 1919 indicated that the adoption of WSP controls was still in its early stage and that much remained to be done. For example, standard specifications for materials going into compounds had been adopted only recently, and, said the speaker, "It is expected that shortly the general purchasing department in New York will be supplying the factories with goods purchased on these specifications." Apparently there was no uniform standard of quality for, "at the present time, the standards of inspection are left almost entirely to the opinion of the foreman and his assistants."[39] According to W. H. Norton, best results were obtained from use of WSP's that dealt with management practices and procedures. For numerous reasons, operational methods varied too much from plant to plant, and changed too rapidly for adherence to a WSP to be practical.

Improved Vulcanizing Methods

Before the introduction of practical methods of curing footwear under pressure, the temperature in the heaters (vulcanizing chambers) was raised very slowly to permit air that had been trapped in the compound to escape without producing sponginess or porosity in the rubber. Consequently, from six to twelve hours were required for satisfactory cures.[40] Since a minute drop of water will expand approximately 1,640 times when heated to 213°F., the great importance of eliminating any air or moisture trapped in the compounds or between layers of material is readily apparent.

In June, 1911, the Mishawaka subsidiary filed an application for a patent on a curing process in which a vacuum was created within hollow aluminum lasts, the bottoms of which had been drilled with small holes. The top of each last was fitted with an attachment for connecting it to a pipe leading to a vacuum pump. Air was withdrawn from the inside of each boot or shoe during the period in the vulcanizing process when the rubber compounds were in their most plastic, stickiest, almost fluid state. This method created an equivalent pressure of about fourteen pounds per square inch against the entire outer surface of the individual boot or shoe. This pressure was maintained throughout the remainder of the curing cycle, virtually eliminating porosity in the rubber stocks and forcing the several layers of rubber and fabric together more firmly than was possible by using handrollers to press the layers together. Sulfur fumes and other volatile matter in the compounds were withdrawn at the same time (Figure 24e). In August, 1912, several special quality rubber boots and rubber mining shoes were added by Mishawaka under the VAC label. Between 1912 and 1915, four cylindrical pressure vulcanizing chambers each measuring 10 feet by 63 feet were installed at Mishawaka. Steam cures were also introduced about 1912.[41]

At about the same time, plans were being made to build pressure heaters at Naugatuck; the first were installed there in 1912. In addition to producing better quality footwear, pressure shortened the cures by about half.

In December, 1916, Dr. Willis A. Gibbons, a young chemist employed at the General Laboratories, applied for a patent on a method he had developed for vulcanizing raincoats or draped rubber fabrics in super-heated steam at atmospheric pressure. Previously, satisfactory vulcanization at atmospheric pressure had required the use of litharge (a yellowish oxide of lead) or a similar accelerator in the rubber compound. Since litharge caused a darkening of the compound, the finished product was almost invariably made black, although white or dark red rubber goods had been produced without litharge, using steam cures in costly, high pressure vulcanizers.

Gibbons' process made it possible to accomplish vulcanization without the use of litharge and thus to produce rubber goods, such as raincoats, carriage cloth, coated rubber substitutes for leather, balloon or airplane fabrics, and white hospital sheeting in colors other than black. Moreover, the necessity for costly construction of large heaters capable of maintaining high pressures was avoided. Years later, a modification of this idea was employed by Gibbons and Sturdevant in the continuous vulcanization of latex thread.

QUICKENED PACE OF DEVELOPMENT

Rubber Regenerating Company Acquired

In December, 1912, with the acquisition of the Rubber Regenerating Company, Mishawaka, Ind., the United States Rubber Company took its first important step toward the organization of a development department.

In 1906, Raymond B. Price had organized the Rubber Regenerating Company of Illinois, which moved to Mishawaka in 1908 and was incorporated in December, 1908 as the Rubber Regenerating Company. In 1894, Price had been the first college-trained chemist to be hired in what was one of the earliest laboratories established in the rubber industry. In 1904, he had patented a rubber reclaiming process that involved use of highly concentrated solutions of caustic soda with a boiling point considerably above the melting point of sulfur. The high concentration avoided infringement on a previous patent obtained by Arthur H. Marks, an Akron chemist who used solutions of low concentration.[42]

The acid reclaiming process had been successful as long as the principal source of scrap rubber had been rubber boots and shoes with low sulfur content. However, with the rapidly increasing production of rubber tires and other items with a relatively high sulfur content, the acid process became impracticable since it merely removed the fabric fiber and did not remove the excess sulfur. In the alkali process the scrap rubber was desulfurized, defiberized, and devulcanized in one step.[43] In 1913, alkali process equipment was installed in the rubber regenerating plant at Naugatuck.

In addition to its Mishawaka plant the Rubber Regenerating Company owned 79% of the capital stock of Rubber Regenerating, Ltd., which operated a plant at Manchester, England. The application, dated Dec. 17, 1912, for listing on the New York Stock Exchange an issue of $6 million of United States Rubber common stock to be exchanged for the capital stock of the Rubber Regenerating Company, stated that the latter derived annual revenue of about $150,000 from royalties on a patented process used in the manufacture of rubber boots and shoes. If similar royalty agreements were made with United States Rubber Company, the additional income would be in excess of $500,000 per annum.

Development Department Organized

The acquisition of Rubber Regenerating Company gave United States Rubber the services of Price, who in 1912 became head of the development department with general charge of laboratories, patents, engineering, and research. In 1912, the company opened a central research laboratory in New Brunswick, N.J., one of the first industrial research laboratories in this country. The following year the General Laboratories were established in rented quarters in New York City, remaining there for fifteen years. The early efforts of the development department were directed chiefly toward making more effective use of the resourcefulness of the different units of the company. Greater flexibility of operations became of vital importance after the outbreak of World War I.

However, special attention was given to development of improved methods in the treatment of crude rubber. Price was particularly impressed with the potential value of the company's recently acquired rubber plantations, although he was not directly responsible for their operation. He was a personal friend of Irenee du Pont, and it is not unlikely that this friendship may have been partially responsible for the latter's early interest in the long-range investment opportunity that United States Rubber appeared to offer at that time.

Colors in Footwear

The use of colors other than black for utilitarian types of rubber boots and shoes was not initiated by United States Rubber. White and red boots and shoes were promoted originally by an Akron manufacturer. Before the adoption of organic accelerators, litharge was the accelerator most commonly used for footwear compounds. During the vulcanizing process, litharge combined with the sulfur in the compound to form lead sulfide, which was black; compounds in which litharge was used were either black, dark gray, or some other dark color, such as maroon. It was the contention of United States Rubber's chemists that, everything else being equal, a black compound would offer better value than a white compound using magnesia or zinc oxide or a compound heavily loaded with white or red inorganic pigments. George H. Mayo later insisted that the best interests of merchants were not served by forcing them to stock more than one color of strictly utilitarian rubber footwear.[44] However, the demand created for white or red boots and shoes was so strong by 1913 that Mishawaka's chemists were testing the aging qualities of white and red compounds. Mishawaka was forced to add these colors in 1915, and United States Rubber's plants at Naugatuck and elsewhere soon followed.

For its first white compounds, Mishawaka used zinc and lithopone (a mixture of zinc sulfide and barium sulfate) for the white pigment, and lime and magnesia for the accelerators. Iron oxide formed the pigment for red compounds, with litharge or red lead for accelerators.[45] For several years, live wet steam was applied directly to the footwear during vulcanization under the VAC process, producing well-cured footwear in as short a time as two hours at a maximum temperature of 290°F.[46]

The introduction of colored rubber footwear caused new and difficult problems for Mishawaka and other plants. Some of the white compounds tended to take on an undesirable purplish hue when exposed to sunlight in a dealer's window for a few days. Worse, some of the red boots and shoes appeared to melt within a short time after they had been shipped to dealers. The defective compounds could overcure and soften to a point where they would first become very sticky, even flow like taffy, then harden and become brittle. Investigation by the company's chemists disclosed that some of the iron oxide used for red pigment was contaminated with manganese.[47] These were not the last of the industry's headaches with colors, or with other new specialized compounds or constructions. They are cited as examples of some of the hazards typical in those years of an industry in which, despite extensive laboratory tests, some detrimental characteristic of a new ingredient or a new construction frequently could not be detected in advance of the production and marketing of large quantities of finished goods. Consequently, costly write-downs occurred. Testing of products under actual service conditions in the field had been conducted for many years, but more extensive and costly programs were later developed that involved testing thousands of pairs of different types of footwear on workers, sportsmen, athletes, and active children. Field tests, more accurate knowledge of the chemistry of rubber, and refinements in equipment and controls have greatly reduced but have not eliminated the unusual risks to which a rubber manufacturer with high quality standards is exposed.

Manufacture of Aniline Oil

An important step toward broadening the scope of the company's production of chemicals was brought about by the Allied naval blockade of Germany during World War I. This stopped the importation of aniline and other coal tar derivatives formerly obtained almost exclusively from Germany.

Not only was aniline essential for the production of dyestuffs for the textile trade, but rubber chemists had been demonstrating that derivatives of aniline and other coal tar intermediates not only made shorter cures of rubber products possible, but, in addition, increased the strength and durability of rubber compounds. The use of aniline and aniline derivatives as accelerators had been introduced in this country in 1906 by George Oenslager, a chemist employed by the Diamond Rubber Company, Akron. He had succeeded in keeping the process a secret for several years, and it was not until a German patent was published in 1914 that its value was generally disclosed.[48] Before the supply of aniline from Germany was cut off, the United States Tire Company's plant in Detroit had converted to use aniline, and needed to find a new source quickly if full-scale production of tires was to be maintained.

By January, 1915, the plant had only four months' supply on hand, and the Naugatuck Chemical Company was asked to develop a process for manufacturing aniline oil and to build a plant for its production. The General Laboratories in New York and central engineering both helped on the project; John E. Caskey was one of several young chemists and engineers sent to Naugatuck to assist in building and operating the aniline plant. They succeeded in expressing the first, still warm drums of aniline to Detroit in time to prevent a shutdown.[49]

Before organic accelerators were developed, about five hours were required to vulcanize a tire. By 1941, an ordinary tire was cured in 40 to 50 minutes. Organic accelerators not only shortened curing times, but enhanced the quality of certain compounds and made it possible for the first time to obtain much lighter and brighter colors. Aniline had a toxic effect and was soon replaced by other safer organic accelerators developed by the General Laboratory. In later years a vast amount of research developed a wide variety of specialized organic accelerators and antioxidants, which resulted in many improvements and refinements in the company's products.

After the outbreak of World War I, Dr. Theodore Whittelsey became the director of research and development, succeeding R. B. Price who went to Washington to devote his time to the war effort.

Carbon Black Compounds

Another pre-World War I development was an exceptionally tough, long-wearing outsole compound formulated by Mishawaka's chemists in 1916. At that time, the outsoles of most leather work shoes were attached by nailing; rubber outsoles previously offered by other rubber companies would not hold the heads of the nails. Mishko, as the new carbon black sole compound was named, could be successfully nailed or stitched to a leather shoe, and in many instances it outlasted the leather uppers. It was the forerunner of United States Rubber's Uskide[50] and numerous other compounded rubber outsoles, which since that time have almost entirely replaced leather for soles of many types of leather shoes. The Mishawaka company decided not to sell Mishko soles to other manufacturers, but rather to enter into the production and sale of a line of leather work shoes with this outsole. First offered for sale in 1917, Mishko sole shoes were an important part of the Mishawaka line for a quarter of a century.

Development Work on Golf Balls

Before 1848, golf balls were made of three pieces of untanned bull's hide (or sometimes sheepskin), stitched wrong side out, with a small

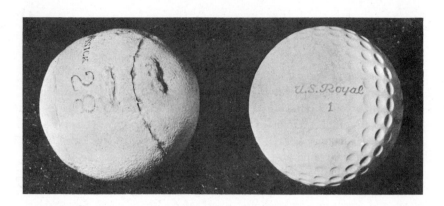

25. Golf balls—old and recent. The one at left, made of sheepskin and stuffed with goose feathers, was used in Scotland 130 years ago. The other was made in 1947 of silicone "bouncing putty."

opening through which, after the leather had been turned outside in, goose feathers were stuffed (Figure 25). Then the hole was stitched shut. The leather balls had good carry as long as they did not get wet. In wet grass, a ball that weighed 28 pennyweight troy at the start of a game might end up a "pounder," and in an important match a new ball might be needed for each hole. In 1848, Sir Thomas Moncrief conceived the idea of making a golf ball out of gutta-percha, a rubber-like substance, and an experimental ball was made by Willie Dunn. It was unsatisfactory. The ball would start away from the club head satisfactorily, but suddenly it would pitch downward. The gutta-percha ball was discarded, but caddies started to play with it. As it began to be nicked by their clubs, a surprising thing happened. The more the ball was nicked, the better its flight. The experiments were renewed and new balls were made, nicked, at first, in lines like the segments of an orange. The flight of these gutta-percha balls was about the same as that of the feather-stuffed leather balls, but the new balls were much more durable and sold for 1 shilling. The cost of the leather balls was 3 shillings, 6 pence.[51]

Development work on the manufacture of golf balls was begun by United States Rubber in 1915 at the plant of the Mechanical Rubber Company, Cleveland, following a suggestion by the factory manager, Arthur Hopkins. The ball had a solid rubber core around which rubber thread was wound. During this experimental stage the golf balls were branded with the trademark of the Mechanical Rubber Company.

In 1917, the development work was transferred to the sundries plant at Providence, where H. Z. Cobb designed and built special machines for winding the rubber thread under carefully controlled tension around the core. A surface resembling in miniature the popular Nobby Tread on U.S. Tires was also developed at the Providence plant, and the ball was named U.S. Nobby. Commercial manufacture began in 1917 following the market survey by Ernest Bradford.

IMPACT OF WORLD WAR I

Prior to World War I, rubber footwear was not an item of general issue in most armies. It was not until December, 1914 that large rush orders for rubber boots and shoes for the British and French forces began to be placed with American manufacturers. During that month, the United States Rubber Company shipped rubber footwear valued at $1.5 million to England and France. Since military equipment was not motorized to any great extent, there was no immediate upsurge in tire sales. On the contrary, tire sales during the last five months of 1914 compared unfavorably with the corresponding 1913 period.

After the declaration of war by the United States in April, 1917, the industry's shipments of replacement tires jumped from 10,782,000 casings in 1916 to 16,754,000 in 1917, and 20,494,000 in 1918,[52] but much of this increase would have materialized anyway as a result of the rapid growth of the automobile industry. It was not necessary to place any restrictions on the private use of motor vehicles, and the company's advertisement in the *Saturday Evening Post*, February, 1918, urged the public to, "Use your automobile more and more for short hauls—railroads can then take care of long hauls" (Figure 26).

It should be noted, however, that at the time of World War I the United States was consuming *annually* only about 60,000 long tons of crude rubber. In contrast, by June, 1941, when the government restricted the use of rubber, consumption had risen to about 70,000 long tons of rubber a *month*.[53] Certainly this situation was far different from that existing during World War II when the Allies were faced with an extreme shortage of rubber.

To prevent rubber from reaching her enemies, Great Britain placed an embargo on shipments of crude rubber, first from colonies in the Far East to ports other than in Great Britain, and later from British ports. Through the efforts of a committee representing British planting and other important interests and a similar committee representing American importers and manufacturers, arrangements were made so that plantation rubber could again be exported to the United States.

For Short Hauls - Passenger
or Commercial - The Automobile

At this present writing, a great railroad man says:

"While the railroads are now congested with both passenger and freight service, the peak has not *yet* been reached."

Therefore—use your automobile more and more (either passenger or commercial) for *short* hauls,

—and the railroads can *then* take care of the *long* hauls.

Keep your automobile always at top efficiency,

—gas in, oil in, motor tuned up,

—and the right tires to give you long mileage and low mileage cost.

Watch the "feet" of your automobile as the officers of an army watch the feet of their men.

United States Tires, for both passenger and commercial cars, have demonstrated their supremacy as the tires of service, of mileage, of low mileage cost.

Proof?—what tire users say about United States Tires—ask them.

Year after year they continue to *use* United States Tires exclusively.

This is proved by the fact that the sales increases of United States Tires are proportionately far larger than the vast increase in the number of automobiles during any given period of time.

For your passenger car, for your commercial car—try United States Tires—and make comparisons.

For Passenger Cars:
'Royal Cord' 'Nobby' 'Chain' 'Usco' 'Plain'

For Commercial Cars:
Solid Truck Tire and 'Nobby' Cord Pneumatic Tire

United States Tires
Are Good Tires

Also Tires for Motorcycles, Bicycles and Aëroplanes

United States Tubes and Tire Accessories Have All the Sterling Worth and Wear that Make United States Tires Supreme.

26. Advertisement, "For Short Hauls—Passenger or Commercial—the Automobile" (*Saturday Evening Post*, Feb. 2, 1918).

As mentioned above, the naval blockade of Germany by the Allied powers spurred the production of aniline by the United States Rubber Company. The new aniline plant was built in 1916; during that year, increased wartime demand for other chemicals led to the construction of another sulfuric acid unit and a new, much larger nitric acid plant.

By the end of 1916, the business of the United States Rubber Export Company was reported to represent about 6.5% of the total business of United States Rubber, whose net sales that year were in excess of $126,750,000. World War I had been in progress for over sixteen months and had brought large demands from abroad for rubber footwear and other rubber products. Total sales for export exceeded $12 million in 1917, but, although the United States had declared war on April 6, 1917, the volume of war orders filled during the year by United States Rubber was only about 5% of its total net sales of $176 million. In 1918, "war business" reached $28,503,000.

In addition to conventional types of rubber products, such as tires and tubes, footwear, rainwear, waterproof blankets, druggist sundries, and insulated wire furnished to the armed forces during World War I, the Providence and Naugatuck plants were called upon to develop and produce a gas mask for protection from the poisonous gas attacks. One of the chemists assigned to that project in 1917-18 was John P. Coe, who later became vice-president and general manager of the Chemical and Synthetic Rubber Division.

After the signing of the Armistice on Nov. 11, 1918, sales designated as "war business" in 1919 fell to approximately $3,476,000.[54] Since exports other than war orders had been maintained at a high level throughout the war, the directors began taking steps toward greatly expanding the company's export business.

---

[1] Henry Hubbard, address to branch store footwear salesmen, Dec. 30, 1915, in Homer E. Sawyer, "Histories of the United States Rubber Company and some of the Subsidiary Companies," 1915, privately printed, p. 51.
[2] "Minutes of the First Annual Sales Service Convention, Footwear Division," 1920, privately printed. p. 4. (Sales of Mishawaka Woolen Mfg. Company were not included in the above figures.)
[3] E. H. White, letter to author, 1962.
[4] E. H. White, interview, 1962.
[5] T. J. Needham, interview, 1962.
[6] "Minutes of the First Annual Sales Service Convention, Footwear Division," 1920, privately printed, p. 66.
[7] R. W. Ashcroft, memorandum, United States Rubber Company archives, Oct. 29, 1934.
[8] T. J. Needham, interview, 1962.
[9] E. H. White, interview, 1962.
[10] V. F. Ludwig, office notices, Mishawaka archives, 1905 to 1915.
[11] Incorporated Feb. 1, 1911.
[12] Peter C. Anderson, letter to author, 1963.
[13] C. M. Carroll, letter to author, 1963.

[14] Ernest S. Bradford, "A Preliminary Report on the Golf Ball Market," 1917, unpublished, company archives.

[15] Advertisement, *Saturday Evening Post* (March 1, 1913).

[16] U.S. Dept. of Commerce, *Statistical Abstract of the United States, 1938* (Washington: U.S. Gov't Printing Office, 1939), p. 370.

[17] *New York Times* (Nov. 27, 1929), p. 2.

[18] Chris Sinsabaugh, *Who Me? Forty Years of Automobile History* (Detroit: Arnold-Powers, Inc., 1940), pp. 147-52.

[19] *Between US*, house organ of United States Rubber Company (August, 1922 and July, 1923). Also see *"U.S." Rubber News*, house organ of United States Rubber Company (July 1, 1924), p. 21.

[20] Leonard Smith, memorandum, 1962.

[21] Hugh Allen, *The House of Goodyear* (Cleveland, Ohio: The Corday and Gross Company, 1943), p. 33.

[22] Walton Hamilton and others, *Price and Price Policies* (New York: McGraw-Hill Book Co., 1938), p. 91.

[23] The above figures pertain to shipments of pneumatic casings. Commercial research department records, company archives. See Table 8.

[24] Advertisement in *Collier's* (July 6, 1918).

[25] E. G. Holt, "Some Fundamental Factors in the American Rubber Industry," *Survey of Current Business* (Washington: U.S. Gov't Printing Office, 1935), p. 18.

[26] Advertisement, *Saturday Evening Post* (Nov. 19, 1910).

[27] United States Rubber Company, "Some Historical Facts About the Tire Division," c. 1950, unpublished, company archives.

[28] Advertisement, *Literary Digest* (Dec. 29, 1917).

[29] Dewhurst and Associates, *America's Needs and Resources* (New York: Twentieth Century Fund, 1947), p. 756.

[30] P. W. Barker, *Rubber: History, Production, and Manufacture*, U.S. Dept. of Commerce (Washington: U.S. Gov't Printing Office, 1940), p. 4.

[31] "Histories of the United States Rubber Company," p. 20.

[32] Chester R. Randall, recollections, 1962.

[33] W. H. Norton, memorandum, 1962.

[34] C. M. Carroll, letter to author, Oct. 20, 1962.

[35] W. H. Norton, memorandum, 1962.

[36] Nancy Paine Norton, "Industrial Pioneer, the Goodyear Metallic Rubber Shoe Company," II, 1950, unpublished dissertation, Radcliffe College, p. 462. Also correspondence with W. H. Norton, 1964.

[37] C. R. Haynes, "Standardization and Development," talk in training course, 1920, company archives.

[38] E. Rung, memorandum, 1962, company archives.

[39] C. R. Haynes, "Standardization and Development," Footwear Division training course, c. 1919, company archives.

[40] Stanton Glover, memorandum, 1960.

[41] Charles Partridge, unpublished, Mishawaka archives.

[42] John M. Ball, *Reclaimed Rubber, the Story of an American Raw Material* (New York: Rubber Reclaimers Association, 1947), pp. 76, 112, 113.

[43] *Reclaimed Rubber*, pp. 69, 99.

[44] George H. Mayo, "The Responsibility of Leadership in the Footwear Industry," *Between US*, house organ of United States Rubber Company, New York, X (March, 1924), p. 7.

[45] Donald L. Zimmerman, letter to author, Oct. 25, 1962.

[46] Charles Partridge, unpublished, Mishawaka archives.

[47] Chester R. Randall, recollections, 1962.

[48] W. A. Gibbons, "The Rubber Industry, 1839-1939," *Industrial and Engineering Chemistry*, XXXI (October, 1939), p. 1199 ff.

[49] John E. Caskey, unpublished paper, 1940, company archives.

[50] C. E. Bradley, conversation with E. A. Saunders, c. 1924, Bradley's notebooks, Mishawaka archives.

[51] Van Tassel Sutphen, *Harper's Weekly*, XLIII (April 8, 1899), pp. 351-52.

[52] Leonard Smith, memorandum, 1962.

[53] U.S. Dept. of Commerce, *Industrial Reference Service, Part 10, "Rubber"* (Washington: U.S. Gov't Printing Office, June, 1941), p. 1.

[54] N. H. Fletcher, letter to author, July 3, 1962.

III
1919 to 1928

5

Erratic Commodity Prices

and Other Problems

SEGER ELECTED PRESIDENT

WHEN THE United States Rubber Company floated an issue of $60 million of 5% first and refunding mortgage bonds in 1917, the bonds were underwritten by a group of banks headed by Kuhn, Loeb and Co., on whose recommendation Charles B. Seger was then elected a director of the company.[1] Seger, who at one time was on the board of directors of more than forty companies, was already connected with the management of many important firms, including the United States Mortgage and Trust Company, Western Union Telegraph Company, International Acceptance Bank, and the Union Pacific.

Born in New Orleans in 1867 of an old New England family, Seger left school at the age of sixteen and went to work for a subsidiary of the Southern Pacific Company. Advancing from office boy through the auditing divisions of the railroad and its subsidiaries, he became, in 1904, auditor of the Pacific System of the Southern Pacific Company. In 1910, he was made general auditor of the Union Pacific and Southern Pacific systems. After the Union Pacific and the Southern Pacific were separated by court order in 1913, he became vice-president and comptroller of the Union Pacific Railroad Company. On March 19, 1918, Seger was elected a member and acting chairman of the executive committee of the Union Pacific, and on July 11, 1918 was elected president of the railroad, the by-laws of which were amended in August, 1918 to provide that the president should be a member ex officio and the chairman of the executive committee. Following his election on Dec. 5, 1918 as president of United States Rubber, Seger resigned the presidency of the railroad com-

145

pany and ceased to be chairman of its executive committee. However, he continued as a director and member of the executive committee of Union Pacific, and on Aug. 12, 1924 also accepted chairmanship of its finance committee.[2]

Upon his appointment as acting chairman of the executive committee of the Union Pacific, his record and the qualities that had been responsible for his rise from the ranks were discussed in *Railway Age*.[3] He was said to exemplify "keen, uncompromising, downright, clear thinking to an unusual degree," and to possess a "remarkable grasp of detail and memory for figures." He was also said to be intolerant of slipshod thinking and fearless in his opposition to theorists or to those whose views were contrary to his own. His subordinates in the United States Rubber Company said that Seger endeavored to give the promising, younger men in the organization opportunities for advancement and that he inspired loyalty and confidence by his own directness, simplicity, and patience.

Nevertheless, it seems evident today that, regardless of Seger's unquestioned qualifications, his lack of knowledge of and personal experience with the problems peculiar to the operations of a rubber company manufacturing diversified lines of products made it difficult for him to recognize and eliminate the main causes of the deterioration of United States Rubber's financial strength and its loss of competitive position. One chief source of weakness was the continued operation of a number of inefficient, high-cost plants resulting in excessive capacity, excessive capital investment, and burdensome overhead. Another source stemmed from overcentralized management.

Probably it is correct to say that Seger saw his primary responsibility to be the conservation of the interests of the bondholders of United States Rubber. In the discharge of this obligation, the circumstances he faced were radically different from those that had confronted Samuel P. Colt. As shall be seen, some of the most serious problems were beyond the control of Seger or any other man. Seger chose to try to meet some of those that were within his control by assuming added personal responsibility—with near disastrous results for United States Rubber.

Until the end of Colt's term of office, United States Rubber had enjoyed an era of almost continuous expansion, acquisition, and diversification, financed largely through repeated borrowings. Net sales had risen from $21,196,000 for the year ended March 31, 1902 to $215,398,000 in 1918. Increased sales and advancing prices had obscured the threat to future profits entailed by the excessive indebtedness. Furthermore, federal income taxes had taken a very small toll prior to 1917.

27. Charles B. Seger.

During the decade from 1919 to 1928 inclusive, when Seger headed the company, the economy was subjected to severe strains resulting from the aftermath of World War I. True, a period of recovery and industrial activity followed, but periods when prices of commodities and crude rubber in particular declined sharply necessitated large write-downs in inventories of materials and finished goods. In 1920 spot cotton sold at 41½¢ a pound in April and at 12⅝¢ in December. The price of rubber that year fell from a high of 56½¢ to 16¢. The difficult situation in which United States Rubber was placed by the constriction of the economy was reflected in the market quotation of the company's common stock, which fell from 143¾ early in 1920 to a low of 53 and closed the year at 60¾.[4] The 5% first and refunding mortgage bonds could be bought in December, 1920 at prices ranging from 70¼ to 78.

The company's net sales dropped to $164,707,000 in 1921, a decline of 35% from 1920. Other years were to follow with their own problems and crises. Keen competition, the consequence of excess production facilities created during the war, frequently forced selling prices of finished goods down to levels that permitted only meager profits, if not actual losses.

Consummate managerial skill, coupled with intimate knowledge of the operating principles that underlie efficient, low cost production would have been required under such conditions to direct successfully the affairs of a company that produced more rubber footwear than all of its competitors combined; was the largest manufacturer of rubber belting, conveyors, and hose; was the second largest manufacturer of tires and tubes; had a large export business; and operated the largest rubber plantations in the world. Unfortunately, that skill and intimate knowledge were not adequately possessed by Seger.

Because he lacked this knowledge and because the comptroller's reports did not include forecasts of future trends, Seger probably relied too much on the judgment and recommendations of senior executives carried over from Colt's administration. Apparently, he believed that these men—Homer E. Sawyer, for example—were well qualified to make the proper decisions, but his confidence in some of his subordinates was misplaced and he was misled by overly optimistic forecasts.

One of the younger executives in the company recalled that Seger had hired an engineer to check over all requests for capital expenditures that were referred for his approval. Seger was said to have told the engineer that every request he received was accompanied by a statement that the expenditure would be recovered out of savings within two years, but that he had not known of one case where this was true.[5]

Under Seger's administration, United States Rubber lost its position of leadership in total sales volume. In 1926, the company's total net sales of $215,528,000 were surpassed for the first time by Goodyear Tire and Rubber Company's sales of a little over $230 million. By the end of 1928, Goodyear's net sales were in excess of $250 million, while those of United States Rubber had declined to $198,089,000. Nor was Goodyear Tire and Rubber the only rubber company that had gained ground during the twenties at the expense of United States Rubber Company's position.

When the sudden fall in the price of rubber early in 1928 made it necessary to take a midyear write-down of $14,148,000 in inventories, the company was threatened for a time with cancellation of its lines of credit with some banks. Seger's approach to the problems that confronted the company during that period, resulting in the conclusion by Kuhn, Loeb and Co. and some important stockholders that he should be replaced as president of United States Rubber, is discussed in a subsequent section of this chapter.

Seger probably felt a sense of relief when he handed over the reins to

Francis B. Davis, Jr. on Jan. 15, 1929. During the previous nine years, the company had had inventory write-downs that totaled almost $79 million, was handicapped by inefficient and high cost operations in the sprawling aggregation of forty-one factories, and was burdened with annual interest charges that for his last four years as president were 3% or more of net sales and averaged in excess of $6 million.

Seger remained on the board of directors until April 16, 1929, when he chose of his own accord to resign, although it had been hoped he would continue as a director so that the rubber company could benefit from his knowledge and experience. He served as chairman of the finance committee of Union Pacific from Aug. 12, 1924 until Jan. 9, 1930, when he again became chairman of the executive committee of the railroad company, continuing in that capacity until Aug. 11, 1932. Seger remained a director of Union Pacific until his death in 1940.

ORGANIZATION AND PERSONNEL PROBLEMS

Personal Rivalries

It will be recalled that the Revere Rubber Company was acquired in 1909 in order to obtain the services of its president, Elisha S. Williams. After his death in October, 1920, the operating departments of United States Rubber were reorganized. Sawyer (first employed in 1885 by the Boston Rubber Shoe Company, a director of United States Rubber since December, 1906, and a vice-president since March, 1914) was placed in charge of the General Division. This division included footwear, mechanical rubber goods and sundries—virtually all the products of the company other than tires and chemicals. The vice-president in charge of tires and accessories was an efficiency expert, J. Newton Gunn, who was also president of United States Tire Company. All overseas activities—including the Export Company and the production, purchase, or trading in crude rubber—were under the supervision of H. Stuart Hotchkiss, who was made a vice-president in 1922. The development and patent departments were under the direction of Ernest Hopkinson, a vice-president who also had general supervision over the Naugatuck Chemical Company and the Rubber Regenerating Company.

In the General Division, reporting to Sawyer, were two second vice-presidents, Edward J. Coughlin, who was in charge of manufacturing, and George H. Mayo, who was in charge of sales.[6] In the Tire Division, reporting to Gunn, were Charles J. Butler, a second vice-president in charge of manufacturing who had been president of Morgan and

Wright, and George S. Shugart, a second vice-president in charge of sales.

Sawyer undoubtedly considered himself the logical and proper successor to Colt; it is probable that Gunn held the same opinion regarding his own qualifications. Had he not been appointed assistant to the president when he joined United States Rubber in 1915? Were not tires and tubes rapidly becoming the most important products of the company? Consequently, when Colt gave up the presidency in 1918 to become chairman of the board, the election by the directors of Seger, the newcomer, as president must have been disappointing to both Sawyer and Gunn. Some of their associates felt that the task faced by Seger in directing the company under the difficult conditions of the 1920's would have been less frustrating had he been given more cooperation by his chief lieutenants. Another serious situation with which Seger had to contend was the lack of sufficient coordination between the activities of the departments of the business under the direction of Sawyer, Gunn, and Hopkinson, and the absence of friendly cooperation between them in furthering the over-all interests of United States Rubber.

Neither Sawyer nor Gunn allowed any interference with the management of the divisions that they headed. Gunn and Seger disagreed regarding the operation of United States Tire, and there was said to be even more conflict between Gunn and Sawyer.

Seger Assumes Direction of Tire Company

Gunn was well-known among the automobile people in Detroit, and perhaps sometimes did not show the deference expected from a subordinate when Seger visited Detroit. Relations between the two men became strained and reached a breaking point in 1923. Gunn left the company, and it was announced that Seger would take over his responsibilities. Organization charts issued during the next several years left blank the space for the name of the manager of the tire division (see organization chart in Appendix E). Assisting Seger in 1924 in directing the operations of the tire division was a divisional tire conference committee, composed of Charles J. Butler, who had been assigned charge of the Manufacturers Sales Department (in other words, responsibility for sales of original equipment tires and tubes); George S. Shugart, in charge of all other tire sales; and Sheldon P. Thacher. (Thacher had been a technical assistant to Gunn, and after the latter's resignation was appointed a second vice-president in charge of manufacturing.) H. Gordon Smith, shown on organization charts of the period as assistant to the president, served as secretary. Seger frequently attended meetings of the committee, whose name was changed early in 1928 to the Tire Division's operating committee with Smith as chairman.

Each member of the group reported directly to Seger; since Thacher, Butler, and Shugart each had full responsibility for their own departments, the committee served chiefly as a coordinating body within the Tire Division, much like the "product-partnerships" that were established after World War II to achieve closer coordination between manufacturing and sales departments. All decisions were subject to Seger's approval, and Seger reserved the right to make the final decision if the members of the committee could not agree. Usually, however, a working agreement was reached.

Management of United States Rubber thus tended to be concentrated in Seger and Sawyer. This arrangement was particularly regrettable since Seger was not only endeavoring to act as chairman of the board and president of United States Rubber, but also as active operating head of the Tire Division, and, after Aug. 12, 1924, as chairman of the finance committee of the Union Pacific Railroad Company. Such concentration of responsibility for management of a highly diversified, multimillion dollar business was an organizational error for which United States Rubber suffered.

Other Organizational Changes

On Feb. 1, 1924, Seger announced the appointment of Herbert E. Smith as general manager of the United States Rubber Export Company, Ltd., and general manager of the export department of United States Rubber Company. In this capacity, Smith reported to Sawyer and was responsible for all international operations (exclusive of those in Canada, of the plantations, and of the General Rubber Company). At the same time, F. H. Hauser and George Bergeron were appointed assistant general managers of the export department. The announcement of these appointments also stated that in the future the export organization would operate as a part of the general sales organization, and that there would be much closer coordination between the two groups.[7]

The value of the overseas inventories was being questioned, and Smith initially knew little about the over-all financial phases of the Export Company's operations. However, he set about getting the facts by asking probing questions. His survey led to write-downs in 1924 and 1925 totaling approximately $3,500,000 in the value of overseas inventories and to a reorganization of the Export Company. Among the divisional sales managers who served under Smith in 1924 and for several years afterwards were:

John B. Tower, export sales manager for tires

Edwin L. Hopkinson, in charge of footwear export sales (brother of Ernest Hopkinson)

Ralph Highlands, in charge of sales of mechanical goods and general products by the Export Company

John D. Clarke, in charge of sales in the area designated as C.A., W.I., & P. (Central America, West Indies, and Peru).

On May 1, 1925, Smith was made general sales manager of the General Division reporting to Sawyer; Charles E. Guest succeeded Smith as general manager of the Export Company.

From Oct. 1, 1920 to Aug. 1, 1921, T. J. Needham was manager of branch store sales, including all sales through the branch stores of tires and mechanical goods as well as footwear. On Aug. 1, 1921, he was appointed manager of branches, including all tire, footwear, and mechanical branches except the Pacific Coast Division. But in March, 1927, it was decided that tires and mechanical goods should have their own managers of sales made through any of the 140 domestic branches and sales agencies that might stock their products. The following appointments were made shortly thereafter:

T. J. Needham, general manager, footwear sales

A. B. Fennell, general manager, U. S. tire sales

W. Gussenhoven, general manager, mechanical goods sales

George E. Goodwin, manager, clothing sales

C. A. Blake, manager, sundries sales.

With the exception of Fennell, who reported to Shugart, second vice-president in charge of tire sales, each of the foregoing reported to Smith, who had been appointed second vice-president in charge of sales for the General Division on Dec. 3, 1925. Sales of all commodities through branch stores on the West Coast were handled by the branch stores in the Pacific Coast Division, of which J. Brendan Brady was general manager. Shortly after the above appointments were made, Sawyer told Needham, while on a train from Boston to New York, that he was to "run the footwear business," and Needham gradually became recognized as the actual general manager of footwear, even before this was officially shown on organization charts. H. E. Smith was made vice-president of the United States Rubber Export Company, Ltd., in 1927, and two years later became president of that company. In April, 1927, Sawyer was named executive vice-president of the company, thereby further concentrating the responsibility for management.

On Aug. 17, 1928, Seger appointed L. D. Tompkins "special representative of the president," and he was so shown on the organization charts of the period, reporting directly to the president (see Appendix E). The organization notice that was issued stated the appointment was made with the understanding that "whatever matters he takes up have been duly assigned to him, and that he is authorized to act for the president."[8] This statement gave Tompkins authority to make certain decisions and commitments in connection with the participation of United States Rubber Company as a member of the Rubber Institute, Inc. It also enabled Seger to utilize the younger man's abilities in certain situations where some United States Rubber executives, who were Tompkins' seniors both in age and in service, had evidenced some reluctance to carry out Seger's wishes.

On Dec. 13, 1928, Seger appointed Tompkins (whose previous experience had been entirely with the General Rubber Company and the plantations) to head the Tire Division with responsibility for all its activities. This appointment of a man who had had no direct contact with the operations of the Tire Division and who frankly disclaimed any knowledge of tire manufacturing or tire sales is indicative of Seger's difficult position, who felt stymied in his efforts to have the Tire Division operated successfully as a profitable and growing division of United States Rubber.

Nevertheless, other factors could be considered as favoring Seger's decision. Tompkins had gained considerable knowledge of the rubber tire industry during the time when he served as a manager of the First and Second Crude Rubber Agencies. He had become acquainted with key executives in both the tire and the automobile companies, and had acquired considerable information regarding certain phases of the tire industry's operations; all now proved valuable in his new position. It seems reasonable also to assume that Seger and others may have been favorably impressed with Tompkins' handling of various problems that confronted the Crude Rubber Agencies during their existence and with his ability to enlist the cooperation and support of the other members of those agencies. Some of the changes in the Tire Division's organization made by Tompkins, as well as the increased sales of tires accomplished under the active direction of F. B. Davis and Tompkins, are discussed in Chapter VIII.

Pacific Coast Division

An exception to the highly centralized organization that existed in United States Rubber for many years prior to 1929 was the Pacific Coast Division, in which Brady continued to exercise broad authority over sales and distribution. He operated through four product managers, appointed by him, who had charge of tires, footwear, clothing, mechanical goods, and sundries.

E. H. White, commodity manager for footwear in the Pacific Coast Division from July, 1925 through December, 1930, said he was the only person in the footwear department on the West Coast who went East to get information about anything connected with footwear. White made four trips a year, and would bring back samples of new and old lines, and information regarding prices and terms. He then held sales meetings with the footwear people at each branch in the division. White was also responsible for control of inventory of footwear at each branch; in addition, the local branch manager was required to have all salary increases for footwear employees of the branch, both outside salesmen and inside personnel, approved by White.

The other commodity managers in the Pacific Coast Division operated in much the same manner. White told the author that the results obtained in the Pacific Coast Division prior to 1929 demonstrated conclusively that capable managers, given complete charge and full authority within their zones or divisions, may produce results better than those obtained under any other form of organization that the company has used.

Coordination Lacking

Today it is difficult to trace the exact shifts in the channels of authority for either production or sales of the United States Rubber Company throughout the years of the Seger administration. In some areas there seems to have been overlapping responsibility, with resultant conflicts and confusion. More serious seems to have been an almost total lack of adequate communication and coordination, not only between divisions of the company, but between manufacturing and sales within each division. The unfortunate absence of coordination between the operating divisions and the development department also contributed to many of the problems faced by the company. In view of the concentration of authority in the persons of Seger and Sawyer, there is no rational explanation for the existence of this situation during the 1920's.

Formation of Industrial Relations Department

Efforts of Rubber Workers to Organize

Prior to the 1930's, relatively few wage earners in the rubber industry belonged to labor unions. Early records show that some unions of **rubber** workers in New Jersey, affiliated with the Knights of Labor, attempted to form a trade union district in 1887. In 1901, the seven existing unions of rubber workers included five made up exclusively of rubber shoe workers, according to a statement made by the Boot and Shoe Workers Union at the 1901 convention of the American Federation of Labor at Scranton, Pa.[9] However, the majority of the workers was not organized, probably because the AFL, organized along craft lines, was not well suited for enrollment of large numbers of workers in such industries as steel, petroleum, and rubber. Moreover, the largest employer in the industry, United States Rubber, had pioneered in adopting plans for stock purchases, pensions, and group insurance, which were designed to help foster satisfactory relations between the company and its employees. Compared with present fringe benefits, these provisions were meager indeed, but at the time they were looked upon as liberal. In any case, they were steps in the right direction. Moreover, R. B. Price is said to have been influential in the establishment at "1790" of a safety department to work toward reduction of the working hazards faced by employees.

"Labor Specialist" Hired

A period of labor unrest ensued after the Armistice on Nov. 11, 1918. The factories in the United States Rubber System were not immune, and Seger welcomed the opportunity in 1919 to employ a man who had demonstrated his ability to bring about improved relations between employer and employees.

Cyrus ("Cy") S. Ching had gone to work in 1901 as a motorman for the Boston Elevated Railway Company. At about that time the transit company began using a new type of individually motorized car, and Ching learned that the company was looking for a man to take charge of equipment. He set about becoming thoroughly familiar with all details of the electric motors and controls, and in 1903 was made superintendent of equipment in service. Not satisfied with his prospects for further advancement, Ching enrolled as a law student in the night classes offered by Northeastern University, Boston, continuing to work 12-hour night shifts (5:30 p.m. to 5:30 a.m.) for the transit company in alternating two-week periods, and paying out of his own pocket for a substitute while he was attending classes. Graduating in 1912 with the degree of LL.B., Ching passed the examination for admission to the Massachusetts bar.

In 1912, Boston Elevated employees were on strike. Ching, through a series of incidents, was instrumental in getting the management to talk with the strikers regarding their grievances and to negotiate a satisfactory agreement under which the men returned to work. He was appointed assistant to the president, and negotiated three separate contracts with the union during the remaining time he was with the Boston Elevated.

It was impossible, however, to obtain authorization from the Public Service Commission for the higher fares needed to cover the rising costs. By 1918, the transit company was headed for receivership, and trustees for the Boston Elevated Company were appointed by the state. Ching remained with the company for a while but soon began looking about for another industry which would offer better opportunity for exercise of his particular talents and ability. He decided on the rubber industry, went to New York, had an interview with Seger, and on April 1, 1919, entered the employ of United States Rubber in the field of labor relations, working out of the executive department in the general office.[10] In October, 1920, he was made supervisor of industrial relations, reporting to the president.

Unsatisfactory Labor Conditions and Relations

Ching felt that there was great room for improvement in the labor relations of most companies. One of the most serious weaknesses was an almost complete lack of communication between management and the worker at the bench. Another weakness was the failure to grasp the importance of proper training and education of foremen, while at the same time relying to a large extent upon them to hire and train the workmen under their supervision. Given virtually free rein in such matters, many foremen practiced favoritism and nepotism, giving cause for grievance and discontent. Prior to the 1920's, Myron H. Clark, general factory manager of the Footwear Division, had set up employment offices in each plant to handle all hiring of factory workers. Considered a radical departure from established practice, it soon demonstrated its merit, and one of Ching's early assignments was to sell the idea to other plants in the United States Rubber System. In trying to carry out this plan, he encountered a major obstacle in the retention of separate corporations, with individual boards of directors and largely autonomous plant operations. It was necessary for him to do a selling job with each one. Consequently, labor management policies practiced by the various plants varied considerably, and not infrequently a considerable time lag developed between approval of a labor policy by top management and its adoption by the several plants.

Shortly after Ching joined United States Rubber, he was asked by Seger to go to Montreal where a strike had occurred at the plant of the Canadian Consolidated Rubber Company. After acquainting himself with the

28. W. A. Eden.

wage rates in the Montreal plant and with the prevailing rates for labor in that area, Ching worked out a proposal with W. A. Eden, then the president of Canadian Consolidated; if the employees returned to work, they could select a committee of their fellow workers to discuss their grievances with the local management. This idea was acceptable to the striking employees, and paved the way for later adjustments in wage scales. Within several months a strike occurred at the Naugatuck, Conn., footwear plants. Ching made a similar proposal to the factory managers, who were reluctant at first to concur in the plan but who came to see the logic of Ching's thinking about the value of better communications between management and the workers. For the second time, his advocacy of frank discussions between management and representatives of the workers led to termination of a work stoppage.

The AFL made relatively little attempt to recruit rubber workers during the 1920's. The only strike of any major consequence in the plants of the United States Rubber System during the decade occurred at the National India Rubber Company, Bristol, R.I., in May, 1920. On May 7, about 4,500 workers struck for higher pay. Apparently responsible leadership for the strike was lacking, and it dragged on for several weeks; tension grew, tempers flared, and toward the end of May three of the strikers were wounded by guards during a riot. The governor of Rhode Island ordered National Guard troops to Bristol and order was restored. On June 3, the plant was reopened and the strike was over.

Ching's Basic Philosophy

Ching collaborated in preparation of a paper entitled "The Human Factor in Industry," which was used in the 1919-20 training course at the Naugatuck plant of the Footwear Division, and which reflects his philosophy of industrial relations. It stressed the importance of fostering the worker's self-respect, of developing his ability to maintain a certain standard of living, and of recognizing his desire to be treated fairly and on a basis of equality. It stated that the wage level should permit a young man "within an average time and with a normal degree of effort" to support a wife and family. The employee's working hours should permit him to have a reasonable amount of time with his family. The tendency of some foremen and of some employers to play upon the employee's natural instinct of fear was deplored; the value and importance of loyalty were stressed.[11]

Efforts to Reduce Labor Turnover

The next section of the training course emphasized the importance of good working conditions and proper indoctrination and training as factors in reducing labor turnover.[12] The need to reduce labor turnover was apparent. Turnover in the Footwear Division during 1919 had ranged from a little less than 50% for the Bristol plant of the National India Rubber Company, with an average force of 4,483 employed during the year, to a high of approximately 215% for the Lawrence Felt Plant, Lawrence, Mass., where the force had averaged 117 employees in 1919. (Probably the fact that the Lawrence plant's production was limited to items largely dependent on severe winter weather for volume sales was responsible for intermittent production, layoffs, and high turnover of the labor force.) Approximate rates for the other important plants in the footwear division were:

	No. Employed	Approximate Percentage of Turnover
Goodyear's India Rubber Glove Manufacturing Company, Naugatuck, Conn.	1,992	60
Alice Mill, Woonsocket Rubber Co., Woonsocket, R.I.	1,599	65
Goodyear Metallic Rubber Shoe Co., Naugatuck	1,568	70
L. Candee and Company, New Haven, Conn.	1,599	90
American Rubber Company, Cambridge, Mass.	1,681	100+
Boston Rubber Shoe Company, Plant No. 1, Malden, Mass.	1,800	115
Lycoming Rubber Company, Williamsport, Pa.	1,594	125—

By comparison the Department of Labor reported that "separations" in the rubber footwear industry in 1939—the last year before labor was significantly affected by the increased industrial activity resulting from World War II—were 38% of the labor force, while "accessions" were 35%.[13]

According to the report, of 17,000 employees who had left the employ of plants in the United States Rubber System during 1919, 1,838 left during the first week of employment; 5,038 during the first month; 8,355 during the first three months; 11,471 during the first six months; and 14,638 left before they had been employed one year. Wages were mentioned by only 740 as a reason for leaving; 3,457 gave "new job" as the reason; 1,563 said they were "leaving the city"; 2,017 left for "unknown" reasons; 1,688 mentioned "ill health"; 1,270 had been laid off; about 1,300 were discharged; and between 500 and 600 left for miscellaneous reasons.

Factory Councils Formed

Ching was convinced that, in addition to unsatisfactory working conditions and poor indoctrination, one of the chief causes of employees' dissatisfaction and the resulting high labor turnover was a lack of adequate communication between labor and management. He was a firm advocate of education of employees in "sound economic and industrial principles." He believed that "one of the greatest obstacles in the way of progress along sound industrial lines is the lack of understanding on the part of the workers." Realizing that the foremen had the most intimate contacts with the rank and file of wage earners, he started in 1919 to encourage classes for foremen and other supervisory personnel of United States Rubber Company so that they might be better prepared to implement proper management principles.

As previously indicated, more enlightened labor management policies had been introduced by Clark in the Footwear Division shortly before World War I. Consequently, Ching found that the men in that division seemed to have a better appreciation of the importance of good relations between the foremen and the workers whom they directed. He said there was also a better attitude in the Footwear Division toward the steps that Ching wished to inaugurate to improve labor-management relations.

One of these steps was the establishment of factory councils, consisting of elected representatives of the employees who dealt with management. He considered the factory council "a means of making the fullest possible use of the ideas and energies of the workers in the conduct of industry," and a method for "providing a systematic and ever-present channel through which workers can express themselves with reference to their work, their relations with management, and all other factors which concern their well-being and the welfare of the company as a whole."

In a paper outlining the functions and purposes of factory councils, Ching emphasized the necessity of cooperation among the four major economic groups—the farmer, the wage earner, the employer, and the professional man, adding that more cooperation between employer and employee would, in turn, benefit all these groups of society. He also stressed the protection of both private property and human rights as essential to the well-being of society.

The factory councils organized at some of the company's plants during the 1920's afforded workers the opportunity to present their views regarding workloads, safety hazards, and other working conditions. Ching had great faith in the successful functioning of the councils, provided that foremen did not try to influence the election of workers' representatives, that all members were honest and sincere in expressing their views, and that the decisions were fair and based on sound judgment. Generally the factory councils served a useful purpose by acquainting the factory management with the viewpoints of workers, and they may be accorded much of the credit for the relatively small number of work stoppages in the company's plants during the 1920's. Formation of factory councils did not cease with the end of the decade; for example, the one at the G & J tire plant in Indianapolis was not formed until 1933.[14]

Unhappy Ending of Stock Purchase Plan

Back in 1919, when the common stock of the company was doubled by an issue of $36 million, holders of common stock were offered the right to subscribe for it at par ($100) pro rata. To encourage employees to subscribe under the Value Sharing Plan for the amount to which they were entitled, the company agreed to accept their five-year notes in payment. Over 4,500 employees took advantage of this plan, and the balance sheet of Dec. 31, 1919 showed $8,576,000 notes receivable given by employees for the purchase of capital stock and secured by this stock. As previously mentioned, from a high of 143¾ early in 1920, the common dropped to a low of 53 before the end of the year and did not regain its par value.

Before the notes came due Oct. 1, 1924, they were extended to 1926 and then to 1928. In December, 1928, the board of directors decided it would be detrimental to morale and the interests of the company to compel payment. The 32,776 shares of common still held as security for payment of the notes were sold to the Meyer Rubber Company, and the signers were released from their obligation. In April, 1929, the newly created executive committee authorized reimbursement to active and former employees of the amounts paid by them on the notes they had given for purchase of the stock. This action brought the matter to an end.

Group Insurance Plan Adopted

By the mid-twenties, some of the larger corporations were offering group life insurance to their employees. The benefits of such relatively low cost protection without physical examination were not fully recognized by many employees, and their reactions were mixed; some approved, some did not, and many were indifferent. On May 1, 1926, United States Rubber offered each of its 10,164 full-time salaried employees under age 60 a plan for life and permanent disability insurance. (Two years later it announced that wage employees would be eligible to participate.) The amount of insurance to which each employee was eligible under the plan ranged from $500 for those with an annual salary or wage of $1,000 or less to a maximum of $10,000 for those whose salaries were $7,500 or over. Employees 60-64 years of age were eligible for $1,000 insurance and those 65 or older for $500.

Premiums of 15¢ a week for each $1,000 of insurance were paid by participating employees, but the expense of administering the plan was paid by the company.[15] The increasing importance and wide acceptance of the insurance plan led to reference to it in the annual report for 1937, and made it a proper subject for comment in each successive report.

FINANCIAL OPERATIONS

Between Jan. 1, 1919 and Dec. 31, 1920, United States Rubber raised $99,400,000 in new money as follows:

Bank loans and accounts payable increased	$42,100,000
Funded debt increased	18,400,000
Preferred stock increased	2,900,000
Common stock sold	36,000,000
	$99,400,000

These funds were used in part for:

Addition to plant	$42,300,000
Increased inventories	52,800,000
Additions to cash	2,200,000
	$97,300,000

On Sept. 9, 1919, the stockholders voted to increase the authorized first preferred from $70 million to $100 million and the authorized common stock from $40 million to $200 million.[16] At the same time, the balance of second preferred still unconverted to first preferred was retired. Common stock valued at $36 million was then offered to holders of common at par, pro rata on a 100% basis. This stock was oversubscribed; a considerable amount of the proceeds was used to liquidate current indebtedness, and the remainder was used mostly for expansion of the productive capacities of the tire plants and for extension of the rubber plantations.

Expenditures upon plants and properties in 1920, including enlargement of tire plants at Detroit, Hartford, Providence, and Indianapolis, were $28,616,000. These funds were raised by issuance of $20 million in ten-year 7½% gold notes secured by $25 million of the company's 6% first and refunding mortgage bonds, series B. However, neither United States Rubber nor most of the other rubber companies had foreseen the collapse of the commodity markets that occurred in 1920.

The yearly averages of wholesale cash or spot prices for crude rubber No. 1, ribbed smoked sheet, are shown in Figure 29. The annual high and low prices also shown indicate that these yearly averages do not adequately portray the extent of the virtually unsolvable problems created for rubber manufacturers during the 1920's by the great fluctuations that occurred from month to month, often from day to day, in the prices of the commodities most essential to the operation of the rubber factory.

As shown in Table 2, the 1920 average wholesale cash price of brown 4/4 sheeting, a typical fabric, was 21.8¢ a square yard, down only by one-tenth of a cent from the average price for 1919. Yet as of Dec. 31, 1920, United States Rubber was forced to write down its year-end inventory of cotton fabrics by $6,425,000, to bring the valuation in line, supposedly, with the current nominal market price. This amount, charged against reserves previously set up in anticipation of such declines, proved to be inadequate, for the average price of the same sheeting in 1921 was only 11.4¢ a yard.

Crude rubber (No. 1, latex crepe, landed in New York) was quoted at the beginning of 1920 at 55¢ a pound; by the end of the year it was selling below 20¢. As of Dec. 31, 1920, the company carried over (either on hand or due to arrive) enough crude rubber to fill requirements for about seven months. The average cost of this carry-over was 26.79¢ a pound. In the chairman's annual report for 1920 he said this figure was below the average cost of production and added, "With the revival of business, the price of crude rubber is certain to advance." Nevertheless, in keeping

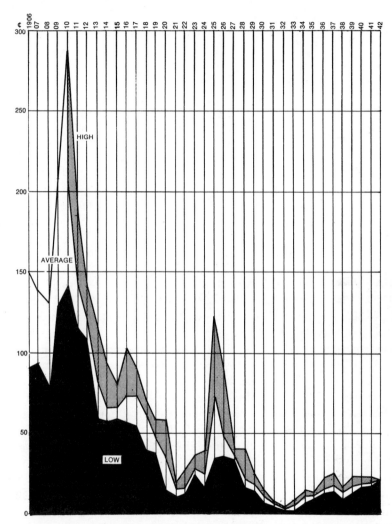

29. Annual high, low, and average wholesale spot prices, crude rubber No. 1, ribbed smoked sheet, 1906-42 (cents per pound, landed New York; see Table A-4).

with proper accounting practice, the carry-over of raw materials was valued at the current market price.

The total write-down on rubber, cotton fabrics, and other materials in inventory on Dec. 31, 1920 was $11,151,444. In addition, $6 million was appropriated out of 1920 income and set up as a reserve to provide for any contingencies that might arise in connection with inventory valuations or settlement of contracts.

TABLE 2.   Average annual prices of cotton middling and brown Pepperell sheeting, 1919-29.

	Cotton Middling. New Orleans (per pound)	Brown Pepperell 4/4 Sheeting (per yard)
1919	$0.319	$0.219
1920	.330	.218
1921	.141	.114
1922	.204	.125
1923	.287	.152
1924	.279	.155
1925	.230	.139
1926	.168	.123
1927	.172	.121
1928	.194	.122
1929	.186	.117

SOURCE: *Statistical Abstract of the United States* (Washington: U.S. Gov't Printing Office, 1925 and 1931).

The balance sheet as of Dec. 31, 1920 showed total debt to be $154,-400,300, with current liabilities of $67,373,500 and funded debt of $87,026,800. Current assets were $187,128,200, and net worth was shown to be $200,312,000.

The annual report for 1921 stated that the amounts written off as of Dec. 31, 1920 proved to be ample for all commodities except cotton fabrics. The report explained that "there was no real market for cotton fabrics" at the end of 1920, and also stated that "throughout the year 1921 the market for cotton fabrics was demoralized." Not only was the reserve of $6 million used, but it was necessary in 1921 to appropriate $6,594,031 from surplus for further depreciation of cotton fabrics on hand or committed for as of Dec. 31, 1920.

No provision had been made in any of the foregoing adjustments for depreciation in value of finished goods in inventory on Dec. 31, 1920. Selling prices in effect at that time yielded a satisfactory net profit, and it had been believed those prices would be maintained long enough to liquidate the inventory. Apparently, United States Rubber Company was not alone in this belief. However, 1921 operations had to absorb approximately $10 million of excess cost of finished goods carried over from 1920 and sold in 1921, as compared with average cost of producing similar goods in 1921. Prices of tires fell in 1921, and prices of most other rubber products also declined (Figures 30 and 31), forcing write-downs in 1921 of $6,113,629 in the value of finished goods in inventory as of Dec. 31, 1920. Of this amount $2,023,000 was charged against

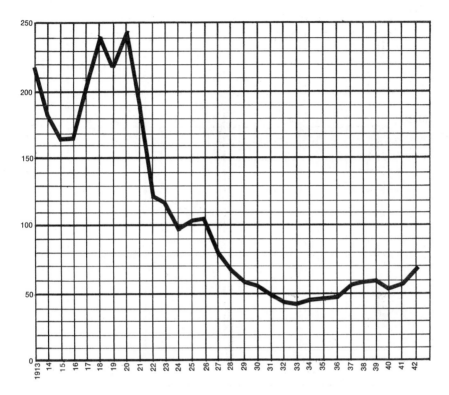

30. Wholesale prices, tires and tubes, 1913-42 (1957-59=100; see table A-10).

reserves previously created, and $4,091,000 was appropriated from sur-
plus. Thus, in one form or another, the charges absorbed in 1921 on
inventories of materials and finished goods as of Dec. 31, 1920, plus
commitments for materials as of that date, totaled approximately $29.7
million.

Contrary to the expectation implied in the annual report for 1920
that the price of crude rubber was certain to advance to over 26.79¢ a
pound (the company's average cost of rubber on hand and due to arrive
as of Dec. 31, 1920), the 1921 annual average price of No. 1, ribbed
smoked sheet, landed New York, was only 16.5¢. For 1922, it was
17.5¢.[17] The base prices at the plantations were said to be well below
the cost of production, especially on the larger plantations.

In 1921, total inventories were brought into better balance with requirements and were reduced by $46,561,000 or by 37.7%. Forward
commitments for raw materials and supplies, which had amounted to

31. National income, industry sales of rubber footwear, and rubber prices, 1920-40.

31a. Industry sales (1921=100) and prices, No. 1 smoked sheet (1920=100).

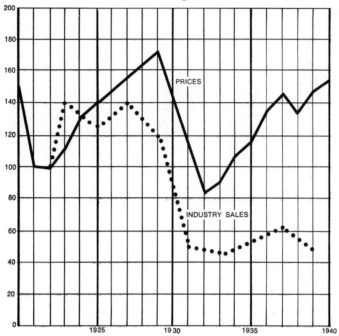

31b. National income and industry sales (1921=100).

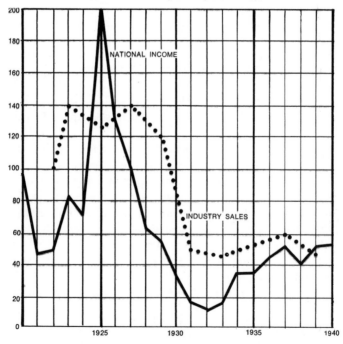

$24 million on Dec. 31, 1920, also were brought down to $7,200,000 by the end of the year.

By Dec. 31, 1921 current liabilities had been reduced to $48,551,000, and Seger reported that "financial obligations, including forward commitments, were reduced $40,681,798" during 1921. Working capital, however, had shrunk from $119,755,000 to $85,104,000.

In August, 1922, United States Rubber sold to Kuhn, Loeb and Co. an issue of $7 million of 5% first and refunding mortgage gold bonds due 1947. In the annual report for 1922, Seger stated, "The Company had an opportunity to sell the 5% Bonds at a favorable price." While it was true that the market price had risen substantially from the low of 70¼ in December, 1920, the "favorable price" in August, 1922 was low enough to enable the banking firm to offer the bonds at 90½ and accrued interest. The proceeds were used to retire, on Dec. 1, 1922, $6 million of 7% secured gold notes, due Dec. 1, 1923, releasing $9 million of the 5% first and refunding mortgage gold bonds that the company had had to deposit as security, and substituting long-term bonds for short-term notes. Through the operation of sinking funds, $970,000 of funded indebtedness had been retired during the year, and the net increase in outstanding funded indebtedness was only $30,000. Moreover, annual interest charges had been reduced by $123,000 by these transactions. No further writedowns on inventories were found necessary by United States Rubber in 1922 or 1923, but in 1924 the liquidation value of the more than $8 million in inventories in its foreign branches was questioned, and, as previously mentioned, H. E. Smith started a detailed study to determine their actual value. In 1924, a write-down of $1,500,000 in the value of those inventories was charged against surplus as definitely allocable to former periods, and in 1925 on the completion of the survey an additional charge of $2,007,242 was made against surplus.

In May, 1924, it was rumored that because of conditions in the rubber industry, particularly with respect to tires, United States Rubber might take steps to adjust (downward) the dividends on its 8% first preferred. This rumor was denied by officials of the company, but on May 28, 1924 the price of its first preferred fell to 66½ on the New York Stock Exchange. A year before, it had stood at $105 a share.

Nevertheless, Seger felt the financial position of United States Rubber had improved enough by Aug. 12, 1924 that he could accept his election as chairman of the finance committee of the Union Pacific Railroad Company. When an interviewer asked him how these additional duties would affect the discharge of his responsibilities with the rubber company, Seger

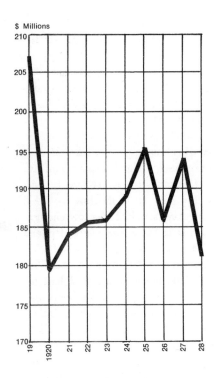

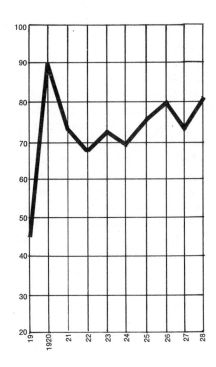

32. Financial trends, 1919-28 (see Tables A-12 and A-13).

(above left)
32a. Net worth.

(above right)
32b. Ratio of debt to net worth.

(below)
32c. Common shares outstanding.

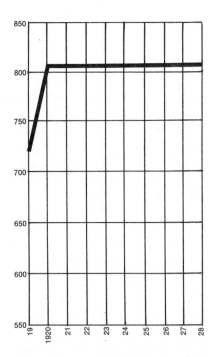

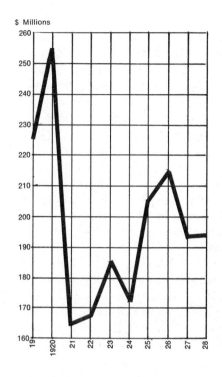

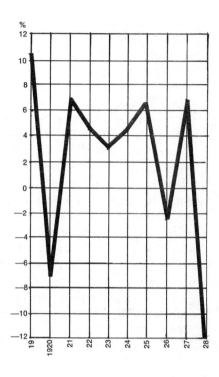

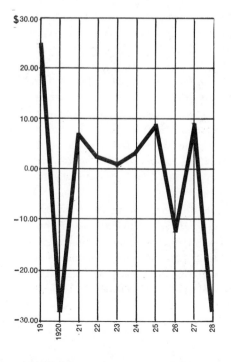

(above left)
32d. Net sales.

(above right)
32e. Net income as percentage of sales

(below)
32f. Earnings per common share outstanding at end of fiscal year.

said it would have "absolutely no effect upon my relations with or active management of the United States Rubber Company. The organization and affairs of the United States Rubber Company have reached a point where I find it possible to take a more active part in the affairs of the Union Pacific."[18] Tending to support his view in some measure was the reduction of notes and loans payable to $31,490,000 as of Dec. 31, 1924, down by almost $30 million since Nov. 20, 1920.

To convert most of the remaining current liabilities to long-term obligations, an issue of $30 million of 6½% serial gold notes, maturing in fifteen annual installments of $2 million each, was sold March 1, 1925. Under the terms of the indenture covering this issue, the net value of the current assets of United States Rubber and its subsidiaries was required at all times to be equal to at least twice the outstanding principal amount of all indebtedness of the company and of its subsidiaries, including the issue of 6½% serial notes but excluding the 1917 issue of 5% first and refunding mortgage bonds, the 1920 issue of 7½% secured gold notes, and the 6% gold bonds of Canadian Consolidated Rubber Company. The indenture further required that the inventories be figured at cost or market price as of the day of computation, whichever was lower. These provisions would become of paramount importance in the first part of 1928.

Another sharp decline in the price of crude rubber began in December, 1925. It was deemed advisable to appropriate out of surplus 1925 earnings $3 million to be applied against cost of rubber to be received in 1926. The entire reserve was used in 1926 for that purpose. The continued drop in the price of rubber brought decreases in prices of finished goods, particularly tires. Inventories of finished goods as of Dec. 31, 1926 were taken at *cost of production*, which was less than current selling prices, according to the annual report. Inventories of rubber and other raw materials were taken at *cost* rather than market. The annual report to the stockholders explained that the violent fluctuations in the price of crude rubber during 1926 was the cause for this action, and added that "current market quotations as of any date are not indicative of the real value of crude rubber inventories."

By not using the current market values for inventories, the company's balance sheet showed that, on net sales of $215,528,000, net income from operations was $17,929,000 *before* interest on funded indebtedness or estimated depreciation of the plants—but after all other charges. *After* interest charges of $6,456,000 and depreciation amounting to $3,711,000, net income from operations was reduced to $7,762,000. A dividend of

$6 million from the United States Rubber Plantations, Inc. enabled the parent company to report net surplus earnings of $8,535,000, after declaring dividends of $5,226,000 on the preferred stock and the minority stock holdings in Dominion Rubber Company, Ltd. However, it was "deemed advisable to set aside this entire amount ($8,535,000) as a reserve against inventories." This action and other prior charges against surplus resulted in a net reduction of $263,000 in surplus. With the help of dividends from the plantations ($6 million in 1926 and $4 million in 1927) and a transfer in 1927 of $8 million from the surplus of the United States Rubber Plantations, Inc., short-term bank loans were found sufficient to finance the parent company's operations until December, 1928.

In 1927, net sales were down to $193,443,000, reflecting an average reduction of 13½% in selling prices. Net income from operations was reported as $12,523,000 "before interest ($6,291,000) on funded indebtedness and estimated depreciation of plants ($3,981,000)." When it was obvious that the market prices of crude rubber would not soon recover to the levels at which purchases had been made in 1926, the entire reserve of $8,535,000—together with an additional amount of $8,911,000 from surplus—was used to bring the value of crude rubber and of the rubber content in finished goods and goods in process to the cost of replacement at market prices current as of Jan. 1, 1927. Using funds received from the plantations, dividends of $5,226,000 were again declared in 1927 on the preferred and on the minority stockholdings in Dominion Rubber. The end result was to reduce stated surplus of the parent company by $652,000 in 1927.

The drop in the New York price of rubber to 20¢ in April, 1928 compelled a midyear write-down of $14,148,000 in the value of United States Rubber's inventories as of June 30, 1928. In the judgment of F. B. Davis, Jr., the lack of the sales-production-coordination system during Seger's administration, which was introduced after Davis became president in 1929, was largely responsible for the excessive inventories of finished goods and crude rubber, necessitating the several large writedowns taken by the company during the 1920's. More serious than the lack of any particular coordinating system was the failure of both the producing and the selling organizations and the auxiliary departments to recognize a community of interests. Too often, management decisions by members of each group were governed principally, if not entirely, by the advantages accruing to the individual department rather than by the ultimate effect on net operating profits.

RUBBER PLANTATIONS AND THE STEVENSON PLAN

By 1919, United States Rubber's plantations in northeastern Sumatra included almost 90,000 acres, contained in an area extending approximately 30 miles at its greatest length and about 20 miles at its greatest width. The planted area was said to be the largest unit planted to rubber in the world. However, with an expansion program designed to more than double the productive capacity of its tire plants by 1920, and in view of the desirability of obtaining a much larger percentage of its rubber requirements from its own plantations, the company acquired in 1919 about 13,000 acres on the Malayan peninsula for rubber plantations. Output of crude rubber on United States Rubber's plantations in 1920 was 13,113,000 pounds. The annual report issued March 8, 1923, said the Malayan properties then included over 22,000 acres of which over 10,000 had been planted. Of these, only about 1,500 were in production.

It was not customary to start tapping rubber trees until about five and one-half years after planting or bud grafting, at which time the annual yield of latex per tree was in the neighborhood of 4½ to 5 pounds (dry rubber content). The yield per tree as well as the quality of the latex increased gradually for about six years, with the best yield starting about the seventh year of tapping and continuing until about the thirteenth year, after which the yield tapered off slowly.

The time lag between the first clearing of the land, planting, and tapping of the rubber trees points up the impossibility of adjusting the current output of the plantations to the current demand for rubber. During periods such as that between 1910 and 1920, when the demand for rubber exceeded the current supply, planted areas were enlarged; the new areas might not become fully productive, however, until supply was much in excess of the immediate demand for rubber. As a result, prior to the development of the synthetic rubber industry during World War II, the crude rubber market alternated between periods of scarcity and glut, with consequent wide fluctuations in prices of crude rubber.

In 1910, when United States Rubber had acquired its first plantations, the total world acreage of all rubber plantations was estimated as 1,125,000 acres. By 1920, 4,500,000 acres were under cultivation, and world production of rubber had increased from 95,000 long tons in 1910 to 295,000 long tons.[19] But in the years following 1920, the maturing trees increased the supply of rubber even though the rubber market was temporarily glutted. (Similar conditions would reoccur in the early 1930's.)

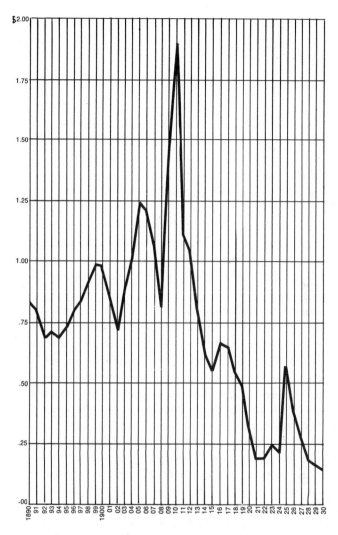

33. Average annual wholesale prices, Para rubber, 1890-1930 (see Table A-3).

The violent fluctuations in the price of crude rubber that occurred from 1923 through 1926 were brought about largely by the adoption of the so-called Stevenson Plan. In the latter part of 1921, the world's stock of rubber stood at about 300,000 long tons, with production for 1922 estimated to be 360,000 long tons of plantation rubber in addition to 30,000 tons of native rubber. Only about 185,000 long tons of crude

rubber were imported into the United States in 1921,[20] and estimated
world consumption in 1922 was not expected to exceed 250,000 long
tons. Prices in Singapore were said to be below the cost of production;
in the third quarter of 1921, rubber had sold as low as 11½¢ per pound.
Under these conditions new plantings were stopped, and a few old rubber estates were actually abandoned. Since British planters then accounted
for about 70% of the total world production and since American factories consumed about 70% of the total world usage, it was only natural
that the British government was pressed for adoption of some plan to
restrict exportation of crude rubber from British colonies in order to
support higher prices.

Late in 1921, Winston Churchill, then secretary of state for the colonies, appointed an old friend, Sir James Stevenson, as chairman of a committee to draw up a recommendation. This committee reported its pro-
posals in May, 1922, and in November, 1922 the Stevenson Plan became
operative.

The quantity of dry rubber produced by any holding in the British possessions during the period from Nov. 1, 1919 to Oct. 31, 1920, plus an
allowance for untapped trees, was established as the standard for that
holding. At the beginning, permissible exportation was set at 60% of
standard. The plan provided that, after the average price of standard
quality smoked sheet rubber landed in London had been not less than
15d. (about 27.5¢ at the rate of exchange in 1922) per pound for
three months, the exportable allowance would be raised by 5% for the
next quarter. If the average price had been less than 12d., the exportable
allowance for the next quarter would be reduced to 55%. Other increases or decreases in the exportable allowance were provided for, depending on the average price landed in London. An export duty of one
pence a pound was levied on the permissible standard of production.

When the allowance was 60% for the quarter, a producer who wished
to export more than 60% of standard would be required to pay higher
export duty on his total export during twelve months. The schedule for
this increase was as follows:

On export not exceeding 65% of standard	4d. per pound
Over 65 but not exceeding 70%	5d. per pound
. . . and so on to 100% of standard	11d. per pound
Over 100% of standard	12d. per pound

A lengthy article in the July, 1923 issue of United States Rubber Company's house organ, *Between US*, referred to losses of over $128 million

reportedly suffered by plantation owners during the period of low prices for crude rubber. The article also said that American rubber manufacturers acquainted with the real facts of the situation preferred a somewhat higher price for crude rubber rather than suffer a famine if planting of rubber trees was discouraged by low prices. According to British sources, the cost of laying down a pound of crude rubber in New York was 17½¢; a price of 32¢ a pound was therefore necessary to give the planters the return of 15% expected on their investment. These costs were said to be based on an average annual yield of 400 pounds per acre, even though 350 pounds might be on the high side.

Writing in the same vein for the *Harvard Business Review* for January, 1924, H. Stuart Hotchkiss, vice-president of United States Rubber in charge of its crude rubber activities, said that much of the criticism of the Stevenson Plan stemmed from lack of knowledge of the real cost of producing rubber. He stated that the objective was to save existing plantations from ruin and to attract capital that would provide additional production of rubber to meet the ever-increasing demand. According to Hotchkiss, 35¢ a pound, New York basis, was not exorbitant until the current average annual yield of 350 pounds per acre from seven-year-old trees was exceeded. Until synthetic rubber could be produced commercially and competitively, it was said to be essential that the price be kept high enough to make planting profitable for reasonably efficient plantations.[21]

The first result of the Stevenson Plan was to raise the New York price of plantation ribbed smoked sheet from the 1922 average of 17½¢ to over 36¢ in January, 1923 (Figure 29 and Table 4 in Appendix). But although demand in this country was increasing, it was not strong enough at that time to support that level. Increasing amounts of native rubber were also being shipped from the Dutch East Indies, and substantial amounts were being smuggled out of Malaya for reshipment from the Dutch colonies. Consequently, prices fell to the point where the limit exportable from British possessions was cut to 50% of standard in the last part of 1924.

Meanwhile, business conditions in the United States had been improving; auto sales were increasing, and balloon tires, requiring about 30% more rubber than the old high pressure tires, were becoming popular. Crude rubber as a percentage of the total weight of a tire rose from 47.9% in 1922 to 49.7 in 1923 and 55.0% in 1924. (With higher prices for crude rubber prevailing in the years immediately following, this percentage declined by several percentage points each year until 1928

TABLE 3.   Average monthly wholesale prices of crude rubber, 1925-26.
(per pound, landed New York)

	Para	Plantation Ribbed Smoked Sheet
January, 1925	$0.318	$0.364
February	.307	.357
March	.346	.411
April	.340	.439
May	.420	.574
June	.619	.772
July	.825	1.048
August	.663	.814
September	.590	.881
October	.773	1.003
November	.853	1.055
December	.764	1.005
January, 1926	.605	.800
February	.526	.623
March	.448	.589
April	.395	.513
May	.383	.485
June	.344	.434
July	.335	.416
August	.337	.392
September	.340	.413
October	.333	.427
November	.286	.401
December	.256	.383

SOURCE: *Bureau of Labor Statistics Bulletin* (Washington: U.S. Gov't Printing Office, July, 1927), p. 213.

when it was as low as 40.4%.) Imports of crude rubber by this country rose from 692 million pounds in 1923 to 735 million in 1924 and 888 million pounds in 1925. Increased demand and curtailed production forced the average price of plantation rubber landed in New York from 36.4¢ in January, 1925 to 43.9¢ in April. In July, the spot price of ribbed smoked sheet rubber shot up to $1.21 a pound, the highest since 1916. Prices remained at above a dollar a pound throughout the last quarter of the year (Table 3).

But by 1926, the Dutch East Indies, which had exported only 72,000 tons of rubber in 1921, had increased exports to 204,000 tons. (United States Rubber Company's chief plantations were on Dutch soil.) This fact, together with increased smuggling from the British possessions and greater use of reclaimed rubber, weakened the effectiveness of the Stevenson Plan. In January, 1926, ribbed smoked sheet rubber averaged 80¢ a pound in New York; in April, 51.3¢; in July, 41.6¢. By December, 1926, the average price was down to 38.3¢.

Crude Rubber Agencies Organized

The American companies that were the principal consumers of crude rubber—the tire companies and, indirectly, the automobile manufacturers—sought to keep the price of rubber in the London market at or above the equivalent of 40¢ a pound to defeat or minimize the effects of further restrictions on exportation that would be imposed by the British authorities if the price fell too low. Virtually all the rubber companies and automobile manufacturers were invited to participate in a crude rubber agency. Most of those invited entered into an agreement, as of Oct. 1, 1926, which had the following objectives:

To acquire and create a national reserve of crude rubber at a price that would protect American industry from foreign restrictions such as the Stevenson Plan;

To offer all rubber companies the right to subscribe on the basis of their 1925 consumption of crude rubber, and to offer a similar right to automobile manufacturers;

To offer to rubber manufacturing companies, not members of the agency, the right of buying or selling crude rubber through the agency;

To encourage investment of American capital in rubber plantations;

To endeavor to eliminate foreign restriction measures that artificially raised the price of crude rubber.

Meanwhile, the minimum average price for any quarter, below which more stringent restrictions under the Stevenson Plan would operate, had been raised by the British and Dutch interests to 36¢ and then to 42¢ a pound. Since it had fallen below 42¢ in the quarter ended Oct. 31, 1926, the price would have to remain above 42¢ for three consecutive quarters before the restrictions on exportable allowance would be reduced.

On Nov. 19, 1926, five tire companies (United States Rubber, Goodyear, Goodrich, Firestone, and Fisk) and the General Motors Corporation agreed to underwrite the operations of the agency. On behalf of the automobile companies, General Motors underwrote 20%, and the tire companies the remaining 80%.

United States Rubber was the only American corporation with a worldwide organization for trading in crude rubber (the General Rubber Company), which could rapidly gather and transmit facts regarding movements of crude rubber in the world markets. L. D. Tompkins was then the president of the General Rubber Company, which maintained offices in New York; London and Liverpool; Para and Belem, Brazil; Colombo, Ceylon; and in Singapore, Straits Settlements. Tompkins was chosen to head up the trading activities of the Crude Rubber Agency, and acted as one of its managers.

Since there was no law authorizing such an agreement between manufacturers, it seems obvious that the companies participating in the agency must have had some sort of informal, tacit assurance from a responsible governmental source that the agreement had unofficial approval and blessing. The fact that no action was taken against the participating companies would support this view. Although no records were found by the author, to indicate government approval, it is known that Tompkins, before completing the organization of the Crude Rubber Agency and accepting responsibility for its operation, went to Washington and gave the Secretary of Commerce and the Attorney General complete data on the agency.

The agency was authorized by the representatives of the underwriting companies to buy 44,000 tons of rubber and actually purchased approximately 39,500 tons at an average cost, including expenses, of 42.648¢ per pound. Between Oct. 1, 1926 and Feb. 25, 1928, several supplemental or continuing agreements were entered into by the members of the agency. At the beginning of 1928, the New York price of crude rubber was one cent above 40¢ a pound, the price which the agency had sought to establish as the floor in order to avoid further reduction of exportable allowances under the Stevenson Plan. However, the exports of rubber from the Dutch East Indies, plus illegal shipments from British possessions, had increased to a point that defied further attempts to stabilize the price. On Feb. 25, 1928, it was found necessary for the underwriting companies to authorize the agency to buy up to 20,000 additional tons, in an effort to keep the price, then at 32¢, from falling further, and to avoid more drastic restrictions on exports of rubber from British possessions.

On March 17, 1928, the Second Crude Rubber Agency was formed, and about 4,000 tons were bought at approximately the 32¢ level. Authorization was also requested to buy an additional 44,000 tons, if necessary, to stabilize the price at a level that would obviate the enforcement of further restrictions on production and exports, and prevent a repetition of the sharp advances in the market price that had occurred in 1926. However, no action was taken on this request, and the price of rubber continued to decline. By March 31, 1928, the New York price was 27¢.

Second Crude Rubber Agency Dissolved

On April 4, 1928, Prime Minister Baldwin announced that the restrictions and export duties imposed under the Stevenson Plan would be removed on Nov. 1, 1928. He pointed out that the plan had failed to maintain the desired minimum price for crude rubber; furthermore, it had encouraged unrestricted production of rubber on plantations in the Dutch East Indies.[22]

Contributing to the failure of the Stevenson Plan had been the unforeseen increase in production of rubber by natives in southern Sumatra and Borneo. For years the Dutch government of the Netherlands East Indies had urged natives to plant rubber trees, had given them large tracts of land, and had not assessed taxes on their production. By 1914, 32 million rubber trees had been set out in the Djambi district of Sumatra and several million had been planted elsewhere, but little attention was paid to the productive capacity of these native holdings until 1923. The rubber trade was said to be "completely surprised" to find that, of the 137,000 tons of rubber shipped from the Dutch East Indies in 1923, 55,000 tons were produced at low cost by natives. Their tapping methods were crude and often injurious to the trees, and the dirt and moisture content amounted to 20-30%; nevertheless, beginning in 1923 and continuing for many years, native production of rubber tended to have a depressing effect on its price.

The New York price of crude rubber fell to 20¢ a pound the day following Baldwin's announcement, and on May 31, 1928 the Second Rubber Agency wrote down to 20¢ a pound its holdings of rubber taken over from the first agency. During July, August, and September, the Second Agency began to dispose of the rubber it held, the average price received during those months being about 19½¢ a pound.

With the expiration of the Stevenson Plan, there was no need for further operation of the Second Crude Rubber Agency. Its holdings were distributed among the members, and the agency was dissolved. While large losses were taken in 1928 as a result of the agency's operations, no one knows whether even greater losses might not have been incurred by American manufacturers had the price of rubber been allowed to fluctuate erratically in 1927 as it did in 1925. Some of those most closely associated with the undertaking were convinced that the agency had served its original purpose and had helped to bring to an end, for the time being, artificial restrictions on the exportation of crude rubber.

The Newton Bill

One consequence of the advances in prices of crude rubber that had occurred in 1923 and the early part of 1924 was the introduction in Congress of the Newton bill. This bill would have amended the Webb-Pomerene Export Trading Act of 1918 to permit users of raw materials (particularly rubber, potash, and sisal) to form associations to import such commodities without running afoul of the antitrust laws. Harvey Firestone, Sr., president of the Firestone Tire and Rubber Company, was one of the active supporters of this legislation, and the endorsement of Secretary of Commerce Herbert E. Hoover was enlisted.

Appearing in January, 1928 before a congressional committee in support of the bill, Hoover pointed out that during the past five years foreign monopolies, either government-owned or government-controlled, were trading in these commodities. Therefore, he said, American buyers were at a disadvantage when forced to deal with such monopolies individually, and were often in competition with each other. In his testimony, Firestone said he hoped the American people would be awakened to the necessity of providing a supply of rubber from its own territory, and said rubber plantations could be established in the Philippines if the laws restricting large holdings of land there were modified. Charles B. Seger also appeared before the committee, saying that American rubber manufacturers still depended mainly on a supply of rubber produced under foreign monopolistic control.

The Newton bill did not become law, and the agitation in its support died down when Prime Minister Baldwin announced that the Stevenson Plan would terminate on Nov. 1, 1928. During the operation of the plan, Great Britain's share of the total world output of crude rubber had declined from 70 to about 50%. (But by 1939, crude rubber from British Malaya rose to 56% of the total rubber imported into the United States.)

PLANTATIONS AID PARENT COMPANY

Guiding Principles of Operation

It should be emphasized that, from the outset, United States Rubber did not look upon the plantations as merely a source of ordinary rubber. The primary purpose and chief concern of management was to produce specialty and superior grades of rubber that could not be obtained in the open market. Referring to a visit he had recently made to the United States Rubber research center established at Kisaran, Sumatra, Herbert Ashplant, the British rubber mycologist of Southern India, wrote in his report entitled "Recent Developments in the Rubber Planting Industry": "Of all the areas visited, none produced so much useful information. Kisaran, the headquarters of these plantations, has become the Mecca of all planters who wish to keep abreast of recent rubber research."[23]

This research center was concerned with means and methods of tapping, collecting, and preserving rubber latex. The relative amounts obtained by different methods and different frequencies of tapping were determined by experiments begun in 1918 and continued for many years. These experiments proved that when a tree was tapped on alternate days, the yield was 97-98% as much as from daily tapping, with large savings in labor and administration. Another test showed that daily tapping in alternate months gave 8.6% greater yield at the end of the third year, compared with the standard method.

The agricultural section sought various ways to increase yield per acre. By 1923, the manuring experiments begun in 1918-19 had proved that regular application of nitrogenous fertilizers could increase the annual yield per acre from about 350 pounds to about 675 pounds or more.

In the early days, trees to be retained in the process of thinning the original planting had been selected on the basis of their size and shape. However on United States Rubber Company plantations, the practice of keeping a record of each tree's yield was soon started so that scientifically controlled thinning could be done about twelve years after bud grafting (Figure 34). The process of bud grafting involved insertion of a bud from a tree of proven high yield under the bark of a seedling about ten to eighteen months old. After the graft had developed a sturdy sprout, the seedling was pruned above the graft, and the sprout became the tree that was ultimately tapped. The group of trees descended through the process of bud grafting from a given mother tree was called a clone. On the United States Rubber Company's plantations, trees in all new plantings were from clones of high yield, and the trees kept after thinning were the healthiest trees with the best yield.

By the late twenties, genetic selection and bud grafting had developed stands of trees capable of yielding annually about 1,000 pounds (dry rubber content) per acre. (See p. 395 for later increases in yield per acre.) On April 19, 1926, Hugh Farrell, associate editor of the *New York Commercial*, wrote in an article entitled "Does Research Pay?" that per-

Flap of bark cut and opened.

Bud inserted beneath flap.

Tree sealed against weather.

Tree pruned above new shoot.   34. Bud-graft-
                                      ing rubber tree.

Bud-grafted tree one year old. 10 ft.

Elephant's foot formation of adult tree.

sons outside the rubber industry felt that United States Rubber's bud grafting experiments promised to solve the problem of producing enough crude rubber to meet the anticipated increases in demand.[24]

The provisions made by the company for the health and well-being of the native workers, provisions which were said to be outstanding and to excel those of other rubber plantations, were also a factor in making Kisaran the Mecca for rubber planters. In an interview just before his retirement in 1962 as vice-president in charge of research and material, Wallace E. Cake, whose intimate knowledge of the company's plantation operations covered forty years from his first assignment to Kisaran in 1922, said that United States Rubber had always pioneered in bettering the conditions of natives employed on its plantations. The hospital on the company's plantations in Sumatra had a capacity of about 800 patients and had "attracted attention throughout southern Asia." The Dutch government showed its appreciation by conferring a medal on the Plantations Company.[25]

As well as improving the living conditions of the natives through its program of providing better housing and adequate medical care, Cake said that the company had aided significantly in the economic development of the northeastern coast of Sumatra. Long before the Dutch were finally expelled from Indonesia in 1949, the United States Rubber Company's plantations employed some native Indonesians as assistant managers, directly responsible to the estate manager. Reporting to these estate assistant managers were native head *mandurs* (head foremen) supervising all tapping on the estate; under these men were several *mandurs*, each of whom supervised an average of twenty tapping tasks. Other natives who had been taught in mission schools were employed in clerical positions.

Commercialization of Latex

The first recorded date of importation into Europe of liquid latex from *Hevea brasiliensis*, preserved by ammonia, was in 1853.[26] However, no important commercial use was made of latex until Ernest Hopkinson began working out practical methods of transporting and processing latex.

As early as 1911, the General Rubber Company had shipped about 30 gallons of latex in 5-gallon tins to New York, followed by about 100 gallons, also in 5-gallon tins, over the next two years. During 1918 and 1919, various trial lots, totaling about 3,000 gallons, were shipped in 50-gallon and 100-gallon drums by the General Rubber Company. Until a practical method for treating rubber latex was discovered, the latex contained in many of these early shipments soured, and some coagulated into a solid mass during transit.

By 1920, shipments of latex were measured in the equivalent of long tons (2,240 pounds) of the dry rubber content. Shipments that year are estimated at 20 dry rubber tons, and at about 50 dry rubber tons in 1921. Before 1921, the chemists in the company's General Laboratories had developed more precise methods for treating rubber latex with ammonia, so that bulk shipments could be made without having the latex

coagulate enroute to the United States. The first bulk shipment of latex
in a steamer tank, containing 422 dry rubber tons, was made in 1922.
A valuable contribution to the future progress of the company had been
made.[27] Ernest Hopkinson, then in charge of the development and
patent departments of the company, was credited with having been
largely responsible for the commercialization of latex. One of those
most closely associated with him on this project was Dr. John M. Mc-
Gavack of the General Development Laboratories. The first commercial
application of liquid latex was made by the Tire Division in the treatment of tire cords. In January, 1924, H. Stuart Hotchkiss wrote that the
company was bringing latex to this country in steamers' tanks for transfer to the company's factories where "it was being utilized on an ever
increasing scale."[28] To handle the growing volume of shipments, loading plants with tank storage capacity were built at Belawan in Sumatra
and at Port Swettenham in Malaya, and storage tanks for receiving shipments were installed at North Bergen, N.J.

The mid-twenties brought developments in methods of concentrating
latex by centrifuging or creaming, so that it was no longer necessary to
transport the high water content (about 65%) of the latex as it came
from the trees. (In both the creaming and the centrifuging operations,
the nitrogen or protein and other nonrubber ingredients of the latex
are reduced, thus minimizing the problems experienced with sprayed
rubber that are discussed in the following chapter.) The Development
Department of United States Rubber did a great amount of experimental work, mainly under the direction of McGavack, on all kinds of
creaming agents and their use. The creaming agent finally adopted was
ammonium alginate (McGavack's invention) that produced a concentrate
of over 70% solids. It was still used in 1964, not only by United States
Rubber but by other companies, and was also being used for concentration of synthetic latex.[29]

By 1925, the company's imports of latex had increased to 4,961 tons
(dry rubber content), and in a press release on Jan. 15, 1926, the company stated that it was importing "large quantities of rubber in the form
of latex."[30] The use of latex would continue to increase until the rubber industry's imports in 1937 were over 34,000 tons, approximately
half of which were imported by United States Rubber.

Benefits of Increased Production

During the operation of the Stevenson Plan, United States Rubber's ownership of extensive rubber plantations, which by that time were supply-

Table 4.   Rubber latex shipments.

4a.   World shipments, 1911-28.
(based on most reliable estimates available)

	Quantity (gallons)		Quantity (long tons)
1911	30	1923	2,308
1912-13	100	1924	2,232
1918-19	3,000	1925	5,822
	(long tons)	1926	3,336
1920	20	1927	2,718
1921	50	1928	3,664
1922	422		

4b.   Imports by United States Rubber Company, 1921-28.

	Quantity (pounds)		Quantity (pounds)
1921	40,320	1925	11,112,640
1922	539,840	1926	8,843,520
1923	5,458,880	1927	5,938,240
1924	4,130,560	1928	6,742,400

Source: Commercial research department, United States Rubber Company.

35.   Transferring latex to barge-borne tank cars, North Bergen, N.J.

ing about 20% of its requirements, helped to cushion the effects on the company of the wide swings in the prices of crude rubber.

At the end of 1926, the company, through its subsidiary plantation companies, had holdings of over 104,000 acres in Sumatra and approximately 30,000 in Malaya (Figure 36). The properties represented an investment of $29,662,000 of which $18,000,000 had been invested by the parent company, with the balance of $11,662,000 provided by the earnings of the plantation companies. Approximately 83,000 acres (about 117 square miles) were planted with more than 7 million rubber trees. About two-thirds of the planted areas were bearing and had produced approximately 23 million pounds of rubber in 1926. Within five years, it was expected that trees on the remaining 30,646 acres would become tappable, and it was estimated that within six years the production of rubber on the company's plantations would be increased by about 75% through additional plantings, maturing of trees already bearing, and by other trees coming into the bearing stage. Costs of plantings were amortized over twenty-five year periods, at the end of which it was planned to replace the old trees with new plantings of clones with a higher yield of latex.

In October, 1927, the company stated that the ultimate annual yield of the areas most recently planted was expected to reach 1,000 pounds per acre. It said that 30,000 acres out of 83,000 were planted with budded stock, an acreage larger than that planted with budded stock by all other persons or firms. As the result of ten years' work, twenty-seven strains of high-yield trees were being used exclusively. According to the press release, United States Rubber had produced 22,908,360 pounds of rubber from 82,583 acres, while in certain British possessions (probably Ceylon) it was claimed 135,509 acres had been required to produce 22,813,285 pounds. On the company's plantations, 51,968 acres were producing, compared with 99,763 acres producing on the British plantations. Average yield per acre had been 441 pounds on the rubber company's properties, but, stated the press release, average yield on the British plantations had been only 229 pounds per acre. Furthermore, United States Rubber's plantations had employed 22,392 in producing slightly more rubber than had been produced by 44,383 persons on the British plantations.

Statistics were compiled in 1928 by the commercial research department of United States Rubber covering the thirteen American-owned rubber plantations then in operation, including four Hawaiian corporations

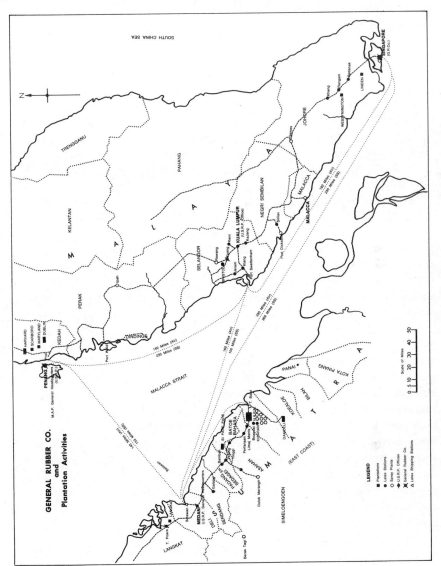

36. Operations of United States Rubber Plantations, Inc., in Far East in mid-twenties.

and four others incorporated in the Philippines. Operations in 1927 by
the three largest compared as follows:

| | Acreage | | | |
	Planted	Tapping	Production (pounds)	Lbs. per Acre in Tapping
United States Rubber Company	87,000	54,053	25,677,000	475
Goodyear Tire	15,500	14,200	5,250,000	370
Firestone	21,077	1,077	378,869	351

In 1927, J. W. Bicknell succeeded W. J. Gallagher as managing director of the company's plantations. Gallagher, who had held the post
from the beginning of United States Rubber's operations in Sumatra, resigned in order to spend most of his time in England. However, he
continued to be available for consultation and participation in plantation
activities from time to time.

The annual report for 1928 said that the largest plantation unit, consisting of more than 44,000 acres, was yielding approximately 550
pounds per acre a year. Twelve months later, the average annual yield
per acre had risen to 570 pounds. These yields compared with 390
pounds per mature acre on all "estates" in the Dutch East Indies in
1929, and with 430 pounds per acre for the same year on holdings by
natives in the Dutch East Indies.[31] The higher yield per acre on the
natives' holdings usually was due to overtapping, which injured the trees.

As mentioned in the section dealing with financial operations, United
States Rubber Plantations, Inc., declared dividends of $6 million and $4
million to the parent company out of earnings for 1926 and 1927 respectively, and also transferred $8 million from surplus in 1927. Quite
understandably, one astute and well-informed observer, not then officially
connected with the company, expressed his judgment that the plantations were the rubber company's best asset.[32] Possibly he was not entirely correct, but their record of earnings during recent years was in
sharp contrast with those of the parent. On Dec. 14, 1927, the *New
York Times* confirmed a report that members of the du Pont family had
acquired about 300,000 shares of United States Rubber common stock
and stated that the du Ponts were said to be interested mainly in the
plantations.

DU PONT FAMILY BECOMES INTERESTED

Members of the du Pont family, particularly Irenee du Pont, had invested in the stock of United States Rubber as early as 1913 and 1918.
His good friend, Raymond B. Price, had first interested him in the
investment opportunity because of the company's large rubber planta-

TABLE 5.   Significant financial ratios, United States Rubber Company, 1924-26.

	1924	1925	1926
Current assets/current liabilities (times)	2.6	5.2	4.6
Inventory/sales%	36.4	39.1	44.1
Receivables/sales%	25.1	24.4	22.0
Net income/sales%	4.0	5.9	2.3
Net income/net worth%	3.6	6.1	2.5
Sales/total assets%	53.3	58.4	60.6
Net worth/total debt (times)	1.4	1.3	1.3

SOURCE: Adjusted annual reports of United States Rubber Company. Prior to 1928, several million dollars of intangible assets were included in "Investments" shown on balance sheet of the company.

The data on which the foregoing ratios have been calculated have not been fully adjusted to conform to current accounting practice, but are based on those facts that would have been known to any analyst in the early months of 1927.

tions; possibly, du Pont also considered the stock attractive because of the acquisition in 1912 of Price's alkali process for reclaiming rubber.

In the first half of 1927, a severe decline in the price of United States Rubber common appeared to offer a good opportunity for buying additional stock. It also aroused questions regarding the financial management of the company. With his brother-in-law, Winder Laird, head of a Wilmington brokerage firm, Irenee du Pont studied the company's financial statements and felt his suspicions were confirmed. The statements revealed (1) excessive inventories, (2) too many receivables on hand, and (3) heavy indebtedness (Table 5). The two men believed these weaknesses could be corrected by utilization of their knowledge and experience and that of their associates. They concluded that it would be necessary to buy enough stock to gain the ear of management, to induce the liquidation of inventories and accounts receivable, and to use the proceeds thus obtained in reduction of the indebtedness.

Since this action would require the acquisition of more stock than du Pont thought he could afford, a syndicate of several members of the family was formed. It was thought that the proper corrective measures, as well as the advantages of the company's plantations, should result in higher prices for United States Rubber stock, and that the members of the syndicate would profit accordingly. Two successive syndicates, formed in 1927, acquired about 155,000 shares of the common stock, or about 10½% of the total voting stock including the preferred, which had equal voting rights. (This percentage was considerably smaller than that indicated in newspaper publicity at the time.)

There is no evidence that either Irenee du Pont or his brother, Pierre, or any other members of the du Pont family had any idea in 1926 or 1927 of replacing the management of United States Rubber. On the contrary, Irenee du Pont's first impressions of Seger were favorable. In December, 1927, he and representatives of Kuhn, Loeb and Co. met with Seger and expressed their views that receivables and inventories were too high. If these could be reduced, the funds thus obtained could be used to buy United States Rubber Company's bonds, which were selling below par (1927 range, 96¾-88). Apparently nothing came of this interview.

Preferred Dividend Omitted

The situation that developed in the early months of 1928 caused du Pont to revise his appraisal of Seger's fitness for the presidency of United States Rubber. The price of crude rubber declined steadily during the first quarter, and United States Rubber faced the possibility of being forced to take a large loss, perhaps as much as $20 million on its inventories of about 100 million pounds of crude rubber and rubber content of manufactured goods. Payment of the April dividend on the company's preferred stock should be omitted, du Pont thought, since conservation of cash was important and, in addition, payment could violate the terms of the indenture covering the 1925 issue of gold notes. Seger hesitated to make such a recommendation to the board of directors. Then, Prime Minister Baldwin announced that Great Britain would discontinue the Stevenson Plan the following November, and the price of rubber immediately fell to 20¢ a pound, New York basis.

On April 5, the directors of United States Rubber voted to omit payment of the quarterly dividend of 2% on the preferred. Seger's announcement of the vote of the directors pointed out that on March 31 the New York price of rubber had been 27¢, but that the price had dropped to 20¢ as a result of the previous day's announcement that the Stevenson Plan was to be abandoned. On the basis of this latest quotation, Seger added, the value of the current assets of the company and of its subsidiaries did not meet the requirements of the indenture covering the 1925 issue of 6½% serial gold notes. The drastic decline in the price of rubber, stated Seger, would not necessarily entail a corresponding loss to the United States Rubber Company, since the ultimate results would depend upon the prices at which its products were sold. Except for the limitations of the indenture, he went on to say, "There is no reason why the regular quarterly dividend should not have been declared at this time."[33]

Regardless of the terms of the 1925 indenture, the company owed about $20 million in short-term loans in the spring of 1928, and there was danger that some of the uneasy creditor banks would force a receivership. It was imperative that United States Rubber conserve cash for meeting maturities on some of its indebtedness. Even before the drop in the price of rubber, and after giving effect to receipt of dividends from the plantations, the "margin of safety" representing net income in excess of fixed charges had fallen from 75% of total income in 1925 to 50% in 1927. It was small wonder that, in the face of Seger's apparent reluctance to conserve cash, the company's creditors had shown concern,[34] while his obvious reluctance to advise the directors to omit the April dividend led du Pont to concur with Kuhn, Loeb's recommendation that a successor to Seger should be found. The business ability of the du Ponts had impressed other important stockholders, as well as investment bankers; they were favorably inclined toward any recommendation the du Pont brothers might offer.

New Issue of Common Stock

When a reduction of $14,148,000 in the value of United States Rubber's inventories as of June 30, 1928 was announced, the Guaranty Trust Company threatened to cut off its line of credit to the company. Other banks also began questioning its ability to meet its obligations.

Kuhn, Loeb and Co. had previously concluded that, to protect the investment of its own customers to whom it had sold the rubber company's securities, more equity capital was needed to bring about a better relationship between risk capital and United States Rubber's indebtedness. In April, 1928, Kuhn, Loeb had suggested to Seger a plan for issuance of additional common stock, but he had taken no action on it. In September, another plan, under which Kuhn, Loeb agreed to underwrite a new issue of common stock, was submitted, and this one was accepted by Seger. When they were informed of this plan, the creditor banks consented to continue the lines of credit they had granted United States Rubber. Under the new plan, the common stock would be changed from shares having a par value of $100 each to shares of no par value. Then, 728,412 shares of no par common stock of United States Rubber would be offered to holders of the common stock, share for share, at $35 a share, to be paid for on or before Jan. 11, 1929.

On Dec. 7, 1928, the stockholders approved the revised plan. As of Dec. 1, the investment in United States Rubber stock by the syndicate of members of the du Pont family amounted to more than $6,576,000. Since subscription by the syndicate for its full allotment of the new issue of no par common stock would involve an additional investment of over $4 million, the du Pont brothers felt that their interest entitled them to nominate someone for membership on the board of directors.

The other stockholders agreed, and Henry Davis was elected a director. On Dec. 13, he was also elected a member of the so-called executive committee, which at that time functioned as a finance committee.

The entire new issue of common stock was subscribed, increasing the stated value of equity capital by approximately $17,300,000. Since the preferred and common stock had equal voting rights, the increase in the number of shares of common gave the holders of those shares greater voting strength. The 125,150 additional shares of the company's common stock purchased by the du Pont syndicate in January, 1929, together with shares of United States Rubber stock then owned individually by members of the du Pont family, brought the group's combined holdings to approximately 17% of the total voting stock then outstanding.

Balance Sheets for 1928 and 1929 Compared

The balance sheet as of Dec. 31, 1928 stated the new value of the common stock as $67.50 a share. A comparison of the balance sheets for Dec. 31, 1927 and Dec. 31, 1928 reveals significant changes in the listing of assets. The 1927 statement included, among other items:

Plants, properties, and investments including rubber plantations, less reserve for depreciation	$183,739,321
Securities of affiliated and controlled corporations not included in United States Rubber Company system	4,236,908
Securities of other corporations not included in the system	1,687,598

The 1928 statement included among the assets of the company:

Properties, plants, and equipment	$144,927,344	
Less reserves for depreciation	39,829,335	$105,098,009
Investment in United States Rubber Plantations, Inc.		18,000,000
Securities of corporations not included in the system		2,621,456
Net investment in intangible capital assets, such as goodwill, patents, after deducting fixed surpluses of subsidiary companies		58,925,372

Since the 1928 statement could not have been put in its final form until after F. B. Davis, Jr. had become president in January, 1929, it appears obvious that he felt the stockholders should have a more clarified accounting of what had been included in the assets of the company. In addition, an effort had been made to appraise more realistically the true value of securities of other companies outside the United States Rubber Company system. At the same time, a reserve of $10 million was created for the closing of plants and disposal of obsolete machinery and equipment.

Earned surplus (adjusted) as of Dec. 31, 1928, was $19,305,000, down by more than $29,500,000 from the earned (adjusted) surplus of $48,826,000 on Dec. 31, 1918 when Seger took over the reins from Colt.

[1] Other directors recommended by Kuhn, Loeb, and Co. were James S. Alexander and William S. Kies. Kies remained on the board only a few years; Alexander continued as director until Jan. 7, 1930, when he retired. He was characterized by F. B. Davis, Jr., as an "experienced banker and able director."

[2] C. W. Rosswarn, letter to author, 1964.

[3] "Charles B. Seger," *Railway Age*, LXIV (March 22, 1918), p. 707.

[4] W. M. Dougherty, speech at sales managers' committee meeting, April 15, 1957, unpublished, company archives. See also Walter Emery, "First Section of History of United States Rubber Company," 1946, unpublished, company archives.

[5] Elmer Roberts, interview, 1963.

[6] Coughlin had started with New York Belting and Packing Company in 1890 and in 1915 had been made general factory manager for mechanical goods. George H. Mayo, the son of William F. Mayo, who was founder of William F. Mayo Company, came with United States Rubber in 1912. Since July, 1917, he had been manager of the Footwear Division.

[7] *Between US*, house organ of United States Rubber Company (February, 1924).

[8] *"U.S." Rubber News*, house organ of United States Rubber Company (September, 1928), p. 5.

[9] Harold S. Roberts, *The Rubber Workers* (New York: Harper & Brothers, 1944), pp. 24-25.

[10] Cyrus S. Ching, interview, 1963.

[11] "The Human Factor in Industry," Footwear Division training course, 1919-20, company archives.

[12] "Employment and Instruction," Footwear Division training course, company archives.

[13] U.S. Dept. of Commerce, *Industrial Reference Service, Part 10, "Rubber"* (Washington: U.S. Gov't Printing Office, May, 1941), p. 1.

[14] Factory councils were declared illegal under the Wagner Act and were discontinued by United States Rubber Company.

[15] *New York Times* (May 11, 1926), p. 39.

[16] Between 1912 and 1920, increases in capitalization of the leading rubber companies were: Kelly-Springfield, 250%; B. F. Goodrich, 250%; Fisk Rubber Corporation, 700%; Firestone Tire and Rubber Company, 700%; Goodyear Tire and Rubber Company, 1100%. See David M. Beights, "Financing American Rubber Manufacturing Companies," 1932, unpublished dissertation, University of Illinois, p. 4, as quoted by John D. Gaffey, in *The Productivity of Labor in the Rubber Tire Manufacturing Industry* (New York: Columbia University Press, 1940), p. 155.

[17] Crude rubber was available in about 300 grades during the mid-twenties; prices of most grades were related to the price of No. 1, ribbed smoked sheet.

[18] *"U.S." Rubber News* (Sept. 1, 1924), p. 1.

[19] P. W. Barker, *Rubber: History, Production, and Manufacture*, U.S. Dept. of Commerce (Washington: U.S. Gov't Printing Office, 1940), p. 45.

[20] U.S. Dept. of Commerce, *Historical Statistics of the United States, Colonial Times to 1957* (Washington: U.S. Gov't Printing Office, 1960), p. 548.

[21] H. Stuart Hotchkiss, "The Evolution of the World Rubber Situation," *Harvard Business Review*, II (January, 1924), p. 136.

[22] *New York Times* (April 5, 1928), p. 1.

[23] As quoted by United States Rubber in advertisement, *Saturday Evening Post* (May 8, 1926).

[24] *"U.S." Rubber News* (May 1, 1926), pp. 8-10.

[25] "Romance of Rubber," Footwear Division, training course, 1919-20, company archives, p. 12.

[26] "Annals of Rubber," reprinted from *India Rubber World* (New York, 1946), p. 12.

[27] Fred S. Carpenter, letter to author, 1965.

[28] "The Evolution of the World Rubber Situation," p. 135.

[29] John M. McGavack, letter to author, 1964.

[30] *New York Times* (Jan. 15, 1926), p. 22.

[31] Peter T. Bauer, *The Rubber Industry, a Study in Competition and Monopoly* (Cambridge: Harvard University Press, 1948), p. 29.

[32] R. B. Price as quoted by H. Gordon Smith, interview, 1952, company archives.

[33] *Financial Chronicle*, CXXVI (April 7, 1928), p. 2163.

[34] *Moody's Manual of Investments* (New York: Moody's Investors Service, 1929), p. 1922.

6

Uncertain Course of

Sales and Profits

CHANGES IN MARKETS AND MARKETING

Effects of Motorization

Large-scale production of motor vehicles in this country began in the 1920's, and revolutionized not only transportation but many other elements of the American economy. The record of factory sales shown in Table 6 only indicates the impact of the motor industry's growth.

The estimated annual miles of travel by motor vehicles rose from 55 million in 1921 to 122 million miles in 1925, and to 206 million by 1930.[1] Improved highways encouraged families in small towns and rural communities to do more of their shopping in county seat towns or larger cities so that, one after another, the small towns "dried up." There was now less need for the heavy, warm clothing and footwear that had been essential in horse-and-buggy days. Fewer children walked country roads to school. Motorized labor-saving equipment was introduced in mining, road building, lumbering, commercial fishing, and farming, and fewer men were employed in these outdoor occupations.

These trends affected the product mix of United States Rubber in the 1920's even before they reached their full momentum. To offset the lessening demand for many types of strictly utilitarian waterproof rubber footwear, style features were promoted, and colors other than black introduced. Greater emphasis was placed upon footwear for recreation and sports wear. Although major shifts occurred in the relative importance of different types of footwear, the company and the rubber footwear industry maintained production fairly well through 1929.

Prices of all types of rubber footwear showed a gradually declining trend throughout most of the 1920's, with the sharpest declines in prices

TABLE 6.   Factory sales of passenger cars, trucks, and buses, 1920-29.

	Quantity			*Quantity*
1920	2,227,349	1925		4,265,830
1921	1,616,119	1926		4,300,934
1922	2,544,176	1927		3,401,326
1923	4,034,012	1928		4,358,759
1924	3,602,540	1929		5,337,087

SOURCE: U.S. Dept. of Commerce, *Historical Statistics of the United States, Colonial Times to 1957* (Washington: U.S. Gov't Printing Office, 1960), p. 462.

of women's gaiters (buckle or slide fastener) and men's rubber-soled canvas shoes. Industry prices of women's gaiters in the years 1927 through 1929 were only slightly above 40% of the 1920 price level, and the index of men's lace-to-toe rubber-soled canvas shoe prices was even lower, about 70% less than in 1920 (Figure 37).

Invention, Skirt Lengths, and Obsolescence

In the days when motors had to be cranked by hand, most automobile drivers were men; but after the electric starter was introduced in 1911, a large percentage of drivers were women. Women soon found that picture hats obstructed their vision and that long skirts interfered with operation of the pedals; thereupon, ankle-length skirts went out of fashion for daytime wear. Shorter skirts lent new interest to footwear fashions, and manufacturers learned that rubber footwear for women and children had to be given eye appeal if it were to be sold in volume. New styles, types, and colors were introduced in the early 1920's.[2] Because the transition was relatively rapid, many of the new styles were short-lived, and both manufacturers and retailers struggled with loss sales of obsolete inventories. Moreover, wartime employment and enrollment of women in the Red Cross and other organizations had popularized year-round wear of low-cut oxfords and pumps. Shapes of shoe lasts changed radically. Women no longer bought high-button shoes with a long vamp that would peek discreetly from beneath floor-length skirts. Only low-cut shoes with much shorter vamps and rounder toes found ready sales.

Large losses were taken by many shoe firms. For example, Foote-Schulz Shoe Company, St. Paul, Minn., a Goodyear Glove distributor, was primarily a manufacturer of women's shoes. It failed to recognize that year-round wearing of low-cut oxfords, T-straps, and pumps was more than a passing fad, and continued to produce expensive, high-cut button or lace shoes. Meanwhile, St. Louis firms gained popularity with their lines of the new low-cut and lower-priced styles. The St. Paul firm, despite repeated price cuts, accumulated a large inventory.

When Foote-Schulz failed in 1926, it was heavily indebted to the
United States Rubber Company. In an effort to salvage as much as
possible of the account, the rubber company took over, at full price,
Foote-Schulz's inventory of Goodyear Glove rubber footwear, much of
it quite old and in bad shape. In 1926, a young tax accountant, William
A. Mitchel, had just been employed by the St. Paul Rubber Company,
a local subsidiary of United States Rubber. Mitchel recalled, when interviewed by the author in 1963, that one floor of the newly organized
Goodyear Glove branch was filled with obsolete rubber footwear acquired from the Foote-Schulz Company. Fortunately, the 1926-27 winter in the Midwest was very severe, and stocks of rubber footwear were
depleted. Consequently, the Goodyear Glove branch in St. Paul was
able to sell the entire lot of obsolete rubber footwear "as is" to one of
the mass distributors whose customers were clamoring for rubber footwear of almost any description. In many other instances, United States
Rubber was not so fortunate and was forced to assume large losses on
inventories of wholesalers taken over under similar circumstances.

The radical changes in shapes of women's shoes posed serious problems for rubber manufacturers whose overshoes could not be fitted satisfactorily over the current styles of leather shoes. Since the highly seasonal character of waterproof rubber footwear required scheduling of
large-scale production months in advance of the peak of retail demand,
a way had to be found to anticipate, by as much as a year and a half,
changes that would be made in shapes of lasts and heels for women's
shoes. This problem was particularly acute with a company such as
Mishawaka Rubber and Woolen Mfg. Co.,[3] which did not operate branches
and sold the bulk of its annual production on advance orders placed
during the first five or six months of the year.

To solve this problem, Mishawaka enlisted the assistance of manufacturers of shoe lasts and made periodic and extensive surveys of the
leather shoe trade in an effort to determine as precisely as possible what
changes might be in prospect. Although skeptical of the value of such a
survey, the many shoe manufacturers and others in the trade who were
visited cooperated generously in providing such information as they were
able to give. Mishawaka was thus able in most instances to revise its
lasts soon enough to keep its rubber overshoes fairly well abreast of
the changes in leather shoes. Because Mishawaka could control its inventory, which was concentrated at the factory, this subsidiary did not
incur losses on obsolete styles and lasts as large as did the other factories
in the System. Similar surveys were made by other plants, but Mishawaka's unique distribution pattern required more extensive study.

37. Rubber footwear manufacturers' bottom prices, 1920-40 (1920=100).

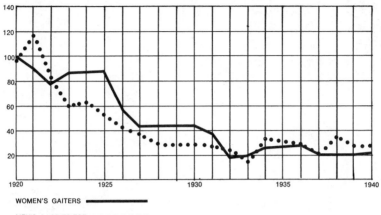

WOMEN'S GAITERS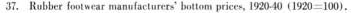

MEN'S LACE-TO-TOE ● ● ● ● ● ● ● ●
RUBBER-SOLED CANVAS SHOES

Red Line Territories

From 1920 until 1927, T. J. Needham was in charge of all sales through the branches (see p. 152). To correct the overlapping of sales activities, he began to assign to each branch an exclusive territory within which it would have sole control of the sale of items carrying the label of the United States Rubber System. (There still were some exceptions, such as a fifty-mile buffer zone that existed for some time between the St. Paul and Chicago territories, wherein either of those branches was privileged to take orders.)[4] Because the outlines of the branch territories were shown on the map in red they were known as "red line" territories. However, on other brands made by companies in the United States Rubber System, the branches still had to compete with jobbers offering the same brands. Sometimes, as previously mentioned, this situation came about because it seemed the best way to maintain distribution of certain brands enjoying strong demand in a given area.

In 1926, according to Mitchel, United States Rubber was operating four wholesale houses in Minneapolis and St. Paul. The Minneapolis branch of United States Rubber Company handled U.S. footwear, tires, and mechanical goods; Beacon Falls footwear was distributed by a Beacon Falls Rubber Company branch; Hub, Lycoming, Duck, and Woonsocket brands were sold by the St. Paul Rubber Company; and the Goodyear Glove brand was sold by Foote-Schulz until the latter went out of business and was succeeded by a Goodyear Glove branch.

Royal Cord

Usco

Nobby

Bathing Caps
and Keds Bathing Shoes

Raynsters

38.   Some 1920 products.

Each branch operated its affairs with little supervision from the parent company, much as though it were an entirely independent unit. Even in the late 1920's, Mitchel recalled, the older salesmen traveling out of St. Paul were inclined to regard branches that had replaced independently owned jobbing firms as competitors, rather than as members of the same corporate family. He said that after 1929 this attitude began to be corrected and was further improved by the mid-thirties.

The history of the Chicago branch well illustrates the long process of consolidation and assimilation that characterized the early growth of United States Rubber. In 1909, the Chicago offices of Central Rubber Co., Banigan Rubber Co., and Standard Rubber Shoe Co. were consolidated in the Chicago Rubber Company, and the name of the branch became Chicago Branch, United States Rubber Company. In 1912, the local Duck Brand Co. was consolidated with Chicago Rubber Company. In 1918, local branches of the Peerless Rubber Co., Eureka Fire Hose Co., Revere Rubber Co., and the mechanical department of the Chicago Rubber Co. were consolidated as the Mechanical Goods Division, Chicago branch.

Various separate offices were maintained in Chicago until 1922, when all except United States Tire Company were consolidated in new quarters at 440 W. Washington Street, Chicago. Beginning in April, 1924, Needham began consolidating Tire Company branches with the general branches in several of the larger cities. The Chicago branch of the Tire Company, with its subbranches in Davenport and Cedar Rapids, Iowa, Peoria, Ill., and South Bend, Ind., was consolidated with the general Chicago branch, making the latter, with combined sales of about $9 million, the largest branch then operated by United States Rubber.[5]

The program of consolidating the Tire Company's branches with the general branches was completed about 1926, Mitchel said. By 1929, with the exception of Philadelphia, Detroit, and a few other cities where a separate Goodyear Glove branch was still maintained, only one United States Rubber Company branch operated in each city.

Compensation of Salesmen

Before World War I the United States Rubber Company's salesmen had been paid a salary with reimbursement for their traveling expenses. If the salesman owned an automobile, an allowance, depending upon the territory, was worked out with him by his branch manager. In some Western districts, and possibly in other areas, new salesmen who did not own a car were given assistance in building up a fund for the downpayment. The company would also back the salesman's arrangements

with the auto dealer for financing his purchase. Salesmen were not required to keep within a fixed expense budget. Until the middle 1920's,
most salesmen traveled by train in the winter because very few rural
highways were in good condition. Auto travel was impractical, and sometimes tires were "cut to pieces in thirty to forty miles" by icy ruts.[6]

After World War I the company began adopting various plans to
provide salesmen with incentives for increased effort and added sales
volume. One plan was based on the average sales per capita for all salesmen operating out of a branch. After the average per capita sales had
been determined for each of the major commodity groups (footwear,
tires, mechanical, clothing, and sundries), they would be reviewed by
experienced management personnel and would be adjusted upward or
downward. Conditions that might be expected to have an important
bearing upon sales for the new season were taken into consideration,
as well as the amount of effort required to reach or exceed the desired
volume. The salesmen were then given quotas and were paid bonuses
based on their accomplishment.

Advertising and Sales Promotion

Since radio was yet to be developed, and since the company's products
with general appeal to the consuming public during the early 1920's
were chiefly tires, footwear, rubberized clothing, and golf balls, it was
possible for United States Rubber to get good results from relatively
few advertisements in magazines of general circulation. Also, full page
advertisements in rotogravure and colored supplements of Sunday newspapers were used effectively. Advertisements in trade journals were also
used, particularly for mechanical rubber goods and for footwear (Figure
39a). In the same period, United States Tires were advertised on permanent billboards carrying interesting historical information (39b). These
had high attention-getting value and were remembered by many motorists long after the billboards had been discontinued.

United States Rubber was an early exponent of effective sales promotions, especially for Keds. In 1922, the Footwear Division inaugurated
a Keds plan that offered free advertising material to all retailers who
placed an advance order for a certain quantity. At least once a month,
the more than 300 stores that participated received a house organ, the
Keds Dealer, containing stories of how other dealers had built up their
business on Keds, and showing photographs of dealer's window displays.
Merchants who had taken the Keds plan were eligible to participate in
two contests, one for window displays of Keds, and the other for sug-
gesting and using original ideas for the sale of Keds. The winners re-

ceived cash prizes, and their sales and advertising programs were pub-
licized in the *Keds Dealer*.

Through the efforts of the city salesman, Vester Duckworth, more
dealers in Atlanta, Ga., participated in the Keds plan in 1922 than in
any other city. Duckworth sold them on taking part in a Keds Week,
during which each store put in special window displays and ran newspaper ads featuring Keds. The results were satisfactory to all concerned,
and in 1924, Duckworth, with the active support of the Atlanta branch
manager, William F. Cairns, promoted a Keds Field Day, with a popular football star, recently on the Georgia Tech squad, in charge of all
arrangements. Boys and girls wishing to take part were required to appear at the park wearing United States Rubber Company's Keds, and
more than 1,000 entered the various events. When all the newspaper
stories and copies of local dealers' advertisements during the promotion
were pasted on a strip of paper, it measured 18 inches by 31 feet.

Other special Keds Weeks and Keds Field Days were promoted dur-
ing the 1920's. In 1924, for example, the Omaha branch tied in Keds
Week with the annual field day of the sixth and eighth grades of the
Omaha public schools. About 8,000 copies of a booklet, *Track and Field
Work*, were distributed through the thirteen participating dealers. In
May, 1928, A. C. Ware, then the local city salesman in Atlanta, ar-
ranged for another successful Keds Field Day, which resulted in an
unusual amount of Keds advertising by retailers over several weeks.[7]

In 1926, Gregory T. Ward, who had joined the company in 1925 as
a salesman for U.S. clothing with a San Francisco territory, was made
the department manager in that branch for footwear, clothing, and sundries. As a salesman he had presented promotion plans to his best accounts. These plans were designed to increase store traffic, and he had
found them very helpful, not only in building sales of the merchandise
he was offering, but also in creating valuable goodwill.

Evidence of the effectiveness of the sales promotions was assembled,
including photographs of store windows and interior displays, as well
as statistics regarding the stores' increase in volume of business on
United States Rubber Company products. This evidence was then used
to convince other dealers and other salesmen for the company that such
promotions were profitable both for the retailer and the company. Considerable skepticism and initial resistance developed toward this virtually
new concept of selling in that territory, so far as the apparel industries
were concerned, but the basic idea of helping the retailer move goods
into the hands of satisfied customers was sound—and it spread.

In the presidential campaign of 1928, Ward had seen a large cloth campaign banner stretched across one of the main streets of Palo Alto. He arranged to get the banner after the campaign and to store it until the following spring, when he had it repainted to read:

U. S. KEDS, the Shoes of CHAMPIONS
FIELD DAY

All of the Keds dealers in the area were invited to participate in the field day, complete with various contests and prizes for children. A police permit to hang the repainted banner across the street was procured, and a motorcycle police escort was arranged for a calvacade of local dealers and United States Rubber salesmen from San Francisco to Palo Alto. The novelty of the occasion created great enthusiasm and intense excitement, with marked increase in the sales of Keds in the area.[8]

The success of these and many other promotions conducted by the company's footwear salesmen was so impressive that effective sales promotions, particularly on rubber-soled fabric footwear for women and children, became the cornerstone of much of the Footwear Division's selling philosophy and practice during succeeding years.

Publicity Efforts

The Footwear Division seized a good opportunity for favorable publicity in February, 1926, when two heavy snowstorms within eight days crippled rail and highway traffic in the New York City area and southern New England. George F. Hichborn, traffic manager of United States Rubber was asked, on the morning of Thursday, Feb. 11, to have several cases of women's rubber galoshes flown from Naugatuck to New York. After two airplane companies had declined the job because their light planes would capsize if they attempted to land on the snow, a biplane, equipped with skids, was flown by the Curtiss Aeroplane Service to a point four miles from the Naugatuck plant where it was loaded. When it arrived back at Curtiss Field, Garden City, Long Island at 3:00 p.m., a Pathe News cameraman was on hand to take motion pictures of the cases of galoshes being unloaded (Figure 39c). The galoshes were rushed to the New York branch and the pictures to the advertising department. By 10:55 p.m., final approval was given for the full page ads that appeared in the first editions of the morning papers that hit the streets at midnight.

Actually, the truck crews that dug their way through deep snow from the Naugatuck plant to the airfield four miles away, and to and from Curtiss Field, had much more difficulty than the plane, which contin-

39. Promotion and publicity efforts.

39a. "140,000,000 Advertisements to Help You Sell Keds" (announcement to salesmen of plans for 1924).

39b. Advertisements for Keds, Atlanta, Ga., May, 1928.

39c. Unloading galoshes at Curtiss Field, Feb. 11, 1926.

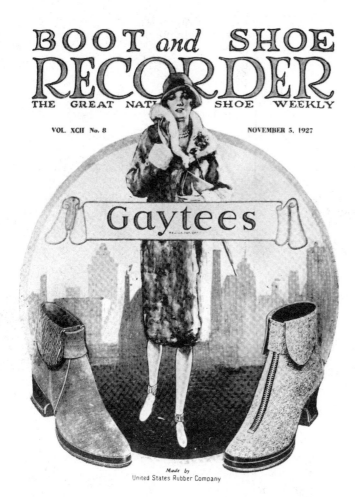

39e. Signboard in New South Wales, Australia.

ued until late Friday afternoon to deliver footwear from the Naugatuck plant to New York.[9]

The year 1926 also saw the erection of two electrical signs on the roof of the headquarters building at 1790 Broadway. These were proclaimed at the time as "the largest ever erected on Broadway." Facing to the north, the letters US were 35 feet high with an 8 foot wide face. In back of these were the words "Rubber Co." and below, flashing alternately, "Keds" and "Royal Cord Tires." The entire sign was 53 feet high and 88 feet long. A somewhat smaller sign faced south.

Sales of Mechanical Goods

The market for industrial rubber goods was served in various ways. In some territories general line salesmen handled sales to industrial jobbers who supplied local industries with their requirements of belting, packing, hose, and other mechanical rubber goods. Where the volume was large enough, full-time salesmen for mechanicals were employed. In the latter part of 1922, it was announced that, thereafter, the initials U.S. would be used in connection with many items of mechanical goods; for example, Rainbow transmission belt would be known as U.S. Rainbow transmission belt. The sales organization was urged to popularize the new names. However, the New York Belting and Packing Company operated much as an independent organization until the early 1930's; it maintained seven separate branches and did not report its sales to the parent company. In 1927, the Eureka Fire Hose Manufacturing Company distributed through fourteen or more agencies. The Fabric Fire Hose Company carried stocks in fifteen branches, and the cut rubber thread department worked out of two branches.

In many instances, mechanical rubber goods salesmen worked primarily with the customers' engineers to arrive at specifications for a particular job. After the engineers were satisfied that the approved specifications had been met, prices were negotiated with the purchasing department which placed the actual order.

The Mechanical Goods Division was rightfully proud of the excellence of many of its products. For example, numerous installations of U.S. Rainbow conveyor belts were giving superior service under very severe conditions. One of these, sold by the Johannesburg, South Africa, branch of the Export Company to the Randfontein Estates Gold Mining Company, was a 4-ply belt, 36 inches wide, with a 3/16 inch "face," or coating of rubber compound, which in 1,327 days of continuous service carried 1,102,964 tons of ore (Figure 40). The branch was informed

40. "U.S." conveyor belt at Randfontein gold mines, South Africa.

that the best record previously made on the same job by any belt had not been over 950 days, and the performance of the U.S. belt was said to have made a deep impression throughout the gold mining area. Issues of the house organs published during the 1920's included many illustrations of United States Rubber Company's oil hose, belting, and other products being used under unusual conditions. With increasing use of turbines, U.S. rubber expansion joints, claimed to be the only ones on the market, were declared to have become "a thoroughly established part of pipe line equipment of the modern power plant," and were used in most of the important ones.

Early in 1927, the Mechanical Goods Division established the motor products department, with headquarters at the factory of the Mechanical Rubber Company, Cleveland, Ohio. Edward Abramson, who had been first employed by Revere Rubber Company in 1897 as a stock clerk in its San Francisco branch, was made head of the new department, and the manufacture of motor products (mechanical rubber goods used in the manufacture of automobiles) was concentrated in the Cleveland factory. Orders for motor products were placed for stated quantities at stated prices for delivery during the automobile manufacturer's model year. Releases for shipment of goods applying against such orders would be furnished by the automobile manufacturer as production schedules required. Other mechanical rubber goods that were sold to the automobile manufacturers for operation or maintenance, such as hose, belts, and packing, were made at other factories of United States Rubber and were sold by the branches.

Coated Fabrics

About 1915, a motor fabrics department for production of rubberized cloth tops for automobiles was organized at the Malden, Mass., plant of the Boston Rubber Shoe Company. Sometime later the Goodyear Metallic Rubber Shoe Company started production of coated fabric under the name Naugahyde. When the sale of automobiles declined in 1920, the two operations were consolidated at Malden. By 1921, coated fabrics under the brands Supertex and Raynbar were being sold to some of the largest automobile companies as well as to wholesale houses, and a good business was being developed on Naugahyde luggage.

New Overseas Branches Opened

Beginning about 1917, under the direction of Fred H. Hauser, there was a growing recognition that worthwhile business could be obtained in other overseas territories, and important branches were quickly opened in several other countries, including Brazil, Chile, and Uruguay, and in India and Australia. Large markets for the company's tires were developed in Brazil and Argentina, and in the latter country for rubber-soled canvas footwear.

The Havana branch, first opened in May, 1915, had thirty-five employees by the end of 1920, and was selling large quantities of Keds. Other important items in the Cuban market were U.S. Raynsters, U.S. Royal Cord and Nobby tires, and the company's mechanical goods, said to be well represented in the island's sugar industry. In December, 1916, another branch, operated through a subsidiary, was opened in Paris. In January, 1919, a separate sales subsidiary, known as India Rubber Products, Ltd., was organized in South Africa. On Jan. 6, 1921, the name of the South African corporation was changed to United States Rubber Company (Proprietary) Limited, and was still so known in 1965.[10]

By the early 1920's, export sales had become an important part of the business of the Canadian Consolidated Rubber Company, partly because of the aftereffects of World War I, and partly because of the limited domestic market in Canada. As related in a previous chapter, some of the earliest sales by the Canadian company had been exports; by 1923, about 40% of the production of the Kitchener tire plant was being exported under the Dominion label, which, by 1919, applied to all the rubber footwear made in the Canadian plants operated by the company. (In 1926, the name of the corporation was changed from Canadian Consolidated Rubber Company, Ltd., to Dominion Rubber Company, Ltd.[11]) The Mishawaka subsidiary also did a small amount of export business, with most of its sales concentrated either in Europe or the British Empire.

By 1923, the Buenos Aires branch, in its new building on the beautiful Congressional Plaza, employed a staff of sixty-five. Other branches were also opened in the Far East, and those in India and Australia enjoyed especially strong demand for United States Rubber's products.

Herbert E. Smith, appointed general manager of the Export Company in March, 1924, was keenly interested in expanding the overseas market, as was also his successor, Charles E. Guest, who had previously been manager of the branch in Manila. In 1925, the London subsidiary of United States Rubber Export Company, India Rubber Products, Ltd. (not connected with the South African corporation) was dissolved and a new distributing subsidiary of the Export Company, Dominion Rubber Company, Ltd., was formed to handle sales in the British Isles. By August, 1927, the Export Company was maintaining thirty-four branches in foreign countries (not including Canada) and had three overseas selling agencies. Four branches were located in Great Britain, five in Continental Europe, four each in Australia, New Zealand, and South Africa, and three in Brazil. There was one branch in Calcutta and Shanghai, and in the capital city of each of the following countries: Mexico, Cuba, Chile, Argentina, Uruguay, Japan, Philippines, and the Dutch East Indies. Overseas branches carried full lines of the company's products, suited for their individual markets, and all had adequate staffs. Sales offices were maintained in other countries where the volume of business did not warrant the operation of a full-fledged branch. The sales agencies were located in Vienna, Milan, and Panama.[12] These branches and agencies served all the important foreign markets (again excluding Canada, served by the Dominion Rubber Company), with the exception of the West Indies (other than Cuba), Central America (other than Mexico), Venezuela, Colombia, Ecuador, Peru, Bolivia, Chile, and the British, French, and Dutch Guianas.

Until about 1932, sales by the Export Company in the regions comprised by these three areas were handled out of the New York office by what was known as the C.A., W.I., and P., department, with a small group of salesmen under the direction of John D. Clarke. One of these representatives was Herbert G. Kieswetter. In 1927, when a branch was opened in Puerto Rico, L. C. Boos was sent to manage the new branch, and that island was no longer served by representatives of the department in New York.[13]

Some men in the Export Company had begun to see the possibility of greatly enlarging overseas volume by opening manufacturing plants abroad. Argentina was selected as the most promising location; in 1928 a proposal for installation of manufacturing facilities was prepared. However, the financial plight of the parent company prevented any action on this project and it was indefinitely postponed.

Export sales volume, approximately $10 million in 1923, rose to $27 million in 1929. The sales of the thirty-one foreign branches operated in 1929 represented about 14% of United States Rubber's total sales.[14]

BITTER COMPETITION ON TIRES

The record of the number of tires shipped by United States Rubber prior to 1915 is not available at this time. In 1915 and 1916, the company's shipments of original equipment tires formed 20-22% of the industry's total shipments of tires for original equipment of motor vehicles. It may be assumed that replacement tires shipped by United States Rubber in those years represented at least as large a percentage of the total shipments of replacement tires as they did in 1917. If this assumption were true, the company's combined shipments of original equipment tires and replacement tires probably totaled about 1,575,000 in 1915 and about 2,325,000 in 1916 (see Table 8).

Prior to 1918, the annual production of tires seldom appears to have been below 75-80% of the capacity of the industry.[15] Tire production caught up with demand in 1920, the first year that total shipments of pneumatic tires did not show a large gain over the preceding year. Instead, industry shipments in 1920 were about 5% below the 1919 total. The temporary slump was halted in 1921 when increasing demand for replacement tires offset the effect of the decline in factory sales of motor vehicles (down to 1,616,000 in 1921 from 2,227,000 in 1920),[16] and tire manufacturers shipped approximately 30 million pneumatic casings.

TABLE 7. Percentage of "practical capacity" used by tire industry, 1921-29.

	Practical Capacity (thousands of tires)	Percentage of Practical Capacity Used
1921	45,600	59.8
1922	46,500	88.1
1923	61,800	73.5
1924	62,000	82.0
1925	64,700	90.9
1926	68,600	87.6
1927	74,500	85.3
1928	86,700	87.1
1929	91,600	76.2

SOURCE: E. G. Nourse and Associates, *America's Capacity to Produce* (Washington: The Brookings Institution, 1934), p. 583. Data originally supplied by Leonard Smith, commercial research department, United States Rubber Company. Percentage of practical capacity was based on production and not on shipments shown in Table 8.

According to the Biennial Census of Manufactures for 1921, tires and tubes represented 63.9% of the total value of all rubber products in 1921.

However, the tire production facilities of United States Rubber and other members of the tire industry had been increased to the point where it was estimated that only 60% of the "practical physical capacity" of the tire plants was utilized that year. Pneumatic tire shipments rose to approximately 44 million in 1923, but the industry's production capacity had also risen, so that only about 74% of capacity was used (Tables 7 and 8).

No amount of sales effort, advertising, or even reduced prices at the retail level had any appreciable effect on the total consumption of tires. Consumption depended on: (1) the total number of motor vehicles in operation; (2) the quality of the tires and tubes; (3) total volume of spare tires sold with new cars; and (4) general business conditions affecting operation of motor vehicles. Consequently, a tire manufacturer faced with excess capacity could hope to achieve full operation of his facilities only if he could take business away from other tire companies; and full production was held essential for profitable operations. Since the value of tire production represented almost 70% of the total value of all goods produced by the rubber industry, the vital importance of profitable tire operations is obvious. Many of the smaller tire companies, constantly contending with wide and sudden fluctuations in the price of crude rubber while they were engaged in a desperate struggle for a share

TABLE 8. United States Rubber Company percentage of domestic shipments of tire casings, 1910-29.
(in thousands)

	Original Equipment Tires			Replacement Tires			All Tires		
	Industry Total	U.S. Rubber Company	Company Per Cent of Industry Total	Industry Total	U.S. Rubber Company	Company Per Cent of Industry Total	Industry Total	U.S. Rubber Company	Company Per Cent of Industry Total
1910	724	n.a.	n.a.	1,525	n.a.	n.a.	2,249	n.a.	n.a.
1911	797	n.a.	n.a.	2,031	n.a.	n.a.	2,828	n.a.	n.a.
1912	1,424	n.a.	n.a.	2,971	n.a.	n.a.	4,395	n.a.	n.a.
1913	1,646	n.a.	n.a.	4,022	n.a.	n.a.	5,868	n.a.	n.a.
1914	2,175	n.a.	n.a.	6,008	n.a.	n.a.	8,183	n.a.	n.a.
1915	3,584	782	21.8	7,871	n.a.	n.a.	11,455	n.a.	n.a.
1916	6,139	1,237	20.1	10,782	n.a.	n.a.	16,921	n.a.	n.a.
1917	7,086	1,011	14.3	16,754	1,684	10.1	23,840	2,695	11.3
1918	4,046	574	14.2	20,494	1,826	8.9	24,537	2,400	9.8
1919	7,249	708	9.8	23,373	2,200	9.4	30,622	2,908	9.5
1920	8,472	805	9.5	20,565	1,412	6.9	29,037	2,217	7.6
1921	8,010	899	11.2	22,480	1,695	7.5	30,490	2,594	8.5
1922	10,447	861	8.2	28,516	2,167	7.6	38,963	3,028	7.8
1923	16,226	1,199	7.4	27,751	1,943	7.0	43,977	3,142	7.1
1924	13,607	625	4.6	35,112	2,613	7.4	48,719	3,238	6.6
1925	18,265	1,377	7.5	39,391	2,748	7.0	57,656	4,125	7.2
1926	18,191	1,432	7.9	39,413	2,778	7.0	57,604	4,210	7.3
1927	15,185	862	5.7	46,415	2,659	5.7	61,600	3,521	5.7
1928	19,919	1,676	8.4	51,791	2,914	5.6	71,710	4,590	6.4
1929	19,389	1,345	6.9	47,085	3,072	6.5	66,474	4,417	6.6

n.a.—Not available.
Source: Department of commercial research, United States Rubber Company.

of the existing market, failed. Some of the larger tire manufacturers who were caught with excessive inventories of rubber and other raw materials also underwent financial reorganization during this period. By 1924, only 132 manufacturers of tire casings remained, a decline of over 30% from the number operating in the previous decade. By 1929, only 79 were in existence.[17]

Competition on Tires for Original Equipment

As the manufacture of motor vehicles became concentrated in a few very large companies, tire manufacturers found themselves dealing with powerful buyers who were well aware of the intense competition between tire companies. As a consequence, contracts for original equipment tires, more often than not, were written at prices that left little if any margin of profit.

Long-term contracts at low prices for a large volume of original equipment tires did assure steady operating schedules, however, and, if costs were allocated properly, could absorb a substantial share of overhead expense. Also, an intangible but valuable benefit from free advertising resulted from the association of the tire company's brand with the product of the motor company.

During the 1920's, United States Rubber's percentage of the total shipments of original equipment tires by the tire industry averaged only slightly more than 7.5%, a sharp drop from the share it had enjoyed during the previous ten years. In actual units, the annual average of the company's shipments of original equipment tire casings from 1920 to 1929, inclusive, was a little less than the average of its shipments for the years 1916 and 1917. At the same time, the remainder of the tire industry had more than tripled its 1916 shipments of original equipment tires.

The Replacement Tire Market

Despite the growing number of cars and their increased mileage, the need for more replacement tires was offset partially by better tires and improved highways. The rapid lengthening of tire mileage is apparent from the following data:[18]

Year Produced	Average Mileage (service given by pneumatic tire casings)
1905	2,000
1910	3,000
1915	3,500
1920	5,000

By 1920, the average life of the straight-side high pressure cord tires then being produced was said to be about eighteen months, compared with an average life of only slightly over ten months for the fabric clincher tires they had replaced.

General adoption, by 1925, of low pressure balloon tires that averaged twenty-seven month's service further reduced the number of replacement tires needed to keep motor vehicles operating.[19] Multiplying the number of pneumatic tire casings produced in each year by the average number of miles in service provides an interesting indication of the contribution that better tires made to the growth of the motor industry. Pneumatic tires produced in 1910 were in service for an estimated 7 billion "tire miles," while those produced in 1925 were estimated to be in service for 588 billion tire miles. The latter figure represents 84 times the amount of service given by tires produced in the earlier year, although the total number of pneumatic tires produced in the latter year had increased less than 25 times.[20] Average mileage of tires produced in 1925 was estimated to be well over three times the mileage received from tires produced in 1910. The lengthening service also contributed toward diminishing the share that replacement tires formed in manufacturers' total tire shipments from an average of 73.6% for 1919-20 to approximately 68.4% average for 1925-26.

The replacement tire business had been fairly profitable under conditions prevailing prior to World War I, but successive cuts in published prices in 1920 and 1921 narrowed profit margins. The competitive situation in 1921 was made even more acute by the growing popularity of cord tires in preference to the fabric tires that most companies were then equipped to manufacture in large volume. In March, 1920, George S. Shugart, then the general sales manager of the United States Tire Company, stressed the necessity of using cord tires to sell fabric tires, which still formed about two-thirds of the company's production.[21]

United States Rubber's share of the replacement tire market fell to 6.9% in 1920 and was only 7% in 1923, the year in which Charles B. Seger, the company president, said tire prices were the lowest ever known. While United States Rubber's shipments of replacement tires increased to over 2.9 million in 1928, the industry's shipments of replacement tires had increased even faster, and the company's percentage of the total volume of replacement tires had fallen to 5.6%. The severity of this loss of position in the industry may be more fully realized when it is noted that, if United States Rubber had continued to maintain its 1917 percentage of 10.1, its shipments of replacement tires in 1928 alone would have been increased by over 2.3 million units.

Weak Price Structure

The fierceness of competition among tire manufacturers is indicated by the drastic drop of about 60% in wholesale prices from 1920 to 1924. Higher prices for crude rubber, prevalent during the first few years that the Stevenson Plan was effective in restricting exports of rubber from British possessions in the Far East, kept the price of tires on a reasonably level basis, although it was still lower than in 1923 when Seger said it had been the "lowest ever known." The sharp and almost uninterrupted decline in crude rubber prices that began by December, 1925 and continued throughout 1926 was finally reflected in the price of tires in 1927, even before the Stevenson Plan was abandoned by the British government in 1928.

The following comparisons clearly illustrate the increased values enjoyed by purchasers of tires in the 1920's. In 1909, a 30″ x 3½″ passenger car tire, the size then used for a Ford car, was priced at $35.05 without tube; in 1925, a much better tire in the same size was priced at $12.30, and by 1929 the price was down to $7.45.[22] Tire prices were cut repeatedly during the last years of the 1920's. Low cost producers, such as Firestone and Goodyear Tire and Rubber Company, could reduce prices and still show a profit. United States Rubber with less efficient plants was at a serious disadvantage. Table 10 in the Appendix indicates that the wholesale prices of tires and tubes in 1928 averaged about 37% less than the average for 1926, but it has been said that discounts and concessions were so generally given by most distributors that list prices were almost meaningless at that time.

Important Shifts in Retail Distribution of Tires

Various factors contributed to bring about the loss of competitive position in the tire industry suffered by United States Rubber in the 1920's: (1) tardy recognition of consumers' strong preference for the more easily mounted straight-side tire instead of the clincher tire on which the company's production had been concentrated during the previous decade; (2) costly delays in conversion of a major portion of its production from fabric to cord tires; (3) excessive concentration of responsibility and authority in the persons of Seger and Sawyer; and (4) a competitor's capture of a large segment of the replacement tire market through a cost-plus contract with a large mass distributor. The effects of that contract, signed in March, 1926 (the details were not generally known until several years later), would be felt by the tire industry for many years.

Within a few years after the contract between the Goodyear Tire and Rubber Company and Sears Roebuck and Company was signed, the mail-order house and other mass distributors were supplying a substantial portion of the retail market for replacement tires. The independent retailers' share of the replacement tire market declined from the 98% they had enjoyed in 1922 to about 85% by 1928. Many tire retailers became discouraged and discontinued selling tires; some sold out to one or another of the major tire manufacturers.

Faced with this new situation, the Firestone Tire and Rubber Company sought to protect its share of the replacement tire market by establishing a nationwide chain of company-owned stores. The Goodyear Tire and Rubber Company inaugurated a somewhat similar program and within a few years opened about 200 retail tire stores. Each of these programs entailed the investment of several million dollars.[23]

United States Rubber continued distributing its replacement tires almost exclusively through independent retailers. Beginning about 1925, the company had organized Quick Tire Service, Inc., which, through various subsidiaries, acquired and operated retail outlets in a number of cities. These stores serviced and sold tires and accessories made by the United States Rubber System; some also sold gasoline. Among the subsidiary selling companies controlled by Quick Tire Service, Inc., during the 1920's and until these retail tire stores were sold or closed in the early 1930's, were: Atlantic Quick Tire Service, Inc.; Newsum Tire Company (Arkansas); Quick Tire Service, Inc. (Kentucky); Quick Tire Service, Inc. (New York); U.S. Tire Service, Inc.; Master Tire Service, Inc.; Royal Tire Service, Inc. (Delaware); Royal Tire Service of Michigan, Inc.; Quick Tire Service of El Paso, Inc.; Royal Tire Service of Birmingham, Inc.; and others.[24]

However, the group of about twenty-two combined service stations and retail stores operated by United States Rubber was not comparable to the national chains established by other tire manufacturers during the late 1920's. Loyalty to its dealers caused United States Rubber to suffer further loss of position at that time in the industry's sales of replacement tires.

Merger Rumors

In June, 1927, there were rumors in the market that a merger of Goodyear Tire and Rubber Company and United States Rubber Company might be effected. The purchase of about 120,000 shares of Goodyear Tire and Rubber Company stock by Edgar B. Davis, formerly a director of United States Rubber, was said to be responsible for these reports, which were denied by officers of both companies.[25] Again, on Jan. 4, 1928, the *New York Times* carried an article regarding rumors circulating among financial circles that Cyrus S. Eaton, prominent Cleveland banker and financier, was promoting a merger of United States Rubber, the Goodyear Tire and Rubber Company, and the Seiberling Tire and Rubber Company. Eaton had been active in promoting mergers of several steel companies; also, holding companies controlled by him were known to have large investments in the rubber industry. The following day the *Times* reported that officials of all three companies had denied that anyone was seeking to bring about a merger of the three firms, but the article added that the reports "persisted in Wall Street in spite of the denials."[26]

Since no merger was ever effected, it appears that the reports were exaggerated. However, it is not unlikely that both Eaton and other large investment interests would have welcomed some feasible way of lessening the ruinous competition between the large rubber companies.

NAUGATUCK CHEMICAL COMPANY

New Accelerators

After responding to the critical need for the production of aniline oil, Naugatuck Chemical had produced in 1917 or 1918 an accelerator, hexamethylene-tetramine, commonly known as "white salt." Unfortunately, it was toxic, and some workers who came in contact with it were liable to suffer dermatitis or to be affected in other ways. Dr. Sidney M. Cadwell, then on the staff of the General Laboratories, was able to develop some good nontoxic accelerators that were produced by Naugatuck Chemical. Among his inventions were the aldehyde amine accelerators; their manufacture was begun in 1922 by Naugatuck. They were suitable for high temperature vulcanization and increased the tensile strength of rubber compounds.[27]

The first operating division to adopt any of the new accelerators was the Mechanical Division, which used them in its production of insulated wire. Before the other operating divisions recognized the value of the new organic accelerators and were convinced they were safe to use, the sharp recession that started in 1920 almost marked the end of United States Rubber's interest in Naugatuck Chemical.

Sale of Chemical Company Considered

After the end of World War I surplus production of sulfuric acid and the other acids made by Naugatuck Chemical forced prices to unprofitable levels. During the same period, the managers of the operating divisions were reluctant to adopt the new accelerators offered by the company; instead, the general preference was for the slower-acting inorganic accelerators, which were familiar and were considered safer. Furthermore, the chief interests of the research chemists in the General Laboratories were then directed toward improvements in the preparation and processing of natural rubber, either dry or as liquid latex.[28]

At that point Seger and Sawyer became thoroughly dissatisfied with the management of both Naugatuck Chemical and the Rubber Regenerating Company and told Ernest Hopkinson he should take charge of both. Hopkinson went to Naugatuck and took along a young engineer in the development department, Elmer Roberts, who had been working with him and who was familiar with both plants.

Roberts later recalled that it rained very hard during their visit to Naugatuck and that the grounds of the chemical company were muddy and dirty. He said Hopkinson was not at all pleased with what he saw, and on the return trip to New York, while the two men were changing trains, Hopkinson remarked he would like to get rid of the chemical plant. Roberts' assignments had brought him into close contact with the work being done at the chemical company and at the General Laboratories, and he believed there was a good future for the new organic accelerators and other chemicals. If United States Rubber wished to sell the chemical company, Roberts thought he might be able to arrange to buy it.

Accordingly, Roberts went to friends in Wall Street and presented the situation to them, explaining that he did not know whether United States Rubber would decide to sell Naugatuck Chemical, and if they did, he did not know how much money would be required to buy it. A million dollars might be needed. His friends gave Roberts a certified check for $1 million and told him he could have another million if needed.

Roberts Appointed General Manager

The next morning Roberts told Hopkinson that if the company decided to sell Naugatuck Chemical he would like to buy it on his own account, provided he was given the patent rights to manufacture the accelerators developed by the General Laboratories. Hopkinson stared at him in disbelief, but, when shown the certified check, was convinced of the sincerity of the offer. However, Roberts' readiness to buy the chemical company caused Hopkinson to revise his appraisal of the future of that company and there was no more talk about selling Naugatuck Chemical. Instead, Hopkinson told Roberts that, because the latter had so much confidence in his ability to operate the chemical company profitably, he was just the man to be made sales manager. Roberts declined that appointment and said that if he were to assume any responsibility for its operations, he would have to be made general manager. Furthermore, he wanted several men in the General Laboratories to be transferred to Naugatuck Chemical, and he specified that production of some of the new accelerators invented by Cadwell and others, including the one adopted by the Mechanical Division for its insulated wire, should be transferred to Naugatuck. Roberts' conditions were agreed to and he became general manager of Naugatuck Chemical on July 19, 1924.[29] Shortly afterwards, funds for construction of new facilities at Naugatuck were appropriated. By 1925, thirty-four different products were being manufactured at Naugatuck in forty-four buildings.

Changing Composition of Product Line

Since most of the factories of the United States Rubber Company were either not prepared or not inclined to use the entire output of Naugatuck Chemical, the policy of selling chemicals to other rubber companies was initiated. Then, as evidence grew that the newer types of organic accelerators offered many advantages, the chemists in the company's fabricating plants found increasing opportunities for their use. For example, the development of thiocarbanilide and other organic types of accelerators made it possible to introduce bright colors in rubber footwear and bathing caps for women and children, substantially increasing the sales of such items. Bright colors also began to be used in beach bags and water toys. In the manufacture of rubber footwear, the sulfur-bearing organic accelerators were generally used in combination with an ultra accelerator.[30]

Writing in *Industrial and Engineering Chemistry* in April, 1925, Geer and Bedford estimated that, with shorter curing times, organic accelerators had saved the rubber industry a capital investment of $40 million; also, through increased mileage from tires, organic accelerators were saving consumers about $50 million annually.[31]

Acids

The production of several heavy acids was gradually discontinued as new conditions arose; for example, the introduction of stainless steel tank cars reduced the cost of transportation and made it less expensive to buy these acids than for Naugatuck Chemical to manufacture them. The first production to be discontinued was hydrofluoric acid, followed in turn by muriatic and acetic acids. Production of nitric acid, for which a new plant had been built during World War I, was continued until the 1940's. (Muriatic and nitric acids, after their production was discontinued, were still handled by the chemical company as part of its service.)

Despite stiff competition on sulfuric acid, Naugatuck Chemical continued to produce and market it. Where the quantity used by customers was large enough, Naugatuck Chemical offered to install storage tanks at its own expense on the customer's property. This service assured the customer of having an uninterrupted supply and at the same time enabled Naugatuck Chemical to make deliveries in economical quantities. Obviously, it also tended to keep the customer "married" to the source. While the competitive situation was such that there was little direct profit in the business of sulfuric acid, it did absorb overhead and was considered helpful to the over-all operations of the chemical company.

Antioxidants

The General Laboratories and Naugatuck Chemical pioneered in the development of organic antioxidants. The first successful antioxidant was offered commercially by the chemical company in 1924, and Sunproof, a wax that "bloomed" on the surface of the finished product and afforded protection against ozone, was placed on the market in 1926.[32] The first commercial antioxidant introduced after Sunproof was known as vGB and was the invention of S. M. Cadwell. (Largely because of his invention of vGB, Cadwell was awarded the Goodyear Gold Medal.)[33]

The development of organic antioxidants marked a noteworthy advance in the rubber industry. The antioxidants tended to minimize the harmful effects of light, heat, oxidation, and ozone in the air. They also tended to retard flex-cracking (the cracking of a rubber product along a line that is subjected to repeated flexing or on a surface of the rubber that is wrinkled or folded for a prolonged period). Without organic antioxidants balloon tires could not have been successfully introduced.

Labels

An interesting incident contributed to the introduction in 1926 of two-color labels made from natural rubber latex. On a visit to Naugatuck,

Elmer Roberts saw a young philatelist at the plant admiring some postage stamps and asked him if he had ever thought of making stamps out of rubber. On Roberts' next trip to the plant this young man showed him several experimental labels made from latex, whereupon Roberts asked the sales manager, E. B. Curtis, if he could sell the Passaic plant on the idea of using such labels on some of its products. Curtis did so, and Naugatuck Chemical began producing rubber labels. Hopkinson, however, did not think the chemical company should be in the business of making labels and ruled that production should be transferred to the Providence plant. However, that plant did not want to take on the label business, so it remained with the Naugatuck company, which developed a large and profitable volume on rubber labels.

Lotols

Experimentation to find other opportunities for direct utilization of rubber latex had been carried on for several years by the General Laboratories. Under Hopkinson's urging, research and development work in colloidal chemistry, particularly with respect to latex, had also been conducted there by W. A. Gibbons and others without arousing much interest on the part of company executives. In 1927, production of heat-concentrated latex-base compounds under the trade name Lotol was begun on a small scale by Naugatuck Chemical. Then, in the fall of 1928, a letter from Collins and Aikman, who were looking for a low-cost backing that would be satisfactory for the carpeting used in automobiles, was brought to Roberts' attention. Naugatuck Chemical was able to offer them a choice of several of the low-cost latex-base compounds that had been developed, and these compounds proved to be so well-suited for their purpose that they offered to contract for a large quantity to be produced over the next two years. This offer enabled Roberts to obtain approval for construction in 1929 of a new building for production of Lotols. Lotol compounds for rubberizing fabrics could be offered with two to three times the rubber content found in ordinary rubber cements. Also, Lotols could be formulated so that they would not harden or crack while in storage. Since the late 1920's, the production of Lotols has further expanded into a wide variety of latex adhesive and penetrating compounds used in the textile, paper, leather shoe, and other industries, as well as in the rubber industry.

As a result of all the expansion into new fields during the 1920's, United States Rubber tripled its sales of chemicals. What once had been referred to as a "very small tail on a very big dog" was being readied for even greater expansion in the following decade.

OPERATING DEPARTMENTS SEEK IMPROVED PERFORMANCE

Progress in Cost Reduction

Pressure vulcanization and organic accelerators, introduced prior to World
War I, made important contributions to lower costs of all rubber products in the 1920's. More efficient millroom equipment, notably the Banbury mixer and larger calenders, also helped cut manufacturing costs.
But as a result of the scattering of production of goods among numerous
multistoried factories, United States Rubber found only limited opportunity to introduce cost-saving techniques such as streamlined layouts,
more efficient processes, and labor-saving equipment. Despite these handi-
caps, progress was made on several fronts, notably in the Tire Division,
where introduction during the early twenties of the flat-band method of
making tires was an outstanding achievement. The plants making mechanical rubber goods, although having to struggle with antiquated buildings and a multiplicity of dissimilar items, managed some savings in
manufacturing costs. Many major economies, however, could not be
accomplished until most manufacture of mechanical goods was concentrated at Passaic in the early thirties.

New Methods Tried

In the period following World War I, the footwear factories of the United
States Rubber System were also trying many new methods of making rubber boots and shoes in an effort to reduce the cost of labor, which averaged 29% of the total production cost of rubber footwear. This percentage compared with only 16% for wages in the rubber tire industry
and with 22% for wages in manufacture of all other rubber goods.[34]
Comparable figures for United States Rubber are not available, but an
undated copy of a talk probably delivered in 1920 at Naugatuck by
G. L. Lawrence during a Footwear Division training course included
charts showing:

	Percentage of Total Production Cost
Direct labor	32.6
Labor expense (foremen, chauffeurs, laborers, clerks)	7.4
Factory expense	8.2
Production material	51.8

In the same talk the comparable percentage of total production costs represented by labor was said to average 12% for the leather shoe industry
and 15.4% for all principal industries.[35] The lower percentage of total

costs represented by labor in leather shoe manufacture was affected by (1) higher costs of leather, the principal raw material, and (2) mechanization of many operations necessarily performed by hand in making rubber footwear.

The larger percentage of total production costs represented by labor in the manufacture of rubber footwear became even more important for United States Rubber because of its product mix. In 1929, the breakdown of the total number of wage earners employed in the rubber products industry was: tires and tubes, 55.8%; rubber footwear, 17.2%; and all other rubber products, 27.0%.[36] Directly comparable figures for United States Rubber are not available, but in 1925, the percentage of all wage and salary personnel employed in each of the three major operating divisions of the company was: tires, 26.0%; footwear, 47.2%; and all other rubber products, 26.8%.[37]

It may be safely concluded that in 1929 rubber footwear still represented a substantially larger share of the total production of United States Rubber than of the rubber products industry as a whole. Thus, United States Rubber's cost of sales tended to be higher than other members of the "Big Four" of the tire industry, but, of course, the proportion of footwear production was not the entire reason. Other factors previously mentioned contributed to these higher costs.

The principles established in the footwear plants before World War I by Myron Clark (p. 129) continued to bear fruit, but many of the processes and operations common in the rubber footwear industry during most of the 1920's were inefficient and costly. One of the younger men who had been stimulated by Clark's management philosophy was Walter H. Norton, who in 1919 had succeeded Henry ("Harry") S. Marlor as superintendent of the G.M.R. plant at Naugatuck. In 1921, Norton was transferred to Williamsport as factory manager of the Lycoming Rubber Company's footwear plant. Within a short time he and his staff initiated a comprehensive program of cost reduction; its first step was the establishment of both factory-wide and departmental objectives, and the policies governing adoption of programs to attain them. Included in the latter were reduction of process time, material savings, motion studies, better layouts, and savings through better use of floor space. Along with the cost reduction programs, efforts were made to improve service to customers and the quality of the merchandise. When changes were made in any area of the operations, the effect on other areas was studied. If it was found that further improvement in performance of any operation depended upon progress in some other field, staff members tackled the problem. Common knowledge of long-range objectives and good team work directed toward their attainment produced results, despite temporary setbacks and disappointments.

Much of this progress had been made possible as a result of pressure cures, which not only shortened vulcanization time but greatly reduced losses formerly incurred from damaged footwear or rejected stocks. Other advantages accruing from pressure cures, organic accelerators, and the development of the ammonia cure are discussed in the section on research and development (page 230).

Progress toward reduction of costs of manufacturing rubber footwear was badly hampered by the continued production of numerous brands; the problems of this practice have been discussed in the preceding chapter. To solve these problems, United States Rubber took steps in the mid-twenties to have all its footwear factories use identical lasts and similar specifications, and to have all fabrics procured through a central purchasing department. Other action taken during the same period substantially improved the quality of the product and did much to establish the U.S. label as the mark of high-grade rubber footwear.

Several plants in the Footwear Division began establishing special departments during the 1920's for the subassembly of parts for footwear. The New Brunswick plant experimented with a system of moving shoes through the making operations in racks like those which were commonly used in leather shoe factories, but found the handling expense prohibitive. Nor had many long, time-consuming movements by operators been eliminated. Standardized units for tables and racks were employed by the Williamsport factory, but the system did not show promise until a new method was devised for delivering lasts in sequence and in waist-high baskets for easy handling. By 1927, the Candee plant was making four-buckle arctics with teams of three men working on each side of a belt conveyor; the belt carried the finished arctics to a "presser" who had special equipment for pressing the outsoles firmly. Harold N. Barrett, who in 1962 became president of the United States Tire Company, was a presser on one of these lines in 1927. In the same year Candee also used similar "two-point teams" for varnished shoes.

About 1928, the American Rubber Company began experimenting in its Cambridge plant with a conveyor on which shoe lasts were carried. Girls were stationed at each side; each one performed a different operation on the rubber shoe as the lasts proceeded along the assembly line. The last with the finished shoe was then removed from the conveyor and placed on a "car" to be taken either to the vulcanizer or to a varnish-dipping tank if a bright finish were desired.

In 1928, the Williamsport plant was leading the other footwear factories of the company in adoption of improved methods and achievement of lower costs. Norton, factory manager at Williamsport, was then brought back to Naugatuck in the same capacity.

Efforts to Control Inventory

Under the management policies of Seger and Sawyer, branch managers were given great latitude in estimating the sales requirements of their distributing branches. Since they did not wish to run any chance of being short of needed merchandise at the height of the seasonal demand for rubber products, whether tires, footwear, or other rubber items, it is not surprising that branch inventories were often larger than necessary. If the winter proved to be milder than expected, or if there were less snowfall than normal in the populous sections of the country, these inventories of rubber footwear were usually excessive. Even if the branch managers reduced their orders for new production, factories would frequently still be scheduled to operate at full capacity as long as possible in order to achieve lower manufacturing cost per unit. The excess production would then be distributed among the branches although, in many cases, a large part of the goods would have to be liquidated at a considerable discount from the established prices—often at less than the actual manufacturing cost.

For example, in 1926, there was a heavy demand for a women's low, cotton jersey snap gaiter with a self-cuff. During the spring of 1927, dealers placed large advance orders for this style, and by late fall United States Rubber's footwear factories were producing it at the rate of 18,000 twelve-pair cases a week. However, in the winter of 1927-28 the snowstorms did not come early enough in the more populous sections to create a large volume of reorders. By Jan. 1, 1928, the Footwear Division had 72,000 cases of these gaiters in stock, and Needham tried to have production stopped. He was not successful, but eventually the factories reduced manufacture to 12,000 cases a week, the minimum production they declared they must have. Meanwhile, a new all-rubber style gaiter for women, introduced by two other companies, had become popular, and by the end of 1929, the Footwear Division owned an inventory of 100,000 cases of women's cloth gaiters. Before this inventory was liquidated, some had to be sold for as little as 25¢ a pair, Needham said.

For several years, the person in the New York office responsible for

preparation of production orders for rubber footwear did not have intimate knowledge of branch operations. The factories were instructed to
pack the production in standard assortments of sizes in each shipping
case, and these assortments were not adjusted to keep the stock in a
branch warehouse properly balanced. Consequently, branches frequently
accumulated surpluses of smaller sizes that were not wanted by their
customers.

At one time, while he was struggling to have production brought in
line with the sales requirements, Needham was asked by Sawyer why the
Mishawaka factory was able to get a better rate of inventory turn-over
than the other factories. Needham reported he had heard that Mishawaka
had installed punch-card tabulating equipment to record orders and control inventory. Sawyer then called a staff meeting to consider adoption
of this system but was informed by the financial manager of branch store
sales that such a system would cost United States Rubber $200,000. In-
stead, one person was hired in each branch to keep a pen-and-ink record
of orders. Needham recalled that the hand-compiled record cost $60,000
a year, and it took so long to compile the information that it was not
of much use. After Needham became general manager of the division in
1929, he had tabulating equipment installed at Naugatuck.[38]

The inventory problems in footwear manufacture, compounded by the
wide range of styles and sizes, were common with other rubber products
prior to 1930. The Detroit tire plant, for example, had a large inventory
of obsolete tires in 1928. Late in that year, William M. Dougherty, previously of the commercial research department, was transferred to the
department of tire sales where he reported to L. D. Tompkins, who had
been placed in charge of the Tire Company's operations in December.
Under Tompkins' direction, Dougherty was placed in charge of production scheduling, but he had no control over distribution to the branches.
As in the case of footwear, some branch managers ordered wisely, but
many did not, and often the inventory of certain types or sizes of tires
was in the wrong place when it was badly needed elsewhere by other
branches.[39] Dougherty's efforts to correct this situation laid the foundation for the company-wide adoption in 1930 of the sales-production coordination system, which will be treated in fuller detail in Chapter VII.

Production Control

Meanwhile, during the 1920's, production control (known as central control until about 1925) was improved in the footwear plants. For example,
girls operating adding machines and trained in the use of material con-

version charts took the ticketed orders for different shoes and accumulated the total number of pieces of any given fabric that were to be cut with the same die. A cutting ticket was then issued to the operators of beam presses and clickers, showing for each part (1) the specified material to be laid on the table in front of the cutter; (2) the standard number of plies to be laid, (3) the identification number of the cutting die set to be used, and (4) the number of cuts to be made. Mass production cutting was thus possible, and the cutters were able to devote their entire workday to the efficient operation of their equipment. Cutting scrap was reduced, and fewer beam presses and clickers were required for the same volume of production; consequently, both floor space and labor were saved.

As the production control department gained experience, the principles of efficient planning and organization were applied to other operations. Production control told the stores department the amount of each material required for the scheduled production and told the plant superintendent how many operators would be needed in each department of the factory. Important savings in costs were thus accomplished, although full benefits could not be attained while the system's production was scattered in so many plants.

The three different approaches to the over-all problems of manufacturing costs, production control, sales-production-coordination, and the shift from individual makers to conveyorized production by multiple-operator teams were laying the foundations for important savings when production would be concentrated, during the 1930's, in a few plants.

Early Moves to Increase Office Efficiency

Soon after the close of World War I, the Mishawaka Woolen Mfg. Co. began an intensive effort to improve its methods of processing orders. The company's products, BALL-BAND rubber and woolen and leather footwear, were being handled by about 50,000 retailers, and since Mishawaka was not then operating any distributing branches, the first general snowstorm of each winter brought an avalanche of rush orders, as well as urgent telegrams and long distance telephone calls from customers. (Distribution of BALL-BAND footwear in New England and greater New York City was handled by Mishawaka's only wholesale account, Dunham Brothers' Company, Brattleboro, Vt. For many years retailers in all other territories were serviced directly from Mishawaka.)

Merchants could not afford to be caught short of rubber footwear in the first few days of the "rubber rush" that usually ensued immediately after the first heavy snowstorm. If Mishawaka hoped to continue as the chief supplier of rubber footwear to any store, it had to convince the merchant that it was to his advantage to send his orders to Mishawaka, rather than to branch warehouses operated by Mishawaka's competitors, or to wholesalers who sold other brands.

Mishawaka had an important advantage over competition in that *all* of its inventory was concentrated at the Mishawaka plant, whereas most other rubber companies were obliged to carry stock in numerous branches. Furthermore, Mishawaka was strategically located in northern Indiana, not too far from the nation's population center. But these advantages were of little value if rush orders were not filled with speed and accuracy.

To accomplish this goal, a number of steps were taken by the company to begin the systematic reorganization of office and warehousing methods. Brief discussion of each step will give a general idea of the extent of the programs.

(1) Over-all responsibility for all phases of order handling was vested in one man.

(2) Order forms were printed to show every 15-minute period from 7:00 a.m. to 5:00 p.m., each operation was given an identifying number, and each person performing any operation (from the mail opening, through sales records, interpreting, credit, stock records, order entry, casing, and dispatching) was required to show the time he had passed the order to the next operation. These time records were reviewed frequently during the day. Any indication that a bottleneck or unnecessary delay was occurring at any point was investigated immediately, and steps were taken to eliminate it, usually by temporarily shifting personnel.

(3) Physical rearrangement of departments and of operations within departments streamlined the flow of orders and eliminated much backtracking.

(4) It was discovered that the total time consumed in actual performance of the several operations on an order was relatively small compared to far longer periods when orders were lying idle waiting to be worked on or to be sent to the next operation. Elimination of idle time was found to be more effective than merely trying to hasten the actual clerical operations in the effort to speed the flow of orders.

(5) Installations of various conveying devices, special belts, carriers, and tubes followed.

(6) Staggered starting times for certain departments, from 6:30 to 8:00 a.m., were instituted.

As a result of these steps, the warehouse office received by 8:00 a.m. a good stream of the "at once" orders that had arrived that morning. Many small orders were entirely processed by the several office departments within less than one hour. As a general rule, approximately 85 to over 90% of all "at once" orders, including those received in the afternoon mail, were shipped during the same calendar day, and the invoice mailed by the following noon. Obviously, on days of heaviest demand such promptness was impossible, since sometimes as many as 3,000 to 5,000 orders were received on the first Monday immediately after the first big snowstorm of the season. (Mishawaka's record of "at once" orders received from retailers, Monday through Friday of one week, was slightly more than 15,000.)

Meanwhile, a punch-card tabulating department for recording bookings by stock number, shipping month, salesman's territory, county, town, and individual dealer replaced the hand counts formerly kept, and substantial savings in costs were made. Clerical expense was also reduced through adoption of new equipment and methods in the stock-records department.

An incentive wage payment plan was specially devised for order-filling operations in the warehouse, resulting in speedier dispatch of orders, large savings in labor, as well as better earnings for the workers.

The program just outlined was the first successful attempt in the rubber footwear industry to ship customers' small fill-in orders immediately so that the goods could be received by dealers in time to satisfy consumers' current demands. Naturally such an extensive program was not completed in one season, or even in two or three years, nor was it the work of only one or two individuals. But the early accomplishments served to stimulate active participation by all department heads, who became increasingly cost conscious.

During the late 1920's, at a time when prices of some items in the line were less than 50¢ a pair, a careful calculation of Mishawaka's average over-all cost of processing and billing an order for one pair of footwear indicated a 50¢ minimum cost. Much later, this type of cost analysis led to adoption of a nominal, but insufficient, service charge on small orders. The cost of handling the total volume of business received annually from small accounts was also scrutinized. It soon became evident that orders for many accounts were being handled at a net loss. Steps were taken to stop soliciting orders from such accounts unless satisfactory evidence of potential growth justified continued sales effort.

No scientific methods-engineering studies were made in the Mishawaka office prior to about 1925; even when such work was undertaken it was rather primitive, judged by present standards. However, such studies served to point up the possibility of further savings in office procedures. Studies were continued and intensified in the 1930's, when more sophisticated approaches to the reduction of clerical expense were introduced;

one noteworthy result was that methods engineering became recognized throughout the United States Rubber Company as an essential function of office management.

RESEARCH AND DEVELOPMENT UNDER SEGER

Ernest Hopkinson, a patent lawyer, first became connected with the New York Belting & Packing Company in 1897 and was in charge of development for that company when the Rubber Goods Manufacturing Company was acquired by United States Rubber in 1905. He had a very active mind and was prolific in ideas for improvements in the product and in methods of manufacture. During Samuel P. Colt's administration, Hopkinson reportedly objected to insufficient interest in development and said that he did not propose to expend his time and talents unless he had an opportunity to gain some personal benefit from his work. Therefore, he had prepared a paper for Colt's signature, authorizing Hopkinson to apply for patents in his own name without assigning his rights to United States Rubber or to any of its subsidiaries. Colt, it is said, granted permission, presumably on the basis that Hopkinson had been employed to do legal work, not invention.

This agreement and the circumstances reportedly behind it explain Hopkinson's obtaining patents in his own name and collecting royalties from United States Rubber on some of them. Several years later, the agreement was revised to grant "shop rights" to United States Rubber. During World War I there was an interruption of development work by United States Rubber, but on April 17, 1919, Hopkinson was placed in charge of development and patents.

Flat-Band Method of Making Tires

As far back as Jan. 4, 1917, Hopkinson had filed an application in his own name for a patent on the method of making tires by what later came to be known as the flat-band method. He was subsequently granted other patents covering improved equipment for this process. It has been said that Hopkinson directed Charles B. Seger's attention to the equipment being designed to build tires by the flat-band method, but that Seger refused to authorize the expenditures needed to perfect the process and the equipment involved. It is probable that Seger did not visualize the important increases in labor productivity that would follow the adoption of the method. Perhaps, however, he knew that one patent on it had been issued to Hopkinson, that at least one other application had been filed, and that Hopkinson was in a position to claim a royalty for use of the invention. Possibly that knowledge made Hopkinson's proposal less interesting to Seger. Possibly Seger was influenced by advice from others in the company who resented Hopkinson's benefitting personally from patents taken in his own name, whereas they, in accordance with the conditions of their employment, were obliged to assign their patents to the company or to one of its subsidiaries, whenever such inventions were made in connection with their work for the company. In any event, Hopkinson is reported to have personally supplied substantially all of the out-of-pocket expense incurred in the development of the invention. It is a matter of record that, until the early 1930's, Hopkinson was paid a royalty by United States Rubber under contract for the right to use the flat-band process.

By 1923, the company was proclaiming in news releases and in its national advertising that the flat-band method was one of "three great recent improvements" in tire manufacture (Figure 41). "Scientific precision in laying the plies" was said to ensure uniform strength with all cords laid at accurately controlled angles and with equal tension so that "every cord bears an equal share of the load."[40] Prior to Hopkinson's invention, all pneumatic tires for automobiles or motor trucks had been built by the "core process," in which the carcass of the tire, consisting of plies of bias cut fabric impregnated with rubber, the rubber tread, and other parts, was built upon a metal form shaped to correspond to the cavity of the tire. Considerable stitching down of the parts by means of stitching wheels or disks was required. The core process was slow, expensive, and required skilled operators who needed several weeks of training before they acquired sufficient dexterity.

The importance of the invention of the flat-band process and the marked increase in labor productivity that followed its adoption merit an abbreviated description of the process as outlined in the patent application. The various layers of rubberized fabric and rubber, or rubberized tire cords and rubber, were laminated on a revolving collapsible drum in a substantially flat pulley-band shape of the thickness and weight needed to produce a completed tire of the desired dimensions. The angle at which each of the cords in this first ply was placed with respect to the edges of the pulley-shaped band was determined precisely so that, when the tire was finally shaped, each cord would be under equal tension. The cords in each successive ply ran in the opposite direction of the cords in the previously applied layer of cords.

When the prescribed layers of tire cord fabric had been applied, the positioning of wire bead rings was controlled by guides built in the machine. Then the edges of fabric were folded over the bead, and other layers of fabric and rubber and tread rubber were applied. The tire, looking much like a flat pulley belt, was then removed and delivered to a vacuum shaping machine where it was sucked out to shape. Toe rings were then clamped onto the beads of the tire to hold it in shape for curing. At this point, the tire was aged for a day or two before being placed in one of several molds stacked and bolted in a "French" hydraulic press, all within a steam chamber. At first, each tire was connected to a manifold through which incombustible carbon dioxide gas under 200 pounds pressure was forced into the tire cavity, while steam of 40 pounds pressure was injected into the vulcanizing chamber. The cure lasted about an hour. Many problems, including leaky manifolds, loss of pressure, and blistered inner plies of the tires demanded solutions. Later the process was changed and an inflatable heavy rubber tube, called a "curing bag," was inserted into the tire preparatory to vulcanization. During the vulcanizing process, hot water and steam were injected into the bag as well as into the curing chamber, forcing the tire tread and carcass against the engraved inner surfaces of the mold, thereby giving the desired shape and surface design to the tire. At the end of the cure the steam chamber was flooded with cold water to cool the molds; then they were hoisted onto an iron rail table where the tires were removed. At the time of its adoption, the flat-band process marked an important advance in the art of building automobile tires, although many improvements in methods, accelerators, equipment, and material handling were developed after that time.

A study of the productivity of labor in those manufacturing industries that had shown the most rapid increases during the period from 1914 to 1927 disclosed the following: [41]

	Percentage of Increase
Tires	292
Automobiles	178
Petroleum refining	82
Flour milling	59
Iron and steel	55

Between 1921 and 1924, the index of labor productivity, as measured by tires per man-hour, increased by over 52%. Boris Stern, who was commissioned by the Bureau of Labor Statistics in 1932 to survey labor productivity in the tire industry, observed that the shift to the flat-band process was the most important major change in the manufacture of

41. Improvements in tire manufacture.

41a. Flat-band process of tire making. Top row (left), the tire is built on a flat drum and (right) the breaker strip is added; bottom (left), the band is placed on a shaping machine and (right) shaped by inflation.

41b.   Hopkinson tower for spraying latex on plantation in Sumatra.

41c.   Removal of sheet rubber from oven where it had been dried and smoked for four days. This equipment was in use on the company plantation in Malaya.

pneumatic tires and was an important reason for the great growth in labor productivity. Writing as late as 1940, another student of the industry said that the flat-band invention was the only innovation in the process of tire manufacture during the previous quarter of a century that could "properly be considered revolutionary."[42]

Due to the development of assembly line techniques in the young automobile industry, one might expect its gain in labor productivity between 1914 and 1927 to be greater than in the tire industry. However, the opposite was true, and this fact tends to support the views here stated regarding the importance of Hopkinson's invention of the flat-band process.

Somewhat similar methods had been previously developed for use in the manufacture of bicycle tires, but Hopkinson appears to have been the first to apply the principle to the building of automobile tires that were both larger and heavier. In so doing, he worked out the complete process. He is therefore entitled to a great deal of credit for the benefits which accrued to the whole tire industry. (The validity of the Hopkinson patent was later contested. See Chapter VII.)

Immersion of Tire Cords in Latex

The second "great recent improvement" referred to in the advertisements and news releases of 1923 was the immersion of the tire cords in latex, resulting in a more positive bond between the cords. Formerly, the cords had been held together by cross-threads. Experiments to reduce tire failures by eliminating these cross-threads had been carried on for several years by United States Rubber before the web fabric of cords immersed in latex was far enough developed for commercial production. This one development was claimed to have increased tire mileage by 30%.[43] According to the advertisements, this important improvement in tire construction was made possible by the fact that the United States Rubber Company's plantations provided a dependable supply of latex.

Tire Tubes

In 1926, United States Rubber adopted a new method of curing tubes for tires in water under high pressure at steam heat. This method eliminated minute bubbles in the rubber compound that might cause failure of the tube in service.

Sprayed Rubber

The third "great improvement" was the development of sprayed rubber. On Jan. 16, 1920, Hopkinson applied for a patent on converting rubber latex to dry rubber by spraying the latex in a chamber filled with heated air. In the application for patent, which was finally granted on July 25, 1922, it was stressed that the spraying process would prevent the loss of solid contents of the latex, which were not obtained when the latex was coagulated by conventional methods.[44] The patent stated that spraying would provide approximately 10% greater yield of dry rubber, that no chemical change occurred in the rubber, that the quality of the rubber would be materially improved, and that the tensile strength and resistance to abrasion would be increased by about 20%.

The first experimental spray tower was erected at the Peerless plant in New Durham, N.J., where the method was tested and improvements were made in the spraying device and in the construction of the heated chamber. In 1922, the first of the "Hopkinson towers" was erected at the headquarters of the rubber plantation at Kisaran, Sumatra. Latex was taken to the port for shipment only if a ship was in the harbor. If no ship was in port or if storage space was not available, the latex was taken directly to the spraying tower. By 1923, United States Rubber's growing demands for latex exceeded the quantity available from the company's plantations. Purchases of latex were made from several other plantations located in the same general area of Sumatra.

The first spray tower erected on the plantations, a wooden structure, burned and was replaced by metal towers in 1923. These towers were somewhat larger at the bottom than at the top. Rubber latex was poured in a steady stream on a rapidly revolving disc located at the top of a heated chamber, about 30 feet high and 30 feet square. A strong blast of hot air, into which ammonia was injected, dehydrated the latex spray as it fell. The dried particles were deposited as a fluffy, tawny-colored mass on removable sections of the floor, which were mounted on low casters. This spongy mass was then transferred to a hydraulic press, which compressed it into a solid block of crude rubber weighing from 150 to 200 pounds.

It was claimed that the spray method retained colloidal proteins that added strength to the solid rubber produced, and that decomposition of these proteins was immediately arrested and prevented by the blast of hot air. Under the best of native methods (Brazilian), or other plantation methods of coagulating latex and preparing rubber for shipment, varying conditions of weather and temperature resulted in varying degrees of uniformity in the rubber as it reached the manufacturer. Under Hopkinson's method, sprayed rubber reached the factories with complete uniformity, which eliminated the necessity of blending batches of rubber from different shipments. It was also found that sprayed rubber vulcan-

ized at a much faster rate than sheet or crepe rubber.[45] The most attractive achievement, however, was the increased yield of rubber by
the spray process. In 1925 alone, this increase amounted to 1,600,000
pounds.

Much publicity was given to the development of sprayed rubber; in a
press release dated Jan. 15, 1926, the United States Rubber Company
stated that practically all the 20 million pounds of rubber received from
the company's plantations in 1925 had been in the form of sprayed rubber, "a development exclusively owned by the Company."[46] However,
sprayed rubber was not destined to play the important role first prophe-
sied for it. Not only did it carry a premium price over No. 1, ribbed
smoked sheet, and even over No. 1, pale crepe, but the fact that it did
retain certain organic nonrubber ingredients contributed to product failures, particularly in tires, sundries, and insulated wire.

Sprayed rubber (or L-S) was also more difficult to process in the mixing mills, especially the type of L-S first produced in which ammonia
had been used to prevent coagulation. (Later, the ammonia was replaced by formaldehyde, which produced a softer L-S that could be
processed with less difficulty.) So, while L-S was exceptionally tough,
the disadvantages outweighed the advantages in most cases. Urged by
Hopkinson, United States Rubber factories used large quantities of L-S
for a time, but various plants began to revert to the use of conventional
types of rubber and to place orders with the General Rubber Company
for rubbers that had been prepared by conventional methods. Meanwhile,
the plantations, influenced by Hopkinson's enthusiastic promotion of L-S,
were continuing to produce a very high percentage of it. In August,
1928, the spraying plants on the plantations were reported to be operating twenty-four hours a day "to keep up with the demand for L-S."

Possibly because they were reluctant to tell Hopkinson that they had
discontinued the use of L-S in the manufacture of tires, the United
States Tire Company is said to have continued to accept large consign-
ments of L-S until there were several million pounds in storage.[47] Meanwhile, the General Rubber Company was compelled to go into the open
market to cover the factories' requirements of smoked ribbed sheet, pale
crepe, and other conventional types of crude rubber. This lack of coordination between the actual consumption by the factories and the types
of rubber being produced by the plantations was partially responsible for
creation of excessively heavy inventories, which resulted in heavy losses
on crude rubber owned by United States Rubber when the market price
broke in 1928.

In view of the limited applications for L-S and its many disadvantages, the company's plantations eventually curtailed production of sprayed rubber and finally discontinued it entirely at the start of World War II.

It frequently happens, however, that unanticipated benefits are obtained as an indirect result of a new development; such was the case with sprayed rubber. Dr. John McGavack said that, under his direction, work was undertaken which resulted in the spraying of a multicreamed latex. Many tons of purified rubber produced by this method (on which a number of patents were issued) were sold at a premium to other companies making insulated wire. This business, developed in the early thirties, continued until synthetic rubber displaced natural rubber for this purpose.

Costly Mistakes

From today's vantage point, it seems obvious that the development department or the General Laboratories should have been provided with funds, personnel, and facilities so that they could have not only analyzed the dry rubber, but also conducted extensive service tests of products incorporating the compounds in which L-S was used. If the thorough testing procedures adopted by United States Rubber's laboratories soon after Davis became president had been followed in the 1920's, the tests probably would have disclosed the harmful effects eventually caused by certain proteins and other organic nonrubber ingredients that remained in the dehydrated floc. Possibly such a testing program would have also identified the most promising areas for use of sprayed rubber. Management undoubtedly would have made decisions that would have avoided the large losses that resulted from rushing into large-scale production and use of L-S.

A similar observation may be made regarding the Tire Division's continued use for several years of certain fillers in tire tread compounds that added nothing to tread life. During the early years, white had been the preferred color for pneumatic tires for passenger cars. In order to introduce a distinctive change in color, carbon black treads were first used in 1912 by another manufacturer, who discovered that the addition of a relatively high percentage of carbon black increased the compound's tensile strength and resistance to abrasive wear.[48] The United States Tire Company continued for several years to produce the bulk of its tires from white compounds and used large quantities of zinc oxide for the pigment. Zinc oxide was an excellent toughener for tire tread compounds, but it was expensive. The Tire Company, shortly after World War I, asked the General Laboratories to try to find some material that would be a satisfactory substitute for zinc oxide, either in whole or in part. Refined clays had long been used by the rubber industry as inert fillers to stiffen, harden, and reinforce some other rubber compounds, and the General Laboratories tested over 200 samples of clays from England and the United States. Finally a clay from a site near Leesburg, Fla., was reported as meeting the requirements of the Tire Company, and the land containing the deposit was acquired.

At first, the clay was sent to the Naugatuck Chemical Company's plant where it was pulverized. Hopkinson decided that a fine dehydrated powdered clay could be best obtained by spraying a slurry of the clay in a heated chamber, using much the same method that was being used to produce sprayed rubber. Following a successful pilot plant operation, a large spraying tower was built on the Florida property.

The leading article in the company house organ, "U.S." Rubber News, for Sept. 15, 1924, proclaimed that this process had revolutionized the preparation of clay for use in rubber compounds, giving the company a finer product as well as a less expensive one. Referring to the search for a substitute for the more expensive zinc oxide, the article stated that all rubber manufacturers had turned to the use of clay. The spray process produced an entirely dehydrated clay powder of very fine particles, free from any lumps, and superior to anything previously produced, according to the author of the article.

The powdered clay worked satisfactorily in the high pressure tires that were being manufactured in the early 1920's, but it was not suited for use in the balloon tires that became popular about 1924. The compounds in which the clay had been used did not stand up under the constant flexing of the balloon tires with their lower air pressures. Bad tire failures resulted; the clay in the tire treads was replaced by carbon black; the Florida operation was discontinued, and the property was sold.

A development department with adequate funds and moral support, and governed by the modern operating principles that were followed during and ever since Davis' administration, would either (1) have found ways to improve each compound before it was adopted commercially, or (2) would have prevented large-scale usage, thus avoiding the costly adjustments and damaged reputation for high quality that the Tire Division temporarily suffered in the mid-twenties.

That such steps were not taken earlier in the 1920's by the development department may have been due to excessive reliance on the limited

testing program then conducted by the Tire Division. Moreover, throughout Seger's tenure of office the appropriations for both the development
department and the General Laboratories were meager. On two separate
occasions during Seger's administration laboratory personnel was drastically reduced. As a result, it was frequently necessary to use graduate
chemists for routine jobs when they should have been engaged in important research and analysis. In years with unsatisfactory profits or even
deficits it was almost impossible to obtain approval of appropriation requests for adequate testing programs. Furthermore, for the same reasons,
some tests that indicated possible weaknesses in the product were not
followed up.

A greater appreciation of the valuable contributions to profit of a
properly functioning development department was evident soon after
Davis became president of the company in 1929. Meanwhile, about
1925, under the direction of S. P. Thacher, steps to re-establish the
quality standing of the company's tires had been undertaken, and by
1929 considerable progress had been made. Under Sidney Cadwell's
guidance, that progress was intensified until U.S. tires were again recognized for outstanding quality.

Rubber Latex Thread

Cut rubber thread had been made for many years by plants of the Revere Rubber Company and the Mechanical Fabric Company, both in
Providence, R.I. Hopkinson early sought to work out a satisfactory
method of forming a continuous thread from rubber latex. Presumably
his interest in this project sprang from knowledge that the tensile strength
of rubber products made from pure natural latex is considerably greater
than that of similar items made from dry rubber, such as smoked ribbed
sheet, pale crepe, and other types of rubber. When the proper antioxidants and other toughening ingredients are added to the vulcanizing
agents in the latex compound to protect against rapid aging and to increase tear resistance, the finished product can be given superior qualities. This is particularly true of a round thread made from natural latex
as compared with a square thread cut from sheet rubber. But it was not
easy to devise equipment that would handle fine filaments of unvulcanized latex.

In April, 1923, as rubber latex was becoming available in commercial
quantities, the development department applied for a patent on an experimental machine that extruded a fine round thread of latex through
nozzles with openings approximately .05 inches in diameter. It was im-

mediately coagulated by passage through a bath of diluted acetic acid. From that bath, the latex thread was carried through other baths of cold and heated glycerol followed by passage through cold water. Next the thread was delivered onto a drying conveyor, and into a bath of vulcanizing solution, after which it was passed onto more drying conveyors to drive off the solvents used for the vulcanizing solution. After another passage through two glycerol baths heated to about 140-50° C., to vulcanize the thread further, it was carried over another drying conveyor. At that point the latex thread was ready to be wound up on a reel; the vulcanizing agents continued to operate after the thread was wound, final vulcanization requiring up to two weeks depending upon the ingredients employed in the solutions. As the latex thread was carried through the process, the linear speed of successive conveyors was increased in order to maintain the proper tension on the thread and keep it lined up properly.

These details indicate the intricate nature of the process originally patented by Hopkinson and W. A. Gibbons in 1925. One can well imagine that Seger, having neither manufacturing nor technical background, found it difficult to understand the operation of the equipment. Probably because he did not understand that the process could be simplified, Seger decided the company should not spend money at that time in further development of what he is reported to have said was "a ridiculous idea," since the company already had a satisfactory market for cut rubber thread. Moreover, in any appraisal of Seger's decision, consideration should be given to the company's financial position at that time.

Several years later the "ridiculous idea" became the basis for the establishment of the profitable Lastex business. Gibbons was placed in charge of the General Laboratories in 1928; at his direction, the experimental latex thread machine was again put in operation. One of the major problems was to find a more practical method of continuously vulcanizing the filament of latex after it was extruded. The development of a continuous process of vulcanization and the rapid growth of the large market for Lastex, the "miracle yarn," are covered in Part IV.

Developments in Rubber Footwear

Before the footwear and sundries divisions could take advantage of the bright colors made possible by organic accelerators, it was necessary for the manufacturers of organic pigments and dyes to develop materials that would withstand the heat and other conditions encountered in vulcanization. United States Rubber's chemists worked with several of these manufacturers for a considerable time in the early 1920's before suitable colors were obtained. The new sulfur-bearing accelerators developed by Naugatuck Chemical Company in those years not only promoted the use of bright colors but were safer to use than the organic bases that had comprised the first group of organic accelerators to be generally adopted by the rubber footwear industry. The earlier organic base accelerators had tended to "set up" while the unvulcanized compounds were being processed or even while they were being held for processing. As a result large quantities of stock had been "burnt" or "scorched" when being calendered and had had to be scrapped.

However, the sulfur-bearing accelerators were not found to be entirely successful in commercial production of rubber footwear until after the adoption of the "ammonia cure." Naugatuck, about 1928, began injecting ammonia gas into the heaters during the vulcanizing process. Not only did the ammonia cure improve the appearance of the footwear, but it was a factor in controlling blisters; surfaces of the goods were less tacky and felt dry to the hand. The more desirable surface also made it possible to transfer the footwear, as soon as it had sufficiently cooled after vulcanization, to moving belts along which the stripping, trimming, mating, inspecting, and packing operations were performed. Moreover, the tensile strength of the rubber compounds was increased; at the same time, cost savings were achieved by lessened need for acceleration and by the shorter length of cure required.

Developments in Mechanical Goods

When Edward Abramson was made head of the motor products department of the Mechanical Goods Division in 1927, with headquarters at Cleveland, he worked closely with the engineers of the various automobile manufacturers. In later years he said he had been unsuccessful in attempts to interest Seger or Sawyer in the development of anything but the ordinary types of mechanical rubber goods and cited two instances in support of his statement.

Engineers at Chalmers Motors (a division of the Chrysler Corporation) had conceived the idea of "floating power," which required the adhesion of rubber supports to metal parts of the motor. Abramson said he worked with the Chalmers' engineers and had made some parts for test purposes, which were seen by Sawyer on a visit to the Cleveland plant. Sawyer ordered the experimental work to be stopped and the metal parts to be discarded, saying they were not going to turn the rubber factory into a steel plant. However, the idea of cushioning motors and other metal units with rubber persisted, and Abramson said that United States Rubber was a prime factor in the development of the process of bonding rubber to metal.

The Cleveland plant also developed a hard-rubber steering wheel, and samples were tested by Ford, Chrysler, and several of the divisions of General Motors. Although favorable test reports were received, Abramson related that Sawyer refused to apply for a patent on the development. Nevertheless, the motor products department succeeded in obtaining business on this item, and one-piece steering wheels made of hard rubber became an established product of United States Rubber for many years.[49]

Another first for the company, according to John Millard of the Passaic plant, was its development of wire-braided hydraulic hose, which was marketed about 1928 under the United States Rubber Company's label. He said that several other companies have claimed to be first, but that written evidence shows that the New York Belting and Packing Company was actually first to introduce this construction, developed primarily for lubricating systems such as Alemite. Willard Cobb said that NYB&P, in its work with horizontal braiders since 1910, had built improved machines with shuttles capable of operating with high tensions, and other equipment for spool-winding of multiple ends of yarn or wire of equal length. These machines made it possible to produce a uniform product of superior quality, braided with cotton yarns for some purposes, or with multiple ends of fine wire (necessary for flexibility). With this development, United States Rubber was able to offer wire-braided hose capable of resisting extremely high pressures with a minimum of elongation or expansion. These features were essential requirements for certain types of practical hydraulic hose demanded by the rapidly expanding automotive industry and especially for applications in aircraft where controls are often actuated by hydraulic pressure.[50]

An important breakthrough in another field was accomplished in the mid-twenties. Working to develop new materials for the leather shoe and other industries, the Cleveland plant of the Mechanical Goods Division was the first in this country to develop fiber products from cellulose pulp to which latex had been added in the beater. The Cleveland plant was thus able to produce unwoven sheeted materials (marketed under the trademark Lexide) that were widely adopted by the shoe industry for findings, such as shoe counters, toe boxes, and midsoles. This development, which became the basis for the present large latex fiber industry, led to the formation in 1929 of the Fiber-Products Department, discussed further in Chapter VIII.

Golf Balls

In April, 1926, United States Rubber announced in a double-page advertisement in the *Saturday Evening Post* (Figure 42) that U.S. golf balls
were made with a perfectly centered "heart" or core of heavier material,
held in a jacket of soft rubber and wound with many yards of fine rubber thread, manufactured in the company's rubber thread factory, the
"largest in the world." The advertisement featured unretouched photos
of cross-sections of six U.S. Royals and of six other golf balls, the cores
of the latter being obviously off-center. For the next two years the company's advertisements stressed the theme, "You can't putt straight with
an egg." These advertisements created considerable interest, and several
independent tests were made by skeptics around the country. As reported in *"U.S." Rubber News*, these tests confirmed the claims made
in the advertisements.

Steps Toward Synthesis of Rubber

Prior to World War I, the attention of Hopkinson and Gibbons had been
drawn to the work of a Russian scientist, Iwan Ostromislensky, a resi-
dent of St. Petersburg in Russia, who had been experimenting with per-
oxides and other nonsulfur agents for vulcanizing rubber. Ostromislensky
and another Russian chemist, A. D. Maximoff, were brought to the company's central research laboratory in New York City, and in 1922 they
set up an experimental cracking plant in the laboratory (Figure 43), and
succeeded in producing the isomeric hydrocarbon, butadiene.

The two continued their experiments, and during the next several
years a number of patents were issued to Ostromislensky in connection
with styrene. In April, 1926, application was filed for a patent covering
production of synthetic rubber latex by polymerizing an emulsion of
erythrene (butadiene) with soap in the presence of a catalyst, and a patent was issued in 1933 to Maximoff, assignor to the Naugatuck Chemical
Company. Gibbons was associated with and, despite the language bar-
rier, supervised much of the work of Ostromislensky and Maximoff in
these experiments.[51]

The United States Rubber chemists had come close to finding a practical method of making synthetic rubber, and, if styrene had been added
to the polymerized emulsion of butadiene in the presence of a catalyst,
they would have been able to anticipate what was later done by German
scientists. Naugatuck Chemical wanted to continue a research and development program on synthetic rubber; however, both butadiene and

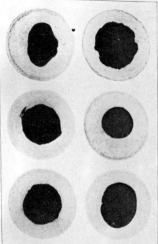

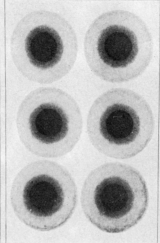

Six X-Rays of golf balls of standard makes other than "U. S." Royal. These X-Rays are typical of some fifty or more in our records, covering practically all the different makes. They are not the worst. Nor are they the best. They are just about average.

The X-Ray above shows one-half of a box of "U. S." Royals, taken out of the stock room at random and put under the X-Ray with all the wrappings and seals intact. No retouching has been done on this photograph or on the others.

Here is the Exclusive "U.S." Royal Construction

THE HEART—A perfect sphere, skillfully compounded of virgin rubber. It has considerable weight for its size, and gives the "U. S." Royal its accurate center of gravity.

THE JACKET—Of soft rubber. On this pliable jacket the rubber winding of the core takes a firm grip, making it possible to secure extremely high tension.

THE CORE—Consisting of many yards of the finest rubber thread, wound on the jacket by specially constructed machines. Tension and hardness are checked on every ball. The rubber thread is manufactured in the United States Rubber Company's own thread factory—the largest in the world.

Below is a "U. S." Royal ready to play. Great distance. Tough cover. Four coats of paint. A ball that will stay white and stand a lot of punishment.

Buy "U. S." Royals from your club professional or authorized dealer—3 for $2.50 or 85c each.

IN the X-Ray photograph above at the right you see why the "U. S." Royal is the *truest putting* golf ball made.

The black center is the heart or "pill" of the ball. The dark gray circle is the soft rubber jacket which encloses the "pill." The light gray circle is the "core" of yards and yards of the finest rubber thread. The outer dark gray circle is the dense, tough cover.

Note that the heart is a *true sphere*. And it is located in the *exact center* of the ball.

The *center of gravity* coincides with the *center* of the ball.

Furthermore, this center of gravity is *fixed*. It does not shift when the ball is hit.

A "U. S." Royal *putts true* on

its first green—and it putts true also on its *thirty-sixth* green.

But true putting is not all of the "U. S." Royal.

There is no ball that will give you more *distance*.

There is none that will *fly* straighter.

None with a *tougher* cover to resist punishment. Or with *paint* that stands up better.

There is no better golf ball made—whether made in this country or abroad, and at whatever price—than the "U. S." Royal.

Buy "U. S." Royals from your club professional or authorized dealers—3 for $2.50, 85c each.

"U. S." Royal—Mesh Marking

United States Rubber Company

The world's largest Growers, Manufacturers and Distributors of Rubber and its Products. Makers of "U. S." Royal Cord Tires, "U. S." Rubber Footwear, Keds, Raynsters, "U. S." Spring-Step Rubber Heels, Uskide Soles, etc.

42. Cross-sections of U.S. Royal and other golf balls (*Saturday Evening Post*, April 17, 1926).

43. Experimental laboratory cracking plant. This device was used by Iwan Ostromislensky to produce butadiene in 1922.

styrene in 1923 were looked upon by many as merely scientific curiosities. Since styrene in particular was costly to produce, little importance was attached to these developments and the management vetoed further work on the project. As there was no prospect of getting enough money appropriated to carry on an adequate program for development of a satisfactory synthetic rubber, the basic styrene process patent was later sold to the Union Carbide Corporation.[52]

Summary

In 1928, the general development department comprised more than 250 scientists, chemists, and analysts. In May of that year Hopkinson announced that the research and development activities of the company would be transferred to a recently built five-story building adjoining the Passaic plant. That move, in itself, was an indication that the work of the department was attaining greater importance. Although significant improvements were made in the quality of the products of United States Rubber during the Seger administration, apparently research was not then considered by the chief executive as worthy of his active encouragement and strong support—certainly not as research is thought of today.

Two Acquisitions

During the latter part of 1919, United States Rubber purchased the property of the Dolgeville Felt Shoe Company, Dolgeville, N.Y., manufacturers of a line of felt shoes and slippers. The former owners continued in charge of operations, and the Dolgeville company conducted its business under its own name.

The sharp recession of 1921 brought financial embarrassment to the Beacon Falls Rubber Company, Beacon Falls, Conn., which had been founded in 1899 by George A. Lewis, former president of Goodyear Metallic Rubber Shoe Company and a director of United States Rubber from 1892 to 1898. (Colt was reported to have purchased a one-third interest in the Beacon Falls Rubber Company prior to 1905;[53] later this interest was acquired by the United States Rubber Company.) When, in 1921, the Beacon Falls Company found it would be unable to meet its financial obligations, it appealed to United States Rubber to come to its assistance. This appeal was seconded by banks and other creditors of Beacon Falls.

United States Rubber then purchased at their face value substantially all the outstanding notes of the Beacon Falls Company, amounting to $3,010,000, under an agreement that payment of the notes would not be enforced prior to May 31, 1926. United States Rubber had until May 31, 1923 to pay the notes' purchase price, with the option of making payment either in its first and refunding mortgage bonds at par or in cash. The company also agreed that within five years it would either buy or find a purchaser for the outstanding stock of Beacon Falls on the basis of $20 for the common and $80 for the preferred stock. During the five-year period, United States Rubber would pay $5 per year on the preferred and $2 per year on the common stock and, in compensation, would be entitled to any dividends declared during the period.

On July 22, 1921, a contract gave United States Rubber management of Beacon Falls Rubber Company for five years and half of the net profits during the period. Frank E. Church was appointed president of Beacon Falls Rubber Shoe Company, which operated its branches as entirely separate and distinct from those of United States Rubber. A listing statement filed with the New York Stock Exchange on Dec. 1, 1928 stated that a subsidiary of United States Rubber then owned most of the preferred and common stock of Beacon Falls Rubber Company, which continued to market rubber and canvas footwear under the Beacon Falls label.

THE CORPORATE ANATOMY IN 1928

What was the United States Rubber Company when F. B. Davis, Jr., was invited to become its president and chief executive officer?

According to the balance sheet, net worth as of Dec. 31, 1928 was $181,451,000 *including* an item of $58,925,000 for "Good Will, Patents, etc.," and $3,730,000 in prepaid and deferred assets. Current liabilities were $43,161,000, and funded indebtedness was $104,475,000 on which $6,098,000 interest was paid in 1928. The decline in the price of crude rubber during the first six months of the year had necessitated a write-down on June 30 of $14,148,000 in value of inventories. After this and other charges, there was a net loss of $10,781,000 for the year.

Net sales of $193,480,000 in 1928 were 69% of tangible assets. As of Dec. 31, 1928, ratio of inventories to sales was 34.4%; ratio of receivables to sales was 22.7% (not including cash receivable Jan. 11, 1929 from sale of common stock).

There were 18,099 holders of the 651,109 shares outstanding of the company's preferred stock, and 7,958 holders of 1,456,824 shares of its no par common stock (including the additional issue of 728,412 shares of common approved by the stockholders Dec. 7, 1928, to be paid for at $35 per share on or before Jan. 11, 1929). Dividends on the 8% non-cumulative preferred had been omitted after the payment on Feb. 15, 1928. No dividends had been paid on the common since April 30, 1921.

Organization chart of the top echelons of management as of Sept. 1, 1928 is shown in Appendix E. The total number of employees on June 30, 1928 was 62,629, of whom about 24,000 were on the rubber plantations. These comprised about 135,000 acres, and had produced 28,-767,000 pounds of rubber in 1928.

The company and its thirty-eight subsidiaries owned more than fifty factories in the United States, Canada, and England; forty-one of these were active, nine were closed as of Dec. 31, 1928. Its principal manufactures were officially listed as "tires and tubes, waterproof and tennis footwear, clothing, belting, hose and packing, insulated wire, golf balls, hard rubber goods, and reclaimed rubber. Other manufactures include chemicals, shoe hardware, felt and felt goods, and cotton fabrics." The major subsidiary corporations owned by the company in 1928 and their principal products are listed in Appendix F.

Channels of distribution were almost as varied and complex as the manufactured products. There were nearly 400 distributing branches or agencies in the United States, Canada, and abroad. Sales to some industrial accounts (especially to the automotive industry) and to some mass distributors, as well as to some wholesalers, were handled by special representatives or executives working out of the headquarters of either the parent company or of one of its subsidiaries. Lines of communication, essential to implementation of company-wide policies, were difficult to maintain. In addition, several subsidiary companies maintained separate sales organizations. Some of these competed vigorously with each other and/or with the parent.

The impossibility of properly and effectively directing and managing the affairs of such a diversified company by the highly centralized organization that was maintained during Seger's tenure of office is obvious.

[1] Motor vehicle registrations in the United States rose from 9,239,000 in 1920 to over 20 million in 1925, and to 26,750,000 by 1930. See U.S. Dept. of Commerce, *Historical Statistics of the United States, Colonial Times to 1957* (Washington: U.S. Gov't Printing Office, 1960), pp. 462-63.

[2] The word "flapper," used to designate a teen-age girl, arose from the practice by teen-agers in the early 1920's of wearing four-buckle arctics with the buckles unfastened.

[3] Upon renewal of its corporate charter in 1922, the name of the corporation was changed to reflect the importance of its rubber business.

[4] W. A. Mitchel, interview, 1963.

[5] "U.S." *Rubber News*, house organ of United States Rubber Company (May 15, p. 3, and June 1, 1924, p. 9).

[6] E. H. White, interview, 1962.

[7] *Between US*, house organ of the United States Rubber Company (June, August, and October, 1922). Also see "U.S." *Rubber News* (May 15 and June 15, 1924, and July, 1928).

[8] Gregg T. Ward, interview, 1963.

[9] "U.S." *Rubber News* (Feb. 15, 1926), p. 9 ff.

[10] Based largely on correspondence with A. E. Denari and E. J. Higgins.

[11] Leslie Roberts, "From Three Men," privately printed, Dominion Rubber Company, Ltd., 1954, pp. 23, 27.

[12] Organization chart, 1927, United States Rubber Company archives.

[13] H. G. Kieswetter, interview, 1963.

[14] A. E. Denari, interview, 1963.

[15] John D. Gaffey, *The Productivity of Labor in the Rubber Tire Manufacturing Industry* (New York: Columbia University Press, 1940), p. 59.

[16] *Automobile Facts and Figures, 1962* (New York: Automobile Manufacturers Association), p. 3.

[17] Leonard Smith, records of commercial research department, company archives.

[18] *The Productivity of Labor in the Rubber Tire Manufacturing Industry*, p. 39.

[19] E. G. Holt, "Some Fundamental Factors in the American Rubber Industry," *Survey of Current Business* (Washington: U.S. Gov't Printing Office, April, 1935), p. 18.

[20] *The Productivity of Labor in the Rubber Tire Manufacturing Industry*, p. 41.

[21] United States Rubber Company, "Minutes of First Annual Sales Service Convention," 1920, privately printed, p. 56.

[22] Ralph C. Epstein, "Concentration and Price Trends in the Rubber Tire Industry, 1930-47," privately printed for submission to the Federal Trade Commission, 1949, p. 45.

[23] *Federal Trade Commission Decisions, January 14, 1936—July 9, 1936*, XXII (Washington: U.S. Gov't Printing Office), p. 232 ff.; also Alfred D. Chandler, Jr., *Strategy and Structure* (Cambridge, Mass.: The M.I.T. Press, 1962), pp. 235-36; also Boris Ammet and John E. Jeuck, *Catalogues and Counters* (Chicago:

University of Chicago Press, 1950), pp. 389-90, 619; also Walton Hamilton and others, *Price and Price Policies* (New York: McGraw-Hll Book Co., 1938), pp. 101-02.

[24]Records of United States Rubber Company.

[25]*New York Times* (June 7, 1927), p. 43.

[26]*New York Times* (Jan. 4, 1928), p. 41, and (Jan. 5, 1928), p. 51.

[27]"Over Fifty Years of Service Through Creative Chemistry," 1955, unpublished, company archives; also S. M. Cadwell, letter, Nov. 3, 1961.

[28] Remarks by George R. Vila, June, 1960, before the Commercial Chemical Development Association; also interview with Elmer Roberts, 1963.

[29] Elmer Roberts, interview, 1963.

[30]Stanton Glover, memorandum, May 3, 1960, company archives.

[31]*Concentration and Price Trends in the Rubber Tire Industry, 1930-47*, p. 60.

[32]"Over Fifty Years of Service Through Creative Chemistry."

[33]Sidney M. Cadwell, letter, Nov. 3, 1964.

[34]Harold S. Roberts, *The Rubber Workers* (New York: Harper & Brothers, 1944), p. 5.

[35]G. L. Lawrence, c. 1920, Naugatuck archives.

[36]*Rubber Products Industry, A Statistical Compendium* (New York: National Industrial Conference Board, 1959), p. 4.

[37]C. M. Carroll, letter to author, 1963.

[38]T. J. Needham, W. H. Norton, and Harold N. Barrett, interviews and correspondence with author, 1962 to 1964.

[39]William Dougherty, interview, 1962.

[40]Advertisements, *National Geographic* (April, 1923) and *Saturday Evening Post* (Aug. 25, 1923).

[41]U.S. Bureau of Labor Statistics, "Productivity of Labor in Eleven Manufacturing Industries," *Monthly Labor Review*, XXX (March, 1930), pp. 501-17. Quoted in *The Productivity of Labor in the Rubber Tire Manufacturing Industry*, p. 81.

[42]*The Productivity of Labor in the Rubber Tire Manufacturing Industry*, pp. 69-90.

[43]United States Rubber Company, "A Brief Story About the United States Rubber Company," 1946, privately printed.

[44]The solids in natural rubber latex, as collected from the tree, are about 38 to 40%, including about 35% in rubber. The remainder is in ash, resins, and proteins. G. R. Vila, "Types of Latex," *The Vanderbilt Rubber Handbook* (New York: R. T. Vanderbilt Co., 1948), p. 264.

[45]*The Science of Rubber*, D. K. Memmler, ed. (New York: Reinhold Publishing Corporation, 1934), p. 127.

[46]*New York Times* (Jan. 15, 1926), p. 22; also "U.S." *Rubber News* (Oct. 1, 1925, pp. 26, 27, and May 1, 1926, pp. 8-10).

[47]W. A. Gibbons, interview, 1963.

[48]The increase amounts to as much as ten times, according to Stanton Glover in talk given at training course, Naugatuck, May 3, 1960.

[49]Morris E. Dry, memorandum of interview with Edward Abramson, Aug. 6, 1952, company archives.

[50]John Millard, interview, 1963; also correspondence from W. H. Cobb, 1961.

[51]*US*, house organ of United States Rubber Company (November, 1942), p. 4; also W. A. Gibbons, interview, 1963.

[52]Elmer Roberts, correspondence with author, 1964; also George R. Vila, untitled paper, June, 1960.

[53]E. A. Saunders, interview with C. E. Bradley, c. 1924, C. E. Bradley's notebooks, Mishawaka archives.

IV
1929 to 1942

7

Scraping Bottom

F. B. DAVIS, JR.

Francis Breese Davis, Jr. was born in Fort Edward, N.Y., Sept. 16, 1883, and was reared on a farm. After graduation from high school, he had accumulated only $200 when he enrolled in the Sheffield Scientific School at Yale University. When the $200 had been spent, a classmate offered a loan to help him finish the three-year course, but Davis refused it and began selling clocks and calendars, and waiting tables. Soon, however, he began the more profitable sale of drawing instruments and other supplies needed by engineering students. Meeting the incoming freshmen at the railroad station in New Haven, he would have them signed up to buy from him all their pens, inks, T-squares, and slide rules before they set foot on the campus.

When Davis had one more year to complete his course, the school decided that these items would be sold to the students through the college co-op. Davis protested to the dean that many of his contracts, signed by students before the school made its ruling, had one more year to run and that the ruling should not be retroactive. Evidently he persuaded the dean that he had a good case, for the latter agreed that Davis could continue to sell the instruments, and, as compensation for giving up the sale of supplies, granted Davis a year's free tuition and a room in the dormitory.[1]

Graduating in 1906 with an engineering degree, Davis got a job in the office of the city engineer, New Haven, at $40 a month. He next worked for the Empire Engineering Corporation on a section of the Erie Barge Canal. From early in 1907 until the summer of 1909, he was employed at Wilmington, Del., by the Pennsylvania Railroad to do engineering work on the maintenance of way of the Philadelphia, Baltimore, and Washington Railroad. In 1909, he joined the engineering department of E. I. du Pont de Nemours & Company. In 1911, he was made division engineer in charge of all black powder engineering. Between 1911 and 1913, he participated in the construction of Du Pont plants at Du Pont, Wash., and Augusta, Colo. In 1913, when the federal government brought about the separation of the Atlas and Hercules powder companies from Du Pont, Davis was appointed as assistant to Lammot du Pont as superintendent of the sporting powder division of the black powder operating department.

In 1915, he was assistant engineer in charge of the construction of the guncotton plant erected by Du Pont for the U.S. government at Hopewell, N.J. For several months he was in charge of operations at Hopewell; then he was transferred to Carney's Point, N.J., and later to Old Hickory, Tenn., as assistant to the engineer in charge of engineering and construction of the new munitions plant. He remained there until the end of World War I. In January, 1919, Davis was named vice-president of the Du Pont Chemical Company, which had been formed to dispose of surplus materials and factories acquired during the war.

The manufacture of explosives contracted sharply after the end of World War I, and a number of younger executives left the Du Pont company. Some—Davis among them—went to General Motors, where Pierre S. du Pont had become president following William C. Durant's resignation on Nov. 30, 1920. Davis later said he wanted experience in GM's decentralized organization, which he admired. After joining GM in 1921, he was appointed assistant general manager in charge of manufacture and sales of products of the Saginaw Division. In that capacity he had frequent contact with men who, at that time or later, were in charge of different divisions of General Motors. These included A. R. Glancy, who in 1925 became general manager of the Oakland Division (later the Oakland-Pontiac Division after the Pontiac was launched in January, 1926[2]). He also dealt with William S. Knudsen of Chevrolet and Harry Bassett of Buick, who were still heads of those divisions when Davis became president of United States Rubber. From that experience, he said, he learned it was harder for a former insider, such as he, to "sell these men" than it would have been for someone who had had no connection with General Motors; a competent buyer resents any implied pressure or inference that his purchases are, or should be, based on any personal consideration or any factor other than price, quality, and service.

Davis returned to the Du Pont Company in 1923 as assistant to the general manager of the pyralin department, becoming general manager of that department on Aug. 1, 1923. On May 1, 1925, the Du Pont Company bought the Viscoloid Company, and Davis was made president of Du Pont Viscoloid, operating that subsidiary profitably until he left to become president of United States Rubber.

In the late 1920's, General Motors was using pyralin on the inside of curtains for automobiles. When automobile bodies with hard tops and glass windows were adopted, Davis tried unsuccessfully to get the company to use safety glass in which a layer of pyralin was sandwiched between two layers of glass. He told the executives that GM would be forced to adopt safety glass because he would sell the idea to their competitors. Under his guidance, the Du Pont Viscoloid Company formed in January, 1928, with Pittsburgh Plate Glass Company, the Pittsburgh Safety Glass Corporation to market safety glass under the trade name Duplate. Duplate was adopted by one or more of the other auto manufacturers before GM yielded.[3] Davis was the first chairman of the board of directors of the Pittsburgh Safety Glass Corporation.

Davis also became president of the Celastic Corporation, jointly organized in April, 1925 by the Du Pont Company and United States Shoe Machinery Corporation for the manufacture and sale of Celastic, an impregnated fabric used in the leather shoe industry.

Irenee du Pont and Kuhn, Loeb and Co. had concluded before the end of 1928 that a change in the management of United States Rubber was essential. On their recommendation, the board of directors on Jan. 15, 1929 elected Davis president of the company and chairman of the board, succeeding C. B. Seger, who resigned from both offices but remained for a time as a director. Davis' practical experience and years of training in Du Pont management philosophy brought to the presidency of United States Rubber a badly needed perception of both the problems and the great advantages inherent in such a widely diversified manufacturing company.

Problems Facing the New President

The problems faced by Davis upon his election as president of United States Rubber were numerous, complex, and even more critical than appeared on the surface. He found that the physical assets shown on the company's balance sheets were not realistic and required heavy charges for depreciation to bring them down to a properly conservative basis in accordance with sound business practice. Responsibility and authority were so centralized that the organization was ill-adapted for efficient management. Morale of personnel was low in many plants or departments. Cost of production was excessive, and the burdensome annual charges for interest on the funded indebtedness would absorb most, if not all, of any early operating profit. In addition, rubber would decline still further in 1930, necessitating a write-down of over $11 million in inventories, plus provision for contingencies, by United States Rubber as of Dec. 31, 1930. This drop was largely unforeseen at the time since the market price of crude rubber was lower in January, 1929 than it had been since before the Stevenson Plan.

The following comparisons give some idea of the serious situation that faced the new president in 1929. Net sales of United States Rubber in 1928 had been only 56.4% of total assets as of Dec. 31, 1928 and only 69% of tangible assets. This record compared with the following for the three leading competitors:

	Percentage of Tangible Assets
Firestone Tire and Rubber Company	114.5
B. F. Goodrich Company	128.1
Goodyear Tire and Rubber Company	120.9

Percentages of net sales reported as net income in 1928 by the "Big Four" were: Firestone, 5.2%; Goodrich, 2.4%; Goodyear, 5.3%; and United States Rubber, a loss of 12.1%. (United States Rubber's net income has been adjusted to conform with current accounting practices.) The ratios of tangible net worth to total debt for each of these companies were: Firestone, 271.6%; Goodrich, 165.6%; Goodyear, 95.1%; and United States Rubber, only 80.3%.

The internal problems that these figures disclosed were compounded by the years of depression that followed the stock market crash of 1929. Management was afforded no quick or easy solution of the company's precarious position. In any consideration of the steps taken by United States Rubber under Davis' direction, it is essential to focus on the interrelation of the different aspects of the several major problem areas. Under more normal circumstances, any one of these areas would have been deemed worthy of top priority.

To avoid confusion, the sections that follow will discuss each phase of management more or less independently of the other operations of the company. However, since management problems cannot be fitted neatly into airtight compartments, this review will seek to reflect the interplay and reciprocal action of the moves undertaken to reduce manufacturing costs, increase sales, lessen interest charges, develop new products, create a more efficient organization, and, simultaneously, to foster better relations with employees, the public, the stockholders, and the holders of the company's financial obligations.

At a dinner given by the United States Rubber Club of Massachusetts in Boston on Feb. 11, 1929, Davis had his first good opportunity to acquaint the company's employees with his management philosophy. He emphasized that (1) the business always must be profitable; (2) management should keep the organization informed regarding its policies and objectives; (3) compensation should be based on worth and merit of the employee; (4) the importance of research and development should be fully recognized; and (5) United States Rubber Company must be kept up to date in methods and policies. In closing his remarks, Davis invited employees to submit suggestions.

A conversation that occurred soon after Davis accepted his new duties reveals something of the characters of the men involved as well as the magnitude of the problems they faced. Davis walked into the office of L. D. Tompkins, who only a few weeks before had been made responsible for the operations of the Tire Division. "What is your inventory turn-over rate?" Davis asked Tompkins, who replied, "I do not know." Davis' next question was, "What is your waste factor?" Again Tompkins said he didn't know.

Davis must have been surprised by this lack of knowledge on the part of the head of the Tire Division, but he continued asking Tompkins such questions as, "What kind of a plant is the Indianapolis plant?" and "What kind of mills are the Winnsboro Mills?" To each question, Tompkins' answer was, "I don't know." Suddenly Davis interrupted his rapid-fire questions with the statement that he had heard the Tire Division was "a mess" and it was not surprising when the top executive knew so little about the division, whereupon Tompkins said, "You and I seem to have much in common."

Davis asked the meaning of this statement, and Tompkins explained his recent appointment and the circumstances connected with it, and added, "You are trying to find out just what is wrong with the United States Rubber Company and what should be done to correct it. I am trying to learn the same things about the Tire Division." Davis recognized the fairness of the comparison and asked Tompkins if he would take him to the tire plants. Tompkins gladly consented to do so, and during the ensuing years the two men worked closely together on a basis of mutual respect and understanding until Tompkins resigned from the executive committee in 1942, when he became Assistant Deputy Rubber Director, War Products Board, in Washington.

44.   United States Rubber Company headquarters building, 1230 Avenue of the Americas. New York City. Its opening coincided with the emergency of the company from a long period of financial stress.

Problems Aggressively Attacked

Davis promptly launched a many-pronged attack on the over-all problem of the company's critical financial situation. (The results are indicated in the synoptic history that follows.) Concurrent programs were inaugurated to reorganize the management, reduce manufacturing costs, increase sales, and to develop and introduce new products that would better employ existing facilities. Above all, a determined campaign was carried on to lessen the staggering impact of the company's heavy indebtedness.

During 1932, the worst year of the depression that began after the market crash in October, 1929, United States Rubber Company's consolidated net sales fell as low as $78 million, with cost of sales just under $77 million, so that operating profit (before interest or depreciation) was only $1.3 million or 1.7% of net sales. After all charges, operations for 1932 showed a deficit of almost $10.4 million. By 1935, profit from operations had risen to 9.6% of net sales, and for the seven peacetime years from 1935 to 1941 inclusive, operating profit averaged 9% of total net sales. Meanwhile, net sales had climbed to $315.3 million in 1941, or 284% of tangible net worth.

For 1929, the first year of Davis' administration, United States Rubber paid $5.9 million in interest on its funded indebtedness; by 1935 this charge had been cut down to $3.5 million, by 1940 to $1.5 million, and by 1942 to $1.3 million. Although United States Rubber continued to show losses in each year from 1928 through 1934, the combined losses for 1933 and 1934 were held to only about $1.15 million, and by 1935 the company was showing a profit. The extent of recovery made by United States Rubber between 1934 and 1939 is shown in Tables 14-15 in the Appendix. This achievement is a good measure of the effectiveness of the programs instituted and carried through by Davis and his staff, notably William de Krafft, during the long depression years.

Coincidental with the company's emergence from its long period of financial stress, the headquarters' offices were moved in March, 1940 to the new United States Rubber building at 1230 Sixth Avenue (since named Avenue of the Americas). When dividends on the common stock of the company were resumed in 1941, the restoration of the company to the sound and preeminent position it had attained was hailed in the press as a particularly remarkable achievement in the light of the conditions that had prevailed since 1929.[4]

THE ORGANIZATION REVAMPED

Decentralization

Davis soon concluded that United States Rubber, a corporation with sales of $190 million, was both poorly organized and in need of extensive changes. He believed that authority had been excessively concentrated when one man, Seger, served simultaneously as chairman of the board, president, chairman of the executive committee, acting head of the Tire Division (until Tompkins was placed in charge of the division in December, 1928), and, particularly, as an active member or chairman of either the executive committee or of the finance committee of the Union Pacific Railroad. Moreover, it was readily seen that too many products, other than tires, and too many activities of the company were embraced in the unwieldy General Division headed by Homer E. Sawyer, executive vice-president of the company, again resulting in overcentralization of authority.

Davis said he discovered that the so-called executive committee actually functioned more as a finance committee. The nearest approach to an executive committee was the president's "conference committee," first appointed by Seger in 1923. In 1928, this committee was composed of:

> Charles B. Seger, president
> William O. Cutter, vice-president and comptroller
> Ernest Hopkinson, vice-president in charge of Development and Patent Departments
> H. Stuart Hotchkiss, vice-president and president of United States Rubber Plantations, Inc.
> Homer E. Sawyer, executive vice-president in charge of the General Division
> Eric Burkman, assistant to the president.

While all except Burkman were directors, Davis found that the committee neither reported to the board nor supervised the commercial operations of United States Rubber. On the contrary, he learned that it had served chiefly to provide opportunity for Seger to talk with the group. Davis discontinued the president's conference committee immediately after he took office and set up instead an operating committee, comprised of Davis as chairman, Cutter, Hopkinson, Tompkins, Edward J. Coughlin, and H. E. Smith (Figure 45a).

The function of this committee was to consult and advise on the steps to be taken in reorganizing and staffing the company, and to supervise operations until an executive committee truly representative of the board of directors could be organized. The operating committee held eight meetings between March 12, 1929 and April 23, 1929, when it was discontinued. On the same date, the members of the operating committee were elected to the new executive committee. (In 1932, the operating committee was reestablished, subordinate to the executive committee, to give operating executives an opportunity to exchange views and to provide a coordinated effort toward the reduction of costs. At that time the operating committee also included A. F. Van Pelt, representing the Treasurer's Department, and W. A. Gibbons, representing the Development Department.)

Having determined the changes he considered essential for efficient operations, the new president issued a letter to stockholders and employees on April 23, 1929 outlining the new plan of organization. The letter, quoted in its entirety in Appendix G announced the division of the company's business into separate departments or companies, each directed and operated by a general manager—or a president in the case of a subsidiary operating under its own name—who would "have control and absolute responsibility for all the operations of his department." Each general manager would be expected to avail himself of the help of nine general service departments. The organization thus set up replaced the centralized control that had existed during Seger's administration with one "designed to give each General Manager the greatest freedom of action, and all the help which can be usefully availed of from each and every department and individual in the company."

Simultaneously, the executive committee was reorganized. Between meetings of the board of directors, the executive committee possessed and exercised, subject to orders and resolutions of the board, all powers of the board in the management of the company except those powers reserved to the finance committee. The executive committee represented the board in the effective supervision of all divisional operations pertaining to manufacturing, selling, development, and research. (In 1935, the executive committee, then comprising Davis as chairman, Coughlin, de Krafft, Smith, and Tompkins, was disbanded and replaced by the operating committee.) The finance committee, also created on April 23, 1929, exercised all powers of the board of directors in the management of the financial affairs of the company. It was also given control and supervision of the work and responsibilities of the comptroller, treasurer, and secretary.

Appendix E includes a chart of the organization as it was set up on April 23, 1929. A comparison with the organization chart dated Sept. 1, 1928, also in Appendix E, reveals the sweeping nature of the reorganization. Although in later years it was recognized that this type of organization was not perfectly suited for a corporation as diversified as United States Rubber, the underlying principle governing the realignment of responsibilities and authority remained basically unchanged for over thirty years. Certainly it was much more efficient than the highly centralized control that it replaced.

Bonuses and Awards

In the letter of April 23, 1929 to the stockholders and employees of the United States Rubber Company, Davis announced his intention to inaugu-

45. Company leadership, 1929.

45a. Executive committee.

William O. Cutter   Ernest Hopkinson   L. D. Tompkins

Herbert E. Smith   F. B. Davis, Jr.   E. J. Coughlin

rate a plan that would provide for "participation in the profits of the Company by those who, by industry and intelligent effort, or conspicuous ability, make outstanding contribution to the Company's success." Accordingly, the company's attorneys were requested to study various plans and submit recommendations to the executive committee. This committee decided that an incentive plan based on one successful in other companies, and modified to suit U.S. Rubber, should be adopted.

45b. Group of general
managers.

ELMER ROBERTS   T. J. NEEDHAM

GEORGE E. GOODWIN   WALTER GUSSENHOVEN   H. W. WAITE

In September, 1929, the finance committee and the board of directors completed plans that were approved by the stockholders by a vote of 1,245,269 shares to 100 shares at the October meeting. The chief features of the plans were revealed in a press release on Sept. 10. They provided for three bonus plans. Class A bonuses would be granted for "conspicuous service of any kind," irrespective of the earnings of the company. Class B bonuses would be granted to those employees "who have contributed most in a general way to the success of the company by their loyalty, industry or ability." These Class B awards, which depended upon the profits of the company, would be made from a special fund to be created by the directors. Class C bonuses could be authorized by the board, providing awards to employees who equaled or excelled standards of performance. Class C awards did not depend upon the earnings of the company, and might be combined with awards under Class A or Class B.

Also approved was a "manager's shares plan" procedure for crediting "employees of the company occupying responsible positions" with shares of common stock of the company, equal in the aggregate to the amount of awards under Class B bonuses. Shares awarded under this plan would cost recipients $5 each. Since Class B awards depended upon net profits earned by the company, awards under the manager's plan likewise would not be made unless such profits were realized. During the first few years after the approval of these incentive plans, the operations showed a loss, and the profit finally earned in 1935 was not large enough to warrant the awarding of Class B bonuses or manager's shares. Therefore, these plans did not become effective until 1936.

Allotments of trust shares under the manager's shares plan were always made by a committee created for that purpose, which did not include any executives eligible for such awards. Awards under Class B were approved by the executive committee, whose members were not eligible for Class B awards.

Changes in Board of Directors

By April 16, 1929, several members of the old board of directors had resigned. They were N. F. Brady, H. E. Sawyer, John W. Davis, Samuel M. Nicholson, and C. B. Seger. In April, nine new directors were elected, including E. J. Coughlin and Herbert E. Smith, designated as second vice-presidents in charge, respectively, of manufacturing and sales in the General Division; and L. D. Tompkins, vice-president in charge of the Tire Division. These men were added to the board because Davis wished to have some of the chief operating executives eligible to serve on the newly reorganized executive committee. Ernest Hopkinson, vice-president in charge of the Development and Patent Departments, was one of the former directors reelected to the board on April 16. He was another operating officer who could and did serve on the executive committee. (John W. Davis continued as general counsel and later returned to the board on March 6, 1940, at the urging of Davis.)

Apart from Davis and the men just mentioned, the only other member of the board of directors elected in April, 1929, who was then connected with the day-to-day operation of United States Rubber, was William O. Cutter, comptroller and vice-president in charge of finances. Ten were chiefly bankers or financial men.

Temporary Reversal of Decentralization

In September, 1929, at Davis' suggestion, Tompkins hired Joseph A. O'Shaughnessy as assistant to the general manager of the Tire Division.

(O'Shaughnessy had been the director of sales for Du Pont Viscoloid while Davis was president of that company.) In 1930, the work on the executive committee began demanding more of Tompkins' time, and in April of that year O'Shaughnessy was made general manager of the Tire Division. In May, 1932, he was made a vice-president of United States Rubber in charge of sales of all products.[5] When the National Recovery Administration (NRA) was established in June, 1933, Tompkins was called to Washington and remained there about nine months. During Tompkins' leave of absence from United States Rubber, O'Shaughnessy was again promoted in October, 1933, with added responsibilities in the company, apportioning his time between Detroit and New York.

The products of United States Rubber were no less diversified in 1932 than they were in 1929, when wide diversification prompted Davis to decentralize its management. However, the depressed condition of business in 1932 may at least partially explain why one man was given control of all sales of the Tire, Footwear, and Mechanical Divisions, thereby deviating from the policy of decentralization so recently established. The company's net sales had fallen from $192,962,000 in 1929, Davis' first year in office, to $114,132,000 in 1931, and to only $78,830,000 in 1932. Under these circumstances, it is not surprising that Davis was persuaded the company needed a hard-driving general sales manager to coordinate and stimulate all its selling activities and to reduce selling costs. He believed that O'Shaughnessy had the ability to revitalize United States Rubber's lagging sales and to lift the company out of its slump.

T. J. Needham, general manager of the Footwear Division, had been in charge of footwear sales since September, 1920, when he became manager of branch store sales. He was now relieved of responsibility for most sales in that division. He remained responsible, however, for quality, prices, and manufacture of footwear for the branches, and for sales and manufacture of private brand footwear for wholesale accounts. In 1931, Needham had also been given responsibility for operations of the Mishawaka Rubber and Woolen Mfg. Co., which was not placed under O'Shaughnessy's supervision.

Closely associated with O'Shaughnessy during his connection with United States Rubber was Lewis M. Simpson. He had first been employed in 1918 as manager of the footwear and clothing department of the Los Angeles branch, and had subsequently been manager for footwear of five other branches in the Pacific Coast Division. When the sales activities of the divisions were reorganized in 1927, the Tire Division felt the need to strengthen its management group, and Needham consented to the transfer of Simpson from the Footwear to the Tire Division, where he became central manager of sales. In May, 1929, Simpson was made general sales manager for tires; on April 19, 1932, O'Shaughnessy appointed him general sales manager for tires and mechanical goods.

Reversion to Decentralized Sales Management

The centralization of sales management lasted only until March, 1934, when O'Shaughnessy resigned and the general managers resumed control of the selling activities of their respective divisions. Shortly thereafter, Simpson and some others who had been associated with O'Shaughnessy left the employ of the company. Tompkins, called back by Davis from service with the NRA in Washington, again took up the duties of general manager of the Tire Division. United States Rubber's second relatively brief and unhappy experience with centralized sales control had convinced Davis that the interests of the company would be better served by a decentralized organization.

Management by Committees

During the Davis administration, maximum use of committee management tended to be the rule in United States Rubber. The organization that existed in 1938 may be taken as fairly typical. The board of directors at that time consisted of fourteen members, with Davis as chairman. Virtually all top-level decisions were made by committees, subject to final approval by the board.

In addition to Davis (who served as its chairman following de Krafft's resignation, effective June 30, 1938), the finance committee in the latter part of 1938 included four members of the board: Lewis L. Strauss, Sir William Wiseman, Henry Davis, and Harry E. Humphreys, Jr.

The operating committee, which functioned until the end of 1938 with Davis as its chairman, had thirteen members including the general managers of six domestic operating divisions. From May 1, 1935 to Dec. 31, 1938, the general manager of each of these divisions was also a vice-president of United States Rubber Products, Inc. The divisions and their general managers in 1938 were: Tire, Tompkins; Footwear and Clothing, Needham; General Products, H. E. Smith; Thread, Smith; Mechanical Goods, Smith; Chemical and Reclaim, Roberts. On Jan. 1, 1939, the operating committee was replaced by a newly organized executive committee, comprised of Davis as chairman, Humphreys, and five directors who had personal experience in managing the operations of the divisions of the company: Coughlin, Needham, Roberts, Smith, and Tompkins.

In 1938, all operations outside the United States were under the supervision of the foreign activities committee of which Roberts was chairman. He also served as chairman of the board of Consolidated Rubber Manufacturers, Ltd. and its associated companies. Other members of this committee were J. W. Bicknell, managing director, United States Rubber Plantations, Inc., and W. A. Eden, president, Dominion Rubber Company, Ltd. (In 1938, Eden also was president of U.S. Rubber Export Company, Ltd.)

Other committees that functioned in 1938, subject to the operating committee, were:

Sales committee (four members), H. E. Smith, chairman
Advertising and commercial research, W. Emery, director
Purchasing committee (five members), E. J. Coughlin, chairman
Purchasing director, G. M. Tisdale
General traffic manager, G. F. Hichborn
Repairs and general maintenance committee (four members), J. A. Barrett, chairman
General technical committee (five members), F. B. Davis, Jr., chairman
Insurance committee (eight members), E. J. Coughlin, chairman
Secretary, W. F. Lund
Three insurance fund trustees
Board of benefits and awards (five members), E. J. Coughlin, chairman
Retirement and savings plan trustees (two members), Central Bank and Trust Company
Manager's shares plan (special committee of board of directors, three members), Lewis L. Strauss, chairman
Henry Davis, Sir William Wiseman, three trustees

Under the supervision of the operating committee were a number of auxiliary departments, whose services were available to the general managers of the divisions; in fact, the general managers were expected to avail themselves of these services. In 1938, these departments and their supervisors were:

Finance and accounts, H. E. Humphreys, Jr.
Distributing branches, F. W. Strong
Auxiliary departments, E. J. Coughlin
Sales and production coordination, real estate, leases, idle plants
Planning and engineering, J. A. Barrett, director
Development, W. A. Gibbons, director
Industrial and public relations, Cyrus S. Ching, director

Legal and patent matters were handled by Arthur, Dry, and Dole.

Advantages of Decentralization

The decentralized organization existing throughout the Davis administration (with the exceptions previously noted) provided much more flexibility of operation than had been possible under the highly centralized organization headed by Seger. For example, the Mishawaka plant, during the early 1930's, attempted to find new products that would profitably employ excess manufacturing facilities and the surplus floor space resulting from reduced footwear sales and the installation of conveyorized making units. The plant began manufacturing rubber floor mats for automobiles, foam rubber cushions and mattresses, and other items quite apart from the range of products previously manufactured and sold by the Footwear Division. Plants in other divisions also branched out into new fields, thereby increasing sales volume.

Not only did the old divisions have more latitude, but new divisions were created as needed. Prior to 1941, the manufacture and sale of textiles had been carried on as a department in the Tire Division, but the increasing importance of sales of textiles to customers outside the company led to the formation of the Textile Division in 1941, with H. Gordon Smith as its first general manager. Later, the defense work performed by United States Rubber during World War II created new divisions.

During the last year of Davis' presidency, ten divisions were operating under the following general managers:

Tire, F. S. Carpenter
Footwear-Fuel Cell, H. S. Marlor
Mechanical Goods-General Products, Lastex Yarn, and Rubber Thread, W. H. Cobb
Naugatuck Chemical-Synthetic Rubber, J. P. Coe
Textile, H. Gordon Smith
Munitions, J. W. McGovern
Shell Loading, E. G. Brown
Explosives, J. E. Caskey
Dominion Rubber Company, Ltd., P. C. Jones, president
Plantations, J. W. Bicknell.

The following auxiliary departments served the divisions in 1942:

Distributing branches, F. W. Strong, general manager
Pacific Coast Division, J. B. Brady, general manager
Industrial and public relations, Cyrus S. Ching, director
War products committee, T. J. Needham, chairman
    War Products Division, W. W. Cowgill, supervisor
Purchasing—G. M. Tisdale, director
Traffic—G. F. Hichborn, director
Business research—A. F. Van Pelt, director
General development—W. A. Gibbons, director
Engineering—C. A. Ostling, director
Advertising—T. H. Young, director
Legal and patent—Arthur, Dry and Dole, general attorneys
Finance and accounts—A. Surkamp, treasurer
Credits and collections—F. A. Cyr, manager.

Foreign activities, other than the plantations and operations in Canada, were organized under:

United States Rubber Export Company, Ltd., L. C. Boos, vice-president and general manager.

Consolidated Rubber Manufacturers Ltd. (and associated companies), Elmer Roberts, chairman.

The foregoing only partially indicates the great diversity of operations of United States Rubber in 1942, since a wide range of only slightly related products were made by a single division.

Observations Regarding Functioning of Committees

The advantages of decentralization of responsibility and authority instituted by Davis when he became president in 1929 are readily apparent. Through their service on management committees, men were enabled to gain firsthand knowledge of operations of other divisions or departments and broaden their corporate viewpoint. The judgment and knowledge of several executives, each competent in his own field, were brought to bear on all matters that came before the committees. Such a practice tended to prevent hasty decisions that might have been made by an executive with a narrow background or strictly departmental viewpoint. Formal presentations, accompanied by descriptions of facilities required, detailed estimates of costs, projected savings, and return on investment lessened the probability that important decisions would be made without sufficient consideration of related factors. Furthermore, in his capacities as chairman of the executive and operating committees (and as a member and sometimes chairman of the finance committee), Davis soon had the opportunity to appraise the managerial ability, technical skill, operating know-how, and judgment of members of his staff.

Over the years, however, it was found that the committee management did not function as well for United States Rubber as had been expected. The broad diversification of the company prevented most managers of operating divisions from becoming familiar with problems of other divisions. Consequently, when a proposal was submitted to the operating committee by a division's general manager, valuable time was often lost while committee members investigated pertinent factors. Top executives were often engaged for several hours debating expenditures of considerably smaller amounts than they were officially required to approve.

Furthermore, presentation to the committees became encumbered with expensive exhibits. Some of the members thought that during the late 1930's the committees had tended to waste time with meetings occasionally marked by prolonged haggling over details. Decisions reached by a majority vote were too often influenced by "division politics" or were the product of compromises. While on occasion these compromises were well-conceived and beneficial, the nature of the compromise occasionally set up conditions that militated against the full success of the project as finally approved by the committee.

Committee management was not abandoned during Davis' administration nor during the war years that followed, but in the postwar period a series of steps was taken that led to a complete revision of the organization at the top level of executive authority. On Oct. 9, 1957, John W. McGovern succeeded H. E. Humphreys, Jr. (whose ill health required a lightening of his responsibilities) as president and chief operating officer. Humphreys, chairman of the board, also served as chief executive officer, with responsibility for the company as a whole. He convinced the directors that the time had come to replace committee management with a line-and-staff organization.

The former executive committee, which had had responsibility for operating the company, was eliminated. Each general manager was given sole responsibility for operating his division. The former finance committee was replaced by a new executive committee, with all the powers and duties of the former, together with any other duties that might be delegated to it by the directors. Previously, twenty-one persons had reported directly to the chairman. Now, only the president and three others, responsible for "corporate" functions, reported directly to him. Only six others, who had "operating" responsibilities, reported to the president. Three years later at the time of McGovern's retirement and the election on Nov. 1, 1960 of George R. Vila as president, the return to individual responsibility for operations was virtually complete. Among the noticeable effects of the simplification of the organization were speedier decisions by top management. Thus did United States Rubber seek to adapt itself to the exigencies of the space age.

DEPRESSION AND DROUGHT

The stock market crash of Oct. 29, 1929 not only erased millions of paper profits in securities, but also wiped out the entire savings of thousands who had purchased stocks on margin. With public confidence badly shaken, the need for retrenchment and conservation of capital ruled out plans for expansion or for any expenditures not absolutely essential.

Lower Sales of Automobiles and Tires

Automobile manufacturers were especially vulnerable, and factory sales of motor vehicles plummeted. *Automobile Facts and Figures, 1962* reported as follows:

Year	Passenger Cars (thousands)	Motor Trucks (thousands)
1929	4,455	882
1930	2,787	575
1931	1,948	432
1932	1,104	228
1933	1,561	329

Sales of tires for original equipment declined directly in line with sales of cars and trucks, and the curtailment of travel reduced the replacement demand for tires. Average monthly manufacturers' shipments of tire casings for the years 1929 through 1933 were as follows (according to information in the *1959 Statistical Supplement to the Survey of Current Business*):

Year	Original Equipment (thousands)	Replacement (thousands)
1929	1,616	3,924
1930	1,001	3,252
1931	791	3,230
1932	502	2,768
1933	874	2,708

The precipitous decline in prices of crude rubber, coinciding with drastic shrinkage of the market for tires, brought a succession of price cuts that carried prices of tires and of some other rubber products well below the cost of manufacture. The buyer was king and knew he was, and drove hard bargains.

Fortunately for United States Rubber, as it seemed at that time, the aggressive sales policies that had been followed by Davis and Tompkins had increased the company's share of the total tire market (p. 309). In 1929 United States Rubber's shipments of 1,345,000 original equipment tire casings had represented only 6.9% of the industry's total shipments of original equipment tires, and the company's shipments of 3,072,-000 replacement tires had been only 6.5% of the total shipments of replacement tires by the industry. In 1933, the company's shipments had risen to 2,871,000 original equipment tires and 5,263,000 replacement tires. More significant were the increases to 27.4% and 16.2%, respectively, of the industry totals in each tire category.[6]

Sharp Decline of Footwear Sales

The early thirties were also marked by severe drought and mild winters that sharply lessened the demand for rubber footwear. Although some parents economized by buying rubber-soled canvas shoes instead of leather shoes for their children, the market was flooded with shipments of extremely low-priced, rubber-soled canvas shoes from Japan; imports from that country in 1933 totaled 4,438,000 pairs.[7] Apparently the Japanese government was subsidizing these exports in order to obtain additional dollar exchange, for the landed price of Japanese rubber-soled canvas footwear in port of entry on the West Coast was less than the cost to American manufacturers of the raw materials, chiefly rubber and cotton fabrics. The manufacture of low-priced rubber footwear for the export market also expanded in Czechoslovakia during the early 1930's. In 1932, for the first time in history, countries other than the United States consumed more than half of the world's crude rubber, a fact reflecting the increased volume of rubber and rubber-soled canvas footwear and other rubber products manufactured with extremely low wages in Japan and Czechoslovakia for export. Japan's annual imports of crude rubber rose from 18,000 tons to 60,000 tons in 1932, and Czechoslovakia increased its imports from 2,000 to 10,000 tons that year.[8]

The sharp curtailment of volume, coupled with drastic reductions in selling prices, resulted in staggering losses for the domestic manufacturers. The desperate industry sought and obtained respite through an act of Congress, effective March 3, 1933; rubber-soled canvas footwear with fabric uppers in which rubber was the component of greatest value became subject to import duty of 35% of the American selling price of like or similar goods of American manufacture. By the same act, imports of waterproof rubber footwear were subject to ad valorem duty of 25% of the American selling price of like or similar goods of American manufacture. This act curtailed the competition from Japan for several years; imports in 1934 were down to 1,338,000 pairs, in 1935 to 934,000 pairs. Intense competition for the slim market that existed prevailed, however, among domestic manufacturers. Any merchant who was interested could buy all the low-grade, lace-to-toe canvas shoes he wanted at less than 40¢ a pair. In addition, retailers were bombarded with offers of "distress merchandise" in all types of rubber footwear at large discounts, so that for several years it was difficult for any company to get a normal markup on its regular production.

Other Divisions Affected

Other divisions of United States Rubber felt the effects of the depression in varying degrees. Practically the entire output of the textile mills was sold within the company; their sales rose and fell with those of the Tire and Footwear Divisions. Since the nation's industrial plants were operating at only a fraction of capacity, the demand for the products of the Mechanical or Chemical Divisions was limited. Sales and earnings of the Export Division and the Dominion Rubber Company declined as the effect of the depression in the United States spread to Canada and other countries. The rubber trees on plantations in the Far East continued to yield more latex than the market could absorb, and with the fall in the price of crude rubber the company's plantations reported losses for 1930, 1931, and 1932, and a profit of less than $80,000 for 1933.

Financial Positions of Customers

The start of the depression found many of the company's customers burdened with high rentals under long-term leases. Some retailers had impaired their working capital by expensive alterations of their stores or through withdrawal of funds for other investments, the value of which was now either greatly reduced or nonexistent. Most remaining jobbers of United States Rubber products could not survive the depression, and the company was forced to take them over to avoid serious credit losses.

Too many of the industrial accounts sold by United States Rubber had succumbed to the widely held belief that expansion could be safely financed almost entirely with borrowed capital. (United States Rubber Company itself was a prominent example of the pitfalls inherent in this philosophy.) The average annual rate of business failures per 10,000 enterprises as reported by Dun and Bradstreet for the years 1925 to 1929, and for each of the years from 1930 through 1933, compared with 1960 as follows:

1925-1929 average rate	105.0	
1930 rate	124.2	
1931 rate	135.9	
1932 rate	154.0	
1933 rate	100.7	(old series)
1933 rate	95.7	(new series)
1960 rate	57.0	

Enlightened Credit Policy

Obviously, many firms were forced to reappraise their credit policies. When President Roosevelt issued the order closing all banks in March,

1933, practically all rubber tire manufacturers stopped billing on open account and adopted a policy of shipping on a C.O.D. basis only. However, Fred Cyr, then the credit manager for United States Rubber, took the position that a customer who had been entitled to credit on the day before the "bank holiday" was still a good credit risk. Accordingly, Cyr ruled that the company would continue to ship and bill such customers on regular terms. Not surprisingly, Cyr's decision was questioned seriously by more than one of United States Rubber's executives, and he was under considerable pressure to revoke or modify his ruling. However, Cyr stood firm and as a result the company carried, through the darkest days of 1933, a number of good accounts that would have been forced out of business had the company followed the practice adopted by other members of the industry. A similar liberal credit policy was followed by the other operating divisions of the company. Thirty years later, John A. Boll, who in 1933 was credit manager for the Tire Division, said he could name a number of good accounts, with current annual purchases from United States Rubber totaling hundreds of thousands of dollars, whose business had been salvaged by the liberal policy of 1933.

Another aspect of Cyr's philosophy regarding extension of credit, Boll said, frequently worked to the advantage of United States Rubber. Whenever he knew that the margin of profit on some product of the company was above average, Cyr favored approval of thirty-day credit terms to marginal accounts, with the definite understanding that shipments would be stopped if invoices were not paid promptly. It was Cyr's contention that, if the customer did fail or go out of business in a year or two, United States Rubber would lose only one month's billings; meanwhile, it would enjoy a good profit on shipments made during previous months.

Changes in Patterns of Distribution

Commenting on developments in distribution during 1928 in its Jan. 12, 1929 issue, *Dun's Review* said, "One of the outstanding developments was an immense expansion of chain-store and mail-order business." Only 220 chains of shoe stores were reported in 1928[9] ("chain" being defined as consisting of two or more stores), but the financial straits of many independent merchants, coupled with the strong demand for lower-priced goods during the early 1930's, speeded the formation of chains; by 1935 chain shoe stores numbered 5,006.[10]

The shoe stores were not alone in the struggle for survival. The problems that had confronted the independent tire dealers during the late

1920's were intensified after 1929. By 1933, their share of the replacement tire market had fallen from the 89.8% they had enjoyed in 1926 to approximately 63.8%.

Patterns of distribution were further dislocated by the rapid "drying up" of many small communities as local customers began to do more of their shopping in county seat towns and larger cities. Consumer loyalties to brands formerly purchased from local merchants were severely tested when these consumers shifted their trading to other towns. Frequently forced by lack of their former purchasing power to look for bargains, they were susceptible to the apparent savings to be had in buying lower-priced merchandise. As a consequence, many manufacturers of first-quality items found their volume shrinking more than was indicated by the total decline in retail sales. According to the *Biennial Census of Manufactures* (1933, 1935, 1937), the annual average wholesale values per pair of all production by the rubber footwear industry for the years 1929 to 1937 were as follows:

	1929	1931	1933	1935	1937
Rubber-soled canvas shoes	$0.69	$0.61	$0.47	$0.52	$0.57
Waterproof rubber footwear	1.43	1.07	.79	.88	.89

United States Rubber was in a better position to meet this situation than companies that did not have any lower-priced grades to offer,[11] but the company did suffer from the lower average unit sales price. Profits were hit even harder, since the average percentage of net profit on the lower-priced grades was less than on the first-quality items.

Painful Decisions

Sharply declining sales and bitter competition confronted United States Rubber's management with the unavoidable necessity of curtailing output while reducing manufacturing costs per unit of production. Davis moved promptly to close the less efficient or less favorably located factories. To ease the impact of closing plants, United States Rubber adopted a policy of paying termination allowances based on length of service and earnings of the individual. While the company was far in advance of most employers in this regard, these termination allowances of necessity were not large. Looking back from the vantage point of over thirty years, one might think other steps could have been taken to lessen hardships caused by the unavoidable decisions, but the men who were making them were compelled to salvage a business that since has provided a remunerative employment to many thousands. All in all, they left a creditable record.

Financial Therapy

On Dec. 31, 1928, just before Davis became president of United States Rubber, the company's long-term debt was $104,475,000, and bank loans and notes totaled $25,750,000. When Davis relinquished the chairmanship of the executive committee on Dec. 31, 1942 (he had resigned as president on Sept. 28, 1942), the company's funded debt consisted of $34,563,000 of 3⅝% first mortgage and collateral trust bonds due July 1, 1958. There were no current bank loans. Annual interest charges had been reduced from $5,918,000 paid in 1929 to $1,332,000 in 1942. This major accomplishment was all the more remarkable because in January, 1929 United States Rubber had been a high-cost producer overburdened with a sprawling aggregation of inefficient, antiquated plants.

Sales of $192,962,000 in 1929, Davis' first year in office, did not compare too badly with the 1928 sales of $193,480,000, but the year ended with a loss of $4,677,000. A drop in the price of rubber to 16¢ a pound made it necessary to write down the inventory by $2,721,000. The closing of six factories resulted in charges of $2,464,000 against 1929 income for extraordinary expenses connected with concentration of operations. With a more realistic reappraisal of properties and equipment, depreciation was increased by $1,490,000 over the normal charge of $5,153,000. Four million dollars more was charged against surplus for "extraordinary charges to be incurred in connection with future changes in organization and for contingencies." Although it was a bleak start for the new administration, its policies were destined within a few years to make United States Rubber a strong, vigorous, and financially sound corporation.

Refunding Operations Conducted by de Krafft

One of the men elected to the board of directors of United States Rubber on April 16, 1929 was William de Krafft. As vice-president in charge of finance for the Baldwin Locomotive Works, Philadelphia, he had been since 1919 the right-hand man of Baldwin's president, Samuel Vauclain, and had demonstrated outstanding ability as a financial manager. Persuaded to join United States Rubber, de Krafft resigned his position with Baldwin late in 1929 and on Jan. 7, 1930 became vice-president of the rubber company and chairman of its finance committee. He served in these capacities until his resignation, effective June 30, 1938. On Jan. 7, 1930 he was made a member of the executive committee and chairman of the board of benefits and pensions. In addition, de Krafft served at various times on the purchasing, operating, tax, plantations, and general technical committees.

De Krafft brought to United States Rubber's critical financial problems exceptional analytical ability, combined with strong convictions about managerial action. During the more than nine years that he was connected with the company, he gave invaluable assistance to Davis in the management of finances and the reduction of the more than $130 million debt inherited by Davis.

Since few foresaw the duration and severity of the Great Depression, sales forecasts proved to be much too optimistic, leading to accumulation of inventories manufactured from materials that had been purchased at prices higher than those prevailing by the time the production could be converted into sales dollars. Faced with the consequent deterioration in the company's cash position, de Krafft still succeeded in 1930 in selling an issue of $15 million of 6% three-year secured gold notes, due June 1, 1933. With the proceeds, supplemented by cash on hand, the outstanding $18,136,000 of 7½% ten-year secured gold notes, due Aug. 1, 1930, were paid at maturity.

By the end of 1930, funded indebtedness was down to a little less than $100 million, and the total of current liabilities plus funded indebtedness was almost $41 million less than on Dec. 31, 1928. However, in 1930 rubber sold as low as 7⅜¢ a pound, landed New York; this price together with declines in prices of other materials, especially cotton and cotton fabrics, forced another downward adjustment of $11,084,000 in the company's assets Dec. 31, 1930. The tangible net worth of the company as shown on the balance sheet was less than $95 million, and its position was vulnerable.

When Davis addressed the annual stockholders' meeting in April, 1931, he reported that the company had not been able to earn depreciation charges in the first quarter of 1931, but that satisfactory progress was being made in bringing expenses in line with the volume of business. Almost as fast as plants were closed, the properties were offered for sale or lease, and the proceeds were used for open market purchase of the company's outstanding bonds and notes, which were selling much below their face value. The operating statements for 1931, 1932, and 1933 included credits totaling over $4 million for the difference between par and purchase price of bonds and notes purchased for redemption.

Any other opportunities for raising cash were seized by de Krafft. At one time he had an earnest conversation with Needham regarding the desirability of liquidating a large part of the footwear inventory as quickly as possible. Even if some surplus inventory had to be sold below the current quotations, de Krafft said he could make more money for the company by using the proceeds to buy its high-interest-bearing obliga-

tions at the very low market prices then prevailing than the Footwear
Division might hope to gain by holding the goods for higher prices.
(For example, United States Rubber's 6½% serial notes were quoted in
December, 1932 at prices ranging downward from 59¼ for those due in
1934 to 38 for the notes maturing in 1939.)[12] Needham explained to
de Krafft that the division was holding a large number of orders for
which credit approval had not been granted. The decision was then made
that the Footwear Division should take full responsibility for releasing
these orders on the premise that losses arising from nonpayment of the
invoices would be more than offset by profits from market purchase
of the company's outstanding notes with the funds thus made available.
When Needham was interviewed by the author in 1962, he said that
losses incurred on the orders thus released were not unduly excessive
and that the gamble proved to be a profitable one for the company.

Total inventories reported as of Dec. 31, 1932 were approximately
$7,200,000 less than at the end of 1931; accounts receivable also were
lower by about $6,500,000. Funds received by de Krafft from all sources
enabled him to meet interest charges of $4,382,000 on funded indebted-
ness in 1932, although profit from operations, before interest or depreciation charges, was only $1,305,000. (In 1932, the company adopted a
policy of not accruing depreciation on inactive plants, which had a net
book value of $18,886,000 as of Dec. 31, 1932.) The desperate struggle
of both producers and distributors for survival had driven still lower the
prices of commodities as well as of finished goods. Crude rubber had
reached a new low level of 4.25¢ a pound in 1931, and, though it
recovered to approximately 5¢ by the end of the year, write-downs in
value of United States Rubber's inventories as of Dec. 31, 1931 totaled
$2,716,000. In 1932, plantation ribbed smoked sheet sold for as little
as 2.7¢ in New York. Inventories were again adjusted downward as of
Dec. 31, 1932, this time by $1,108,000.

Continued Losses Endanger Survival

As the depression deepened, net sales of the company plummeted. As
soon as it became evident that manufacturing schedules were in excess
of customers' requirements, production was curtailed through shorter
workweeks and layoffs of production workers. All salaries, including
officers' salaries, were reduced, and economies were effected wherever
possible; still the company was unable to bring overhead and indirect
operating costs in line with the rapidly shrinking sales volume.

The lower price levels that were necessary to meet the savage competition during the depression years did help to maintain sales volume

and to hold down production costs per unit, but the sharp curtailment in cash flow intensified the company's financing problems. Nor did the economies resulting from consolidation of manufacturing operations into fewer and more efficient plants fully compensate at once for the heavy charges for inventory adjustments, depreciation, and "extraordinary expenses incident to concentration and reorganization of operations."

On June 10, 1932 the 8% preferred stock, with par value of $100, sold as low as 3⅛ a share, and the common stock hit bottom at 1¼ on June 2. The high market prices for 1932 were recorded on Aug. 30, with 10¼ for United States Rubber common and 20¾ for the preferred. Combined losses incurred during 1930, 1931, and 1932 totaled almost $42 million, and at the end of 1932 the surplus account showed a net *deficit* of $26,952,000. With tangible net worth shrunk to $75.6 million, total debt as of Dec. 31, 1932 stood at $85.1 million. Almost $8,700,000 of the 6% three-year secured gold notes, due for payment June 1, 1933, were still outstanding. Some observers questioned whether the United States Rubber Company could survive.[13] Indicative of the market's skepticism was the low price of 41 asked in December, 1932 by holders of the company's 5% first and refunding mortgage gold bonds.

The first three months of 1933 were marked by the rapid deterioration of the national financial crisis, culminating in the bank holiday declared by President Roosevelt on March 6. As doubt increased that United States Rubber could weather the storm or fully discharge its current obligations, the market price of its three-year notes fell from 91¼ in January to 71½ in March, even though the maturity date was only sixty days away. On March 31, with $8,513,000 of that issue still outstanding, Davis announced a plan of exchange which offered the note holders payment of 30% in cash and 70% in a new issue of 6% three-year gold notes, secured by pledge of the company's 6% bonds first and refunding mortgage, series B, to the extent of 250% of the principal amount of the notes, as compared with 133% security for the old notes.

Under the plan, deposits of the notes maturing in June were requested, the exchange for the new notes to be completed when the plan was declared effective by the board of directors. The holders of the old three-year notes were slow about agreeing to the plan and depositing their notes for exchange, so that only $2,800,000 had been deposited by the time of the annual stockholders' meeting in April. Vice-President de Krafft reported that the cash balance as of April 18 (exclusive of cash held by subsidiaries) was approximately $6,600,000, down from $12,300,000 on Dec. 31, 1932. It was explained that the decline was caused chiefly by seasonal expansion of inventories and by a larger than normal increase in accounts receivable due to the bank holiday declared in March.[14]

At that point, John S. Dole of the legal firm Arthur & Dry (later Arthur, Dry and Dole) made a timely suggestion. Searching for ways to conserve cash and reduce expenses, de Krafft had taken advantage of a clause in the indenture covering the 1917 issue of $60 million of first and refunding bonds. It permitted United States Rubber Company to be self-insured in part, provided the premiums for such insurance were paid into a separate trust fund created by the company but held and administered by individual trustees.[15] Dole now proposed to de Krafft that the balance then in the insurance trust fund could be used, legally and properly, to purchase the old three-year notes in the open market as an investment of the trust fund. In April, 1933, they were selling at about 70, and de Krafft lost no time in acting upon Dole's suggestions. The trustees of the insurance fund immediately deposited the purchased notes under the plan of exchange.

These purchases not only reduced the number of undeposited old notes outstanding (and ultimately afforded the insurance trust fund a tidy profit when the new issue of 6% three-year notes for which they were exchanged was paid in full), but they caused the market quotations on the old notes to firm up, giving the note holders a better feeling with respect to the new financing plan. Increased tenders of the old notes for deposit under the plan promptly followed. The *Commercial and Financial Chronicle* quoted Davis on May 1, 1933 as saying that the holders of more than 51% of the notes had deposited them. On May 23, the directors of United States Rubber Company declared that sufficient notes had been deposited and the plan was effective; depositing note holders were thus bound to accept the new notes upon their issue on June 1. Davis was also happy to announce that sales during the first two weeks in May had been larger than in the corresponding 1932 period, the first time in three years that the trend had changed for the better.[16]

On June 5, President Roosevelt signed an act of Congress invalidating any gold clause in public or private obligations. If the directors had not been able to declare the refinancing plan effective and the new notes had not been issued on June 1, prior to the enactment outlawing gold payment clauses, the holders of the old three-year secured gold notes could (and undoubtedly would) have demanded cash payment in full rather than accept new notes that would not contain a gold payment clause. Probably United States Rubber would have been unable to redeem the old notes in cash, and receivership and reorganization would have resulted in several million dollars expense to the stockholders.

United States Rubber then owned plants in about thirty states. If the company had been found to be in default, in addition to the primary receivership in the district of the federal court exercising original juris-diction, there would have been ancillary receiverships in each of the other federal districts in which such property was situated. United States Rubber Company had outstanding issues of 5% first and refunding gold mortgage bonds, $6\frac{1}{2}\%$ serial gold notes, the 6% three-year secured gold notes, preferred and common stock. Also outstanding was an issue of 6% gold bonds of the Dominion Rubber Company. In addition, there were other outstanding notes and unsecured creditors. To ensure that all classes would be treated with equal fairness, a protective com-mittee would have been formed for holders of each class of security, each with a secretary and its own legal counsel. The bondholders' pro-tective committee would probably have been sponsored by the invest-ment bankers who had sold the issue to the public; they would have been represented by attorneys as would the trust companies serving as depositaries. Representatives of each protective committee would have formed a reorganization committee, and charges would have been heavy for printings and mailings, advertisements, and other solicitations aimed at persuading security holders to deposit their securities with the trust companies appointed as depositaries. Attorneys' fees, court costs, and fees to trust companies for performing procedural functions and serving as depositaries might easily have been well in excess of $1 million. This calculation does not include compensation of the receivers since it probably would have corresponded roughly to the compensation of top executives of the corporation whom the receivers had replaced.

A receivership for United States Rubber would have been complicated further because it had many subsidiaries, some of which had minority stockholders who could have been expected to form their own protective committee. The company also owned subsidiary companies with proper-ties outside of the United States, factories in Canada, rubber plantations in the Far East, and branches and warehouses in many other countries.

Eventually, a mortgage foreclosure sale would have occurred pursuant to a reorganization plan worked out by the reorganization committee and approved by the court. Since the first and refunding mortgage bonds would not normally have been disturbed, it would have been almost impossible to interest outsiders in supplying the funds needed to make the reorganization possible; it would have been necessary to obtain them by an "assessment" on the stockholders. Upon payment of the assessment, stockholders who had deposited their shares with the reorganization committee would be entitled to certain of the same rank of securistockholders to pay the assessment, it would have been fixed at someties of the new company as those given to satisfy creditors. To induce what less than the estimated value of the package of securities offered. If a stockholder did not pay the assessment within the specified period, he would forfeit his right to participate in the reorganization plan. Inasmuch as the reorganization plan would have provided for formation of a new company with lower fixed charges, the holders of at least some classes of interest-bearing obligations would have had to accept obligations of the new company with lesser face amount or reduced rate of interest, or to accept stock for at least a portion of their claims. In addition to the other expenses mentioned, the holders of stock and the junior interest-bearing obligations would have had to meet in one way or another the underwriters' commission on the new issue. If that commission were no more than 5%, it would amount to $5 million on a hypothetical issue of $100 million of securities of the new company.

United States Rubber's annual report for 1932 showed 13,443 holders of preferred stock and 13,572 holders of common stock. In a few instances, large blocks of stock were held by individuals, syndicates, or financial firms, but many share holders were persons of relatively limited means; some owned less than one hundred shares each. In the depression year of 1933, they would have been hard pressed to bear their share of an assessment of several million dollars; in view of the low market prices for United States Rubber Company's securities, many of the stockholders would have undoubtedly felt themselves unable to meet the assessment and would have lost their investment. Even if it is assumed that the reorganization managers would have endeavored to assist stockholders who were unable to make other arrangements to finance their participation in the plan, it is likely that in the financial climate existing in 1933, many would have not availed themselves of the offer.

As financial officer of the Baldwin Locomotive Works, de Krafft had seen the results of a number of reorganizations of railroads. He knew that in each case the holders of their securities had suffered losses of several million dollars, either as expenses connected with the receivership and reorganization or in the reduced value of the new securities issued by the reorganized company. On more than one occasion, de Krafft told John Dole he was determined to protect, if it was at all possible to do so, the stockholders of United States Rubber from such expense and loss.[17] He must have felt much relieved when the new three-year notes were issued on June 1, 1933, for the crisis had been met successfully; he had saved the company from receivership and reorganization. Despite dissatisfaction expressed by some of the note holders, all but about 0.3% eventually accepted the new notes in accordance with the plan offered.

Beneficial Use of Adverse Tax Ruling

During World War I the United States Rubber Company had greatly expanded its productive capacity to meet wartime demands. Contract terminations at the end of the war left the company with expanded and unneeded facilities directly and indirectly related to the war effort. While the government gave some recognition to claims based on unamortized special facilities, the allowances were inadequate, and in the late 1920's the company filed refund claims exceeding $1 million in tax money against the government. The controversy continued for more than fifteen years to affect tax allowable deductions. With the advent of World War II and spiraling income tax rates, company management decided to forego its claims for refund and to close the open tax years with what amounted to minimal payments covering all open issues. In the process, the company restored millions of dollars of property to the basis used for depreciation deductions during the war and postwar years when higher income tax rates and excess profits taxes were levied.

Thus the company ultimately converted an adverse tax ruling to a substantial benefit.

The Tide Turns

By Dec. 31, 1933, the surplus account showed a deficit of $27,558,172. However, the tide was turning; the 1933 statement showed the year's deficit to be $606,000. Profit from operations had risen to $10,385,000 in 1933, up from only $1,305,000 in 1932. Interest on funded indebtedness had been reduced to $3,846,000. One more year of loss would go by before United States Rubber Company would show a net profit ($3,531,000 for 1935), but the worst was over. Davis and de Krafft could begin to feel their efforts had not been in vain.

However, the difficulties encountered in profitable management of United States Rubber during the 1930's continued to be aggravated by what Lord Keynes referred to as "frightful fluctuations" in the price of crude rubber. Writing in *The Economic Journal,* he said,

"There has only been one year in the last ten in which the high price of the year has exceeded the low by less than 70%. The average excess of the year's high over the year's low has been 96%. In other words, there is on the average some date in every year in which the price of rubber is approximately double its price at some other date in that year."[18]

It is a tribute to the management policies of Davis and de Krafft that the company made such marked progress during that difficult period. During the first six months of 1938, sixteen subsidiary companies were dissolved, including General Rubber Company, United States Rubber Plantations, Inc., and the Meyer Rubber Company. These sixteen additional subsidiaries were included for the first time in the interim consolidated report as of June 30, 1938.

On July 1, 1938, United States Rubber consummated a memorable refunding operation when it called and paid at 105%, plus accrued interest, the entire outstanding issue of 5% first and refunding mortgage gold bonds, issued in 1917 and due Jan. 1, 1947. The major portion of the funds to retire this issue was provided by sale at par on July 1, 1938, without public offering, of an issue of $45 million of 4¼% first mortgage and collateral trust bonds, series A, due July 1, 1958, to the Metropolitan Life Insurance Company, The Equitable Life Assurance Company, The Prudential Insurance Company of America, and the trustees of the company's insurance fund. The $7,500,000 remainder of the $52,500,000 required to retire the old bonds at 105% was drawn from the company's cash without recourse to other borrowing. The indenture covering the new issue provided for a maximum issue of $75 million of new bonds and required the company to redeem at par $1 million on each July 1 and Jan. 1, plus, starting with July 1, 1940, an amount equivalent to 10% of consolidated net earnings for the previous calendar year.

As of Dec. 31, 1937, the consolidated earned surplus account had shown a deficit of $10,471,627, which was converted to a capital surplus of $11,159,633 on June 30, 1938. The steps taken to accomplish this surplus included stockholders' approval, on March 31, 1938, to change the common stock from shares of no par value to shares of $10 par value. There were 1,567,261 shares of common stock outstanding on June 30, 1938. The previously stated value of these shares was $100,895,-401. Their new stated value was $15,672,610, and the difference of $85,222,791 was used to create a capital surplus account. The other financial changes made June 30, 1938 are described in Table 9.

De Krafft resigned on June 30, 1938, and Harry E. Humphreys, Jr. was elected director, vice-president, and a member of the finance committee. Davis assumed the chairmanship of the finance committee at the same time.

Freed from the restrictions of the indenture covering the 1917 issue of bonds, four additional subsidiaries, including United States Rubber Products, Inc., were dissolved after June 30, 1938.

TABLE 9.   Financial changes, June 30, 1938.

Consolidated Earned Surplus

Consolidated earned surplus (deficit) Jan. 1, 1938 ....$10,471,627
Loss for six months ended June 30, 1938 1,284,280
Adjustment of property, plant and equipment values, including $10,791,-
400 to reduce plants not required for manufacturing purposes to esti-
mated recovery values 11,575,503
Refinancing expense, including 5% premium of $2,456,190 2,780,988
Miscellaneous net charges   134,568

Consolidated earned surplus (deficit) June 30, 1938..$26,246,966
Dividends received from plantation subsidiaries out of earnings of previ-
ous periods 6,568,511

Deficit of June 30, 1938 transferred to capital surplus $19,678,455

Consolidated Capital Surplus

Capital surplus arising from change of common stock from
shares without par value to shares having a par value of
$10 each $85,222,791
Less goodwill, patents, and so on, now written off...............$57,662,405
Deficit of June 30, 1938 transferred from earned surplus 19,678,455   77,340,860

                                                                                                            $7,881,931
Net aggregate equity of surpluses of subsidiaries included for
the first time in the consolidated statement as of June 30,
1938   3,277,702

Capital surplus, June 30, 1938 .... $11,159,633

Formation and Dissolution of United States Rubber Products, Inc.

Prior to 1929, dividends received by the parent company from a subsidiary were fully taxable. In 1929, corporations were permitted to file
consolidated returns, offsetting losses that might be incurred by one subsidiary against profits earned by another subsidiary. Then the Revenue
Act of 1932 introduced for the first time the penalty concept, whereby
dividends paid by a subsidiary to its parent corporation and included in
the latter's consolidated return were subject to an additional tax of 0.75%.
At that time this provision was academic insofar as United States Rubber
was concerned, since the company did not earn any profit in 1932,
1933, or 1934. However, under the act of 1934, a corporation filing a
consolidated return was no longer permitted to offset the losses of some
subsidiaries against the net income of other subsidiaries. Neither was a

corporation permitted in 1934 to carry forward any losses incurred during the tax year. These changes in the revenue acts led United States Rubber to take action.

Under the indenture covering the 1917 issue of $60 million of 5% thirty-year first and refunding mortgage gold bonds, United States Rubber had covenanted that the net unencumbered quick assets of its wholly-owned subsidiaries, excluding General Rubber Company and its subsidiaries, should at all times equal at least $30 million. Consequently, United States Rubber was not free in 1934 to consolidate all its subsidiaries with the parent company. It chose, however, to consolidate all but seven of them in United States Rubber Products, Inc.[19] On Sept. 1, 1934, approximately twenty wholly-owned subsidiaries transferred to United States Rubber Company all their operating assets and contracts; on the same date, United States Rubber Company sold and transferred to United States Rubber Products, Inc. all of its operating assets and contracts (*other than real property*). On April 18, 1935, a written agreement between United States Rubber Company and United States Rubber Products, Inc. confirmed this transfer and provided for lease to United States Rubber Products, Inc., as of Sept. 1, 1934, all real estate used in the manufacturing and operating end of the business. The Rubber Company also granted to the Products Company right to use its trademarks, copyrights, and so on, and granted the Products Company a license to use all its patents.

United States Rubber Products, Inc. thus became and remained the principal operating subsidiary of the company until Dec. 31, 1938. On May 1, 1935, the vice-presidents of the parent company (with the exception of de Krafft) resigned and became vice-presidents in charge of the same operating units in the Products Company. When United States Rubber Products, Inc. was dissolved on Dec. 31, 1938, the vice-presidents of the Products Company once more became vice-presidents of the Rubber Company. This arrangement explains why service records of several of the officers of the Rubber Company showed gaps in their tenure of office with the parent company from May 1, 1935 until Jan. 1, 1939.

On Dec. 31, 1938, the full consolidation consisted of the parent company and thirty-five subsidiary companies, all fully owned except seven in which there were minority interests. By March, 1941, the number of subsidiaries had been reduced to twenty-nine.

Improved Financial Condition Recognized

When Davis had been made president in January, 1929, the long-term debt of United States Rubber was by far the highest of any of its chief competitors; by the end of 1938, the long-term debt had been brought down to $44,950,000 and was next to the lowest of any of the leading rubber companies. Davis attributed much of this reduction to the use of funds obtained from the sales of idle plants and equipment, and from the reduction of inventories through the operation of the sales-production coordination system introduced in 1929.

Further indication of the improved financial position of United States Rubber was shown when, effective July 1, 1939, the holders of the first mortgage and collateral trust bonds reduced the interest rate from 4¼% to 3⅝% and also waived the sinking fund payments of Jan. 1, 1940 and July 1, 1940. By Dec. 31, 1942 the amount of the long-term debt had been reduced to approximately 23% of the capital structure of the company on that date. Following is a comparison with the capital structure as of Dec. 31, 1928, before giving account to the receipt of $23,276,000 for 728,412 shares of common stock paid for on Jan. 11, 1929:

	Dec. 31, 1928		Dec. 31, 1942	
	($1000)	Per Cent	($1000)	Per Cent
Value of common stock and surplus	$34,141*	16.7	$49,608	33.2
Preferred stock	65,109	32.0	65,109	43.6
Funded debt	104,475	51.3	34,563	23.2

*After deduction of $58,925,000 intangible assets carried on the books as of Dec. 31, 1928.

It is readily apparent why the financial houses considered United States Rubber had become a much better risk, fully entitled to favorable interest rates.

Resumption of Dividends

The financial reorganization of the company as of June 30, 1938 enabled the directors of United States Rubber to resume declaration of dividends on the noncumulative preferred stock of the company out of earnings available after June 30, 1938. The company was incorporated under the laws of New Jersey, which specify that no dividends can be paid when a capital deficit exists or when an impairment of capital would result, even though net earnings are realized in such years; payment of such dividends would be an impairment of capital, expressly forbidden by New Jersey law. United States Rubber had had net earnings in 1935, 1936, and 1937 of $3,531,000, $10,774,000, and $4,861,-000 respectively, but the consolidated surplus account (adjusted) had shown the following deficits as of Dec. 31 for the same three years:

$24,570,403, $15,332,572, and $10,471,627. Therefore no dividends on the noncumulative preferred stock had been paid in any of these years.

Dividends on the preferred stock were resumed with a payment of $4 a share on Dec. 23, 1938, and in March, 1939, two further dividends of $2 per share from 1938 earnings were declared on the preferred stock. Thereafter, dividends totaling $8 a year per share on the preferred were declared and paid out of each year's earnings.

Net income for 1941 amounted to $4.86 per share on the outstanding common stock after payment of $8 per share on the preferred, and a total of $2 per share was declared on the common stock, thus ending twenty consecutive years without dividends on the common. A holder of the 8% noncumulative preferred stock tried to enjoin payment of dividends on the common stock until 8% dividends had been paid on the preferred stock for the years 1935, 1936, and 1937, to the extent of the net earnings realized in each of those years. The Federal District Court for New Jersey (later affirmed by the Court of Appeals for the Second Circuit) held that the rights of the stockholders of United States Rubber Company were governed by the laws of the state of New Jersey, under which it was incorporated. The court also held that net profits are not synonymous with net earnings, and that net earnings may be productive of net profits or reductive of a deficit. Net profits were defined as the gain remaining after deducting, from the gross earnings of the business, the expenses incurred in its conduct, the losses sustained in its prosecution, and the capital invested. No dividend out of net profits is earned, said the court, until a balance of assets over liabilities arises from the business of the corporation.

During the years in question, United States Rubber had used its annual net earnings to reduce the capital deficit, and the court found no source from which dividends could have lawfully been paid. The court found that the reserves set up by United States Rubber during 1935, 1936, and 1937 were consonant with good business judgment only; they had existed prior to the three years in question and were still existing in 1941.

The court's decision made references to the following doctrines established in several other cases dealing with payment of dividends on noncumulative preferred stock:

> (1) A company could not declare dividends on common stock until it had paid the full dividend on preferred to the extent such dividend had been earned;

(2) Dividends on noncumulative preferred stock were still cumulative to the extent earned in each year;

(3) Dividends on noncumulative preferred stock could not be paid unless net profits were available for such dividends in such year.

The court therefore found in favor of the defendant, United States Rubber Company, and the suit of the plaintiff was denied.[20]

REDUCTION OF MANUFACTURING COSTS

Work of Central Engineering Department

Even before World War I, it is said that Raymond B. Price had been instrumental in establishment of a central engineering department at the company headquarters at "1790." The department worked closely with the shops at New Haven, Conn., where special equipment for the manufacture of rubber footwear was designed and built for use in the System's plants. Central engineering performed technical services and also had helped the Tire Division produce most of the molds used in the manufacture of tires. Certain special machinery and equipment required for the manufacture of mechanical rubber goods were also developed by central engineering and either produced by it or by the plants of the Mechanical Goods Division.

In the 1930's, all divisions placed increased emphasis on the development of labor-saving devices, which contributed in no small measure to the reduction of manufacturing costs during that decade.

Corrections Needed in 1929

Shortly after becoming president of United States Rubber, Davis made a personal survey of the company's tire plants. A keen observer, Davis understood manufacturing problems and was quick to recognize the effects of a manager's operating philosophy, good or bad. He found the following matters needed correction: (1) excessive amount of fixed investment in plants and equipment; (2) substantial obsolescence of equipment; (3) production methods not using assembly line techniques; (4) research and development insufficiently encouraged; and (5) inadequate coordination between sales requirements and production schedules, resulting in low rates of inventory turn. Davis surveyed other plants operated by the company and found similar conditions in many.

Consolidation of Mechanical Goods Division Proposed

In the early 1930's, the company made more than 1,000 items of mechanical rubber goods (including different sizes of the same item). Transmission, conveyor, and elevator belting formed the most important group, with different types of hose second. These two classifications comprised about 55% of the mechanical division's volume, with packings and miscellaneous goods making up the remainder. In sales of hose, garden hose was most important, followed by water, fire, steam, air, and filling station gasoline hose.

Of the eight domestic subsidiaries of United States Rubber that were manufacturing mechanical goods in 1919, six were still operating in 1929, when a report was prepared recommending consolidation of most operations at the Passaic plant.[21] Since the policy of the company had been to maintain the identity of brands of the different subsidiaries, each plant in the Mechanical Goods Division was producing some goods for other plants in the division. For example, New York Belting and Packing Company's plant at Passaic produced goods under the brands of New York Belting and Packing Company; Mechanical Rubber Company, Cleveland; Mechanical Rubber Company, Chicago; Revere Rubber Company; and United States Rubber Company. Passaic also produced rubber tubes and other material for Eureka Fire Hose Company and for Fabric Fire Hose Company.

The principal items manufactured at Passaic were belting and a full line of hose, with the exception of fire hose and heavy suction hose, which was made at the Chelsea plant of the Revere Rubber Company. Cleveland made a general line of mechanical goods, including automotive products, packing, tape, vacuum hose, and rubber jar rings. The Bristol plant made insulated wire; hard rubber goods were made in Providence. Many products were made in two or more plants with wide variations in costs, while the antiquated and peculiar setup on fire hose production at Passaic, Sandy Hook, and Jersey City was reported to involve transfer of considerable material and manufactured parts between the three plants; none, it was said, possessed modern or efficient equipment for this work.

Of the plants operated by the Mechanical Goods Division in 1929, Passaic was the most modern, both in buildings and equipment. If all plants were to be kept operating, immediate expenditure of almost $500,000 for modern and efficient equipment in the mill and calender room of the Cleveland plant was said to be required, as well as $200,000 at the Chicago plant to replace condemned boilers on which the time limit would expire in 1930.

The proposal for consolidation was accompanied by an estimate of possible savings if all production of the Chicago and Chelsea plants were moved to the Cleveland factory. However, the author of the report believed savings of $1,599,000 a year (including $817,000 in overhead) would be possible if all production of mechanical goods, other than wire, were consolidated at Passaic—and certain other recommended changes in procedure were adopted. Such a move would require added factory space at Passaic. The total expenditures involved were estimated as:

Purchase of land and construction of buildings at Passaic	$2,100,000
Purchase of additional equipment	640,000
Relocation expense	832,000
Total of these items	$3,572,000

Completion of the various projects detailed in the report was expected to take about three years, with a little more than half the expense to be incurred the first year, one-third in the second year, and the remainder in the third year. By the end of the third year, savings of $1,480,000 were projected.

Reorganization along functional lines was recommended, together with improved scheduling procedures. It was claimed that with proper controls the inventory of raw materials could be reduced from an over-two-months position to two weeks, but estimated savings were based on attaining only a four-weeks position. In-process inventory should be cut from approximately $800,000 to about $278,000. Substantial savings in carrying charges were forecast.

The report stated that if the proposed changes had been effective throughout 1928, when the Mechanical Division's net sales were $22,516,-000 (exclusive of $3,331,000 by the Wire Division), 1928 gross profit would have increased from 30.30% to 36.53% and net operating profit from 8.17% to 14.36%.

The operating committee approved the proposed consolidation, and, by the middle of 1930, the job of transferring operations and equipment and of closing down the plants of the Mechanical Goods Division at Chicago, Cleveland, and Chelsea was well under way; the entire consolidation required about four years to complete. Closing of the Eureka Fire Hose Company's plant at Jersey City was completed about 1934-35. The original proposal called for closing the Sandy Hook plant of Fabric Fire Hose Company. However, Willard H. Cobb, who had been transferred to Passaic in 1929 as technical superintendent to ensure that all the details connected with factory specifications and technical and manufacturing standards were properly handled during the consolidation, did not favor closing the Sandy Hook plant because it consistently produced a profit. By March, 1934, Cobb had been appointed general factory manager of all the plants in the Mechanical Goods Division, and his decision that operations should be continued at Sandy Hook prevailed.[22] The production of wire at Bristol and of mechanical goods at Providence was also continued.

According to a staff member of the Mechanical Goods Division at that time, the changes connected with these consolidations created a general feeling of instability and lack of security. However, he added, this situation was corrected with Cobb's appointment as the general factory manager of the division.

Actual costs incurred in consolidating so many operations at Passaic were considerably higher than estimated. One major unforeseen item was the added cost of steel piling required for the foundations of the new building near the river bank at Passaic. Nevertheless, the ensuing improvement in earnings of the division fully justified the move.[23]

Tire Division's Merry-go-round

On an early trip to the Detroit plant Davis told Tompkins that Arthur J. Brandt had recently formed (in June, 1929) a firm of consulting engineers. Davis had known Brandt when both men worked for Du Pont at the Old Hickory plant, and later, when Davis was with General Motors and Brandt was vice-president of the Pontiac division in charge of production. Davis said Brandt had done some good work on plant layouts and in conveyorizing production units. Brandt was in Detroit at the time, and before Davis and Tompkins returned to New York they had engaged the Brandt company to devise better tire-making methods and more efficient factory layouts.

One of Brandt's partners was Carl Ostling, who had been his chief of standards and factory manager at Pontiac. Ostling had been responsible for the factory layout of the Pontiac division's new motor car plant at Pontiac, Mich., which at that time was the largest manufacturing plant ever put under one roof. Neither Brandt, Ostling, nor either of the two other partners in the Brandt company knew anything about the rubber business, but they could readily see opportunities for rearranging the Detroit plant to improve the flow of the work. While the flat-band method of making tires had greatly increased productivity, an individual operator still assembled or "built" an entire tire. Considerable motion was wasted in reaching for the different materials that went into the tire—fabrics, intermediate layers of rubber, wire bead, and outer rubber tread.

Brandt had been doing some work for the Footwear Division and knew about the rotary conveyorized units that the American Rubber

Company's Cambridge plant had developed. He and Ostling now conceived the idea of mounting a series of tire-building machines on a rotary conveyor with nineteen stations for workers performing the successive operations. Such an installation would substantially reduce trucking and handling of material, would lessen the dependence on skilled labor, shorten the training period, and make it possible to employ women on some of the lighter operations. During an interview in 1952, H. Gordon Smith stated that a similar idea for a conveyorized tire-making unit had been discussed even before J. Newton Gunn resigned in 1923. The suggestion was not adopted because "probably no one in manufacturing quite realized the possibilities," Smith said.

When interviewed by the author in 1963, Ostling recalled that when he presented his drawings of the proposed conveyorized unit to the factory management, the consensus of the group was that the probable actual savings would not justify adoption of his proposal. After leaving the meeting, he said he met F. B. Davis, Jr., who happened to be in Detroit at the time. Ostling told him about his idea for a conveyorized tire-building unit; Davis asked to see the drawings and inquired about the cost to set up a pilot unit. On the basis of Ostling's "off-the-cuff" estimate of $30,000, he was told to go ahead. The unit was built and manned with an entirely "green" crew. Only one tire was produced the first day; then about 13 tires were produced the following day, followed by production of 26, then 39 tires a day.

Months were spent trying to "work out the bugs" in the unit. Finally, Curtis Moody, who was then factory manager of the Detroit plant, assigned to the unit an experienced foreman, John Donahue, who had a record of solving difficult production problems. It was decided to remove four of the tire-building machines from the unit, to regroup the operations, and to perform some subassemblies adjacent to the unit. The results were encouraging. After a few more months of testing this pilot installation, it was decided to eliminate the original conveyor and to install ten tire-building machines on a circular turntable that soon became known as the "merry-go-round" (Figure 46). More than fifteen of these circular units, each containing ten tire-building machines, were later built and used in the Tire Division. The output of each merry-go-round ranged from 3,000 to 3,300 tires per twenty-four hour day.

Experience proved that an unskilled crew could be trained in about ten days instead of several years as had previously been required. Understandably, the merry-go-round was described by Davis as a "real revolution" in tire manufacture. While the units finally designed and oper-

46. Merry-go-round tire-building unit in operation at the company's
Detroit plant.

ated were radically different from the original conveyorized unit, it has
been said that without the Brandt organization's idea of installing tire-
building machines on a chain conveyor, the merry-go-round probably
would not have been developed, certainly not at that time.[24]

At about the time the first conveyorized tire-building unit was installed, the Detroit plant was making its initial tests of unit vulcanizers.
The pilot installation indicated that substantial savings could be realized
by replacing the twenty-foot deep pit vulcanizers then in use. The Brandt
organization now rendered valuable assistance with preparation of new
layouts that provided for installation of ranks of unit vulcanizers with a
capacity commensurate with the tire-building units, and located on the
same floor.

By 1941, the company's total daily manufacturing capacity had
reached 60,000 tires. When Ostling was interviewed in 1963, he said
the exceptional advantages of the merry-go-round units were again demonstrated after World War II. When the wartime production of tires for
passenger cars was prohibited, most of the units were dismantled
and the space used for the production of fuel cells and other military
items. At the end of the war, the Tire Division submitted appropriation

requests for reinstalling a number of merry-go-rounds, but Ostling thought they might have been outmoded by new automatic devices developed at Akron during the war. He referred the requests back to the division engineers with the recommendation that, before spending about $150,000 for reinstallation of each unit, they carefully investigate the newer equipment and methods. After each investigation, the engineers concluded that the merry-go-round units still offered the most economy. Even the tire plant in Kitchener, Ontario, which had not had any of these units prior to World War II, installed them when reconverting to peacetime production of passenger car tires. Several more years would elapse before developments in automation through the use of computers and electronic controls would render the merry-go-round obsolete.

Patents on Flat-Band Process Contested

In 1933, the United States Rubber Company filed suit against the Firestone Tire and Rubber Company to collect damages for alleged infringement of Hopkinson's basic patent 1,374,505 and of six related patents, which were claimed to relate to the method of building automobile tires by the so-called drum or flat-band process. The lower court decided in favor of United States Rubber, saying in part, "The Hopkinson patent discloses a complete departure from the core process of molding tire casings and while other and earlier methods are suggested in singular form they do not anticipate the revolutionary combination which is found in Hopkinson invention." The Firestone Tire and Rubber Company appealed, and on Oct. 10, 1935 the Circuit Court of Appeals, Sixth Circuit, reversed the findings of the lower court with respect to the Hopkinson patent and some of the related patents, but held that United States Rubber was entitled to "the usual relief for infringement of the apparatus claims of Abbott Patent No. 1,507,563." United States Rubber appealed to the Supreme Court, which refused to grant writ of certiorari; however, under the ruling of the Circuit Court, United States Rubber continued to collect royalties from tire companies licensed to manufacture tires under patents that were not held invalid.

Footwear Production Consolidated and Conveyorized

The steps taken in the Footwear Division to reduce manufacturing costs are discussed at some length, principally because the cost of sales in that division was higher than average. Rubber footwear manufacture required more hand operations than most other rubber goods.

Within two months after Davis became president of United States

Rubber, production of rubber footwear was discontinued at the plant of L. Candee and Company. Before the end of the year four other plants had been closed, and six factories, together with other obsolete plants closed in previous years, were offered for sale. By the end of 1932 all production of rubber footwear and of rubber-soled canvas footwear had been concentrated at Naugatuck with the exception of BALL-BAND (Red Ball) footwear made at the Mishawaka plant. The following footwear factories then had been closed: American Rubber Company, Cambridge, Mass., footwear only; American Rubber Company, Stoughton, Mass.; Boston Rubber Shoe Company, Malden and Melrose, Mass.; Beacon Falls Rubber Shoe Company, Beacon Falls, Conn.; L. Candee Rubber Company, New Haven, Conn.; Lycoming Rubber Company, Williamsport, Pa.; Woonsocket Rubber Company, Woonsocket, R.I. and Millville, Mass.; Lawrence Felting Company, Millville, Mass.; and McCord Norton Shoe Company, St. Joseph, Mo. (leather footwear).

The Naugatuck plants of the Goodyear Metallic Rubber Shoe Company and the Goodyear India Rubber Glove Company had been revamped to handle the concentrated production. All manufacture of footwear lasts had been consolidated at the Shoe Hardware Company, Waterbury, Conn., and the felt shoe plant at Dolgeville, N.Y., had been sold.

Needham, before his appointment in 1929 as general manager of the Footwear Division, had been employed in the commercial phases of the division. To acquaint himself with manufacturing operations and to gain the cooperation of the factory managers, he visited the various plants; these trips paid good dividends.

When Needham proposed closing the plants at Malden and Melrose, he forecast a saving of $540,000 in fixed overhead. His judgment was seriously challenged by members of the executive committee, who were not convinced that the Naugatuck plants could satisfactorily absorb the additional production, or that, if they could, the projected savings would be realized. However, de Krafft reminded the members of the committee that, under Davis' new plan of operation, the general manager of each operating division had been given full authority and responsibility for profitable operation of his division. Needham's staff had carefully checked all aspects of the proposed consolidation, and he now confidently proceeded with the proposed move. In addition, the Lawrence Felting Plant at Millville was sold to the American Woolen Mills, and the Boston Rubber Shoe Company's footwear last plant was sold to United Shoe Machinery Corporation. The combined net savings accomplished by all these moves far exceeded his estimate of $540,000.

Consolidation of manufacturing operations made a program of modernization feasible. The steps that had been taken at some of the footwear factories during the 1920's to increase their efficiencies now began to bear fruit. The conveyorized making units, first introduced at the Cambridge plant about 1928, eventually enabled the company to install specially designed automatic equipment, such as sole and heel presses. These and other devices eliminated many hand operations and also ensured that controlled pressure would be applied uniformly at all times on soles, heels, and other critical areas. At about the same time, more of the prefitting and subassembly operations began to be performed by women working alongside flat rubber conveyor belts. The assembly was then passed under a roller, which pressed the parts together. Thus the quality of the footwear was improved as costs were reduced. About 1929, a new heavy duty straight-line boot conveyor, equipped with a new type of jack that positioned the boot last for each operation, was designed by the Footwear Division's central mechanical department and was installed at Naugatuck.

Before the Cambridge plant was closed, Needham had seen a conveyorized unit specially equipped to press together the several parts of buckle stays for arctics. However, he was unable to convince the central engineering department that the possible labor savings would pay for the installation of more similar conveyors, which he was told would cost between $3,000 and $4,000 each. Needham was not satisfied with this answer, and the Naugatuck staff built two conveyors for $1,000 each, which in thirty days saved 15% of the labor cost.

Naturally, in the efforts to improve efficiencies, intermediate changes were made in methods and equipment. For example, in the early thirties, Mishawaka devised large movable reels for temporary storage of long strips of sheeted, unvulcanized stocks for footwear uppers. The sheeted stock could be fed as desired from the reels to moving belts, where cutting or other preparatory operations were performed. These reels were an improvement over the long, unwieldy frames of cotton sheeting formerly used to transport single lengths of unvulcanized upper stocks from the calenders to the cutting room, where the frames were stacked in front of the cutters' benches. The reels made it possible to use the moving belts at considerable cost savings, but they occupied a great deal of floor space. They were eliminated later by coordinating calendering with subsequent operations so that continuous sheets of rubber could be fed directly to the moving belts and passed through presses or self-cutting rolls, which also eliminated costly hand cutting. The cutting scrap from high-quality, high-cost upper stocks could then be fed back immediately into the calender. Since unvulcanized rubber suitable for uppers deteriorates rapidly, it had previously been necessary to blend upper scrap with stocks worth about one-fifth as much. The new system reduced in-process inventory, investment in equipment, storage space, and labor costs. Better layouts and improved methods of servicing the making units with lasts and parts reduced nonproductive trucking costs and also did away with much of the need for placing cut parts in "books" for the "makers."

In the mid-thirties, the Footwear Division began to evolve methods for more efficient operation of conveyorized units. The delivery of cut parts and other materials to each unit was timed so that no operator would be forced to wait for material. Operations along the conveyor were divided into work cycles. Since different types of shoes were made on the same conveyor, loaded and unloaded cycles occurred at different points. Wherever possible, heavily loaded cycles were lightened, perhaps by having some parts pre-assembled or by installation along the line of a machine for positioning the last for the operator, or for doing some other operation such as rolling. The contract with the union permitted filling of unloaded cycles at any time without changing the rate. Sometimes careful revision of work loads resulted in a more even balance between operations, so that the unit could function more efficiently, with increased earnings for the workers while costs per pair were reduced.

Other conveyors were introduced to transport materials and lasts to and from the assembly or making departments, or to carry finished (but unvulcanized) footwear through varnishing tanks. It was also found possible, within an hour after the vulcanized footwear had left the heaters, to perform stripping, trimming, mating, inspecting, and packing operations along a moving belt.[25]

Improved System of Production Control

Tied in with these improvements in manufacturing layouts and methods were refinements in the Footwear Division's system of production control, initiated in the 1920's. The production control department now began to issue its schedules in the form of "brackets" that specified the total number of pairs of each style that would be assembled on a given day by the group of operators working on each conveyor. By determining how many hours or fractions of hours would be required for making the pairs in each bracket, each unit was provided with the proper amount of work for the hours it was scheduled to operate.

Similar scheduling procedures took place in the millroom and other preparatory departments whenever this could be done without impairing customer service or creating burdensome inventories of either finished goods or goods in process. Down time of expensive equipment and waiting time for workers were thereby reduced.

The transfer to Naugatuck of all the brands and types of footwear that had formerly been made in the closed plants rendered it impossible to rely on the ability of scheduling clerks to remember all the detailed information regarding construction of each item, including compounds, fabrics, die numbers, and cutting information. Working with representatives of International Business Machines Corporation, a system was developed whereby specifications for each item were punched into tabulating cards. By running these cards through an IBM printer, an abstract could be prepared and accurate copies made of the daily brackets scheduled for production.

Benefits of Consolidation

W. H. Norton, factory manager at Naugatuck from November, 1928 to August, 1941, has listed some of the benefits accruing from consolidation in the 1930's of footwear manufacturing at Naugatuck and Mishawaka, together with installation of conveyorized units, paced production groups, and better scheduling procedures:

1. About 400% greater utilization of floor space
2. An orderly straight flow of work
3. Reduction of losses on scrapped processed materials and parts
4. Savings in labor effort, with resulting lower costs, from utilization of motion studies, and introduction of labor saving devices
5. Reduction in training expense
6. Simplified computation of payrolls
7. Less in-process inventory
8. Lower overhead costs per unit of production
9. Improved service to customers.

Some of the ideas for improvements in manufacturing procedures originated with employees of the Footwear Division; others were developed by representatives of the central engineering department, some by consulting engineers and suppliers of equipment. Any sound proposal was accepted, regardless of its source. The policy was to have consulting engineers advise plant management on a process, but not to organize or handle the installation. This policy prevented serious mistakes that sometimes occurred when the consultants were involved in operating details or making the final decisions.

Remarkable savings resulted from the combined effect of better layouts and methods, conveyorized production units, efficient production
control department, and proper functioning of the sales-production-coordination department. In the 1920's, the manufacturing cycle for
rubber-soled canvas footwear required seventeen working days from the
first writing of the making tickets until the shoes were in the warehouse
available for shipment. This period was cut to a regular schedule of
nine days, thereby reducing the value of in-process inventory. The
greater flexibility also made better customer service possible. When
necessary, rush orders could even be scheduled for production in four
working days. Comparable but less spectacular reductions were made
in the production cycles on waterproof rubber footwear.

As a consequence, the Naugatuck footwear factories, built to produce
40,000 pairs of rubber footwear daily on a one-shift basis but producing
in 1928 only 17,000 pairs per day, now had a capacity of 130,000 pairs
per day, operating with two and three shifts. They actually produced as
many as 110,000 pairs a day in the late 1930's. During the period from
1929 to 1936 inclusive, the actual productivity per square foot of much
of the Naugatuck plant was said to be increased 4 to 5 times without
constructing any new buildings.[26]

The critical cash position of the company in the early thirties had
caused de Krafft to require that any expenditures for new equipment
or layouts must be recovered out of savings within six months. But
during 1930, 1931, and 1932, savings accomplished at Naugatuck
amounted to thousands of dollars per day, according to Norton. By
1936, said Needham, not only had production costs of the late 1920's
of footwear been reduced by about half, but the quality had improved
at least 50%. Meanwhile, de Krafft was able to use some of the savings
in redeeming more of the company's high-interest bearing securities at
the exceptionally low prices that prevailed during the depression.

Other Consolidations

In 1930, the Naugatuck Chemical Company and the Rubber Regenerating Company were consolidated in the Chemical and Reclaim Department of the United States Rubber Company. However, Naugatuck Chemical Company retained its corporate identity until 1934, when the corporation was dissolved and the Naugatuck Chemical Division was created.

In October, 1931, both manufacturing and sales operations pertaining to automotive mechanical rubber goods going into the fabrication of
automobiles were transferred to the Detroit tire plant. As new automotive

mechanical goods were developed by the Footwear and General Products Division, this policy was modified.

The production of rubber surface clothing and rainwear was discontinued at the Cambridge plant of the American Rubber Company, finally closed in 1934; this production was then transferred to Mishawaka, where it remained until after World War II.

Sales-Production Coordination Inaugurated

Reference has been made to work of W. M. Dougherty of the Detroit tire plant towards better coordination of sales requirements and production schedules. In 1929, Harmon F. Newell was manager of planning and sales service for the Du Pont Viscoloid Company. F. B. Davis had a high regard for Newell's work in balancing production with sales needs and in controlling costs, and, at Davis' recommendation, Newell was hired in February, 1929 by the Tire Division. He was placed in charge of the operation that has since been designated in the United States Rubber Company organization as sales-production coordination (SPC). Other divisions soon learned of the improved balancing of tire production with sales requirements, and the SPC procedure was adopted as a company-wide practice.

In United States Rubber the SPC procedure required each sales manager to submit to the general manager of his division an annual sales estimate showing estimated units and sales dollars for each quarter. After approval or revision by the general manager, this estimate became the official sales forecast for that sales unit and was then referred to the SPC department. The department took existing inventories of finished goods into account and prepared long-range manufacturing schedules that were used by the production manager or factory manager in determining additional or possibly reduced production requirements, whether related to equipment, floor space, or personnel. The purchasing department was also furnished by SPC with information that could be the basis for forward commitments for materials and purchased parts.

The sales departments were also required to submit to SPC, usually by the tenth of the month, their estimates of net sales for the following month in units and dollars, and the twelve-month forecast was revised each quarter for the ensuing twelve-month period. In this manner, sales forecasts and manufacturing schedules were being continually revised on the basis of sales performance, thus reducing the likelihood of excessive inventories. Production curves were improved, and peaks and valleys in manufacturing operations were lessened. The adoption of the

SPC system enabled the company to decrease the inventory/sales ratio from 34.4% in 1928 to an average of 26.3% over the next eight years. The accelerated turnover of inventory made additional cash available for retirement of part of the funded indebtedness.

Cost Savings Accomplished

The combined effect of these and other cost-saving innovations caused at least some members of top management to feel that, by the end of 1933, United States Rubber was the lowest-cost producer of mechanical rubber goods, and had achieved tire costs that compared favorably with the average for the industry.

United States Rubber always has been by far the largest producer of rubber footwear, which required more hand labor than tires, mechanical rubber goods, or most other products of the industry. During World War II, members of the rubber footwear industry making items for the government were required to submit their costs, broken down between direct and overhead charges. The government then reported back to the participating manufacturers (without identifying the sources) the lowest, average, and highest cost reported, also the lowest, average, and highest overhead charges. These reports indicated that the Naugatuck footwear plant's figures, for both direct costs and overhead charges, were as low as any of its competitors and lower than most.[27] However, it should not be considered altogether strange that United States Rubber's overall cost of sales during the 1930's never was as low as the average for the entire rubber industry. The company was laboring under the necessity of operating a number of old plants where streamlined operations were not possible. Furthermore, several of these were located in high labor-cost areas. After World War II the company took effective steps to correct this situation, but in the period under discussion it did not appear feasible to embark on a program involving such large capital expenditures.

[1]*US*, house organ of United States Rubber Company (January, 1943), pp. 20-21; "U.S. Rubber, I, The Corporate State," *Fortune*, IX (February, 1934), p. 53.

[2]Chris Sinsabaugh, *Who, Me? Forty Years of Automobile History* (Detroit: Arnold-Powers, Inc., 1940), p. 201.

[3]F. B. Davis, Jr., notes of interview, 1951, United States Rubber Company archives; also "*U.S.*" *Rubber News*, house organ of United States Rubber Company (February, 1929), pp. 1-2.

[4]"United States Rubber Declares Dividend on its Common Stock." *Rubber Age*, XLVIII (March, 1941), pp. 400-402.

[5]*New York Times* (May 22, 1932), Sec. 9, p. 5.

[6]L. S. Smith, untitled report of the Commercial Research Department, 1934, company archives.

[7]U.S. Dept. of Commerce, *Statistical Abstract of the United States, 1935* (Washington: U.S. Gov't Printing Office, 1936), p. 524.

[8]*New York Times* (May 13, 1934), Sec. 8, p. 5.

[9]U.S. Dept. of Commerce, *Historical Statistics of the United States, Colonial Times to 1957* (Washington: U.S. Gov't Printing Office, 1960), p. 523.

[10]*Statistical Abstract of the United States, 1936*, p. 809.

[11]An example was the Mishawaka Rubber and Woolen Manufacturing Company's shipments of waterproof footwear (Mishawaka archives):

	1929	1931	1933	1935	1937
Pairs shipped (in thousands)	8,425	3,589	3,281	4,219	4,961
Percentage of total industry	14.8	12.3	9.2	10.3	11.0

[12]*Bank and Quotation Record*, V (Dec. 9, 1932), p. 93.

[13]"U.S. Rubber, I, The Corporate State," pp. 52 ff., 126.

[14]*The Commercial and Financial Chronicle*, CXXXVI (April 22, 1933), p. 2812.

[15]Indenture, Feb. 15, 1917, p. 131; Art. VI, Sec. 17. The insurance trust fund was created Nov. 14, 1932 with William de Krafft, Edward J. Coughlin, and Eric Burkman as trustees (letter from C. M. Carroll, 1963).

[16]*The Commercial and Financial Chronicle*, CXXXVI (May 6, 1933), p. 3179; (May 27, 1933), p. 3738.

[17]John Dole, correspondence with author, 1965. Also see Max Lowenthal, *The Investor Pays* (New York: Alfred A. Knopf, 1936), pp. 255-68; John Evarts Tracy, *Corporate Foreclosures, Receiverships and Reorganizations* (Chicago: Callaghan and Company, 1929), pp. 13-23, 80-94, 265-72; Nathan L. Jacobs, "The Interstate Commerce Commission and Interstate Railroad Reorganizations," *Harvard Law Review*, XLV (Cambridge: The Harvard Law Review Association, 1932), pp. 866-83; Warner Fuller, "The Background and Techniques of Equity and Bankruptcy Railroad Reorganizations—A Survey," *Law and Contemporary Problems*, VII, No. 3 (Durham: Duke University School of Law, 1940), pp. 379-81.

[18]J. M. Keynes, "The Policy of Government Storage of Food Stuffs and Raw Materials," *The Economic Journal*, XLVIII (September, 1938), pp. 450, 451.

[19]A minor selling subsidiary, United States Rubber, Inc., had been incorporated in Delaware in 1928. In June, 1932, its name had been changed to United States Rubber Products, Inc. In August, 1934, it filed application to increase its capital stock from $25,000 to $15 million (*New York Times* [Aug. 24, 1934], p. 23). The seven subsidiaries not consolidated included, in addition to United States Rubber Products, Inc., Mishawaka Rubber and Woolen Mfg. Co., New York Belting and Packing Company, Fabric Fire Hose Company, Meyer Rubber Company, United States Rubber Export Company, and General Rubber Company. (Statement to author by Herbert M. Kelton, 1963.)

[20]*Lich v. United States Rubber Company*, 39 F. Supp. 675, aff'd 123 F. 2d 145. Also see *Bassett v. United States Cast Iron Pipe and Foundry Co.*, 75 N.J. Eq. 539, 73 A. 514; *Day v. United States Cast Iron Pipe and Foundry Co.*, 95 N.J. Eq. 389, 123 A. 546, aff'd 96 N.J. Eq. 736, 126 A. 302.

[21]Unsigned memorandum, believed to have been prepared in 1929 by W. C. Bowker, assistant general manager, Mechanical Goods Division, company archives.

[22]W. H. Cobb, letter to author, Oct. 12, 1964. "The identity of the original company (Fabric Fire Hose Company), its product and its method of operating, have not changed substantially. Capable management has produced a continuing profit with a sound, improved product. This is really a reflection of the sound judgment of top management in a large corporation."

[23]Information obtained in correspondence with W. H. Cobb, 1963. An interesting commentary on the benefits of increased efficiencies and greater productivity resulting from modernization of equipment, better factory layouts, and consolidation of operations was made to the author by H. W. Willard in an interview in September, 1963. Willard said that present prices of several items of mechanical rubber goods are lower than those shown on comparable items in an old price list printed in the 1880's.

[24]Evan B. Alderfer and H. E. Michl, *Economics of American Industry* (New York: McGraw-Hill Book Co., Inc., 1942), p. 273. Also, Edward B. Erickson, letter to author, 1965.

[25]Based largely on information supplied by T. J. Needham, W. H. Norton, and H. N. Barrett.

[26]Correspondence with W. H. Norton, 1964.

[27]Correspondence with W. H. Norton, 1964.

8

Progress Toward Marketing Objectives

Original Equipment Tires

In 1929, as F. B. Davis, Jr. began his tenure of office, sales of rubber footwear and mechanical rubber goods by United States Rubber already represented a major share of the total market. However, in 1928 the company had shipped less than 7% of the rubber manufacturers' total shipments of pneumatic tire casings. Consequently, Davis devoted his personal efforts toward increasing the company's share of the tire market. The best immediate hope for success appeared to lie in a determined campaign to win more of the original equipment tire business placed by the various divisions of General Motors.

GM had attained leadership in the motor industry and was the only one of the three largest automobile companies that did not have a close working arrangement with a rubber company. (The close relations between the Ford Motor Company and Firestone Tire and Rubber Company are well known. United States Rubber had supplied a substantial portion of the tire requirements of the Chrysler Corporation and of its antecedents prior to 1929, but shipments had fallen off sharply; in a new arrangement, Goodyear Tire had become the supplier of virtually 100% of Chrysler's original equipment tires.[1]) Davis thought his acquaintance with several of the GM executives whom he had known before and during the time he had been employed by GM would be of help in gaining an increased share of the tire market for his company.

United States Rubber had sold original equipment tires to several divisions of GM for a number of years. In 1926, for example, sales to the Oakland-Pontiac and the Cadillac-LaSalle divisions had amounted to

$2,272,000. In 1928, sales of $2,669,000 to the same divisions had been supplemented by Chevrolet's $751,000 purchase. However, Davis found that it was difficult to persuade the responsible men at GM that they should give United States Rubber a larger share of their tire business. On the contrary, United States Rubber's sales to GM declined from 524,000 tires in 1928 to 442,000 in 1929, recovering to only 465,000 in 1930 despite the combined efforts of Davis and L. D. Tompkins.

Their difficulties arose in part from serious problems that the rubber company had once experienced with the quality of its tires. Due to the company's tardy recognition during the 1920's of the superiority of carbon black compounds for treads and the use of sprayed rubber and a wrong accelerator, tire failures had been excessive during the twenties. However, development of better tires had been under way for some time, and, by the end of 1929, tests made by the Detroit plant indicated their new passenger car tires wore about 30% better than competing brands.

But quality was not the only problem. Shortly after being placed in charge of the Tire Division, Tompkins visited various key executives in the automobile industry in Detroit. He soon discovered that the Tire Division's sales representative then assigned to the auto companies did not enjoy frank, friendly relations with the buyers, a condition important for mutually helpful contacts between supplier and customer. One of the junior salesmen, Emmet Sheehan, so impressed Tompkins with his potential ability that Tompkins appointed him manager of manufacturers' tire sales. Sheehan proved to be an excellent choice; his exceptional sales ability, coupled with an unusually warm, friendly nature, won him a cordial reception in the offices of both present and prospective customers. With Sheehan alert to exploit every possibility for additional sales volume, the way was prepared for Davis and Tompkins to conduct their campaign for a larger share of GM's tire requirements.[2]

Convincing GM executives of the new tire's superiority was difficult, but GM's tests, together with the prices quoted, were apparently convincing enough to obtain favorable consideration by some divisions. General Motors had not yet centralized purchases of tires and other materials and, until that policy was inaugurated, each division tried to get a better bargain than the others. The Oldsmobile division placed substantial orders with United States Rubber in 1929, and the Cadillac-LaSalle division bought a large portion of its requirements from the company. Buick, however, bought only 5% of its 1929 requirements from United States Rubber, while Chevrolet declined to use any of their tires that year. Knudsen, president and general manager of Chevrolet, declared that the rubber company did not appreciate the advertising value that a contract to supply tires to Chevrolet would have. Had the company been appreciative of this fact, contended Knudsen, it would have supplied Chevrolet with tires at cost.

Early in 1930, GM seriously considered undertaking the manufacture of rubber tires for itself. Company inspectors visited practically all the tire plants in the country, including those of United States Rubber, whose officials later testified they did not know the underlying purpose of the visits.[3] This survey convinced Charles E. Wilson of General Motors that such an undertaking would be less profitable than if GM took advantage of the depression prices then prevailing for rubber, cotton, and other materials, and entered into a long-term contract with one of the existing tire companies for a major portion of GM's tire requirements. He proposed to his finance committee, therefore, that the company furnish crude rubber and raw cotton to be fabricated by the chosen tire company. He believed that GM would thereby get its tires at much lower prices, since the costs would not be based on the higher costs of the rubber and cotton that the rubber companies had in their inventories from the predepression period. Such a contract would also enable the selected tire manufacturer to produce more economically, he thought, and thus the price paid by GM for its tires would be further reduced. Wilson's proposal was approved by the committee in September, 1930.

In the civil action brought by the Justice Department against the Du Pont Company and members of the du Pont family for conspiracy to obtain control of GM and United States Rubber with the intention of increasing trade between each of the three corporations, Wilson testified that he had first presented his proposal to Goodyear Tire and Rubber Company. Goodyear was not interested, possibly reasoning that such a contract would complicate relations with its other important customers, which included Sears, Roebuck and Company and the Chrysler Corporation. His proposal was then submitted to B. F. Goodrich Company. Prices quoted by Goodrich were not satisfactory, and the plan was then laid before United States Rubber. Under this plan the price to GM would be based on the costs to the rubber company of crude rubber and raw cotton, and all other costs (including profit) in manufacturing a set of four tires.

GM was to purchase the crude rubber at the prevailing market price through the purchasing facilities of United States Rubber, which would act as GM's agent. The latter would then reimburse the rubber company and sell back the rubber when it was used in manufacturing tires under the contract. A somewhat similar arrangement was made for cotton. (To avoid disclosing to competitors the actual price of the finished tires to GM, a preliminary "billing price" was used, which was adjusted periodically to the contract prices.[4])

Features of the proposed contract were advantageous for the rubber company. It would be assured of at least 50% of the tire business of each division of General Motors, including Chevrolet. The company would also be relieved of the financing of purchases of rubber and cotton, and the risk of fluctuations in the market prices of those commodities. Davis and Tompkins knew, however, that they would have to quote a favorable price if they were to get the contract, and they decided to disregard current unit costs, which were too high because of low volume. Therefore, the prices quoted were based on anticipated cost savings, and were calculated to get back "cash costs" plus a moderate profit. The two men planned to achieve the lower costs and show a profit, not only through the added volume, but also by a comprehensive program of disposal of obsolete plant and equipment, consolidation of manufacturing operations, development of more efficient manufacturing methods, improved inventory turn, and reduction of ratio of accounts receivables to sales.

Lengthy negotiations followed, and the contract was finally signed on March 31, 1931, effective as of Jan. 1, 1931. United States Rubber still had to compete against the other tire companies for the remaining 50% of the requirements of each of the GM divisions, since the placing of that portion was left to the discretion of the divisional purchasing agents. The prices and terms for the base 50% applied to orders for additional quantities. Even so, United States Rubber did not at once receive any orders above the contracted 50% from either Chevrolet or Buick, the two largest divisions. However, the Tire Division could be proud that in a year like 1933 such prestige cars as Cadillac, LaSalle, and the Rolls Royce in America were exclusively equipped with United States Rubber tires.[5]

There is no need to go into more detail concerning the various contracts on original equipment tires that were made between United States Rubber and GM; enough has been said to indicate that the financial interest of members of the du Pont family or of the E. I. du Pont de Nemours and Company had not eliminated hard bargaining between the rubber company and the automobile manufacturer. On the contrary, the bargaining may have been intensified as each party strove to prove that his decisions were motivated by nothing except the best interests of the company that he represented.

United States Rubber also had a substantial volume of original equipment tire business with Packard, Graham-Paige, Mack Truck, and others. (The sales of replacement tires to the Atlas Supply Company, to Montgomery Ward and Company, and to other mass distributors are discussed in the following section. After United States Rubber had taken on these accounts, and was thereby enabled to acquire strategically located tire plants and to achieve lower manufacturing costs through increased production, the Tire Division was in a better position to compete for the business of other motor companies.) Its share of the tire industry's shipments of original equipment tire casings rose from 6.9% in 1929 to 12.1 in 1930, and to 32.5 in 1931. For the next several years, its share continued to be in the neighborhood of 28% or better (Table 10). In 1930, Emmet Sheehan was able to sell 700,000 tire casings to the Ford Motor Company, more than twice the quantity sold to Ford in 1928; United States Rubber continued to sell to Ford until the late 1930's, in some years supplying as much as 20% of the motor company's requirements. By 1934, it was reported that United States Rubber was supplying original equipment tires to three-fourths of the automobile makers.[6]

United States Rubber continued to sell GM its original equipment tires on a contractual basis until May 8, 1942, when the contract was terminated as the result of World War II. In 1933, the original agreement was modified by a provision that prices to GM would be no higher than the lowest prices charged by any of the "Big Four" to GM or to other buyers of original equipment tires, with the added provision that United States Rubber would not be required to furnish tires to GM at less than cost.

During the first few years, while the rubber company was going through a period of reorganization and until it began to benefit from improved production methods and equipment, it was hard pressed to show an operating profit on the contracts. By 1937, however, the company had a reasonable net operating profit attributable to sales of original equipment tires to GM.

Replacement Tire Market Enlarged

The volume of replacement tires sold each year by the rubber industry was much more stable than that of original equipment tires, which fluctuated with the highly cyclical production of motor vehicles. For

TABLE 10.   Manufacturers' shipments of tire casings, 1929-42.
(in thousands)

	Original Equipment Tires			Replacement Tires		
	Industry Total	U. S. Rubber Company	Company Per Cent of Industry Total	Industry Total	U. S. Rubber Company	Company Per Cent of Industry Total
1929	19,389	1,345	6.9	47,085	3,072	6.5
1930	12,016	1,458	12.1	39,021	3,053	7.8
1931	9,493	3,086	32.5	38,756	5,312	13.7
1932	6,028	1,699	28.2	33,217	5,124	15.4
1933	10,487	2,871	27.4	32,494	5,263	16.2
1934	13,276	3,752	28.3	32,276	5,093	15.8
1935	19,264	5,401	28.0	29,406	4,816	16.4
1936	21,446	6,903	32.2	30,867	5,586	18.1
1937	22,353	6,494	29.1	29,886	6,745	22.6
1938	11,516	3,381	29.4	30,567	6,484	22.2
1939	18,208	4,759	26.1	38,022	9,114	24.0
1940	22,253	5,999	27.0	35,346	10,929	30.9
1941	24,780	6,908	27.9	39,894	11,382	28.5
1942	6,680	1,748	26.2	8,872	1,843	20.8

SOURCE: Department of commercial research, United States Rubber Company. Unpublished memorandum, company archives.

TABLE 11.   Correlation between sales of motor vehicles and tires.
(1937=100%)

	Factory Sales, Motor Vehicles	Manufacturers' Tire Shipments		U.S. Rubber Co. Tire Shipments	
		Original Eqpmt.	Replacement	Original Eqpmt.	Replacement
1937	100%	100%	100%	100%	100%
1938	52.9	51.5	102.3	52.1	100.6
1939	74.4	81.5	127.2	73.3	135.1

example, between 1929 and 1932, production of motor vehicles fell by about 74%, and shipments of original equipment tires declined by approximately 69%; shipments of replacement tires in 1932, however, were about 29% less than in 1929 (Table 10). The decline in shipments of original equipment tires would have been even greater but for the practice adopted by automobile manufacturers in 1929 of furnishing a spare tire with each new car. Previously, spares usually were sold by the local tire dealer. Conversely, if the new practice had not been inaugurated at that time, shipments of replacement tires would have declined even less. The statistics for 1937, 1938, and 1939 further indicate the correlation between factory sales of motor vehicles and shipments of original equipment tires, and the absence of such correlation with respect to shipments of replacement tires. The replacement tire market in the late 1920's and early 1930's was influenced by the growing volume of retail tire sales by Sears Roebuck and Company. Since United States Rubber did not have at that time the capital necessary to establish a chain of retail tire stores comparable to those being operated by other members of the "Big Four," the decision was made to go after the tire business of the oil companies and of other mass distributors of replacement tires, especially Sears' major competitor, Montgomery Ward and Company.

In 1929, the Colonial Beacon Company, a subsidiary of Standard Oil, began to purchase a private brand tire from United States Rubber and B. F. Goodrich Company for distribution in a limited New England territory. In 1930, a further entry was made into the states of New York and Pennsylvania through sales on a cost-plus basis to another subsidiary of Standard Oil, the Atlas Supply Company, Newark, N.J. United States Rubber then entered into a five-year contract in July, 1930 to supply 50% of Atlas' private brand tires to be sold through Standard Oil stations.

Starting from a negligible amount in 1929, United States Rubber sold 315,000 tires to Atlas in 1930. By 1933, about 1,700,000 Atlas tires (of which United States Rubber presumably supplied 50%) were sold by about 30,000 stations operated by or for the Standard Oil Companies of New Jersey, Ohio, Kentucky, Indiana, and California. By 1936, United States Rubber's share of the Atlas tire business amounted to over one million tires, and when B. F. Goodrich bowed out in 1937 as a supplier, United States Rubber supplied 100% of the Atlas requirements. A similar contract was made in 1930 by United States Rubber to supply Acme tires to the Arkansas Fuel Oil Company, the southern division of Cities Service Company.[7]

The oil companies looked upon the tire business as a means of spreading overhead costs over more dollar sales—but as a definite sideline. Stations stocked few tires compared with the inventories usually carried by independent tire retailers, and relied instead upon the warehouse stocks maintained either by the oil companies or the tire manufacturers. More important, survival of the station did not depend upon any profit it might make on tires. The stations, therefore, felt able to do business on a closer margin of profit than the regular dealers required. In 1931 and 1932, Atlas tires were priced at retail about 10% below standard first-line tires and about 10-15% above Sears' prices on its All-State tires.

Prior to 1930, Montgomery Ward and Company had been buying tires from several small companies. Davis interested the president of Montgomery Ward in the advantages of buying the bulk of Ward's tire requirements from United States Rubber, and a cost-plus contract for delivery of over one million units was signed in the latter part of 1930. Effective March 1, 1931, United States Rubber was to supply 90% of Ward's private brand tires. The Dominion Rubber Company also negotiated a cost-plus contract with the Atlas Supply Company of Canada about the end of 1930.

With no private brand tire business in 1928 and little in 1929, United States Rubber's private brand tire sales in 1930 amounted to 1,841,000 units, exceeding all its sales that year of original equipment tires; this relationship continued to be true in subsequent years.

Other important contracts with mass distributors of replacement tires included those made later with Western Auto Supply and Gamble Skogmo. The added volume of all these contracts not only reduced United States Rubber Company's unit costs, but indirectly helped to influence at least one General Motors executive in favor of a cost-plus contract with United States Rubber. W. F. Armstrong, who at that time was acting as assistant to Wilson at GM, concluded that the large volume of replacement tire business at United States Rubber would help reduce the rubber company's cost of producing tires so that, under a cost-plus contract, GM would get its original equipment tires at a still lower cost.[8]

The effect of all these efforts to increase the United States Rubber Company's share of the replacement tire market raised its percentage of total industry shipments of replacement tires from 5.6 in 1928 to 13.7 in 1931, 16.2 in 1933,[9] and to 22.6 by 1937. By 1940, the company's shipments of replacement tires represented 30.9% of the industry total.

Cost-plus contracts could have advantages for both parties. The customers obtained the benefit of lower prices, assured quality, and the intangible advantage of capitalizing indirectly on the prestige of the United States Rubber Company (reputed after 1931 to be the world's largest supplier of original equipment tires). For the tire manufacturer, cost-plus contracts offered: (1) a guaranteed margin above agreed-upon elements of cost; (2) greater production, resulting in lowered unit costs; (3) justification for larger expenditures for research and development; and (4) volume warranting acquisition of additional facilities.

United States Rubber enjoyed another benefit from cost-plus contracts—lower selling expense. Annual statements did not separate selling and administrative expense from other operating costs until 1935, but for the six peacetime years, 1935 to 1940 inclusive, selling and administrative expense averaged only 14.73% of net sales, a substantially lower ratio than shown by the rest of the tire and rubber industry. These lower expenses offset the higher cost of sales, and contributed to the favorable operating profits, which averaged 8.4% of net sales during the same six years.

However, other cost-plus contracts have frequently been known to lessen the employee's urge to improve his efficiency and thus reduce manufacturing cost, since this reduction would decrease the amount of money representing the percentage agreed upon as his fee. Probably United States Rubber was not always immune to the negative consequences experienced by other companies while long-term, cost-plus contracts were in effect.

On the other hand, United States Rubber had made, and was continuing to make, major contributions towards better tire performance at lower cost per mile. By 1936, as the result of more efficient manufacturing methods, economies in distribution, and about a tenfold improvement in tire quality, the industry was able to supply tires at a cost per mile, when measured in absolute units, that was about one-eighteenth the cost per mile in 1906. In 1920, the tire cost per 10,000 miles was estimated to average about $163; this figure had been reduced to an estimated average of $38.30 per 10,000 miles in 1936. These savings had been brought about despite the greatly increased horsepower, acceleration, and braking power of automobiles, as well as higher driving speeds.[10]

Distribution of Branded Tires

It should not be thought that the company was slighting the replacement market for its own brands. Only about one-third of the total tire sales was of private brand tires; the remainder was of tires carrying the company's own brands. Not only did the original equipment tires carry the U.S. brand, but during the 1930's the company had wide distribution through approximately 30,000 retail tire dealers. This figure represented a large percentage of the independent tire dealers whose numbers had declined from 120,000 in 1926 to 60,000 in 1936.[11]

Tires sold to them included U.S., U.S. Royal, U.S. Royal Master, Gillette, Federal, Peerless, and G. & J. Fisk was added to the brands marketed by United States Rubber after the Fisk Rubber Corporation's assets were acquired in December, 1939.

At the beginning of the decade United States Rubber had twenty-eight subsidiary corporations operating "Tire Service" retail stores, which both sold tires and provided service to users of the company's tires. Twenty of these subsidiaries were either dissolved or otherwise discontinued during the depression years from 1930 to 1933 inclusive; six more were disposed of in 1934. In the first part of 1935, the Tire Division had submitted to the operating committee a plan for expansion of the company-owned retail tire stores. But the operating committee rejected the plan thinking, undoubtedly, that the serious financial problems faced by United States Rubber during those years were over-riding considerations. Atlantic Tire Service, Inc. and Royal Tire Service, Inc. (Maryland) were dissolved in 1935. Properly qualified buyers of the stores were found within the next two or three years, and United States Rubber ceased to operate any retail stores. Not until well after the end of World War II would the company re-enter that channel of distribution.

About twelve years after the operation of retail tire stores was discontinued, a survey was made of the operating results obtained by the new owners. The findings were gratifying to the executives of the Tire Division. All of the dealers were still in business; all were 100% U.S. Royal dealers. In a number of instances, particularly where the purchaser had formerly been employed by the company as either a store manager or in some other capacity, extended credit terms had been granted by United States Rubber. In each case, the debt had been paid in full. In addition, the report showed that both sales of tires and profits had improved greatly. Some of these dealerships had grown to the point where they had earned a place among the top dealers in the entire country.[12]

NEW ACQUISITIONS

Samson and Gillette Acquired

As it became increasingly evident that efforts to enlarge the United States Rubber Company's share of the market of both original equipment and replacement tires were successful, the necessity of obtaining

strategically located plants with modern equipment was apparent. Fortunately, the way was open to acquire two existing tire factories.

In October, 1930, the directors of the company authorized acquisition of the Samson Tire and Rubber Corporation of Los Angeles (established in 1916). The Los Angeles corporation had outstanding 165,000
shares of no par value common stock. A plan was worked out whereby
the holders of the common stock of Samson would exchange their holdings for preferred stock in a new corporation. Under this plan, a new
company, the Samson Corporation, would be organized under the laws
of Delaware with authorized capital stock of 200,000 shares of 6% noncumulative preferred of par value of $10 per share; 200,000 shares of
Class A common, of no par value; and 200,000 shares of Class B common, also of no par value. United States Rubber would purchase for
$600,000, 120,000 shares of the Class A common stock and 50,000 shares
of the Class B common stock of the new corporation, and the latter would
then purchase 60,000 shares of unissued preferred stock of the Samson
Tire and Rubber Corporation of Los Angeles, which would use the proceeds to retire its current obligations. Details were finally agreed upon
and approved by the stockholders of Samson and the directors of United
States Rubber. The acquisition was formally announced in January,
1931.

Also acquired in January, 1931 was "a substantial stock interest"
in the Gillette Rubber Company, Eau Claire, Wis. (established in 1914).
After acquisition of the controlling interests in Samson and Gillette,
United States Rubber installed additional equipment, raising the capacity of Samson from 5,000 to 6,500 tires per day, and of Gillette
from 9,000 to 11,000 tires and tubes per day.[13]

These acquisitions placed United States Rubber in a better position
to supply the tire requirements of Montgomery Ward and Company,
using the facilities of the new plants to service Ward's needs on the
Pacific Coast and in the Middle West. The lower transportation costs
to all parts of the country, which the acquisitions made possible through
the transfer of tire molds from one plant to another, was also an important consideration in United States Rubber's negotiations with General
Motors, the Atlas Supply Company, the Arkansas Fuel Oil Company,
and other mass distributors.[14]

Assets of Fisk Rubber Purchased

By 1939, United States Rubber's tire sales were taxing the full capacity
of its plants. The company learned that the tire plant of the Fisk Rub-

ber Corporation at Chicopee Falls, Mass., was operating at only about half its capacity, and attempted to have Fisk make some tires for United States Rubber. This negotiation failed. Subsequently, L. D. Tompkins reported to the executive committee that one of the following alternatives must be chosen:

1. Reopen the closed tire plant at Hartford, which would entail considerable expense;

2. Build a new plant, preferably in the East, which would increase the total capacity of the tire industry, already burdened with much more capacity than was being used; or,

3. Purchase the property of the Fisk Rubber Corporation, which had been making bicycle tires since 1895 and pneumatic automobile tires since October, 1899.

The plant at Chicopee Falls was reported to be modern and efficient, with a daily capacity of 13,000 tires, 15,000 tubes, and 6,500 bicycle tires. Fisk also had a tire cord mill at New Bedford, Mass., with 60,000 spindles, producing 1,400,000 pounds of yarn and cord a month.

Negotiations for the purchase were conducted, and on Dec. 6, 1939 statements by F. B. Davis, Jr. and by Colonel Charles E. Speaks, president of Fisk, appeared in the *New York Times*. Davis referred to United States Rubber's need for additional production, and Speaks said that, if the purchase were made, a separate division of United States Rubber would continue to manufacture Fisk tires at Chicopee Falls. Speaks added that Fisk tires would be distributed through the Fisk dealers' organization.

The *Times* reported the following Monday that the directors of Fisk had approved sale of the business and assets of the corporation, subject to its liabilities, to United States Rubber Company for $6,687,-330 cash plus 109,981 shares of United States Rubber common stock, subject to approval by stockholders of Fisk at a special stockholders' meeting on Dec. 29, 1939. According to newspaper accounts, holders of 35,277 shares of Fisk preferred stock would receive cash of $110 a share; holders of 439,553 shares of Fisk common stock would receive cash of $6.75 for each share plus one-fourth of one share of United States Rubber Company common stock. On the basis of 40 7/8, the closing price of United States Rubber common on Dec. 8, holders of Fisk common would receive the equivalent of about $17 a share. (The closing prices on Dec. 8 for Fisk preferred and Fisk common were 104½ and 14¾ respectively.)

The newspaper quoted the Fisk management as saying that United States Rubber wished to operate the plants at Chicopee Falls and

New Bedford "at increased capacity for the production of tires to be sold by Fisk under Fisk trade names and for additional tires under the trade names of U.S. Rubber. Should U.S. not acquire Fisk, it contemplates building additional facilities in the East." Although Fisk stockholders overwhelmingly approved the sale, a minority unsuccessfully endeavored to obtain a court injunction to block it.

On Jan. 20, 1940, the secretary of Fisk Rubber announced that "United States Rubber had paid to Fisk cash and stock valued at $11,227,330, the authorized purchase price, and had taken control of Fisk properties." In March, 1940, Fisk stockholders voted to dissolve the corporation, and its officers were instructed to turn over the remaining assets to United States Rubber. In his annual report for 1939 to stockholders, Davis said that, in addition to the plants at Chicopee Falls and New Bedford, United States Rubber had obtained "a going business which had $17,268,000 of sales and net operating earnings of $806,000 in the year 1939." As the average market price of United States Rubber's common stock was $40 on Dec. 30, 1939, the new issue of 109,981 shares was included in the company's capital stock liabilities at the par value of $10 a share, or $1,099,810; the remaining $30 a share, or $3,299,430 was added to capital surplus.

After the acquisition, an attempt was made to have the same salesmen sell both United States Rubber and Fisk tires. This arrangement did not work well, and in October, 1941 a separate Fisk sales organization was set up; it functioned until production of tires for civilian use was discontinued in 1942.

Valuable Trademark Acquired

Among the assets of the Fisk Rubber Corporation acquired by United States Rubber in 1940 was the famous Fisk trademark, a boy and the slogan, "Time to Re-tire." The yawning boy in his one-piece sleeper was the creation in 1907 of Burr E. Giffen, an eighteen-year-old artist in the advertising agency employed by Fisk. Originally sketched for use on a 24-sheet poster, the slogan and drawing were copyrighted June 1, 1910; they first appeared in an advertisement in the *Saturday Evening Post* of March 7, 1914, and were registered as a trademark on July 21, 1914. About 1918, another professional artist, Edward M. Eggleston, made an oil painting of the boy. Fisk spent millions of dollars publicizing the trademark, which was registered in over ninety countries. Publicity releases prior to 1928 said the Fisk boy ranked among the leading trademarks and was as well known universally as "The Little Dutch Boy" or "His Master's Voice."

47.   Advertisement illustration, "Time to Re-tire."

In 1928, Fisk decided the boy should be smiling instead of yawning; in 1930, when the Air-Flight tire was announced, he was further changed to "a happy, smiling 100% American boy in his little two-piece pajama, radiating good cheer, ruddy-cheeked and tousle-headed, snappy and wide awake, standing in the old-time pose but with a new design Fisk Air-

Flight tire over his shoulder."[15] But in 1934, the boy was changed back to his sleepy self. The original artwork had been so changed by all the retouching that in 1941 the Metropolitan Museum was commissioned to restore the painting. A number of artists were consulted as to whether a new boy should be painted, but they were unanimous that the charm of the original could not be improved upon. Consequently, Eggleston's original conception continued to appear in Fisk advertisements, on every Fisk tire, and in numerous other ways. (By the time the fiftieth anniversary of the Fisk boy was celebrated, three-dimensional models, six feet high and made of Vibrin, a polyester resin produced by United States Rubber, were being furnished to Fisk tire distributors for display.)

Divestiture of Tire Business Advised

For at least several years, Irenee du Pont appears to have taken a dim view of United States Rubber's manufacture of tires. Almost immediately after Davis' election as president of the rubber company, du Pont recommended that the tire business be disposed of to the Goodyear Tire and Rubber Company, commenting that this transfer would "drop the most precarious branch of our business and one which has not paid in the past." At the same time, he advised that United States Rubber should lease the rubber plantations operated by Goodyear. Davis opposed the disposal of the tire business, for he was determined to make it a successful operation. His decision received the support of the directors.

Through the joint efforts of Davis, Tompkins, and others in the Tire Division, additional volume on both original equipment and replacement tires was obtained; in 1933, tires and tubes provided about 40% of United States Rubber's total sales. Apparently, du Pont remained unconvinced that the rubber company had a profitable future in the tire business. He still did not favor enlarging the operations of the division, and in 1934 he again recommended disposal of the facilities, this time to one of the three largest automobile manufacturers. Since the property was pledged under the indenture covering the 1917 issue of first and refunding mortgage bonds, he suggested that a lease for thirty or fifty years be arranged with a provision for later purchase by the lessee if the lessor could work out means for accomplishing the transfer of title. In support of his recommendation, du Pont claimed it was only logical that the automobile companies should produce their own tire requirements, and that if any one of them did go into the manufacture of tires, he was sure the others would soon follow suit.[16] If and when that occurred, he believed a tire manufacturer who had not disposed of the tire business to one of the auto companies would "be out on a limb." For this reason, he considered it unwise to expand operations in the manufacture of tires. Nevertheless, United States Rubber acquired in 1934 a cotton tire cord mill with 23,000 spindles, the Shelbyville Mills, Shelbyville, Tenn., thereby materially increasing the rubber company's capacity for production of cord. Obviously, Davis was determined to make the Tire Division a profitable and important part of the company.

United States Rubber's large share of the original equipment tire business enabled the company to benefit from the increased production of automobiles from 1933 to 1937, inclusive. Furthermore, total shipments of replacement tires by the industry in 1941, the last year before wartime restrictions became effective, were less than 85% of the 47,085,-000 replacement casings shipped in 1929, but United States Rubber increased its percentage of the total from 6.5% in 1929 to 28.5% in 1941. Units increased from 3,072,000 in 1929 to 11,382,000 in 1941 (Table 10).

BUILDING FOOTWEAR SALES

Means Used

As a result of the severe competition and lessened demand for rubber footwear that prevailed throughout the early 1930's, prices were "all over the lot." It was evident to T. J. Needham, general manager of the Footwear Division, that United States Rubber could not expect to meet by price alone the competition of all the smaller manufacturers of rubber and canvas footwear. Under his direction, therefore, the Footwear Division adopted a firm sales policy stating that, because of the superior quality and better service that United States Rubber believed it offered, the company was justified in asking higher prices for its products. This policy required the sales force to impress upon dealers the opportunities for greater sales if they handled the company's product.

The increasing mechanization of the American economy was changing the living and working conditions of the nation, and lessening the demand for most types of utilitarian footwear. Therefore, the Footwear Division emphasized promotion of footwear suitable for leisure or recreation or that had style appeal.

In a previous chapter, mention was made of sales promotions on Keds held in Atlanta, Ga., Palo Alto, Calif., and elsewhere. Needham had been favorably impressed by these promotions, particularly by the results obtained under the direction of Elmer H. White, sales manager for footwear, Pacific Coast Division. Needham appointed White manager of footwear branch sales, and in 1931 White refused to accept the depression as an excuse for poor sales. He tirelessly drove himself and his sales force and sparked an intensive campaign of eminently successful sales promotions throughout the country, working closely with Thomas H. Young, advertising manager for the Footwear Division. The salesmen were equipped with "evidence books" showing how other merchants had increased business on Keds and selected items of waterproof rubber footwear through promotions planned by United States Rubber. The salesmen were also equipped with full-color illustrations of advertisements to be run in leading magazines. In addition, they were instructed how to develop and present plans tailored to the individual merchant's store and designed to help him move his stock at a good profit.

Colorful, washable, rubber-soled fabric footwear for women was offered in a limited way by United States Rubber in the mid-thirties. The first attempts at styling this line were not too successful, but the men responsible for sales policy were convinced that a large volume of business could be obtained with a properly designed line, backed up by national advertising and an aggressive, well-conceived program of sales promotions. United States Rubber launched its first line of Kedettes in the fall of 1937 with twenty-five styles in twenty-two color combinations.

Needham sought and obtained an advertising appropriation of $150,000 for Kedettes from W. M. de Krafft, then the chairman of the finance committee, and the first advertisement for Kedettes appeared in *Good Housekeeping*, April, 1938 (Figure 48). It was demonstrated that such ammunition enabled salesmen to obtain active cooperation from good dealers. Advance orders for Kedettes that first season were over $3 million. Also, as a result of the planned promotions, retailers spent more money than the United States Rubber Company in advertising Keds and Kedettes.[17]

Footwear Sales to Mass Distributors

H. S. Marlor, assistant general manager of the Footwear Division, was given responsibility for increasing the volume of business from the company's major accounts with mass distributors. The following examples illustrate the success of this arrangement. When interviewed in 1962, Needham recalled that United States Rubber's sales to Montgomery Ward were more than quadrupled during four years in the early 1930's. He

48. First advertisement for Kedettes.

attributed this success to Marlor's resourceful salesmanship, which convinced buyers of the advantages of purchasing better quality footwear
specially designed for their account. During the same period, the rubber company's sales to the G. R. Kinney Company were more than doubled in one year. The foundations laid at that time for close and friendly
relations between buyer and seller were destined to continue for many
years with substantial benefits for both parties.

VENTURES ABROAD

International Trade Barriers

Worldwide repercussions of the depression of the early 1930's forced
the closing of many of the overseas branches of the United States Rubber Export Company. Efforts to foster local industries were made as
country after country faced a faltering economy and growing unemploy-
ment. Protective tariffs, drastically curtailed import quotas, and restrictions on currency exchange virtually excluded American-manufactured
rubber footwear and rubber-soled canvas footwear from many markets.
Exports of other rubber products were affected adversely in varying
degrees.

The Export Company found its sales sharply reduced. Great Britain in
1931 was among the first to impose import quotas on rubber products.
That year the Export Company's sales fell to about $13 million, about
$14 million less than in 1929. Britain's action was followed quickly by
erection of trade barriers in Germany, France, Argentina, and other
important markets for the company's products. By 1932, its exports
were down to approximately $6 million.[18]

In more than one country it would have been an opportune time to
establish overseas manufacturing facilities, but United States Rubber was
short of cash and in no position to embark on such ventures. However,
the Dominion Rubber Company's factories enjoyed the benefit of the
preferential tariffs granted Canada by members of the British Commonwealth. This privilege enabled Dominion to continue a lively business
on footwear and Uskide soling material with England and the British
colonies. Dominion also had good sales of waterproof rubber footwear and
rubber-soled canvas footwear in Continental Europe. The Export Company had built up a large volume of sales in Argentina and other countries in Latin America, and was able to salvage much of this business
with goods made in Canada because of the lower manufacturing costs
in that country.

In 1931, William A. Eden, president of Dominion Rubber Company, Ltd., succeeded Charles E. Guest as president of the United States Rubber Export Company, Ltd. Since the bulk of the company's footwear exports was from Canadian factories, the footwear department of the Export Company, under the direction of Edwin L. Hopkinson, moved to Montreal in January, 1932. The Tire and Mechanical Goods Departments of the Export Company continued to operate out of New York. Eden maintained his headquarters in Montreal and visited the New York office about once a week to coordinate the overseas activities of the two companies.

Investments in Sweden and Argentina

For a few years, except for the activities of the Dominion Rubber Company in the sterling area, United States Rubber conducted a holding operation, more or less, seeking to maintain a foothold in important export markets until its improved finances would permit broadening of operations. By 1938, United States Rubber was in a position to enlarge its foreign investments. The first important move was a contract in 1939 to supply technical assistance to the largest Swedish rubber company, Svenska Gummifabriks, A/B, Gislaved, Sweden. The contract provided that the Swedish firm would manufacture tires and other rubber products under the U.S. label, and in accordance with United States Rubber's specifications, for sale by the Export Company. Many of the materials used in tire manufacture, particularly rubber chemicals, tire cord, and crude rubber, would be supplied by United States Rubber Company. The relationship with the fine Swedish firm proved to be most satisfactory. Similar negotiations for manufacture of Dominion tires were entered into with North British Rubber Company, Ltd., Edinburgh, shortly before the outbreak of World War II. United States Rubber did not have a financial interest in either firm at that time. (During the war, Svenska Gummifabriks locked in a vault the formulas supplied by United States Rubber and informed the German occupation officials that they could do nothing about supplying these formulas. This verdict was accepted by the Germans.)

Elmer Roberts succeeded Eden as president of the Export Company on Jan. 1, 1939. The plans for construction of a factory in Argentina for manufacture of tires and rubber-soled canvas footwear for the Argentine market, first proposed in the late 1920's, were revived and approved in 1939. Such a factory would enable United States Rubber to recapture the volume of sales it had enjoyed in that country; impetus was added by the desire of the Atlas Supply Company to extend its tire sales through the

Standard Oil subsidiary operating in Argentina. A site for the factory was purchased, some of the building material had been delivered, plans to begin operations by Sept. 1, 1940 were announced, and some of the personnel had arrived when World War II began. All plans had to be discontinued. A similar proposal for a plant in Cuba was postponed at the same time.

In the face of this disappointing setback, a ten-year contract was made in 1939 to have tires made for the Export Company, according to its specifications, in the tire factories operated by Firestone in Brazil and Argentina, using tire molds supplied by United States Rubber. Since United States Rubber was supplying 100% of Atlas' tires in the domestic market, it felt a major responsibility for cooperating fully in the efforts of the Atlas Company to enlarge its overseas distribution. At the same time, Firestone was not in a position to furnish as many tires as United States Rubber wanted. However, an equitable allocation of the available production between Atlas and other customers was worked out. Wartime restrictions prevented normal operations, however, and it was not until much later that United States Rubber was able to arrange for a more adequate supply of tires to its customers in Argentina and Brazil.[19]

Other Developments

It will be seen that prior to World War II the business of the United States Rubber Export Company was almost entirely confined to the shipment and sale abroad of goods manufactured in the United States or by the Dominion Rubber Company in Canada, to the acquisition of goods from foreign manufacturers with whom United States Rubber had agreements for supplying technical assistance, and to the sales by its foreign subsidiaries of the goods so acquired. In addition, a limited volume of business was done on goods manufactured abroad by other American companies for the account of the Export Company.

By 1939, approximately 10% of the total consolidated sales of the United States Rubber Company and its subsidiaries was made by subsidiary companies located outside the borders of the United States. Of the foreign manufacturing and distributing subsidiaries, by far the largest was the Dominion Rubber Company with headquarters in Montreal.

Virtually all of the exports from Canada by Dominion and its subsidiaries were sold by the United States Rubber Export Company. About 71% of the net sales of the Dominion Rubber Company were in Canada, with a large part of the remaining 29% in sterling area countries, where Canadian exports enjoyed the benefit of preferential import duties.

Although Dominion's business was similar to that of the parent company, there were important exceptions. The textile mills operated by Dominion were not producing any rayon tire cord in 1939. When the production of synthetic rubber was begun in the United States in 1942, wartime shortages of critical materials influenced the decision to put off the construction of similar facilities in Canada at that time. Furthermore, during the ensuing period, the Canadian company's research and development devoted most of its efforts towards discovering and developing new and improved types of chemicals suited for use in the rubber industry.

In March, 1940, Edward H. Marsh, Jr., succeeded Elmer Roberts as managing head of the Export Company; however, demands for war products that could be made by the Mechanical Goods Division were so heavy that, at the request of Willard H. Cobb, Marsh was appointed assistant general manager, General Products, Lastex, and Mechanical Goods Division. He was succeeded in the Export Company by Ludwig C. Boos, who had been connected with that company since June, 1926 and for eight years prior to 1940 had been the branch manager in Havana, Cuba. Appointed acting general manager of the Export Company in May, 1941, Boos was made general manager in the following September. On Aug. 1, 1942, he became vice-president and general manager, and moved up to the presidency of United States Rubber Export Company in December, 1945.

Boos was firmly convinced that the expansion of the company's business was contingent upon establishment of manufacturing plants in strategically located areas, taking into account nationalistic trends as well as transportation, climatic condition, supply of suitable labor, accessibility of raw materials, and nearness to important markets. He had an earnest manner and could present impressively the projects he recommended. He won considerable support for his views of the steps that he believed should be taken as soon as the war ended.

Meanwhile, the nation's war effort required that existing rubber footwear factories in Central and South America be kept operating. In 1942, Desiderio Garza, president of Cia. Hulera Mexicana S. A., Mexico City, visited the New York office of United States Rubber, seeking technical assistance in the use of GRS (government rubber styrene). F. E. Worley, Al Myers, and Herbert G. Kieswetter, the assistant general manager of the Export Company, went to Mexico to see if United States Rubber Company could help. After inspecting the factory, they recommended that United States Rubber purchase a 25% interest in the Mexican corporation. This recommendation was approved, and purchase of the minority interest was negotiated. Except for the Canadian plants and the interests that the company had in the foreign companies making Lastex yarn, the investment in Cia Hulera Mexicana S. A. was the first foreign manufacturing operation entered into by United States Rubber. It marked an important broadening of the scope of its international activities. A few years later, all the capital stock of the Mexican firm was acquired.

THE LASTEX STORY

During the difficult days of 1932, Davis is said to have told the staff at the Providence plant, "The fate of the United States Rubber Company is hanging by a thread, a Lastex thread, and I hope it is a golden thread."[20] The comment was almost literally true, for even the relatively small amount of profit made on Lastex yarn during the next few years did help United States Rubber weather the financial crises of the early 1930's.

Percy Adamson's Idea

Percy Adamson, born in the heart of the English textile industry, had come to this country in 1910 as the sales agent for several English textile companies. He conceived the idea of making a fine elastic yarn by wrapping silk, cotton, wool, or any other nonelastic fibrous thread around an elastic core and using the resulting yarn in a knitting machine.[21] When he found that a rubber thread fine enough for his purpose could be made by United States Rubber by extruding an elastic core from latex, he applied for a patent. (The extruding invention had been developed and patented by Ernest Hopkinson and W. A. Gibbons.) During the early part of 1930, Adamson assigned his rights under the patent to the rubber company, which then set about providing adequate manufacturing facilities. Adamson was appointed exclusive selling agent with complete control of distribution of Lastex (the name of the new product was coined from the words "elastic" and "textile").

Basically, the patent issued to Adamson on Sept. 8, 1931 covered, but was not limited to, the manufacture of a fine elastic yarn having a core of elastic material under tension and a covering of relatively inelastic fibrous material. Lastex gave knitted fabric the capacity to stretch in any direction. Adamson visualized its use in the manufacture of hosiery, foundation garments, surgical bandages, bathing suits, and other wearing apparel. Having the idea was important, but it was equally essential to create a market and to develop equipment and methods that would prove commercially feasible and profitable.

In 1930, Gibbons supplied Adamson with some black latex thread that had been produced in the General Laboratories. Adamson had this thread covered by the Frank W. Gorse Co., Needham, Mass., a firm that made elastic yarn by covering cut rubber thread. Adamson then persuaded Scott and Williams, manufacturers of machines for knitting hosiery, to knit an experimental pair of socks, using the Lastex yarn in the cuffs. With this sample, he obtained an order from the manufacturers of Hole-proof Hosiery, the first important sale of Lastex. A year of intense activity followed.

Commercial Production of Lastex Begun

The reaction of other manufacturers of hosiery, foundation garments, and swimsuits was so favorable that in 1931 it was decided to install equipment for commercial production at the General Products Division's Providence plant. The only machine then in existence for producing extruded latex thread was the one developed from the original device. Davis gave Gibbons only six weeks in which to design and build a larger machine for installation at Providence that would be capable of producing latex thread in the quantities required to meet the rapidly growing demand. Gibbons called a meeting of the development chemists and engineers most familiar with the problem and made it clear that all necessary decisions would have to be made then and there; no time was available for making changes in the equipment.

Difficult technical problems were involved in the continuous processing of a fine thread of latex from the moment the unvulcanized liquid was extruded as a fine filament through any one of a rank of porcelain nozzles until the vulcanized and dried thread was ready for transfer to the winding machines, where it would be covered and converted into Lastex yarn. The most serious problem was how to cure the continuously moving thread. Gibbons and Earl G. Sturdevant successfully applied the principle embodied in the method Gibbons had patented before World War I for curing rubberized fabric and raincoats in steam at atmospheric pressure. (The patent granted for their method of vulcanizing rubber thread was one of the first industrial applications of a continuous vulcanizing process.) The proper decisions were promptly made, a machine to produce fifty pounds of Lactron in a twenty-four hour period was built, and the deadline set by Davis was met.

The Providence plant had been making cut rubber thread, and its old customers advised Harlow Waite (general manager of the General Products Division) not to get into the manufacture of Lastex; they claimed the wrapping would slip on the core. On the other hand, should Lastex prove to be practical, Waite would be putting himself out of business. Despite their warnings, work continued on the project. Among those closely associated with it were Alexis W. ("Skipper") Keen; E. G. Sturdevant, B. F. Foster, and F. D. Chittenden from the General Laboratories; John E. Congdon, plant engineer; A. G. McKinnon, development manager at the plant; H. E. Cooper, Ray Frost, and J. J. Orr.

Orr, an electrical engineer associated with the A. J. Brandt Company, was sent to Providence early in 1931 to help develop equipment. The major problem was to wind the cover on the fine latex core with greater precision than was possible with the belt-driven machines then used for covering cut rubber thread. Orr decided that the solution lay in using a separate motor for each spindle, a method which had been introduced only recently in the production of rayon. It so happened that B. F. Perkins and Son, Holyoke, Mass., manufacturers of electrical equipment for paper mills, had developed an experimental machine (somewhat similar to a twisting frame) for winding silk around a cotton core as a means of obtaining a lower cost yarn that could be substituted for pure silk in the price-conscious market then prevailing. Orr interested the Perkins firm in revising its machine according to his criteria, which embodied use of adjustable frequency to supply the power to each spindle. This machine may have been the first industrial application of adjustable frequency. The number of turns of the covering thread per inch of the latex core was controlled by vacuum tubes, one of the first industrial applications of electronics. Each of the winding frames required 48 AC fractional horsepower motors (96 motors if double wrap was specified) of an entirely new design, specially built by General Electric.[22]

While United States Rubber's technical and production men were perfecting the equipment, Adamson was endeavoring to broaden the interest of the garment industry in the use of Lastex. Waldemar Kops, whom Adamson persuaded in 1931 to use his elastic yarn, was the first corset manufacturer to use Lastex, and is reported to have sold 12,000 girdles made with Lastex in two months. Adamson also showed some Lastex yarn to George Rutledge, head of the Chicago company making Vassar foundation garments, in 1931. Rutledge was not receptive at first but finally consented to knit some girdle panels with Lastex. They were then made into a girdle and modeled. Rutledge was so impressed with the fit of the garment that he is said to have accompanied Adamson back to New York and to have offered an advance payment of $1 million to ensure that the Vassar line would have a preferred position in the allocation of Lastex yarn. United States Rubber declined to accept the check. As desperately as the rubber company was striving to obtain cash, the management must have had compelling reasons for not accepting Rutledge's offer. He may have asked for some security that, under the conditions of the indenture covering the 1917 issue of first mortgage and refunding bonds, the company was not in a position to furnish. Or possibly Rutledge stipulated unacceptable restrictions on the distribution of Lastex yarn and garments made with Lastex.

In the annual report for 1931, the following paragraph appeared: "A new elastic yarn has been developed by our research laboratories. This is being marketed under the trade name of 'Lastex' for use in the textile and other fields. Its acceptance indicates a wide use." This was indeed an understatement.

When the contract with the A. J. Brandt Company was canceled in 1931, Orr entered the employ of United States Rubber, and in May, 1932, succeeded John Congdon as plant engineer at Providence. By 1932, one hundred winding machines of forty-eight spindles each had been installed at Providence, but they were not sufficient to supply the rapidly growing demand for Lastex. In May, 1933, Orr received a telephone call from de Krafft, asking him to get a quotation from B. F. Perkins and Son for one hundred more machines. The men from the Perkins company came to Providence on Memorial Day, 1933, and gave him a quotation of $3,600 per machine; de Krafft told him to buy the hundred. Orr was a relatively young man, only recently employed by United States Rubber as an engineer, and he did not have authority to make purchases; neither did he know the prescribed procedure, and he told de Krafft so. But de Krafft evidently thought the price was favorable and was anxious to have the order placed immediately, so he instructed Orr to write out the order. Taking into account the hundreds of specially built motors and other auxiliary equipment involved, together with the expense of installation, the young engineer estimated the total commitment would exceed $1 million.

When it is remembered that this action was taken when the nation was in the depths of the depression, and when United States Rubber had faced a critical financial deadline only the previous week, it is obvious that Lastex was already a promising additional source of profits. Even more remarkable was management's faith in Adamson's ability to establish a market for Lastex, evidenced by the initial investment of more than $1 million in 1930 and 1931.

Rapid Growth of Lastex Sales

Sales of Lastex in 1931 totaled about 69,000 pounds. In 1932, they jumped to over 450,000 pounds, and in 1933 to over 850,000 pounds at a price reported to average over $3 a pound. Although United States Rubber did not disclose its profits on this commodity, an authoritative estimate of $500,000 net operating profit was made.[23]

By 1934, garments were being manufactured that contained from 8 to 75% Lastex yarn, depending upon the type of garment. By utilizing variations in the size of the covering threads, in the diameter, elongation, or tension of the Lactron core, a wide range of stretchable fabrics was produced. In the early thirties, about 80% of the production of Lastex was used in foundation garments, underwear, hosiery, and swimsuits. Just when the depression was creating a demand for lower priced goods, Lastex, the first elastic yarn fine enough to be used in the needles of a knitting machine as well as in the shuttle of a loom, freed garment designers from the limitations of unyielding, conventional fabrics. This freedom made possible the mass, low cost production of form-fitting foundation garments, swimsuits, and other items.

As the market for Lastex yarn broadened, it became apparent that United States Rubber should be prepared to furnish Lastex in coarser sizes than could be produced efficiently on the equipment at Providence. The Frank W. Gorse Company, whose equipment could be readily modified to produce the coarser sizes, was acquired in 1933 by an exchange of capital stock. However, the operations of that company were not reflected in the consolidated statement until 1939. By about 1939, specially processed lightweight leathers were being backed by finely woven fabric made with Lastex for use in the manufacture of "elasticized" shoes.

The rotogravure section of the Sunday *New York Times*, Nov. 12, 1933, carried a full page advertisement for "Living Clothes" made of a fabric containing Lastex, "the miracle yarn" (Figure 49). Acceptance of this innovation in men's suits was less enthusiastic than hoped for. The fabric had a relatively high cost and could not be dry cleaned. However, thirty years later, an even finer Lastex yarn with a core of extruded Vyrene spandex, a synthetic elastomer developed by United States Rubber, was successfully promoted for women's wearing apparel. Stretch fabrics had become popular for women's ski pants, slacks, and other garments. The soundness of Adamson's belief in the universal appeal of the fitting qualities provided by apparel made with elasticized yarn had been conclusively demonstrated.

49.   Lastex in fabrics.

49a.   Swimsuit
of Lastex yarn,
U.S. R u b b e r
bathing cap, and
Kedettes.

European Market Entered

Early in 1932, United States Rubber sent to Europe the general manager
of its fiber products department, R. P. ("Phil") Rose. He negotiated
contracts for the manufacture and distribution of Lastex yarn in the
European market with Dunlop Rubber Company, London; Pirelli
Societa per Azioni, Milan; and the Hungarian Rubber Goods Com-
pany, Budapest. These negotiations led to the formation of the Pirelli
Lastex Societa Italo Americana, Filo Elastico, Milan, and the Dunlop-
Revere Thread Company, Ltd., London. (A news release in Novem-

49b.   Advertisement, "Living Clothes" (*New York Times*, Nov. 12, 1933).

ber, 1932 said that the latter company, jointly owned by the United States Rubber Company and Dunlop, would handle the interests of both concerns with respect to latex thread throughout Great Britain and Europe. It was also announced that the new company would not manufacture fabrics or finished articles made from latex thread. On May 23, 1944, the name of the company was changed to Lastex Yarn and Lactron Thread, Ltd.)

In September, 1932, H. E. Cooper was sent to Europe to help the three European firms set up manufacturing operations. A forty-spindle wrapping machine was built for Dunlop by a small Cotswold firm in the surprisingly short time of thirty to forty days. After this machine had successfully wrapped Lactron thread and Cooper had received the New York office's approval of the sample yarn, Dunlop placed orders for additional machines. Meanwhile, Cooper was also working with the Italian and Hungarian firms. The head of the latter was Dr. Paul Klein, later described by Cooper as a genius, combining scientific knowledge, technical skill, and managerial ability. Klein's firm began two months later than Dunlop to set up for production, yet actually went into production a short time before Dunlop. This achievement was made despite the fact that the Hungarian firm had to convert all measurements on the blueprints to the metric system before it could build the necessary equipment, and also had to convert each of the special parts obtained from a German firm.

To coordinate all operations with respect to production and marketing of Lastex in the European market, Rose was also instrumental in the formation on May 30, 1935 of Consolidated Rubber Manufacturers, Ltd. (and "associated companies").[24] Elmer Roberts was made managing director and chairman of the board of directors of that company.

TECHNICAL DEVELOPMENTS

Differing Approaches

The administrations of Charles B. Seger and F. B. Davis, Jr. differed markedly in many areas, but perhaps nowhere was this difference more evident than in their approaches to research and development. Apparently, Seger did not grasp the importance of strong, consistent support of such work. While he readily approved projects that promised early financial returns, such as the spraying of latex, he probably did not see the wisdom of expenditures for developments that held out only slim prospect for immediate profits. Not unlikely, he believed his position justified by the difficult financial situations he faced.

Even more serious crises confronted the management team Davis headed during the depression of the early 1930's, but from the first Davis stressed well-directed development work. In the editorial columns of at least one trade paper, United States Rubber's research laboratories in 1929 were said to be the finest in the rubber industry, and by 1941 to rank among the finest in the world.[25] The operating divisions were not only encouraged to broaden their markets through development of new items, but were prodded and expected to evolve and commercialize new products that gave reasonable promise of ultimate profit, even though these new items might be quite different from current output. At the same time, an unrelenting drive to eliminate causes of product failure or of customer dissatisfaction was carried on.

The urgent need to enlarge United States Rubber's tire sales focused attention on the rapid improvement of that product along with steps to reduce costs. The personal interest taken by Davis in the implementation of tire development programs gave them new impetus. John P. Coe, who had been appointed manager of tire development in June, 1928, served until he was transferred to the Naugatuck Chemical Company in 1930 as special assistant to the general manager. For about a year, S. P. Thacher was in charge of the tire development department; then Sidney M. Cadwell was appointed its director, and under his leadership great strides were taken that placed United States Rubber's developments in tire quality once more in the forefront of the industry.

Tire Development Program Expanded

Under Cadwell's direction, facilities for development and testing were enlarged and improved, and United States Rubber began to forge toward the forefront of the tire industry. In 1933, Martin Castricum, who had almost twenty years' experience in the development of tire fabrics (fourteen years with Fisk Rubber Corporation and five earlier years with Brighton Mills), joined United States Rubber. Almost immediately he was assigned the important job of developing a successful rayon cord tire. When interviewed in 1963, Castricum said he had been fortunate in working for a company like United States Rubber and under the direction of a department manager like Cadwell who encouraged him, furnished him with the necessary equipment, and then demanded results. Castricum said that, although the tire development department "had to fight" for additional appropriations during the depression years, he could honestly say he had never been turned down on any request for tire-testing facilities. These included, in addition to more test wheels and other laboratory equipment, more road service tests and more controlled mileage tests of tires on bus fleets and trucks.

Rayon Cord Tires Developed

Manufacturing tires that can withstand normal usage on modern cars, buses, trucks, and industrial equipment calls for all the skill that rubber chemists, engineers, and tire designers can offer. The primary consideration is safety under adverse weather and road conditions, at high speeds, on cars equipped with power brakes and power steering, and capable of high acceleration. In addition, the public demands and gets riding comfort, easy steering, low wind drift, good balance, minimum tread noise, and maximum mileage with reduced cost per mile (see footnote 10).

Before World War I, United States Rubber had been a pioneer in the use of cotton cord instead of the woven fabric then widely used for the tire carcass. In the early 1930's, the company began experimenting with rayon cords; it was hoped this material would provide greater strength in the carcass of the tire and lessen the build-up of heat in the sidewalls. Attempts made between 1930 and 1932 to substitute rayon cord for cotton ended in failures. It became evident that satisfactory results would not be obtained unless the physical characteristics of the rayon could be modified. The General Laboratories in Passaic worked closely with Du Pont's scientists, and by 1934 progress warranted an active program of experiments in the development department of the Detroit tire plant.

Among the problems connected with the use of rayon yarn in tire cord were (1) lack of suitable adhesive for the dipping solution used in treating the smooth surface of rayon tire cord; (2) unsatisfactory fatigue resistance of the early samples; and (3) excess cost. The cotton tire cord in general use in truck tires at that time was described as a 23/5/3 cord, indicating that five strands of #23 cotton yarn had been twisted together, and that three of these twisted yarns had then been twisted together in the opposite direction. Technologists working on a similar development for another of the "Big Four" tire companies had substituted a 275 denier rayon yarn for the #23 cotton yarn and then duplicated the standard construction for the cotton tire cord. The cost of rayon, however, was about 80% higher than that of cotton.

Castricum's study of the properties of the 275 denier rayon submitted by Du Pont convinced him it offered possibilities of improvements in tire quality and lower cost. He had before him the results of the work done by O. Edward Kurt of the tire development department on the build-up of heat. He reasoned that if the higher strength of the rayon yarn could be used in a thinner carcass, a cooler-running tire would result. Such a tire would have longer carcass life and improved tread wear.

Meanwhile, in 1933 and 1934, the chemists at the General Laboratories were perfecting a highly satisfactory low-cost adhesive; Castricum considered it an outstanding job. The Du Pont technical personnel had also produced a rayon filament possessing greater fatigue resistance and other physical properties more suitable for tire cord. Through the joint efforts of the development department at Detroit and the General Laboratories at Passaic, a method of completely drying the tire cords after dipping was also worked out.

After an extensive series of laboratory and tire tests involving a wide range of tire cord and tire constructions, it was found that a tire made of a 275/4/2 cord and a carcass thickness of .62" (compared with 1.00" for a cotton tire) had low heat build-up, the required strength, improved tread mileage (about 24% more in truck tires and about 15% in passenger car tires), and relatively low cost. In August, 1934, Cadwell reported that "wheel tests" of tires made with rayon cord showed they far outperformed similar tires made with cotton cord.[26]

The service requirements of large truck tires were so demanding that it was necessary to use an expensive long-staple Egyptian cotton. The new rayon tire not only used fewer pounds of rayon but required substantially fewer pounds of rubber. Cost studies indicated that the company could pay 80¢ per pound for the rayon yarn, yet still break even with cotton cord tire costs. The figure was questioned by top management but was proven to be accurate. Evidently the significance of this breakthrough was soon grasped by the rayon producers, who shortly thereafter took steps to enlarge their production facilities. (In 1935, F. C. Kennedy, who had been Castricum's assistant at Fisk from 1926 to 1933, entered the employ of United States Rubber, and Castricum and Kennedy thereafter worked as a team in the development of the rayon cord tire.)

A substantial additional cost reduction in rayon tires was achieved by the discovery that an 1100/2 cord could be used to replace the 275/-4/2 construction. It cost considerably less per pound to produce 1100

50. Rayon tire
cord before dip-
ping in latex.
The cord is first
threaded through
porcelain eyelets.

denier rayon than to produce four strands of 275 denier rayon, but equally important was the fact that the rayon producer could expand his capacity more quickly and with less capital investment. The elimination of one twisting operation also contributed to cost reduction. Several patents were obtained by United States Rubber in the development of these constructions.

After several thousand road tests of rayon cord tires of various constructions, United States Rubber introduced the Fleetway Rayon tire in March, 1937. Adjustments on this tire proved to be only about half as many as those normally made on cotton cord tires of otherwise comparable quality and construction. The Royal Master Rayon tire was introduced by the company the following year.

According to Cadwell, United States Rubber's thin-wall rayon cord tire improved the performance of truck tires by about 50%. In correspondence to the author, Cadwell has asserted his conviction that the high speeds at which buses and heavily loaded trucks now operate have been made possible by this improvement in tire construction. Also, the savings accruing annually to the trucking industry as the direct consequence of added tire mileage and the faster operating speeds under heavy loads have run into millions of dollars. To the extent that those savings are reflected in lower transportation charges, all industry has benefited.

Demand for Rayon Cord Exceeds Supply

The technical difficulties of producing the rayon tire had been virtually overcome by the latter part of 1938, but now the Du Pont company's facilities for production proved to be inadequate to meet demand. The additional facilities that were under construction did not come into production until 1939; as a result, Du Pont was obliged to allocate its production of tire cord among the different tire manufacturers. Fortunately, United States Rubber had anticipated this possibility and, largely through the efforts of Castricum, had established friendly relations with other rayon producers, including American Viscose and Canadian International Paper, Ltd. (The latter's development of a rayon yarn produced from wood and suitable for tire cord became especially important in later years when government subsidies on cotton raised the price of cotton linters used for production of cellulose for rayon.)

About 1939, the Du Pont company submitted to various tire manufacturers, including United States Rubber, the first samples of nylon yarn for tire cords. They were first used in truck tires, and were found to have some excellent qualities but too much elongation. The progress that has been made since 1942 in taking advantage of nylon's greater strength and excellent fatigue resistance, nylon's capture of a major share of the tire market, and the improvements that the producers of rayon have made in their product do not fall within the scope of this present study.

Results of Leadership

In a brief prepared by Ralph C. Epstein for submission to the Federal Trade Commission, data indicated that the cost to the consumer of a Buick tire (32″ x 4″), based on number of miles run, had been reduced from $1.26 per hundred miles in 1910 to 5¢ per hundred miles in 1935. The 1910 cost per hundred miles for a Ford tire (30″ x 3½″) was 87¢; the 1935 cost for the larger tire then used for Ford cars (4.40-21) had been reduced to 4.3¢. Epstein pointed out that mileage obtained from tires varies greatly with speed, temperature, and type of road. The figures quoted and those used in Figure 51 "represent the average experience of several companies with test fleets and elaborate surveys of tires in the hands of actual consumers."[27]

51. Mileage and cost per mile to consumer of tires, 1910-47 (two popular sizes).

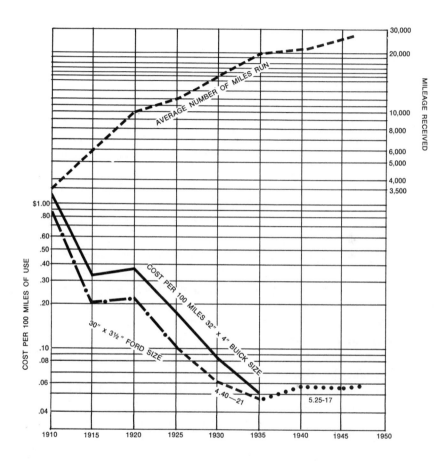

From the mid-thirties until the war brought a halt to production of tires for civilians, Cadwell and his associates could have gratifying assurance that they were leading the industry, a leadership reflected in the improved attitude of dealers and consumers towards tires made by United States Rubber, whether under its own brands or under private brands. An additional benefit was the fine *esprit de corps* that naturally followed among both the company's salesmen and inside personnel. But more important in Cadwell's judgment was the fact that his staff of scientists and technicians could now be allowed sufficient time for thorough investigation, research, and analysis. No longer were they pressed for hasty decisions that might later prove to have been less than advantageous to the company.

Automobile Floor Mats and Foam Rubber

Until 1931, the Mishawaka plant had been almost exclusively used for the manufacture of footwear. However, the drastic drop in sales in 1930 and 1931, and the changes made in equipment and manufacturing processes, meant that the large additions to the factory built in the twenties were no longer needed. George W. Blair, who had been general superintendent of the factory, was assigned to develop new products that would utilize the unused facilities. Since the Mishawaka plant was equipped to make felt boots as well as rubber footwear, Blair hit upon the idea of making rubber floor mats, backed with a felted material, for automobiles. This idea was the start of a business that had annual sales of better than $1,200,000 by 1940. The Mishawaka plant pioneered in the production of automobile floor mats on engraved calenders; other manufacturers had always made these mats in molds. The calender method had obvious limitations. It was not practical for production of the contoured mats, for example, but it speeded up the process and reduced costs. The manufacture and sales of these floor mats brought the Mishawaka organization into close contact with the automotive industry for the first time, and led to its development of other automotive products.

In 1931, Blair spearheaded Mishawaka's efforts to increase the "breathability" of canvas uppers for tennis and basketball shoes. Fred Schott, a development man on Blair's staff, sought a latex adhesive in which bubbles would form and collapse during the vulcanizing process, thus providing porosity in the layer of backing cement between the outer fabric and the lining. Part of an experimental latex compound, accidentally left in a laboratory beaker near heat, vulcanized into a spongy foam. Blair and Schott experimented with this interesting material, and in about a year developed an improved foam sponge. Means of whipping the latex compound into foam, then stabilizing, coagulating, and curing it, were worked out, and various patent applications were filed.

The automotive market for foam rubber seat cushions was the first to be explored, and the first important commercial application was in 1934 for bus seats. Sales efforts were gradually extended to other fields, and foam rubber cushions were installed in some railroad cars and private automobiles. In connection with the early marketing efforts, photographs were made to show how a cutaway section of foam rubber cushion conformed to the shape of a seated or reclining person. These pictures proved that established beliefs regarding weight distribution needed to be revised; it was clearly demonstrated that many cushioned seats then on the market had been improperly designed for maximum comfort.

Foam rubber mattresses were first installed in railway sleeping cars for the new streamlined trains. Because these mattresses had been developed by the Mishawaka plant, they were marketed originally as the Red Ball Sleep Cushion and carried the Red Ball trademark, but it was soon decided that this important new field should be exploited under the trademark of the United States Rubber Company and that all sales efforts should be concentrated in promoting the distribution of a single brand. (In 1938, United States Rubber displayed its foam rubber mattresses at the New York World's Fair, and the first advertisement for U.S. Royal Foam Sponge mattresses and cushions appeared in the March 11, 1939 issue of the *Saturday Evening Post.*)

By 1935, the manufacture of foam rubber cushions was on a production basis. As sales to automobile companies continued to expand, installation of equipment for large-scale production basis was recommended to the executive committee. However, the proposal entailed an expenditure of almost $700,000, and approval was not forthcoming at that time.

In 1938, a second automobile manufacturer adopted Mishawaka's foam rubber cushions. To meet the company's requirements, it was necessary to install as quickly as possible a production line capable of continuous mass production. Many engineering and technical problems had to be solved speedily and, at Blair's request, Eugene A. Luxenberger, chief industrial engineer at the Mishawaka plant, was given the assignment. Despite disagreement among the technicians and operating men as to the methods, these differences were resolved in one way or another and the customers' delivery schedules were met. Better still, substantial savings over original cost estimates were made.

In March, 1941, the name Koyalon was adopted as being better suited to the wide diversity of uses for the company's foam rubber products. Advertising and sales promotion programs were increased,

52. Foam rubber. Above, foam rubber, after whipping, pours into mattress mold. Below, vulcanized Koylon foam rubber is ready for use in foam cushions and mattresses.

53. Parts of a golf ball.

and sales of Koyalon rubber cushions and mattresses expanded rapidly during the next few months until the outbreak of World War II. (The name Koyalon was changed later to Koylon.)

The continued addition of uses for rubber in all types of motor vehicles created large markets. In 1939, $155,530,000 of tires and tubes were used on motor vehicles plus almost $28 million of other rubber products (or almost 18% of the value of the tires and tubes).[28] In 1940, the average automobile contained about two hundred different parts made of rubber, and United States Rubber shared in this growing market to a greater extent as the direct result of the emphasis Davis had placed on development of new products.

Golf Balls Improved

Few, if any, commercial rubber products demanded as much precision in their manufacture or permitted as little tolerance in the finished product as did golf balls. Approximately eighty distinct operations had to be performed, and the core had to be kept in the exact center throughout. In the 1920's, United States Rubber had greatly improved golf balls by perfecting means of keeping the core properly centered, and by replacing the hard cores previously used with resilient cores of various types of

materials. U.S. golf balls were further improved in "feel" and "click" in
the 1930's by the change to a liquid center core (Figure 53). Two rubber hemispheres, molded to form a hollow center, were filled with a nontoxic chemical formula that would be unaffected by normal temperature
or atmospheric changes. Around the core, rubber thread under high tension was wound to a diameter of 1.61 inches. (The kind and size of rubber thread used and the degree of tension could make the difference
between a fine and a poor golf ball. Latex thread was used for a brief
period but was found unsuited for this purpose.) The wound core was
then placed between two hemisphere covers made from balata or gutta
percha; the covered ball was placed in a mold, pressure and heat were
applied, and a dimpled ball emerged. Correct size and shaping and
placing of the dimples as determined by aerodynamic testing were essential if the ball was to give a long true flight.

Vulcanization of the covers presented a difficult problem because the
high temperatures usually employed would take the tension out of the
rubber thread wound around the core and ruin the liveliness of the ball.
Until a vulcanizing method involving the use of lower temperatures was
developed, the covers were thermoplastic and were easily cut or knocked
out of round when hit. In the early 1920's, William C. Geer, a chemist
employed by the B. F. Goodrich Company, had invented a method of
partially curing the cover at a temperature of about 210° F. to 220° F.
for about three minutes, after which the balls were cooled and allowed
to air-cure at ordinary room temperatures from four to seven days. The
curing was achieved by using a rapid accelerator in the balata compound
used for the cover, special precautions being taken to prevent premature
vulcanization of the stock while it was being milled or during the preliminary molding operations. The vulcanized cover was much tougher,
but balata was an expensive material and the flash that formed when
the hemispherical halves of the ball cover were pressed together could
not be reworked. The flash and any imperfectly formed balls had to be
scrapped.

Cadwell had begun working in the late twenties to develop a process
that would not have the disadvantages of Geer's. He succeeded in vulcanizing the cover at still lower temperature, after the ball had been
molded. In this process, the cover stock contained only part of the ingredients needed for vulcanization. It could be milled, sheeted, and
molded without danger that vulcanization would occur during these operations or in storage of process inventory. After the balls had been molded,
they were subjected to an emulsion of carbon disulfide, which diffused

into the cover stock and reacted with diphenylamine to form a powerful vulcanizing combination. Cadwell's invention produced a cover so tough that it withstood cutting to a remarkable degree. Since it was also possible to reuse the unvulcanized flash and to remold any unvulcanized balls having an imperfect surface, cost savings resulted. The patents obtained by Geer and Cadwell were so basic and so valuable that all golf ball manufacturers took out licenses to make the famous Cadwell-Geer golf ball cover. After Geer's patent expired, licenses to manufacture under Cadwell's patent continued to be taken by the industry.

In conformance with the standards of the United States Golf Association, the finished ball could not be less than 1.68 inches in diameter and not more than 1.62 ounces in weight. In the 1920's, about twenty-eight days were required for the manufacture of a golf ball; after World War II, this period was reduced to about nine.[29]

Expansion in Chemicals

Between 1929 and 1930, both Matthew Adgate, vice-president and general manager of Naugatuck Chemical Company, and E. A. Anderson, general manager of Naugatuck Regenerating Company, died. F. B. Davis, Jr. decided the two units should be consolidated under one management and appointed Elmer Roberts as general manager of the chemical and reclaim department. (The Naugatuck Chemical Company retained its corporate name until 1934 when the corporation was dissolved.) After Roberts took over the general supervision of rubber reclaiming, a survey was made to determine the types of reclaim desired by the rubber industry, and new types were placed in production. Lemuel Foutz and John P. Coe assisted Roberts in the coordination of the two operations. (Coe had been sent in 1927 to Detroit to organize the tire development department, then was transferred to New York in 1930 as assistant to the general manager of the chemical and reclaim department.)

The Naugatuck Chemical Company greatly expanded the scope of its activities during the years following 1929. It was the largest producer of chemicals for the rubber industry and is believed to have supplied from 35 to 40% of these chemicals in the 1930's. Much of the expansion was the natural consequence of close cooperation with the General Laboratories in the continued development of organic accelerators and antioxidants that were better suited for certain specific uses than were those previously introduced. One of the new antioxidants, known as BLE, was a successor to VGB, which had been sold to other members of the rubber industry. In 1931, William P. ter Horst, a talented chemist employed in the General Laboratories, was granted a patent on his invention of BLE. Over the years, it became the preferred antioxidant for both tire tread and carcass compounds, and was purchased by other rubber companies in large quantities. (By 1948, BLE was being used in more than one-third of all the tires made in the United States.) With the creation of the synthetic rubber industry during World War II, BLE was widely used as the stabilizer antioxidant for the raw synthetic rubber.[30]

The work done with aqueous dispersions led to development of new LOTOL compounds and to new uses of them: for carpet backing and for new treatments of felt, paper, and other fibers. The phenomenal growth of Lastex sales called for new types of accelerators and antioxidants specifically tailored for that product.

In 1930, the Aromatics Department of Naugatuck Chemical was organized under the guidance of Burton T. Bush, a dealer in essential oils, who had been associated with a European firm. Bush found that heptaldehyde, produced in large quantities by Naugatuck Chemical for rubber accelerators, was a good base for blending with essential oils in the manufacture of perfumes. First engaged on a consulting basis, he became an employee of the company in February, 1933.

In 1931, Coe was made factory manager of the rubber reclaiming operations. On his recommendation, the reclaiming plant at Mishawaka was closed, and all rubber reclaiming operations were consolidated at Naugatuck. Coe also reduced the number of types of reclaim offered by Naugatuck; for the first time in several years, the reclaim department began to make money.

Facilities for reclaiming rubber were enlarged when relations between Japan and this country worsened in 1940. This decision was timely, for by 1942 it became necessary to substitute reclaim for new rubber to the fullest possible extent in the manufacture of rubber footwear and many other items. The three-year average monthly consumption of reclaim for 1941, 1942, and 1943 jumped to 22,143 long tons, an increase of 69% over the monthly average for the previous five years.[31]

As usually happens during extended experimentation and research in a given field, no immediate use had been seen for many of the organic chemicals developed by the General Laboratories during the 1920's. Those chemicals were held in reserve, however, for possible future applications, and in the late 1930's, ter Horst was assigned by Gibbons to try to find commercial uses for some of them. A prospectus outlining ter Horst's program of developing chemicals for the agricultural field was presented to the executive committee by Roberts and Gibbons. Little enthusiasm was shown for the project, but work was continued; farm tests were made, and it was found that ter Horst had developed a successful agricultural chemical (Gibbons named it Spergon), a seed protectant applied before planting that prevented harmful fungi in the soil from attacking the seed. Other agricultural chemicals were developed, and about 1939, a small acreage was purchased near Naugatuck and an experimental agricultural station was established at Bethany, Conn. The agricultural chemical department, formally organized in 1940, gained national recognition as a leading manufacturer of fungicides, miticides, growth regulants, herbicides, growth retardants, seed protectants, fruit set hormones, and feed additives. In addition to Spergon, the products included Aramite, a miticide that was registered for use on more than twenty-seven crops, including cotton, fruits, vegetables, row crops, and trees, and MH, a growth retardant, used to retard sprouting of onions and potatoes in storage, growth of suckers on tobacco plants, and other unwanted growth.

These and other agricultural chemicals marketed by United States Rubber became important factors during the war years in helping food growers meet the problem of producing ever more per acre with less and less available labor.

SEPARATE DIVISION FOR TEXTILES

When F. B. Davis, Jr., became president of United States Rubber Company on Jan. 15, 1929, H. Gordon Smith was a second vice-president of the company and general manager of Winnsboro Mills, which functioned as one of the departments of the Tire Division. The entire production of the two textile mills at Winnsboro, N.C. was confined to tire cord for use by the Tire Division.

When Davis resigned the presidency in September, 1942, the manufacture and sale of textiles were the responsibility of the Textile Division, which had been organized as a separate division on Nov. 24, 1941, with Smith as its general manager, reporting to the president.[32] In addition to Winnsboro Mills, the Textile Division in September, 1942 was operating:

	Year Acquired	Spindle Capacity
Stark Mills, Hogansville, Ga.	1931	35,000
Shelbyville Mills, Shelbyville, Tenn.	1934	23,000
Fisk Cord Mills, New Bedford, Mass.	1940	60,000
Reid Mills, Hogansville, Ga.	1942	13,000

Production in September, 1942 included various weights and types of duck and sheeting; a waterproof fireproof fabric, Asbeston, was made at the Stark Mills. Sales were no longer limited to the requirements of the Tire Division but were being made to other divisions of the United States Rubber Company, to outside companies, and to the military forces.

A number of factors had combined to bring about this expansion and broadening of the activity in textiles. With the acquisition in 1931 of Samson Tire and Rubber Corporation of Los Angeles and the Gillette Rubber Company of Eau Claire, Wis., United States Rubber's shipments of tire casings increased from 4,511,000 in 1930 to 8,398,000 in 1931. Because the demand for tire cord exceeded the capacity of the Winnsboro Mills, Stark Mills, Hogansville, Ga., with 35,000 spindles and annual capacity of 10 million pounds of tire cord, was purchased from Callaway Mills, Inc. in March, 1931. Stark's personnel was retained, and some employees were transferred from Winnsboro to Hogansville to assist with enlargement of production facilities and control of quality. In the announcement of the acquisition it was stated that the mills' output of tire cord would be increased by 50%.

To keep pace with the upward trend of tire sales, Shelbyville Mills, Shelbyville, Tenn. (organized in 1926 as successor to Sylvan Cotton Mills, established in 1902), a mill with 23,000 spindles for manufacture of cotton drill and sheetings, was purchased in 1934 and converted into a tire cord mill. By removing looms and adding twisting equipment, production was more than doubled. The effect of these acquisitions on the total output of United States Rubber's textile mills is shown in Figure 54.

The first diversification came with purchase of the Shelbyville Mills, which, when acquired by the rubber company, had many looms equipped for production of chafer duck. Further diversification was achieved when equipment for production of yarns for fire hose, gasoline hose, vacuum, garden, and other special purpose hose was installed at Stark Mills beginning in 1937.

Through purchase of the assets of Fisk Rubber Corporation, United States Rubber acquired, early in 1940, one of the largest tire cord mills in the country, the Fisk Cord Mills, New Bedford, Mass. This mill contained 60,000 spindles producing 1,400,000 pounds of yarn and tire cord monthly. With this acquisition, the combined output of United States Rubber's textile mills in 1940 was said to consume the cotton grown from approximately one out of every 150 acres in the United States.[33]

Additional diversification was made possible in January, 1942 with the purchase from Callaway Mills, Inc. of another plant in Hogansville,

54. Annual production of Textile Division, 1917-42 (in thousands of pounds).

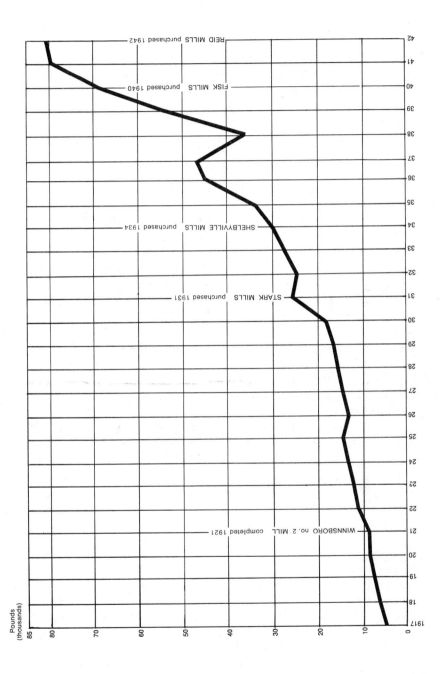

only a "stone's throw" from Stark Mills. The new mill, named Reid Mills after D. G. Reid, superintendent for twenty years under three different owners, had 12,096 spindles and 124 looms. These looms were operated by the Textile Division for production of some of the heavier grades of duck, such as hose duck and belting duck used by United States Rubber and numbered ducks required by the Army and Navy.

In the mid-thirties, Winnsboro Mills had found that by making certain adjustments rayon could be handled on cotton twisting and weaving equipment, and the plant had been producing rayon tire cord for several years prior to World War II. By 1942, Winnsboro was producing rayon fabric for use in bullet-sealing fuel cells for combat aircraft and for combat tires.

The war brought other radical changes to the Textile Division. When production of tires for civilian use was curtailed, the textile mills were quickly converted from spinning yarns for tire cord to spinning yarn for duck for military equipment; facilities for weaving duck were greatly enlarged. All production of tire cord went into tires for military vehicles and aircraft and for essential trucks and buses. In cooperation with the General Laboratories, engineers of the Textile Division had developed yarns of asbestos blended with cotton, called Asbeston. Only a limited application of Asbeston had been found prior to the war, but it was now incorporated in fire-fighting suits and in ducts for conveying exhaust gases and heated air in military aircraft. Equipment to weave Asbeston fabric was installed at Stark Mills, and the fabric, after being made water repellent by a subcontractor in New Jersey, was fashioned into fire-fighting suits at the Mishawaka plant of the Footwear Division. Ustex, another specialized product of the Textile Division, was a cotton yarn spun from the grades of cotton staple available in large quantity, which was approved by Wright Field for use in parachute harnesses.

OTHER ACQUISITIONS

Dispersions Process, Inc.

On Aug. 13, 1929, the company applied to the New York Stock Exchange for listing of 7,547 shares of its common stock issued as payment for 8,000 shares of second preferred and 38,000 of 75,000 authorized shares of the common stock of Dispersions Process, Inc., together with certain licenses from Dispersions to use, under the patents owned by the latter company, aqueous dispersions of rubber. Dispersions Process, Inc., had been established only the year before and was operating in a plant in Oaks, Pa., on the premises of the Philadelphia Rubber Works, a subsidiary of B. F. Goodrich Company. It had a capacity to convert 300,000 pounds per month of dry rubber, either natural or reclaimed, into aqueous dispersions, and held a number of patents on the process. Elmer Roberts was largely responsible for the decision to acquire this company, which had shown a loss of $28,571 during its first year of operations, and in the first six months of 1929 had sustained a further loss of $35,094. United States Rubber's purpose in acquiring control was not to obtain earnings on the stock of Dispersions Process, but, as previously stated, to be able to manufacture artificial dispersions of rubber under the patents held by the latter firm. The laboratory and facilities were transferred to the chemical company's plant at Naugatuck and the office to New York.

Latex Fiber Industries, Inc.

The formation of a new unit, the Fiber Products Department, with R. P. Rose as its general manager, was announced in September, 1929. Unwoven fiber products containing natural or artificial latex were manufactured by the department at Cleveland, Ohio and Rock City Falls, N.Y. Then in March, 1932, United States Rubber Company in conjunction with the J. P. Lewis Company, Beaver Falls, N.Y., formed Latex Fiber Industries, Inc., with H. S. Lewis as president and Rose as vice-president. Production of fiber products was transferred to the Beaver Falls plant of Lewis, Slocum & LeFevre Company. Fifty-one per cent of the capital stock of Latex Fiber was held by United States Rubber, which granted the new corporation licenses under a number of patents owned by United States Rubber and pertaining to the use of latex and fibrous materials. The existing sales organization of the Lewis company marketed the products of Latex Fiber Industries, Inc., which were used primarily in the shoe, artificial leather goods, and automobile industries.

Acquisitions which followed during the 1930's included:

1933   Frank W. Gorse Company; organized in 1922 as successor to F. W. Gorse, established in 1890; factories located at Central Falls, R.I., and Needham Heights, Mass.; equipped to manufacture covered rubber thread from latex cores made in other United States Rubber plants.

1935   Firestone Footwear Company; organized 1926; succeeded Firestone-Apsley Company, established 1921, which had succeeded Apsley Rubber Company, established 1892, as successor to Goodyear Gossamer Company, established 1885; plant in Hudson, Mass., had manufactured line of waterproof rubber footwear and rubber-soled canvas footwear; sales small and plant closed in February, 1936.

1936   Combined Carbon Company; manufactured carbon black, used as a toughener in rubber compounds, chiefly in tire treads and soling material; plant at Sanford, Tex.; United States Rubber sold its interest in 1936 to United Carbon Company in exchange for stock.

1938   Chatham Manufacturing Company; plant at Portland, Conn., established 1920; manufactured square-cut rubber thread; plant was closed in 1940, and activities were transferred to the Providence plant of United States Rubber.

Problems of Coordination

Davis did not favor the relatively loose supervision exercised by his predecessors over many of the operating policies and practices followed by local management personnel of companies acquired by the parent corporation. He recognized that a coherent corporate image could not be presented to employees, customers, or the general public unless there was reasonably consistent adherence to common policies, whether these applied to production, sales, financial operations, quality standards and controls, employee relations, or public relations.

So far as the older plants were concerned, the consolidation of production in fewer factories during the early thirties did much to resolve the matter. But the problem reoccurred with each new acquisition. Probably only those men who were intimately involved in attempting to bring about proper coordination of operations of newly acquired companies with those established by United States Rubber could adequately conceive the difficulties faced. The advantages accruing from the acquisitions were accompanied by many occasions in which understanding, diplomacy, persistence, and patient indoctrination needed to be exercised until agreement was reached. During the conversion process, it not infrequently happened that modifications of policies and procedures resulted that were beneficial to both groups.

Plantations and International Rubber Regulation Committee

Rubber Prices Below Production Costs

In 1935, United States Rubber celebrated the twenty-fifth anniversary of its operation of rubber plantations. The previous year had seen production rise to a total of 50,986,000 pounds (dry rubber content) from almost 11,000,000 trees on the five plantations in Sumatra and six on the Malay Peninsula. The combined area then operated by the company was approximately 99,000 acres.

The climbing production of these plantations pointed up one of the major problems of rubber plantation owners—the time lag between the planting of rubber trees, the initial tapping, and their period of maximum yield. During the depression years, natural rubber continued to be produced far in excess of world consumption. Huge surpluses piled up, and the wholesale price of No. 1, ribbed smoked sheet, landed New York, averaged a little less than 3½¢ a pound for 1932. The lowest price was reached in June, 1932 with the price in London at 1⅝ pence a pound and the New York price about 2⅝¢. These prices included freight, landing, and delivery charges[34] (see Figure 29, p. 163).

In 1933, the annual average wholesale price, landed New York, had risen to almost 6¢ a pound, but the price at the plantations was still well below cost. Production costs on the plantations were variously estimated at 8¢ to 12¢ a pound (U.S. currency).[35]

One commentator claimed that most of the large estates, as a result of increased yield from more mature trees and improved methods of culture, could produce and ship rubber for less than 5¢ a pound.[36] The persons responsible for this statement may have taken into account only current cash-out-of-pocket expenditures during a period when subsistence wages were paid, without allowing for such items as depreciation of trees or interest on the investment during the years before new plantings could be tapped. On that basis they may have been correct in 1933, but the producers would not agree that such a low figure represented their real costs. True, certain field activities such as upkeep and sanitation were postponed during the worst of the depression, but cost penalties were incurred later when these activities could be deferred no longer.

IRRC Formed

After more than four years of discussion and negotiation, a five-year plan for restriction of production and export of crude rubber was signed in London on April 28, 1934 by representatives of the countries producing about 98% of the world supply: Great Britain, Netherlands, India, Burma, French Indo-China, North Borneo, Sarawak, and Siam.[37] The plan prohibited planting of rubber trees in additional areas, except for 31,000 additional acres in Siam; placed tight controls on stocks of crude rubber held in the controlled area; limited replanting to 20% of existing areas; and forbade the exportation of planting materials to territory not covered by the agreement. The plan also established maximum export quotas for each year from 1934 to 1938 inclusive (Table 12).

Table 12.   Crude rubber export quotas, 1934-38.
(as amended by supplementary agreements 1935-38; thousands of long tons to nearest 500)

	1934	1935	1936	1937	1938
Straits Settlements	504	538	569	589	602
Netherlands East Indies	352	400	500	520	540
Ceylon	78	79	80	81	83
Sarawak	24	28	30	32	32
Siam	15	40	40	40	40
North Borneo	12	13	14	16	17
India	7	13	13	13	13
Burma	5	8	9	9	9
Total	997	1,119	1,254	1,299	1,335

Special arrangements were made for French Indo-China, because France imported about four times the amount produced in that colony. All the participating governments, except Sarawak's and Siam's, were invited to levy a tax on exports of rubber to cover the cost of research to discover new uses for the resource.

An International Rubber Regulation Committee (IRRC) was formed to exercise the controls and was given discretionary powers in setting production and export quotas. Each delegation was entitled to one vote for each 1,000 tons of the quota established for the country it represented. The United States was invited to be represented, without vote, on an advisory panel of manufacturers. A. L. Viles, president of the Rubber Manufacturers' Association, served as a member of this panel and William de Krafft was one of the alternates; F. B. Davis, Jr., also attended some meetings. The combined quotas of the British possessions gave them the predominant strength in determining what percentage of the basic quota should be established for each month. Since in the 1930's the "value of rubber exports was about one-quarter to one-fifth of that of all domestic exports from the (British) Colonies," we can understand why the operations of the IRRC loomed so important in the thinking of the British members.[38]

The aim of the IRRC was to hold the price of rubber landed in New York at about twice the cost of production, which would have resulted in prices ranging from about 16 to 24¢ a pound in this country. However, the agreement between the governments of the producing countries made no reference to price and did not establish any machinery for directly setting them. It relied instead on the controls established over production and stocks of crude rubber. Annual world production of rubber was estimated as 1 million long tons, with consumption run-

WORLD ABSORPTION OF CRUDE RUBBER

WORLD STOCKS OF CRUDE RUBBER

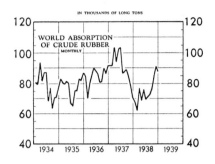

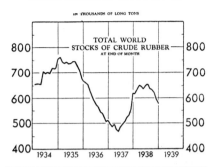

U. S. CRUDE RUBBER CONSUMPTION

STOCKS OF CRUDE RUBBER IN THE U. S.

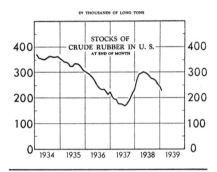

U. S. AUTOMOBILE PRODUCTION

U. S. STOCKS OF TIRES AND TUBES

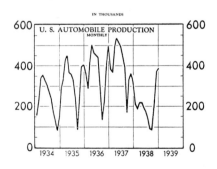

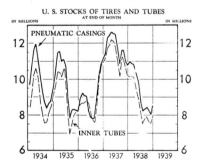

55. The rubber situation, 1934-38.

Source: *Commodity Year Book, 1939* (New York: Commodity Research Bureau, Inc., 1939), p. 373.

ning at the rate of about 931,000 long tons in 1934. World stocks of rubber on hand early in 1934 were estimated to be approximately 650,000 long tons, sufficient for about eight months. (Other estimates were as high as 735,000 long tons.) Disagreement soon arose with Dutch interests, who generally advocated higher quotas than the British favored.

The IRRC set the initial quotas on exports for August/September, 1934 at 10% less than the basic quotas, with a further reduction of 10% for October/November and again for December, 1934. The price of rubber, landed New York, rose to 16¢ a pound in August, but reports of disagreements between the British and Dutch, with the possibility that quotas might be set somewhat higher than British interests would have preferred, lowered the price to 13⅛¢ by Dec. 31, 1934. The IRRC met in October, but was unable to agree on quotas for 1935 and adjourned, with Holland contending for a larger quota for the East Indies because of difficulty (if the London price rose above 6½ pence a pound) in controlling shipments by native producers. They had shipped 14,000 tons more than the quota for the Dutch East Indies, despite heavy export duties.

Since Holland controlled approximately 25% of the votes of the IRRC, its support was essential to the success of any restrictions on exports, so the committee adjourned and met again in November when the exportable percentage of the base quotas was set at 75% for the first quarter of 1935. This figure was a compromise between those who wanted the exports restricted to no more than 70% and the manufacturers supported by the Dutch interests who had held out for 80%. However, world stocks of crude rubber on Sept. 30, 1935 were reported to be 714,622 tons, only 1,621 tons less than twelve months earlier. Because so little progress was being made in bringing world stocks of rubber more in line with consumption, the export quotas established by the IRRC were reduced to 60% for the fourth quarter of 1935.

Effect of Restrictions

The effect of these restrictions was to reduce the profit of the United States Rubber Plantations, Inc. from $1,735,842 in 1934 to $967,695 in 1935, due to reduction in shipments from 50,872,000 pounds in 1934 to 40,004,000 in 1935. Therefore, the unit cost of production had been increased without a compensating increase in price.

Exports of rubber from the producing areas were restricted in 1936 to 60-65% of the revised quotas. By the end of 1936 estimates of world stocks of crude rubber ranged from 464,000 long tons to 511,000 long tons, down by approximately 245,000 long tons since the end of

1934. World stocks then represented only about five and one-half months' current consumption and the New York price of ribbed smoked sheet rose to 20¢ a pound by the end of 1936.[39] Meanwhile, the United States had been slowly recovering from the worst of the depression. Factory sales of motor vehicles rose from only 1,332,000 vehicles in 1932 and 1,890,000 in 1933 to 4,461,000 in 1936. Manufacturers' shipments of tires climbed from 39,245,000 in 1932 to 52,313,000 by 1936; and 496,000 long tons of rubber were imported into the United States in 1936 as compared with only 427,000 tons in 1932 and 437,000 tons in 1933. The increased demand for rubber raised the New York price from the 1935 average of 12.4¢ a pound to the 1936 average of 16.4¢, and to 27⅛¢ a pound in March, 1937, even though the IRRC had permitted 75% of the basic quotas to be exported during the first quarter of 1937.

The higher prices for rubber enabled United States Rubber Plantations, Inc., to show a net profit of $1,914,000 for 1936. Then in 1937, a 39% increase in pounds of rubber shipped by the company's plantations under the liberalized export quotas set by IRRC, together with the higher prices that prevailed during most of the year, swelled the net profits of United States Rubber Plantations, Inc., to $4,590,000. But United States Rubber Company executives had been apprehensive that the higher prices for rubber would not continue. Consequently, a reserve of $1,300,000 had been set aside in 1935 to provide for contingencies arising from fluctuations in prices of rubber and cotton. A further reserve of $700,000 was set aside for the same purpose in 1936. The wisdom of these steps soon became apparent.

Recession of 1937-38

In mid-1937 the federal administration acted to curb what it considered excessive speculation in some commodities. The reaction was probably more severe than had been expected. The recession that started continued through 1938 and came to an end only with the beginning of World War II. The IRRC, not anticipating this turn of events, increased the export limit for the last half of 1937 to 90% of the standard production quotas. World stocks of crude rubber climbed; the New York price of rubber fell sharply and closed the year at 14 9/16¢ a pound. The reserves held for inventory adjustments and other contingencies were now used by United States Rubber, which wrote off $3,648,000 in adjusting inventories to market prices on Dec. 31, 1937.

The IRRC then cut the export limit for the first two quarters of 1938 to 70 and 60%, respectively, of the standard quotas, and to 45% for the last six months. This action came too late, however, to boost rubber prices in 1938. Factory sales of motor vehicles in the United States fell to 2,489,000 in 1938, almost 50% less than 1937 sales of 4,809,000. Likewise, shipments of original equipment tires in 1938 were down to 11,516,000 casings, little more than half of the 22,353,000 shipped in 1937; consumption of rubber in the United States decreased from 543,- 600 tons in 1937 to about 437,000 tons the following year. By the end of March, 1938, the New York price of rubber had fallen to 10⅜¢ a pound. It recovered to 16 5/16¢ by Dec. 31, and the average for the year was 14.7¢. Earnings of United States Rubber's plantations for the first six months of 1938 were only $198,718 after depreciation, amortization, and all other charges.

With the outbreak of war in Europe in September, 1939, the price of rubber began to climb. In June, 1940, Congress created the Rubber Reserve Company, which began to stockpile a strategic reserve of crude rubber in this country. The American consulate general at Singapore repeatedly suggested that it would be helpful if the authorities controlling rubber production would alter their system so as to prevent interference with the actual production and exportation of rubber. World stocks of crude rubber, however, were excessive, and, with the existing rates of production and exportation, the price structure would have been undermined had it not been for the United States government's purchases for the reserve stockpile.[40]

Although the IRRC increased the exportable limit for the last quarter of 1941 to 120% of the production quotas, complaint was made that production was still being arbitrarily limited. It was contended that the "smallholders" of rubber plantations in Malaya had not been permitted to equal the production rate they had had in the early days of 1934, immediately before the IRRC became operative; on the other hand, production quotas assigned to estates (holdings of 100 acres or more) were more than 45% above their 1934 rate of production. It was believed that a similar situation prevailed in the Netherland East Indies and Ceylon.

However, native ingenuity again appears to have been more than a match for governmental restrictions. Claims have been made that the IRRC "favored the planters and was definitely unfavorable to Asiatic peasants, with the result that the trend toward natural rubber's becoming more and more a peasant crop was stopped." But exports of natural rubber that represented production of Indonesian natives increased from 40% of the total in 1933 to 48% in 1938 and to 50% in 1940. Conversely, exports from Indonesia that represented production by "Europeans" declined from 60% in 1933 to only 50% in 1940. Rubber was perhaps the only agricultural commodity that did not reflect increased production by the Western owners of estates, at the expense of Indonesian natives, during those years.[41] With the overrunning of southeastern Asia and the East Indies by the Japanese army in the early months of 1942, the International Rubber Regulation Committee passed out of existence, but lasted officially until 1944.

The depressed prices for rubber during the early years of the 1930's operated to prevent regular replacement of old rubber trees in accordance with the twenty-five year schedule that United States Rubber's plantations favored. Consequently, when the company again gained possession of its plantations (1948 in Malaya and 1951 in Sumatra) many of the trees were from plantings made before World War I. Extensive replanting of higher yielding rubber trees was done over the next several years.

However, during the period of IRRC limitations the research department at Kisaran had not been idle. One of its lesser projects was improvement of the containers in which dry rubber was shipped to this country. Burlap and fiber mattings had been used to wrap bales of rubber; other bales had been packed in containers made of plywood or heavy fiberboard. None of these materials was entirely satisfactory; the packaging was often damaged in transit, and pieces of wood, burlap, or other foreign material were embedded in the rubber. United States Rubber has been credited with development of an improved method of packing ribbed, smoked sheet rubber. A pile of sheet rubber, measuring about 22″ x 18″ and weighing approximately 242 pounds, was wrapped with rubber sheet of equal quality. The stack then was pressed in a baling machine and held in clamps for half an hour. By that time the natural adhesive quality of the rubber held the bale together without use of straps. In 1941, the Netherlands India Rubber Trade Association made test shipments to the Rubber Trade Association of New York. The "bareback" bales, affording savings in handling, arrived in excellent shape.

THE NRA AND THE RUBBER INDUSTRY

Creation of National Recovery Administration

The large number of business failures from 1930 through 1932 made many believe that excessive competition could result in injury to the general public as well as to owners of business and their employees. Increasing numbers advocated federal legislation to permit cooperation between businessmen in the establishment of rules and standards that would fix floors for prices and wages, and thus eliminate or at least lessen the destructive effects of excessive competition and "chiseling." Labor also sought permission to organize and bargain without interference from employers. Out of these demands came the passage on June 13, 1933 of the National Industrial Recovery Act (NIRA), signed by President Roosevelt on June 16, giving the President control of industry.

General Hugh S. Johnson, who had organized and directed the selective draft in World War I, was appointed administrator of the National Recovery Administration (NRA) under the industrial recovery section of the act. The President also appointed a committee under the chairmanship of the Secretary of Commerce to act in accordance with the provisions pertaining to industrial recovery. This committee included General Johnson, the Secretaries of Commerce, Interior, Agriculture, and Labor, the Attorney General, and the chairman of the Federal Trade Commission.

Instead of concentrating its efforts on a few basic industries, such as coal, oil, steel, and lumber, NRA attempted to control all phases of all branches of industry. Representatives of the industries involved were assigned the primary responsibility for drafting the code governing each industry, subject to review and approval by NRA. Within two years, 764 industry codes and supplements had been approved by the NRA. Provisions for price-filing were contained in 444 codes. In 421 selling below cost was prohibited; 365 of the 421 prohibited sales below the individual member's cost, 7 below the lowest representative cost, and 4 below the average cost. Prohibitions against sales below cost were also contained in 38 distribution codes. Sales below invoice cost plus a uniform markup were prohibited in 13 of these; 9 prohibited sales below invoice cost plus transportation; 7 below individual cost; 6 below manufacturers' or wholesalers' list price, and 3 below invoice price plus individual markup. More than 200 of the codes prohibiting sales below cost also contained provisions for dissemination and adoption of uniform accounting procedures; of those submitted for approval, however, only 40 were approved, and only 29 of these were in effect when the NRA was declared unconstitutional by the Supreme Court on May 27, 1935.[42]

L. D. Tompkins was one who went to Washington to assist Edward R. Stettinius, Jr., in formation of the Industrial Advisory Council under NRA. Later, under General Johnson, Tompkins was for a time industrial advisor to various code authorities including those for the rubber industry; he also served as a special assistant to General Johnson.

Code for Rubber Industry (Except Tires)

The Rubber Manufacturers Association assisted in preparation of Code 156 for the industry. That code governed nine divisions of the industry, excluding tires. It prohibited sales below cost as determined by the RMA accounting manual, and provided for special procedures pertaining to prices, discounts, deductions, allowances, extras, commissions, and terms of sale. It also contained prohibitions against rebates, refunds, gifts, or bribes, and against inaccurate, deceptive, or misleading advertising.

The code proposed for the rubber footwear industry provided for filing prices with the code authority, prohibited sales below the cost of the member whose cost was the lowest, and regulated terms and conditions of sale. The provisions regarding lowest representative cost were never put into effect, for four of the smaller manufacturers refused to file, claiming that they would be unable to compete with the manufacturers whose products were nationally advertised if the existing price differentials were eliminated. Members who had filed prices then requested and received exemption from the price filing requirement. The rubber footwear code also prohibited incorporation into the product of any features beyond the approved standard unless a proportionately higher price were filed.

One of the smaller manufacturers in the rubber sole and heel industry contended that disclosure of prices under the price filing requirement tended to make all prices uniform, and that consequently his customers preferred to buy the better known products. In February, the industry obtained an indefinite stay of the price filing provision.

On June 7, 1934, NRA issued Office Memorandum No. 228, which provided for establishment of emergency minimum prices whenever any filed price adversely affected small enterprises, or wages or labor conditions, or when monopoly or other acute conditions tended to defeat the purposes of NRA. Following the issue of this memorandum, emergencies were declared and minimum prices established in nine industries only, including the retail rubber tire and battery industry.[43]

Pressure for Adoption of Tire Industry Code

The intense and unrelenting competition that had prevailed in the rubber tire industry since 1920 had taken its toll of both manufacturers and distributors. More than 200 manufacturers of rubber tires and tubes existed at the close of World War I, but the number had fallen to 104 in 1926, and declined to 32 in 1933.[44] In 1920, independent retailers had enjoyed 98% of the total sales of replacement tires. By 1926, their share of this market had slipped to 89.8%. Tire manufacturers had shipped 39,413,000 replacement tires in 1926; by 1933 shipments had decreased to 33,217,000 casings, and the independent tire retailers sold only 63.8% of the reduced market.

On the other hand, the mail order houses and chain stores had increased their percentage of the replacement tire market to 13.2% by 1933, up from about 2% in 1920 and 8.6% in 1926. Oil companies, whose filling stations had sold less than 1% of the replacement tires in 1926, had increased their share to about 9% in 1933, and stores owned by some of the tire manufacturers accounted for about 8% of the replacement market, up from less than 1% in 1926. Also by 1933, the practice of furnishing a spare with each new car had become almost universal, so that the automobile manufacturers were supplying about 5% of the replacement tire market in this manner.

Under these conditions, pressure was strong for the adoption of codes for the rubber tire manufacturing and distribution industries, which would impose tight restrictions on production and fix price floors, both at the manufacturing and the retailing levels. Small manufacturers and independent retailers sought the incorporation of such controls in the NRA codes, but they were opposed by the Administration as well as by other members of the industries. None of the proposed controls was approved.

In March, 1933, Sears set the prices on its All-State tires at only 10% less than the manufacturers consumers' list prices on first line tires. Also, from March to September, 1933, Sears endeavored to follow the policy on trade-in allowances that was followed by the independent tire dealers. Due principally to these two policies, as well as to increased competition from Montgomery Ward and from such chains as Gamble Skogmo and Western Auto Supply, and from the oil companies, Sears' tire sales fell from 2,526,000 in 1932 to 1,843,000 in 1933, a decline of 27%, although manufacturers' shipments of replacement tires had slumped only 2.2%. Sears' share of the replacement market had fallen from 9.6% in 1929 to only 5.4% of the greatly reduced total replacement tire volume in 1933. In November, 1933, to recover its position, Sears began giving 20-30% trade-in allowances on used tires. Hundreds of complaints poured in to NRA and, after prolonged arguments, a code for the rubber tire industry was adopted in December, 1933, which, it was hoped, would prevent reckless markdowns.[45] On Feb. 2, 1934, NRA called a conference, and an agreement to discontinue excessive trade-in allowances was reached.

The mail order houses then reduced tire prices, whereupon, to help the independent retailers meet the competition, manufacturers rebated to dealers part of their losses. Again complaints were made to the NRA. A forty-day truce was agreed upon, but the terms were disregarded by many before the period expired. Pursuant to the emergency price provisions of the code, the NRA established retail prices on first-line tires at a level of 77½% of Goodyear's consumers' list price. The level set by the code authority was intended to cover the selling costs of the smallest dealers and to provide them with a small operating margin. The price floors on second- and third-line tires were established at 70 and 60%, respectively, of Goodyear's list price. The floor on first-line tires was below the prices Sears had been using in 1934 before the price wars, but within a couple of weeks both Sears and Montgomery Ward had reduced their prices to the new floors. The tire manufacturers who were operating their own retail stores promptly met these prices in their stores. Independent tire dealers had to fall in line, and again complaints poured in to NRA.

Small tire manufacturers and their independent dealers claimed that with virtually uniform prices consumers preferred to buy the brands advertised by the "Big Four." Montgomery Ward and various chains gave similar testimony. The small manufacturers also claimed a disadvantage in a rising market for crude rubber; they were not able to carry large stocks and had to pay higher prices for raw material. The larger manufacturers and Sears were said to have several months' supply of crude rubber purchased at lower prices. However, the Administration was opposed to setting price floors higher than necessary to protect the lowest cost producer and distributor, and in the face of the mass distributors' strong opposition to higher prices NRA refused to approve them.

Another attempt to create a differential between the prices on tires of the large manufacturers, the small manufacturers, and the mail order houses was made in August, 1934, but when one of the large manufacturers refused to raise prices, the other companies did not raise theirs. Many tire retailers did not adopt the new schedules. When the emergency period for price determinations expired in October, 1934, no further effort to control tire prices was made by the code authority.[46]

Cotton Textile Code

The fixing of price floors was only one of the controls by which NRA sought to prevent destructive competition. Attempts were also made to control production in order to prevent individual members of an industry from producing more goods than the market could absorb. Thus the pressure to dispose of surplus inventory at less than cost would be avoided. The cotton textile code provided that extraordinary limitations of plant hours could be imposed whenever there was danger of excessive accumulation of stocks or price cutting. During the 695 days this code operated, ten such extraordinary limitations were ordered, usually calling for a 25% reduction in hours of operation and curtailing use of any equipment not operated during a specified period, usually six months prior to the effective date of the curtailment.

Those tire manufacturers who operated their own textile mills to supply tire fabrics repeatedly but unsuccessfully tried to have the code limitations modified so that they would not be forced to go into the open market for part of their requirements. However, the code authority opposed their efforts to obtain exemptions, and the NRA usually chose to support the code authority.

Some Reasons for Failure of NRA

The preceding account of problems connected with attempts to control industry under the NRA indicates the impracticability of controls in a competitive market and a free economy. In addition, NRA lacked competent personnel to administer the multiplicity of code regulations. As regulations proliferated, the dearth of informed, competent administrators became increasingly acute.[47] The inflexibility inherent in all bureaucratic controls operated to defeat the express purpose of the NRA—the recovery of the national industrial economy.

On May 27, 1935, the Supreme Court in a unanimous decision declared the National Industrial Recovery Act unconstitutional. On May 30, President Roosevelt called a press conference and talked for two hours to the correspondents about the decision, characterizing it as an effort to restore the days of the horse and buggy. National progress along economic and social lines would be impossible in the light of the decision, Secretary of the Interior Harold Ickes quoted him as saying.[48] The efficacy of NRA was over, although, in the opinion of some informed observers, that decision was fatal only because NRA had attempted to cover too much ground and had overextended the physical and intellectual capacity of its staff. All provisions of the NRA delegating powers to approve or prescribe codes of fair competition and providing for enforcement of such codes were repealed on June 14, 1935.

ROBINSON-PATMAN PRICE DISCRIMINATION LAW

Background

In the twenty-two years between the establishment of the Federal Trade Commission on Sept. 26, 1914 and the enactment of the Robinson-Patman law in 1936, the FTC had issued forty-three complaints under the price discrimination provisions of the Clayton Act. Thirty-one of these complaints had been dismissed; cease-and-desist orders had been issued in only twelve cases, and four of these were appealed and were reversed.

The Clayton Act of 1914 was intended to prevent discrimination that would "substantially lessen competition or tend to create a monopoly." The act provided that discrimination on account of differences in "grade, quality or quantity" or in "cost of selling or transportation" was permissible. Discrimination was also permitted when "made in good faith to meet competition." The record of the years since the act had been entered on the statute books disclosed three major sources of difficulty in its application. First, the courts were reluctant to apply the act to those discriminations that tended to reduce competition between the seller's customers, if competition between the seller and his competitors was not reduced. Second, since the Clayton Act permitted discrimination "on account of differences in the quantity of the commodity sold," the courts tended to exempt quantity discounts regardless of their amount or their effect. Third, application was limited to the initiators of discrimination; those that followed and who met competition in good faith were exempted from the provisions of the act.

The rapid growth during the early thirties of chain stores, particularly those dealing in foods, created a strong demand for enactment of legislation that would curb the buying power of chain stores and of other firms who were in a position to exert pressure upon their suppliers for concessions in price or conditions of sale. Agitation steadily increased for legislation that would restrict differences in price or conditions of sale based solely or largely on the quantity of purchases without relation to differences in costs. The result was the introduction in Congress in 1935 of the Robinson-Patman bill, amending Section 2 of the original Clayton Act.

There was general agreement with the bill's avowed purpose to keep large buyers from using their purchasing power to obtain unfair concessions from sellers, but opinion differed considerably as to the best way to accomplish this. Consequently the act approved by President Roosevelt on June 19, 1936 was different from the original bill. It had been greatly modified in Congress, and had been further revised at the hands of the Senate-House conference committee.

Section 2(a) of the Robinson-Patman Act prohibited "discrimination in price between purchasers of commodities of like grade and quality where there was reasonable probability of effects injurious to competition." It introduced a new concept: previous laws seeking to eliminate price discrimination had been concerned with the extent to which such discrimination had reduced *existing* competition, but the new law included the effect or possible effect of discrimination in the *prevention* of competition. Discrimination was still permissible under the Robinson-

Patman Act, but only if it represented "due allowance for difference in cost of manufacture, sale or delivery . . . resulting from differing methods or quantities," or if made in good faith to meet competition.

One weakness of the act was that, while it sought to curb the purchasing power of large buyers, the means were focused upon the sellers. Under Section 2(f) it was unlawful for a buyer "knowingly to induce or receive a discrimination in price which is prohibited under this statute." But what constituted such knowledge was not clearly stated. It was also difficult to apply the act to cases that involved the granting of functional discounts. For example, a manufacturer might be selling a product to independent retailers at the time he was also selling it to national chains, to wholesalers, or to other manufacturers for use in their finished product. Other problems arose when the seller marketed some goods under a nationally advertised brand and somewhat similar goods under a private brand.

U.S. Tire Dealers Mutual Corporation

To conform to the provisions of the Robinson-Patman Act, the United States Rubber Company formed the U.S. Tire Dealers Mutual Corporation, which began on Jan. 1, 1937 to distribute tires and related products to independent dealers. Dealers were told that the initial price at which U.S. tires would be billed to them would be based on competition. Sales made by United States Rubber to private brand volume buyers—for instance, the Atlas Supply Company—or to the U.S. Tire Dealers Mutual Corporation were made at a uniform factory cost plus a uniform percentage profit. At the end of each quarter, actual costs of production were checked, and at the end of the year an adjustment was made in the selling price to the private brand buyer and to the U.S. Tire Dealers Mutual. Mutual took over, as of Jan. 1, 1937, the commercial operations of the Tire Division, its branches, salesmen, advertising, and so on, on an "arms length" agreement. These distribution costs (borne by U.S. Tire Dealers Mutual Corporation) plus profit were added to the previously determined manufacturing costs, and the difference, if any, between this figure and the price that had been charged was refunded to the dealers purchasing from Mutual.

The aim of this arrangement was to enable United States Rubber to continue selling tires and related products to its private brand customers. At the same time, the company could automatically adjust the prices to independent dealers on the basis of a legally cost-justified differential in price of U.S. brand tires, resulting from the differing methods by which the tires were sold. Generally speaking, the independent dealers were happy with the operation of the plan, and the FTC did not take exception to the principle on which it was based.[50]

FTC Complaint and Findings

On Jan. 6, 1939, the FTC issued a complaint against United States Rubber Company and the U.S. Tire Dealers Corporation, in which the FTC charged the Rubber Company with illegal discrimination based on: (1) the sale of goods for resale under private brands to Montgomery Ward and Company, Atlas Supply Company, Western Auto Supply Company, and Arkansas Fuel Oil Company; (2) sale of regularly branded tires to certain large consumers at lower than regular prices; (3) retail sales, through stores owned by the rubber company in twenty principal cities, of regularly branded tires at a discount to so-called commercial accounts; (4) payment of commission of 7½% to Socony Vacuum Oil Company, American Oil Company, Pan-American Petroleum, and Tide-Water Associated Oil Company in the form of sales-commissions on sales made directly by the rubber company to jobbers and filling stations whose primary business was the sale of petroleum products of the oil companies. (The payment of commission to the oil companies was intended as compensation for their sales help in getting the distributors to buy U.S. tires.) In its findings, the commission charged the company with injury to competition and a tendency to create monopoly by its sales of private brand tires, with limited probability of injury to competing retailers from concessions made to commercial accounts, with probability of injury to competition among buyers, and with a tendency toward monopoly in its concessions to large buyers.[51]

The FTC's cease and desist order, dated April 25, 1939, was issued with United States Rubber's consent and was concerned largely with practices that had prevailed prior to presidential approval of the Robinson-Patman Act. It directed the rubber company to cease paying commission to oil companies that were *customers* of United States Rubber, unless such commissions were available proportionately to all other customers. United States Rubber discontinued payment of commissions to oil companies to whom it sold tires for resale; but to other oil companies that were not customers, it continued to pay sales commissions on sales made directly to jobbers or filling stations affiliated with those oil companies.

The consent order also required some other relatively minor changes to be made by the rubber company in its mutual plan system, namely, that the cost of U.S. brand tires be computed separately so that no profit or loss on sale of private brand tires would be taken into consideration; that distribution costs should not include any interest payments to the parent company by the subsidiary, U.S. Tire Dealers Mutual Corporation; and that part of the cost of the company's advertising should be charged to original equipment sales. These orders were complied with. Prices to buyers of private brand tires continued to be based on cost-plus contracts. Prices on U.S. brand tires to dealers and distributors continued to be higher by amounts representing the computed differentials in costs. No retail tire stores were owned or operated by U.S. Tire Dealers Mutual Corporation after Dec. 31, 1938.

The volume discount schedule shown in the company's report of compliance, filed June 20, 1939, required larger volumes to earn discounts that were somewhat smaller. Discounts in the new schedule ranged from 1 to 2.5 per cent on annual volume of purchases ranging from $15,000 to $50,000 and over. Other tire companies appear to have adopted, at least temporarily, similar discount schedules following publication of the compliance report.

Writing in 1959, Corwin D. Edwards of the University of Chicago, a former long-time staff member of the FTC, reviewed twenty years of experience under the Robinson-Patman Act, then made the following statement:

> "The cases of unsystematic price discrimination and private brand discrimination that have been reviewed have shed little further light on the cost defense in price discrimination cases. Only in the case involving United States Rubber [Docket 3685] do problems of cost appear to have been seriously considered. In other instances, the selective nature of the discrimination apparently precluded any successful cost defense. In the U.S. Rubber case, the new feature is the use of the uniform salesprice at the level paid by the most favored customers and the segregation of the further costs of distribution incurred in selling to other customers, so that when the surplus above the segregated additional costs is refunded to the buyer, the price differentials will automatically correspond. It is surprising that there has not been further experiment with such devices."[52]

INDUSTRIAL RELATIONS IN THE 1930's

Assistance to Employees of Closed Plants

When the L. Candee and Company plant at New Haven, Conn., was closed in March, 1929, Cyrus S. Ching was not the only one in management who was deeply concerned about employees, especially those with longer periods of service, who could not be transferred to other factories. Under the pension plan inaugurated in 1917, payments to pensioned employees were small, and on Ching's recommendation a scale was adopted for payment of dismissal wage to employees with ten or more years of service. One week's wages for each year of service was paid (1) to all employees forty-five years of age or older, with ten or more years of service, and (2) to all employees with fifteen or more years of service, who were ineligible for pension.[53] Because of the serious financial situation of United States Rubber in 1929 and for several years afterwards, it was not possible to do anything better at that time.

To further assist employees whose service was being terminated by closing the Candee footwear plant, an employment office was set up where other prospective employers could interview them. The Industrial Relations Department worked with various employers' associations in the New Haven area and the local Chamber of Commerce, and, as the result of this effort, practically all the former employees of the Candee plant who continued to live in or near New Haven obtained other employment. The pattern established at the time of the closing was followed in its essential details when other plants of the United States Rubber Company were closed during the years immediately following 1929.

Strike at the Mishawaka Plant

After 1920, no serious strikes hit any of the factories of United States Rubber or its subsidiaries until 1931. The Mishawaka Rubber and Woolen Mfg. Company[54] suffered a drastic curtailment of its sales in 1930 and 1931 as the result of the depression, the widespread drought, and warm, dry winters. In an effort to spread the available work rather than lay off workers who would be unable to obtain other employment, working schedules were reduced from six days a week to five. As it became evident that even this shorter workweek would produce many more pairs of footwear than customers would buy, the plant was scheduled to work fewer and fewer days per week. It was the first time in the memory of most of the workers that they had not had full-time employment, and they found it hard to believe that the company did not have a large backlog of unfilled orders.

The Mishawaka plant had lagged behind the other rubber footwear factories in the System in the adoption of multiple-man crews or of installation of conveyorized units for the "making" operations. The first important moves to introduce more efficient, less costly methods were made after Davis became president of United States Rubber Company. Many of the workers, both men and women, had had long years of service with the Mishawaka company, during which their work habits had been disturbed little if at all. Consequently, they found it difficult to adjust to the new methods. When, at the same time, the schedules called for fewer days per week and fewer pairs per day, unfounded rumors began to circulate that this was all part of a plan to force the employees to accept a lower pay scale. On May 18, 1931 about 2,400 of the workers at Mishawaka went on strike for about three weeks. The settlement provided that workers would be permitted to elect shop committees to represent them in discussions with factory management regarding working conditions and other matters.

Labor Enters a New Era

A new era in labor relations was inaugurated with the passage of the NIRA in 1933. Section 7(a) gave labor the right to organize and bargain collectively through representatives of their own choosing, without interference by their employers. On June 30, 1933, the President established the National Labor Relations Board to administer the labor provisions of the NIRA. After the Supreme Court in May, 1935 declared unconstitutional Title I of NIRA, that board passed out of existence.

Then Senator Robert F. Wagner sponsored the act that created a Labor Relations Board of three members. This so-called Wagner Act, which became law on July 5, 1935, confirmed the right of labor to bargain collectively with representatives of its own choosing, provided for workers' elections of their representatives, and established regulations covering "unfair practices." The act declared that the findings of the Labor Relations Board were to be binding, and it provided for prosecution of such "unfair practices" through the courts.

During the three years from 1933 to 1935 inclusive, the work days lost in labor stoppages averaged almost 18,840,000 a year. Membership in the AFL climbed to 3,400,000 by 1936, but the insistence of union leaders on organization along craft lines and the relatively slow progress in unionization of the steel, rubber, textile, and automobile industries led to the formation by John L. Lewis of the Congress of Industrial Organizations (CIO) in 1935. Intense organizing rivalry followed.

When the Wagner Act was passed, Ching concluded that the eventual unionization of the rubber company's factories was inevitable. Therefore, he bent his efforts toward developing a policy that would promote good relations between the company and its employees. He decided that the company should pursue a neutral course, and neither take action to promote formation of union locals nor take steps to interfere if the unions were successful in organizing the employees. Councils had been formed at most of the factories operated by the company or its subsidiaries, and thus the workers were accustomed to electing their representatives. Those councils and the policy followed by Ching now served to bring about a smoother transition to union representation of the workers in the company's plants than was experienced by other major rubber tire manufacturers. Disagreements and some work stoppages did occur during the years up to and during World War II, but, comparatively speaking, disputes with labor in that period were ironed out with little trouble.[55] Ching had reason to believe he had taken the right course. In 1941, United States Rubber was the first multiple plant company in the industry to negotiate a company-wide contract with the United Rubber, Cork, Linoleum and Plastic Workers of America, International Union, and its affiliated local unions.

Retirement and Savings, Group Insurance Plans

On May 1, 1931, United States Rubber inaugurated a retirement and savings plan under which employees were permitted to make deposits amounting to 2% of their salary or wages in order to qualify upon retirement for participation in the service fund (contributed by the company out of profits). Employees also had the privilege of making additional deposits as savings, and interest at the rate of 4% was guaranteed by the company on all such deposits. The funds were held by the Central Hanover Bank and Trust Company. A similar plan was operated by the Canadian subsidiary, and those funds were held by the Royal Trust Company of Canada.

The first contribution made by United States Rubber to the service fund amounted to $55,000 out of profits for 1935, the first year to show a profit after the plan was adopted. Other and larger contributions were made by the company in subsequent years. At the annual meeting of stockholders on April 16, 1940, the guaranteed interest rate was reduced to 3% and the service fund was replaced by a new retirement allowance plan whereby employees who qualified through age and length of service would receive retirement allowances to augment old age benefits provided by the Social Security Act. In 1941, in consequence of the Investment Company Act of 1940, the retirement savings plans of the company and its Canadian subsidiary were discontinued, and the funds totaling approximately $7,960,000 were returned to the employees.

The number of employees who took advantage of the group insurance plan of 1926 had grown over the years until, by the end of 1942, 45,769 employees had coverage totaling over $61 million.

[1]"Post-trial Brief of the United States Rubber Company, Nov. 30, 1953," in *United States of America v. E. I. du Pont de Nemours and Company,* et al (N. D., Ill.) p. 75. (Complaint filed in 1949.)

[2]Statement made to author by L. D. Tompkins, 1963. Sheehan, who remained in charge of tire sales to automobile manufacturers until his death in 1947, was described by Tompkins as one of the ablest salesmen he had ever met.

[3]"Post-trial Brief," p. 45.

[4]"Post-trial Brief," p. 14, ff. The government eventually dropped its charges against United States Rubber Company in this case.

[5]"U.S. Rubber, I, The Corporate State," *Fortune,* IX (February, 1934), pp. 126-27.

[6]"U.S. Rubber, I, The Corporate State," pp. 126-27.

[7]Information obtained in correspondence with Noble Ashley, 1962, 1963.

[8]Statement by L. D. Tompkins, 1963.

[9]In 1933, sales of tires were reported to represent about 40% of United States Rubber Company's total business. See "U.S. Rubber, I, The Corporate State," p. 52 ff. It also has been stated that, in the late thirties, tires accounted for about 60% of the company's sales and about the same percentage of its profits.

[10]W. A. Gibbons, "The Rubber Industry, 1839-1939," *Industrial and Engineering Chemistry,* XXXI (October, 1939), p. 1199 ff. Also see John D. Gaffey, *The Productivity of Labor in the Rubber Tire Manufacturing Industry* (New York: Columbia University Press, 1940), p. 39.

[11]Lloyd G. Reynolds, "Competition in the Rubber Tire Industry," *American Economic Review,* XXVIII (September, 1938), pp. 459-68.

[12]Information obtained in correspondence with Howard N. Hawkes, 1963.

[13]Memorandum regarding certain acquisitions, United States Rubber Company archives. By March, 1940, United States Rubber had acquired 93% of the common stock of Gillette Rubber Company and offered to buy the remaining shares at $29 a share until March 29, 1940. Gillette was dissolved and ceased to exist as a separate corporation on March 31, 1940. See *New York Times* (March 2, 1940), p. 24.

[14] Information obtained in correspondence with Noble Ashley, 1962.

[15] R. G. Bath, quoted by Andrew M. Howe, "Don't be Afraid to Improve Your Trade-Mark," *Printers' Ink* (March 27, 1930), pp. 10, 12. Also see *New York Herald Tribune* (Jan. 15, 1941).

[16] A few years later, spurred probably by labor troubles in Akron, the Ford Motor Company did build a tire plant as part of its River Rouge, Mich., motor car complex. Completed early in 1938, it was said to be the "world's most advanced tire plant." It had a potential daily capacity of 16,000 tires and tubes, but did not produce its millionth tire until mid-March, 1939. In late 1942, the U.S. government requested the plant to be dismantled and shipped to Russia under the lend-lease program. *New York Times* (March 19, 1939), p. 7; also (Nov. 3, 1942), p. 22.

[17] T. J. Needham, interview, 1962.

[18] A. E. Denari, interview, 1963.

[19] Largely based on statements made to the author by Denari and Herbert G. Kieswetter, 1963.

[20] Statement made to author by H. E. Cooper, 1963. Lastex is the registered trademark of the United States Rubber Company.

[21] Geoffrey T. Hillman, "Two-Way Stretch Adamson," *Forbes* (April 15, 1934), p. 15.

[22] Based on statements made to the author by J. J. Orr and H. E. Cooper.

[23] "Two-Way Stretch Adamson," p. 15.

[24] Statement to the author by H. E. Cooper, 1963. The "associated companies" were the Italian and Hungarian firms, Pirelli Societa per Azioni and Hungarian Rubber Goods Company.

[25] "United States Rubber Declares Dividend on its Common Stock," *Rubber Age,* XLVIII (March, 1941), p. 400.

[26] Sidney M. Cadwell to Walter L. Pipes, Aug. 21, 1934, company archives.

[27] Ralph C. Epstein, "Concentration and Price Trends in the Rubber Tire Industry, 1930-47," privately printed for submission to the Federal Trade Commission, 1949, pp. 45-47.

[28] U.S. Dept. of Commerce, *Industrial Reference Service, Part 10, "Rubber"* (Washington: U.S. Gov't Printing Office, April, 1941), p. 1; "Romance of Rubber," privately printed, United States Rubber Company, 1941, p. 31.

[29] Information obtained from S. M. Cadwell and S. I. Strickhouser, and from company records.

[30] Information obtained from correspondence with J. P. Monahan, 1963; also see *The Story of United States Rubber Company,* privately printed, p. 34.

[31] U.S. Dept. of Commerce, *Business Statistics, 1959 Biennial Edition* (Washington: U.S. Gov't Printing Office, 1959), p. 45.

[32] On Dec. 5, 1945, he also was made a vice-president of United States Rubber Company; on Oct. 1, 1951, he became executive vice-president and vice-chairman of the executive committee.

[33] "Romance of Rubber," p. 45.

[34] Peter T. Bauer, *The Rubber Industry, a Study in Competition and Monopoly* (Cambridge: Harvard University Press, 1948), p. 31.

[35] *Business Week* (Feb. 23, 1935), p. 22.

[36] "U.S. Rubber, II, Sumatra," *Fortune,* IX (February, 1934), p. 128.

[37] *Business Week* (May 5, 1934), pp. 22, 23.

[38] *The History of Rubber Regulation, 1934-1943,* ed. by Sir Andrew McFadyean for the International Rubber Regulation Committee (London: George Allen & Unwin, Ltd., 1944), p. 47 ff.

[39] W. J. Gallagher (see Chapter III, p. 87) appears to have played an important part in the formation of the *IRRC*. At the 1936 meeting of the shareholders of the Java Amalgamated Rubber Estates, Ltd., Gallagher was reelected a director of the corporation. The shareholders remembered "with gratitude the part he played in bringing into force the present scheme of regulation." *India Rubber World*, XCI (London, April 11, 1936), p. 446.

[40] U.S. Dept. of Commerce, *Industrial Reference Service, Part 10, "Rubber"* (Washington: U.S. Gov't Printing Office, December, 1940), p. 1.

[41] Karl J. Pelzer, "The Resource Pattern of Southeast Asia," and Justus M. van der Kroef, "Economic Origins of Indonesian Nationalism," in *South Asia in the World Today* (Chicago: University of Chicago Press, 1950), pp. 115, 179. Also see Julius H. Boeke, *The Evolution of the Netherlands Indies Economy* (New York: Netherlands and Netherlands Indies Council, Institute of Pacific Relations, 1946), p. 23.

[42] Charles Albert Pearce, *NRA Trade Practice Programs* (New York: Columbia University Press, 1939), pp. 46, 47, and 81.

[43] *NRA Trade Practice Programs*, pp. 62, 63, and 149.

[44] *Federal Trade Commission Decisions, Findings, Orders, and Stipulations*, XXII (Washington: U.S. Gov't Printing Office), p. 302, ff. Leonard Smith, manager of commercial research department, United States Rubber Company, said in an interview in May, 1963, that the actual number of manufacturers of rubber tire casings had declined from 132 on July 1, 1924, to 79 by Jan. 1, 1929; to 29 by July 1, 1938; to 27 by Jan. 1, 1941; to 24 by Jan. 1, 1946; to 22 by Jan. 1, 1950; and to 17 by Oct. 1, 1962.

[45] "U.S. Rubber, I, The Corporate State," p. 127; also, *Federal Trade Commission Decisions, Findings, Orders, and Stipulations*, XXII (Washington: U.S. Gov't Printing Office, 1939), p. 302.

[46] *NRA Trade Practice Programs*, pp. 169-74.

[47] Walton Hamilton and others, *Price and Price Policies* (New York: McGraw-Hill Book Co., 1938), p. 21.

[48] Harold L. Ickes, *The Secret Diary of Harold L. Ickes* (New York: Simon and Schuster, 1954), p. 197.

[49] Corwin D. Edwards, *The Price Discrimination Law, A Review of Experience* (Washington: The Brookings Institution, 1959), pp. 6, 7. In discussing the Robinson-Patman Act, the author has drawn heavily on Edwards' authoritative treatise.

[50] *The Price Discrimination Law*, pp. 471, 472; also statement made to author by Morris E. Dry, 1962.

[51] *The Price Discrimination Law*, p. 472. See *New York Times* (Jan. 10, 1939). Also Federal Trade Commission, Docket 3685; *Federal Trade Commission Decisions, Findings, Orders, and Stipulations*, XXVIII (Washington: U.S. Gov't Printing Office, 1940), pp. 1489-1506.

[52] *The Price Discrimination Law*, p. 483.

[53] "The Dismissal Wage," *Factory and Industrial Management*, LXXIX (March, 1930), p. 536.

[54] When the corporation's charter was renewed in 1922, the name had been changed from Mishawaka Woolen Mfg. Company, in recognition of the major importance of its rubber footwear business.

[55] Statement made to the author by Cyrus S. Ching, 1963. Following World War II, United States Rubber's higher labor costs, resulting in considerable measure from the work standards in effect in its plants, placed the company at a competitive disadvantage with other leading tire manufacturers. A basis for correcting this situation was laid in 1963, but only after costly strikes had occurred at several plants.

9

World War II Begins

Production of Fuel Cells

The need to develop self-sealing fuel tanks (or "cells") for combat air-craft was demonstrated in World War I, and by 1927 several patents had been issued on self-sealing constructions. These usually involved a metal tank covered with rubber or rubber-coated fabric. The leaking gasoline was supposed to cause the rubber to swell, thereby closing the opening.

In July, 1938, Ernest Eger of the Tire Division had demonstrated to the Army Air Corps and the Navy Bureau of Aeronautics what are believed to have been the first successful self-sealing fuel tanks made in this country. The metal tank was covered on the outside with plies of rubber and fabric, but this construction had a serious weakness. A projectile that tumbled in flight through the container left a large hole on its way out. The metal edges of the opening frequently flowered outward, pre-venting the rubber plies from closing. This fault was at least partially corrected by inserting a rubber cell with three layers: a fuel-resistant lining; a sealant, usually semivulcanized rubber or a modified GR-S compound[1] (spread-latex sheet was used until it became unavailable); and a retaining section, consisting of outside layers of rubber-coated cord fabric or tough tire-tread stock. When the cell was punctured by gun-fire, escaping fuel caused the sealant layer to swell rapidly, thereby clos-ing the first opening, and the outward flowering of the metal where the projectile left the tank did not affect the sealing action of the rubber cell inside.

In World War II, during the Battle of Britain, captured German planes were found to have self-sealing fuel cells with a liner of oil-resistant compound, an inner "sandwich" of raw rubber, and an outer casing of rawhide leather. The Detroit plant of United States Rubber used these as models in some of its early development work. In 1940, the Tire Division of United States Rubber made and shipped to England enough ST sandwich sealant to cover the fuel tanks of 467 Allied planes. These planes are said to have been "the first and only planes so protected to reach combat during the early critical period in the defense of England."[2] ST was made of a soft rubber center layer sandwiched between sheets of resilient rubber that were stretched and held under tension during the vulcanizing process. Any puncture resulting from gunfire was immediately closed by the compressive force resulting when the tension was relieved.

Mareng Cells

In 1937, the engineering department of the Glenn L. Martin Company had patented the Mareng cell (*Mar*-tin *eng*-ineering), which was formed from cured neoprene-coated airplane cloth with the seams sewn and cemented with neoprene adhesive. Mareng cells were flexible and shaped to fit into fuselage or wing cavities, and were fastened at various points to the housing. When a self-sealing construction was specified, a three-ply rubber sandwich with a sealant inner layer was attached to the neoprene-coated fabric. At first Martin made Mareng cells for the Martin B-26 bomber. On July 1, 1940, a contract, negotiated primarily by W. R. Yaw of the Tire Division, granted to United States Rubber exclusive rights to manufacture and sell Mareng cells except for those Martin continued to make for its own use.

The Mishawaka plant was chosen to begin manufacture of the cells. There were good reasons for this choice. The Tire Division was straining to meet heavy demands; on the other hand, Mishawaka had factory space available. Furthermore, the Mishawaka engineering and manufacturing organization, effectively led by George W. Blair, had demonstrated considerable resourcefulness in connection with new products, such as automobile floor mats and foam rubber items. In October, 1940, Mishawaka received a substantial order from Martin for self-sealing cells for the B-26 bomber and made its first shipment in December of that year.

Meanwhile, the Naugatuck plant was set up to make self-sealing Mareng cells for the M-187 bomber, which was produced by Martin for Britain, and began to make shipments in April, 1941. Fuel cell sales and engineering activities were centered at Mishawaka. United States Rubber also produced Mareng cells for the Navy flying boat, PBM-3, and for several boat companies. However, most of the cells for use in boats had a rigid, nonmetallic construction. After military requirements exceeded the capacities of both the Mishawaka and Naugatuck plants, fuel cells were also produced at the company's plants in Detroit, Los Angeles, Chicopee, Mass., and St. Jerome, Canada.

Extraordinary Problems

The problems facing manufacturers of self-sealing fuel cells were formidable. The cells had to be capable of holding fuel for long periods at −40° to 160°F. without disintegrating or cracking; they must not contaminate the fuel; and they had to seal bullet openings in less than two minutes. To determine the sealing qualities of each construction, small cells enclosed in aluminum shells were set up on a firing range, 25 yards from a .50 caliber machine gun, and were subjected to gunfire from different angles. United States Rubber's plants at Mishawaka, Naugatuck, Detroit, and Los Angeles maintained full-time gunfire test programs. The plant at St. Jerome conducted firing tests on a part-time basis.

When a .50 caliber bullet traveling at about 2,750 feet per second hit the fuel in the tank, tremendous kinetic energy (known in the industry as "hydraulic ram") was immediately concentrated against the opposite wall. The wing structures of many of the early combat planes were demolished by this force. Hydraulic ram would also tear a 2″ x 4″ (or larger) hole in the metal structure supporting the cell. United States Rubber pioneered in the development of backing materials placed between the supporting metal shell and the self-sealing fuel cell that provided support and prevented the metal edges from holding the hole open. The most important of these new backings was called V-board.

In December, 1941, H. F. Jordon of the General Laboratories called the attention of the Mishawaka development department to the possibility of using a new thermosetting resin as an aromatic-resistant liner for fuel cells. With his characteristic energy and leadership, Blair expedited work on this suggestion, which led to the use of V-board (a laminated sheet of fiber glass and resin) as a supporting material. V-board had exceptionally high tensile strength and did not shatter at −40°F. Especially important, the material did not flower around a bullet hole. V-board was approved by the Air Force in April, 1942, and was produced by Mishawaka in large quantities. Its application as fuel cell liners is believed to have been the first successful commercial use of a fiber glass-resin laminate; a wide range of applications for this material has created a large market since World War II. Out of the work done by

United States Rubber to develop stronger nonmetallic casings for fuel cells came a plastic sheeting material that was commercially marketed later as one of the family of Vibrin resins.[3]

Industry Technical Committee Formed

Nine days after the attack on Pearl Harbor, the Air Corps Material Center at Wright Field, Dayton, called a meeting, which was attended by representatives of United States Rubber and the four other manufacturers of fuel cells for combat aircraft. Also in attendance were representatives of the Bureau of Aeronautics, Navy Department, and the British Air Commission. General George C. Kenny told the manufacturers that it would be necessary to immediately change the compounds used in fuel tanks, hose, and other fuel system parts. Materials would have to be found that were resistant to fuels containing up to 38 percent aromatics (benzene, toluene, and xylene), because these were the only fuels available in theaters of operation. Cells and hose in current production were lined with neoprene, which would disintegrate on exposure to aromatic fuels. At the recommendation of the Army, a lacquer of zinc chromate was sloshed inside the existent cells or hose, the excess was drained, and the deposited film dried. This emergency treatment proved fairly successful.

Other objectives of the meeting with manufacturers at Wright Field in December, 1941, as outlined by Lt. Col. F. C. Carroll, were to work toward standardization of materials and construction; to effect free exchange of technical and manufacturing information between the different fuel cell manufacturers; and to initate the formation of a manufacturers' technical committee to facilitate such exchange. A technical committee was formed with two representatives from each manufacturer and two from Wright Field. G. W. Blair and A. W. Bull were the first representatives for United States Rubber on this committee. The other companies represented were Firestone, Goodrich, Goodyear Tire, and Hewitt Rubber Corporation.

A tentative agreement was drawn up, subject to approval by the legal counsel and officers of each company, for full exchange of technical and manufacturing information pertaining to fuel cells. The participating manufacturers were to make their materials available to each other to the greatest possible extent; inventions pertaining to fuel cells were to be available to the other parties to the agreement. An unusual provision was that contracts for self-sealing fuel cells would be let exclusively to the companies entering into the agreement, and that the government would exempt these companies from prosecution under the antitrust laws for the action taken in accordance with the agreements. It was considered essential that, if the participating companies were to expend large sums in developing fuel cells to meet government specifications and were to make their findings and know-how available to their competitors, they should not be exposed to competition from manufacturers who were not bound by such obligations. The five participating companies were able to meet the requirements for fuel cells and continued to be the only sources used by the armed forces during the war.

At the first meeting of the technical committee on Dec. 27 and 28, 1941, it was found that the five companies were producing over fifty different self-sealing constructions. The need for standardization was obvious. The adoption by the committee of joint Army-Navy specification AN-T-49 was considered a major accomplishment enabling the companies to produce and service the large number of fuel cells required during the war. Technical data, including results of gunfire tests, were made available to all members, thereby saving large sums for independent research and testing, and, more important, speeding production. The technical committee also performed a valuable service in maintaining the functional qualities of the fuel cells as the supply of natural rubber dwindled and it became necessary to use ever increasing amounts of new synthetics. Natural rubber had been used in the first fuel cells for all parts except the liner, but, by the end of the war, its use had been limited to a small percentage of guayule in the sealant compound that increased the compound's tackiness and sealing properties. In the developmental work, numerous problems had to be overcome; the new materials had unfamiliar properties that in many cases were inferior— at least, initally—to those of natural rubber.

Early Steps Toward Production of Synthetic Rubber

As early as 1860, C. Grenville Williams had isolated and identified isoprene as one of the products of the dry distillation of rubber. He was the first to observe the manner in which the atoms of hydrogen and carbon are grouped in the natural rubber molecule, and had shown that isoprene had the same hydrogen-carbon ratio. In 1879, Gustave Bouchardat polymerized isoprene, changing it to a rubberlike substance, and Sir William Tilden proved in 1892 that polymerized isoprene could be vulcanized with sulfur. The chemists had come within a step of synthetic rubber.

During World War I, German scientists attempted to relieve an acute shortage of natural rubber and developed the polymerization of dimethylbutadiene. During the last years of the war, Germany produced about 2,350 tons of what was known as methyl rubber. It was used chiefly in hard rubber tires, but these developed flat spots when vehicles were parked for any extended period.

After the Nazi party came to power, intensified research was ordered in 1933, and each of the German factories making tires or other rubber goods was required to use compulsory quotas of buna-S ("bu" for butadiene, "na" for natrium [sodium], and "S" for styrene). By early 1937, the first commercial plant was reported to be producing synthetic rubber at the rate of 200 tons a month. In the same year, a tire plant in Hanover was said to be making 200 tires a day out of buna-S; about 25% of the plant's production of mechanical rubber goods was also reported to be made from this compound.

Since the German chemical, rubber, and automotive industries did not possess sufficient resources to develop a synthetic rubber industry, a heavy duty on imports of natural rubber was imposed in May, 1937 for two years, and the revenues were earmarked for that purpose.[4] The reported goal was construction of plants capable of producing 6,000 tons a month. Government agencies in this country believed German production of synthetic rubber—mostly buna-S but including some quantities of buna-N ("N" for acrylonitrile, a relatively costly synthetic chemical)—to be about 3,000 tons in 1937, 10,000 tons in 1938, and between 20,000 and 25,000 tons in 1939.

By 1938, it was claimed tires made in Germany with 70% of buna-S and 30% of natural rubber were giving satisfactory service; in January, 1939, I. G. Farbenindustrie A. G., the principal German combination of chemical manufacturers, supplied small quantities of buna-S to several American tire companies, including United States Rubber, for experimental purposes. Tests of tires, however, did not yield satisfying evidence that they could compete successfully in the American market with tires made of natural rubber. Consequently, United States Rubber, as well as other American tire companies, did not feel it could afford to engineer and construct facilities at its own expense, for producing a synthetic that cost more than natural rubber, was considerably more difficult to process, and did not produce tires as good as those made from natural rubber. Even two months after the outbreak of World War II, the Army and Navy Munitions Board said it had no funds or authority to assist in a development program on buna-S. Not until May, 1941 did

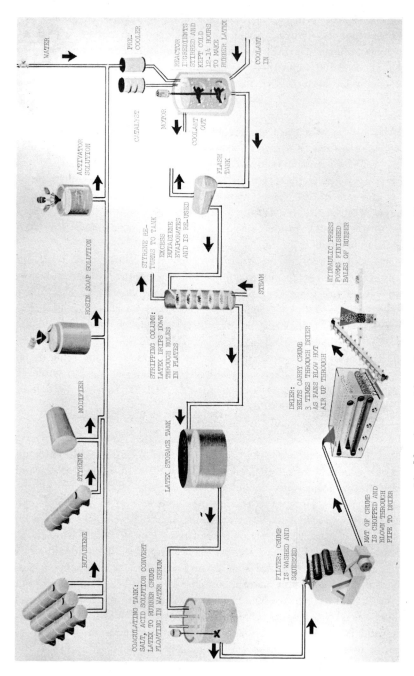

56.　Manufacture of buna-S, general purpose synthetic rubber.

the international situation cause the government to take action toward the creation of a synthetic rubber industry.

Types of So-Called Synthetic Rubber

Strictly speaking, the elastic polymers that had been produced could not properly be termed "synthetic rubber," but buna-S, buna-N, and some other new products were sufficiently similar to natural rubber (in chemical composition, in physical properties, and in their resistance to chemical reagents and mechanical forces) to be used in certain products. Despite drawbacks, buna-S offered the best possibilities. Butadiene, one component of buna-S, could be produced either from a petroleum base or from alcohol (either synthetic or from grain); styrene, the other principal component, was obtained from benzol, a coal tar derivative. The early discoveries made by Iwan Ostromislensky and Maximoff while employed in the General Laboratories of United States Rubber have been related in Chapter 6.

Approximately three parts of butadiene gas were combined with one part of liquid styrene, and the mixture was emulsified in a water solution. The temperature was raised and a catalyst and other modifying chemicals were added, causing copolymerization of the butadiene and styrene. Next, excess butadiene and styrene were removed. Small droplets then formed crumbs in the coagulating tank; these rose to the surface and were screened off, washed, filtered, pressed to remove excess water, dried, and finally pressed into 75-pound bales for shipment. Production of buna-S in this country during the war and for several years afterward was by government-owned plants.

In the United States, buna-N, for the most part, was made in private plants. Several types were produced by varying the ratio of butadiene and acrylonitrile. Buna-N was more resistant to oil, gasoline, and aromatic solvents, and was used for some types of hose, mountings, compounds for lining self-sealing fuel cells, packings, covered wire, and fuel cell fittings.

Neoprene had been developed and marketed by the Du Pont Company in the early 1930's. It was made by polymerizing chloroprene, which was produced from vinyl acetylene and hydrogen chloride. Neoprene was used where resistance to deterioration was desired; however, it was not impervious to fuels containing aromatics, and had to be protected by a coating of a special lacquer when used as a liner in fuel cells.

Butyl, developed by the Standard Oil Company of New Jersey, had an interesting history. In 1932, I. G. Farbenindustrie, A. G., had experimentally polymerized isobutylene, producing a slightly elastic substance that resembled crude rubber. However, it could not be vulcanized. In 1937, two of Standard's research chemists found that vulcanization with sulfur was possible when a small proportion of butadiene was added to the chain of isobutylene molecules.[5] Butyl, as the new synthetic was named, lacked the strength and resilience of natural rubber, and was not compatible with natural rubber for blending purposes. However, butyl was almost impervious to air or gas and was resistant to sunlight; these qualities made it useful for inner tubes, balloons, and gas masks.

Other Substitutes for Natural Rubber

Of the "Big Four" rubber companies, only United States Rubber lacked facilities for producing fuel resistant synthetics. The company was therefore forced to use substitutes until larger supplies of buna-N became available. Such a substitute was Thiokol, a rubber-like synthetic used by the Footwear Division. Thiokol resisted aromatic fuels, but had excessive "cold flow"; the material would creep under pressure, causing leakage around compression fittings. By the middle of 1942, the supply of buna-N was increasing to the point where 100% conversion from Thiokol could be accomplished. Until that time the Tire Division used a specially treated polyvinyl alcohol called Royalin, which had excellent resistance to aromatic fuels but had other characteristics that prevented it from being entirely satisfactory.

Urgent Assignments

Meanwhile, in January, 1942, the Mishawaka plant received an urgent call from Wright Field for aromatic resistant fuel cells to be installed in the outer wings of B-17 bombers to increase their range. Three days after the first conference, three different cells with varying degrees of rigidity were delivered to the field. Wright Field ordered one set, consisting of ten Mareng self-sealing cells of varying shapes and dimensions, for each wing. Despite the fact that all forms, fittings, metal parts, and so on had to be made in the shops of the Mishawaka plant, the set was delivered in ten days. These cells enabled planes to carry 1,100 more gallons of fuel and to bomb distant islands from Australian bases during the early days of the war.

Immediately after, Mishawaka had a call for help in increasing the range of twenty-six B-25 Mitchell bombers for a secret mission. On Feb. 1, 1942, engineers from the Martin company and the United States Rubber Company met with Army officers at Wright Field, and Mishawaka was given the job of producing two additional tanks for each plane with all possible speed. One tank would occupy a place in the bomb bay, and Mishawaka was also asked to make the plastic housings for it. Again there was no time to utilize facilities of outside suppliers. The factory's carpenter and machine shops, and the fuel cell department went on a 24-hour, seven-days-a-week schedule, and the fifty-two fuel cells and twenty-six plastic housings were delivered by March 15, the date set by Lt. Col. James H. Doolittle. Training operations of the bombing squadron at Eglin Field, Fla., revealed the need for additional fuel capacity; this problem arose partly because some of the plastic bomb bay housings, which were slightly too small, caused the cells to buckle. Only nine days were left in Doolittle's schedule. The decision was made to replace the small housings and to install another cell in the rear gun turret.

The additional cells, each a two-foot cube with 60-gallon capacity, and the necessary plastic housings were completed in the allotted time, picked up at the South Bend airport by special transport planes, and flown to Sacramento, Calif., where the squadron had been transferred. With the help of F. A. Sawyer of the Mishawaka organization, these were installed within about six hours. The work was completed on March 25; on April 18, American planes under the command of Doolittle flew 688 miles from the aircraft carrier Hornet and bombed Tokyo. On May 21, the company received a telegram from recently promoted Brig. Gen. Doolittle, which stated that the planes Mishawaka had helped to equip had carried out this raid, and thanked the company for its efforts. This was one of many rush orders for secret missions that illustrates the coordination between groups possessing different skills and abilities.

Difficult Problem with B-29 Wing Cells

Self-sealing wing cells were developed by United States Rubber for the Boeing B-29 Superfortress, which had a fuel capacity of about 9,000 gallons. The fuel was contained in the fuselage cells and the eleven cells of each wing (these had a total capacity of over 5,800 gallons). Cells made of standard six-ply construction developed leaks and severe fires when fired upon. After numerous tests in which fire destroyed several wing sections and many test cells, it was discovered that the hard brittle aluminum forming the heavier metal structure of the plane wings was being torn out in jagged pieces by the projectiles, and that these pieces were "chunking out" the sealant. United States Rubber finally solved the problem by putting in a layer of sealant thick enough to provide swelling that would close the wound. This construction was approved by the

Army Air Forces and was adopted by all the companies that made wing cells for the B-29.

Fuel Cell Division Organized

About the middle of 1942, the Navy began to receive reports of unsatisfactory service from certain fuel cells made by United States Rubber. Cells were being produced by both the Tire and Footwear Divisions and in seven different plants (Los Angeles, Detroit, Indianapolis, and Chicopee in the Tire Division, and at Mishawaka, Naugatuck, and St. Jerome, Canada in the Footwear Division). To establish centralized responsibility for quality as well as to achieve closer coordination between the various plants, the Fuel Cell Division was organized on Aug. 1, 1942 with Henry S. Marlor as general manager. When reports of unsatisfactory service continued, further steps were taken to ensure that correct procedures and practices were followed and the correct materials used in all plants. Mishawaka was established as the divisional headquarters with George W. Blair as active manager, reporting to the general manager. There was a complete divisional staff, including managers of development, production, production and sales coordination, sales, engineering, and quality control. All manufacturing changes were thereafter cleared through the headquarters at Mishawaka.

Under the energetic and resourceful leadership of Marlor and Blair, the reorganized division not only won the approval of the Navy, but in less than two years a representative of the Navy Bureau of Aeronautics stated before the technical representatives of all fuel cell manufacturers that the bureau received fewer unsatisfactory reports on fuel cells manufactured by United States Rubber than on those from any other producer.[6]

Fuel Cell Field Service

It was discovered that many of the reported failures of fuel cells were caused by improper handling, storage, and installation, and in February, 1943 the Fuel Cell Field Service was organized in the division. Its activities do not fall within the period covered by this history of the company, but it would be a mistake not to mention the fine work done by the men in this group. Most of them came from other divisions of the company. Before the war, some had been salesmen for tires, footwear, or other products of United States Rubber. They were given technical training and sent into sections of the United States and to the theaters of military operations: the China-Burma-India area, Saipan, Pearl Harbor, Australia, New Guinea, Tinian, Tarawa, Makin, England, and the Mediterranean.

United States Rubber was the only fuel cell manufacturer offering a complete field service, and its representatives serviced cells made by other manufacturers as well as their own. By explaining why some imperfection was not serious or by showing how it could be repaired, this service was said to have saved thousands of fuel cells that otherwise would have been scrapped. United States Rubber also provided service manuals showing how to prevent fuel cell failures caused by faulty handling, storage, or installation. Letters of commendation received by the company testified to the good work done by this group of men.

Storage Tanks

In addition to fuel cells for aircraft, United States Rubber developed portable collapsible tanks capable of holding up to several thousand gallons of fuel, oil, or water. Production of these began in October, 1942. During the war, the company produced enough flexible storage tanks to hold almost 45 million gallons, approximately the capacity of 4,500 tank cars of the type then in common use.

Major Source of Natural Rubber Lost

The abortive efforts of the Allies to stem the rapid progress of German armies through the Low Countries collapsed in the early months of 1940. These reverses and the steady deterioration of relations between Japan and the United States caused the federal agencies and the business leaders in this country to realize that the United States might be cut off from the source of 97% of its requirements of natural rubber.[7] Before America entered World War II, about 75% of the rubber consumed in this country went into tires and tubes. The civilian economy depended in large measure upon an adequate supply of tires, and it was apparent that involvement of our armed forces would greatly increase the production of motorized equipment. It was essential to guard the nation against serious crippling of defense efforts through lack of this vital material.

Rubber Reserve Company

Stocks of crude rubber in this country as of Dec. 31, 1939 were 125,800 long tons. On June 25, 1940, the Rubber Reserve Company was set up by the federal government under the Reconstruction Finance Corporation (RFC) for the primary purpose of accumulating a strategic stockpile of natural rubber. (Actual authorization to stockpile and to control the distribution of all natural and synthetic rubber was issued June 28,

1940.) Half of the stock of the company was to be owned by the government, and half by private companies in the rubber industry. The original plan was to accumulate in 1940 through regular trade channels 150,000 tons at between 18 and 20¢, c.i.f., New York. Later this authorization was broadened to include an additional 180,000 tons in 1941 at 17½-19¢ a pound, f.o.b. ports of origin, and provision to secure additional tonnage whenever stocks in the hands of manufacturers fell below 150,000 tons.[8]

The United States Rubber Company aided in the acquisition of the stockpile, and at the same time enlarged its own facilities for production of reclaimed rubber. Imports of crude rubber in 1940 totaled 811,564 long tons; consumption in this country was 648,500 long tons, leaving 288,864 on hand Dec. 31, 1940, of which the government stockpile was 112,494 long tons.[9]

Controls over Rubber Established

An unlimited national emergency was proclaimed by the President on May 27, 1941. On June 21 the Federal Loan administrator announced that, effective June 23, the Rubber Reserve Company (which previously had bought rubber for the government stockpile only) would become the sole buyer for all crude rubber exported from the British and Dutch possessions in the Far East. Existing contracts were not affected, nor was any restriction placed at that time on private purchase of natural rubber from Latin America, Africa, the Middle East, or from other countries in the Far East (French Indo-China, for example).

Also on June 21, 1941, the Office of Production Management, Division of Priorities, issued order M-15, the first control placed over a commodity in which a shortage did not exist at the time of the order.[10] The quantity of crude rubber consumed by each company during the twelve-month period ended March 31, 1941 was established as a base. Each rubber-consuming company was ordered to limit its consumption of crude to percentages of the base, declining monthly from 99% in July, 1941, to 80% in December of that year. Defense orders were to be given priority, but no one in or out of government claimed to have any trustworthy data regarding the amount of crude rubber that had been used for defense purposes in the last twelve months or that was expected to be required in the next twelve months. Although it was said to be the "most far reaching single development this industry has ever faced,"[11] M-15 was to be amended repeatedly, each amendment more stringent than before.

Construction of Synthetic Rubber Plants Authorized

Throughout most of 1940, discussions had been carried on between representatives of private industry and various governmental agencies regarding what action, if any, the government should take to create facilities for production of synthetic rubber. In August, 1940, at a meeting of a subcommittee of the Council of National Defense with industry representatives, tentative agreement was reached that industry would engineer plans for government-financed plants to produce 108,000 tons per year. Subsequently this amount was increased to 150,000 tons annual capacity. Included in this figure was a proposal by United States Rubber, in cooperation with Standard Oil of New Jersey, to undertake the preparation of plans and estimates for construction of facilities to produce 25,000 tons of buna-S annually. However, in October, 1940, the RFC took over the synthetic rubber program. In November the government's tentative financial commitment was limited to $30 million, resulting in a reduction of the proposed construction to four plants with capacity of only 10,000 tons each, the cost to be 75% financed by the government, 25% by industry. Even this reduced program was deferred, pending re-examination of the necessity for synthetic rubber.

Why was this reappraisal ordered? Possibly, there was concern whether England and Holland would favor creation of an industry competing with natural rubber. In addition, the fear was often voiced that the new industry would always need protection against natural rubber, with an adverse effect on official trade policies. Overconfidence in the might of our military and naval forces, together with gross underestimates of the length of time required before volume production of synthetic rubber would be obtained from plants that were not even on the engineers' drawing boards, probably had considerable weight. The persons charged with appraising the newly gathered statistics concluded that, even if the country were cut off from all further supplies, there was enough crude rubber on hand to meet its requirements for three years. The 40,000 ton program was then replaced by one calling for construction of four plants, each to have only 2,500 ton capacity. Each company was to agree to produce a minimum of 625 tons during the first year of operation, and to use at least 50% of the tonnage produced in the manufacture of tires and tubes. The government was to have the right to purchase 25% at actual production cost. This ruling meant that during the first year each plant might produce only about one ton of rubber for tires each day.

Many persons in the government as well as those in private industry felt that the facts demanded a much larger program. Efforts were continued to have at least four 10,000-ton plants authorized, and on May 9, 1941, William S. Knudsen, one of the directors of the Office of Production Management (OPM), wrote Jesse Jones recommending that the decision should be made immediately to build plants capable of producing 40,000 tons annually, adding that "we may want to multiply this production to 100,000 or even 200,000 tons of synthetic rubber." Jones promptly took steps to reinstate the 40,000-ton program that had been first tentatively agreed upon in August, 1940. A meeting to review the technical phases was held in Washington on May 21, 1940, and Sidney Cadwell, then the director of tire development for United States Rubber, was one of seven technical experts invited.[12] The period of indecision was coming to an end, but before the reinstated program could be implemented, the RFC authorized through its subsidiary, the Defense Plant Corporation, lease agreements with the four largest rubber companies, Firestone, Goodrich, Goodyear Tire, and United States Rubber. The companies were to construct and operate synthetic rubber plants, each producing 2,500 tons of synthetic rubber a year and costing $1,250,000. Obviously these small plants could only give the operating companies some practical experience in synthesizing rubber, since they could provide only a token contribution toward the nation's projected annual requirements. In peacetime, these needs had been running about 600,000 tons, but military requirements were raising the estimated needs to 800,000 tons a year.

On July 1, 1941 the RFC authorized expansion of these four synthetic rubber plants from a combined capacity of 10,000 tons a year to 40,000 tons. In August, 1941, E. G. Holt of the Rubber Division of the Bureau of Foreign and Domestic Commerce wrote that prospects were dim for the construction of synthetic rubber plants capable of producing enough rubber. In the same article, he urged the appointment of one central authority to head all activities pertaining to rubber, and the formation of a central plan for integrating the actions of all agencies dealing with rubber. Over a year would lapse before this plan was carried out.

Decision to Concentrate on Buna-S

On the recommendation of rubber manufacturers, the decision had been made to concentrate on production of buna-S in the government-owned plants. Buna-S possessed qualities that closely resembled those of natural rubber, the raw materials were readily available, and it could be processed on standard equipment. Another decisive consideration was that buna-S was resistant to abrasive wear and therefore particularly well suited for use in tire treads.

Although not a controlling consideration, GR-S (government-rubber-styrene) compounds took and retained sharper impressions from molds, calendered rolls, and extruders than did natural rubber. This characteristic had advantages, especially in the manufacture of rubber footwear and some mechanical rubber goods as well as in tire treads. After the war, chemists developed experimental variations of the GR-S polymer, and over 400 modifications were scheduled; many of them were made by October, 1947.[13] But for the duration of the war, these modifications were not permitted to interfere with production of the maximum tonnage of GR-S. This product did have drawbacks. It was more difficult to process and fabricate, and it did not have the tackiness of natural rubber; layers of compounds containing GR-S would not readily stick together. Extra cementing and other operations were required. Other important differences between GR-S and natural rubber forced chemists and production men of the rubber industry to alter methods and compounds, accelerators, antioxidants, the type and quantities of carbon black used, and so on, but the advantages far offset the drawbacks.[14] Although GR-S was not a fully satisfactory substitute for natural rubber, it served so well that the limited stockpile of natural rubber was made to suffice for the most essential needs of the war effort.

The readiness of so many manufacturers of rubber goods to subordinate the interests and preferences of their individual companies in order to expedite the establishment of a synthetic rubber industry was noteworthy. Their collaboration in the adoption of the operating formula for large-scale production of GR-S and with respect to basic plant designs accomplished an unparalleled chemical engineering feat.

After Pearl Harbor

Ground was broken at Naugatuck in September, 1941, for the first synthetic rubber plant to be operated for the government by United States Rubber. The Japanese attack on Pearl Harbor on Dec. 7, 1941 was followed almost immediately by the attack on the Philippines, the invasion of northern Malaya and the capture of Penang (location of the headquarters of the Malayan plantations of United States Rubber), and the overrunning of the Dutch East Indies. Immediate and radical revisions of all plans were required. The Naugatuck plant's capacity was increased to 30,000 tons a year, and on July 1, 1942 the United States Rubber

57. Government-owned synthetic rubber plant, Institute, W. Va. This
plant was constructed and operated by the United States Rubber Company during World War II.

Company formally created the Synthetic Rubber Division with John P.
Coe, general manager of the Naugatuck Chemical Division, serving also
as general manager of the new division. Production of synthetic rubber
was begun at the Naugatuck plant on Sept. 4, 1942, a creditable accomplishment.

Trial lots of GR-S were distributed, under government allocation, to
the factories making tires, footwear, mechanical goods, sundries, clothing, and other rubber products so that they could acquire experience
and "work out the bugs" connected with processing GR-S. The experience
of German rubber companies indicated that the existing rubber processing equipment would be able to handle only about 45% as much material made with GR-S as would have been processed with natural rubber compounds. If this limitation had not been overcome, additional
equipment would have been required to maintain former production
rates, and production of all types of rubber products would have been
seriously reduced. But by the latter part of 1942, the capacity to manufacture rubber goods with GR-S had been increased from 45% to two-
thirds or three-fourths of the capacity when natural rubber was used. By
1943, as the result of experimental work done with plasticizers at Naugatuck and elsewhere and because of improvements in the technique of
polymerization, it was possible to process GR-S compounds on existing
plant equipment almost as well as natural rubber.[15]

Meanwhile, the Rubber Reserve Company and the RFC had decided that larger synthetic rubber plants must be built, and United States Rubber was given another contract to build and operate a synthetic rubber plant at Institute, W. Va., with rated annual capacity of 90,000 tons. The Carbide and Carbon Chemicals Corporation was given a contract at the same time to build and operate an adjoining plant for the production of butadiene and styrene, the butadiene to be made from alcohol derived from corn and requiring 27,700,000 bushels of corn a year. (It took about 1¾ bushels of corn to produce enough butadiene for the GR-S needed to make one passenger automobile tire.)

Military requirements in World War II were enormous: millions of tires for all types of vehicles, motorized equipment and aircraft, millions of pairs of rubber footwear and rubber-soled jungle boots, millions of feet of hose, and thousands of miles of insulated signal wire. The list of other military items in which rubber was essential seemed endless. The quantities of rubber used in various types of munitions were much larger than the average citizen realized. For example, one B-17 Flying Fortress bomber used half a ton of rubber and the later larger planes used considerably more; a typical armored tank of 1942 required almost a ton; a battleship might use 75 or more tons. In World War I, 32 pounds of rubber were used per person in military service; in World War II, 194 pounds were used for every person in service.[16]

Baruch Committee

When the government decided that plants capable of producing 800,000 tons of synthetic rubber annually should be built as speedily as possible, and that production should be concentrated on GR-S, contracts were let providing for production of 75% of the necessary butadiene from a petroleum base and 25% from alcohol. Almost immediately, the farm bloc in Congress, supported by the alcohol interests, charged that the oil companies had been given undue preference. A bill (Senate 2600) was passed by both houses to set up a special agency to see that a larger share of the butadiene came from farm crops. (Considerable argument also concerned the relative amounts of strategic materials needed for the construction of the plants.)

Because the bill contained several objectionable provisions that would have hampered the war effort, it was vetoed by President Roosevelt on Aug. 6, 1942. In his veto message, the President announced the appointment of Bernard M. Baruch as chairman of a Rubber Survey Committee to study the supply of crude rubber, and to submit recommendations regarding policy. The other members of the committee were Dr. James

B. Conant, president of Harvard University, and Dr. Karl T. Compton, president of Massachusetts Institute of Technology; a staff of experts assisted.[17]

The committee's report, dated Sept. 10, 1942, stressed the dangerous situation facing the country because of the shortage of rubber. The crude rubber position was described as follows:

	Long Tons
Crude rubber on hand July 1, 1942 (stockpile)	578,000
Estimated imports, July 1, 1942 to Jan. 1, 1944	53,000
Total supply	631,000
Estimated military and other essential demands, July 1, 1942 to Jan. 1, 1944 (no allowance for tires for passenger automobiles)	842,000
Deficit that must be met by production of synthetic rubber before Jan. 1, 1944	211,000

The report affirmed that military and export demands would exhaust stocks of crude rubber before the end of the next summer, and that tires on civilian cars were being worn down eight times faster than they were being replaced.[18] To conserve tires, a national speed limit of 35 miles an hour and rationing of gasoline that would reduce the national average use of civilian cars to 5,000 miles a year were recommended. The committee also proposed that the existing program be speeded up and supplemented by new facilities to produce annually 36,000 additional tons of Thiokol that could be used for recapping tires, 100,000 tons of "quickie" butadiene, 140,000 tons of GR-S, 20,000 tons of neoprene, and 100 million gallons of grain alcohol (useful for production of either butadiene or explosives). If it seemed wise six months later, the report added, a plant to produce 27,000 tons of butadiene from grain and an associated polymerization plant to produce 30,000 tons of synthetic rubber might be built in the grain belt.[19]

Charges were made that millions of dollars were being thrown away in the construction of synthetic rubber plants that might be obsolete before they were completed,[20] and that ample supplies of natural rubber might be better obtained from the jungles of South and Central America. In reply, the committee pointed out that such a program would require moving nearly half a million natives into the Amazon valley.

The Baruch committee was critical of costly delays in the synthetic rubber program resulting from the number of government agencies that exercised overlapping and confusing authority. Therefore, the committee urged that authority for the entire program be centralized in a rubber administrator, appointed by and responsible to the chairman of the War Production Board.

In general accordance with this recommendation, William M. Jeffers, president of the Union Pacific Railroad, was appointed National Rubber Director, reporting directly to the President, with full authority over all government agencies with respect to all matters concerning rubber, natural or synthetic. Bradley Dewey, a chemical engineer with wide industrial and executive experience, became Deputy Rubber Director, and on Oct. 7, 1942, Lucius D. Tompkins, a vice-president of United States Rubber, was made Assistant Deputy Rubber Director as head of the division of operations and allocations.

Another recommendation was that the United States should take advantage of the Soviet Union's offer to exchange information regarding the manufacture of synthetic rubber. Russia's experience in large-scale manufacture of the original buna type synthetic was not thought to include the emulsion polymerization method used in Germany and America; nevertheless, information regarding Russia's findings might be useful. Jeffers therefore appointed a four-man American Rubber Mission to the Soviet Union, including W. A. Gibbons, director of general development for United States Rubber, who represented all American rubber manufacturers. Lengthy negotiations took place regarding right of access to the manufacturing plants, and the mission spent considerable time in the Soviet Union. However, it was able to visit only one plant, and the knowledge obtained did not include any important new technical data. (To brief Gibbons for this mission, George R. Vila, then a technologist in Naugatuck Chemical's research and development department, was assigned to compile all that was known in this country concerning synthetic rubber. In 1943, Vila became United States Rubber Company's research and development manager for synthetic rubber. He pioneered in the development of experimental varieties of GR-S tailored for specific end uses, and in the application of statistical quality control concepts to the manufacture of synthetic rubber.)

A Modern Miracle

The young chemists and engineers assigned to design and erect the synthetic rubber plant to be operated by United States Rubber at Institute, W. Va., were faced with new and difficult situations. The only synthetic rubber plant previously built and operating in this country was the small plant at Naugatuck, which was not much more than a pilot plant. Before specifications for construction could be drawn up, new equipment had to be designed and layouts approved. The government ordered several successive increases in capacity and, with each increase, new plans had to be drawn. By the time the plant was completed, it was estimated that thirty-five acres of blueprints had been produced.

Two simple statistics indicate the magnitude of the project. The processes required enough water to supply the needs of a city the size of Los Angeles in 1942; half as much electrical energy was called for as was then being generated for the state of Delaware.[21] Wartime shortages had to be overcome by substitution of other materials, and, when it was impossible to have some equipment built elsewhere on time, the parts were ordered and the equipment was assembled on the spot. For a year, chemists on the job at the Institute plant averaged seventy hours a week, knowing that large quantities of synthetic rubber were essential to the war effort.

Butadiene and styrene were "extremely violent and tricky" materials. To lessen the danger of explosions, the plants were spread over seventy-seven acres, and much of the installation was not enclosed. The winter of 1942 was severe; chemicals froze in the pipes, and the steam lines installed to warm them also froze. Insulation was not obtainable, but construction continued. For the last several weeks, construction crews worked twelve hours a day, seven days a week. On March 31, 1943, after the final twenty-four hour stretch without adequate rest, George Graham, plant manager, opened a valve at 9:04 a.m. starting the flow of butadiene into the synthetic rubber plant from the adjacent butadiene plant operated by Carbide and Carbon Chemicals Corporation. A major advance toward winning the war had been achieved.

Institute was the first of the larger synthetic rubber plants to come into production and was the largest operated by any one company during World War II. Its planned annual production of 90,000 tons of rubber was said to be equivalent to the annual yield from 18-24 million rubber trees. Such a plantation would have required the work of about 100,000 natives, according to one writer. The cost of the complex at Institute was approximately $56 million; $80 million was one estimate of the cost of acquiring and developing a rubber plantation of about 27,000 acres that would produce an equal amount of natural rubber, together with the necessary facilities for handling, processing, and transporting it. Furthermore, five years would have to elapse before the new rubber trees would begin producing.

United States Rubber also erected and operated for the government a 30,000-ton synthetic rubber plant at Los Angeles, which was put into production in 1943. At the close of that year, the three plants were producing at about 90% of their total rated capacity, and the Institute plant was then operating at an annual rate of approximately 100,000 tons. Although official sources had been predicting as late as October, 1941 that several years would be required to develop plants capable of producing enough synthetic rubber to equal half of the nation's requirements, the peak annual rate of production of GR-S, reached by all the synthetic plants in the country during the war, was 755,532 long tons, achieved in June, 1944. Production of all other types of synthetic rubber reached its high point for the war period in the same month with an annual rate of 91,140 long tons, making the combined annual rate 846,672 long tons.[22]

Meanwhile, the Naugatuck Chemical Division of the Dominion Rubber Company had expanded its plant at Elmira, Canada. Originally designed to supply aniline oil and diphenylamine to the Canadian Department of Defense Production, the Elmira plant had become the only producer in Canada of specialty organic chemicals for the Canadian rubber industry. When the supply of natural rubber was cut off, Elmira was equipped to produce Thiokol. This was the first production in the British Commonwealth of a synthetic substitute for natural rubber.[23]

In addition to providing a vital substitute for natural rubber during the war, the creation of the synthetic rubber industry has served in the postwar years to stabilize the price of natural rubber. This stablization of the price of its principal raw material has been of incalculable benefit to all segments of the industry.

A YEAR OF WAR

Few who were not active in the rubber manufacturing industry in 1941 could fully appreciate the cataclysmic effects of the Japanese attack on Pearl Harbor and the subsequent loss of the rubber-growing areas in the Far East. Steps had been initiated by the federal government as well as by private firms to guard against the possible loss of the major sources of crude rubber, but those steps were inadequate.

Seizure of the Dutch East Indies and the Malayan Peninsula by Japan meant loss of the world's largest rubber plantations. By 1941, United States Rubber Plantations, Inc., comprised over 104,000 acres on the island of Sumatra, in the residencies of Sumatra East Coast and Langkat, and almost 31,000 acres in the native states of Kedah, Selanger, and Johore, British Malaya. They had produced over 65 million pounds of rubber (dry content) in 1940 from 89,380 acres of mature trees, an average yield of more than 740 pounds per acre, a new record. (Some of the better land, planted with trees from higher-yielding clones, had produced 2,000 pounds per acre.)[24]

Like other rubber manufacturers, United States Rubber was confronted simultaneously with several other major problems. Any one of these, under ordinary circumstances, would have seemed insurmountable. One staff member has referred to "the endless crises we went through and nightmarish disasters that were constantly threatening." Yet somehow the problems were solved and the disasters avoided. The combined know-how of production men, industrial engineers, technicians, scientists, purchasing departments, transportation experts, top executives, middle management personnel, and a host of rank-and-file employees faced each situation, found answers, and kept production in full swing.

Use of Rubber Further Restricted

Within three days after Japan's attack on Pearl Harbor, the Office of Production Management limited the types and quantities of rubber products permitted on orders not having a priority rating of A3 or better. The restrictions were mild compared to those that were to come; for example, the definition of "rubber" did not then include reclaimed rubber, and November, 1941, was made the base month for measuring the subsequent rate of manufacturing. Supplementary orders, however, extended the restrictions. In February, 1942, reclaimed rubber was included in the definition, and the order further limited the kinds of products containing rubber permitted for civilian use to those essential to the economy or to the health and welfare of the public. The weight of rubber that could be used in each permitted item was also limited. The use of natural rubber in civilian items was severely restricted; in many products it was replaced largely if not entirely by reclaimed rubber until GR-S became available. For the five years ended Dec. 31, 1940, reclaimed rubber had formed approximately 28% of total new rubber consumed in the United States; in 1942 it leaped to 64.6%.

By April, 1942, the imminent exhaustion of the strategic stockpile of rubber before sufficient quantities of synthetic rubber would be available brought an order listing many items in which "no rubber shall be used in manufacture for the U.S. Army even though the use of rubber therein may be called for by the army purchase orders or the army specification." In addition to many items of sundries and mechanical rubber goods, the list included such items as gym and basketball shoes and raincoat fabric.

The maximum amount of rubber, natural (dry or latex) or synthetic, that each manufacturer was allowed to use each month in the production of permitted civilian and military items was stipulated by the War Production Board acting under directions of the Office of the Rubber Director. As the natural rubber supply situation worsened, these restrictions became progressively tighter. (United States Rubber was appointed by the government as the custodian of all latex in the country.)

Wartime Demands on Rubber Companies

As these restrictions became effective, the rubber companies were urgently pressed to develop and produce in great quantities many military items that had to perform satisfactorily under severe conditions, and withstand extremes of heat or cold far beyond those to which commercial products had been subjected. The lives of thousands of men depended upon speedy solutions to baffling technical problems. Even those military items produced by United States Rubber that were similar to peacetime products—such as footwear, tires, clothing, and many items of mechanical goods—usually had to be redesigned or made with changed rubber compounds that would meet the rigorous demands of combat use. Others, including self-sealing fuel cells, collapsible storage tanks, inflatable lifeboats and life rafts, barrage balloons, asbestos fire-fighting suits, diving suits, gas masks, pontons, and tank treads, were far removed from the commercial items produced by the company in its ordinary course of business.

The response of United States Rubber to the needs of the military forces increased the percentage of the company's total sales represented by direct government orders from about 1% in 1940 to 13% in 1941 and an average 55% in 1942 (exclusive of any production in plants operated by the company for the government). In December, 1942, war production averaged 66% of the company's output.

In that critical period, the thin-wall rayon cord construction for tires developed by Martin Castricum and pioneered by United States Rubber proved a tremendous asset. Early in the war it was evident that neither the existing tire-making facilities nor the rayon-producing capacity would be adequate for the over-all military and essential civilian requirements. Castricum said he conceived the idea that if two 1100 denier rayon yarns were laid together, the additional strength would make it possible to reduce the number of plies in truck tires—for example, from 12 ply to 10 ply, or from 10 to 8. The rayon producers then said they could produce many more pounds of rayon in 2200 denier than in 1100. Thus three bottlenecks would be relieved: the production of rayon yarn, tire cord twisting capacity, and tire-building capacity.

L. D. Tompkins, then serving as Assistant Deputy Rubber Director in charge of operations, called a joint meeting of representatives of the tire and rayon industries, who approved the thin-wall rayon cord construction. The direct result was the production of many more truck tires with existing facilities. In tests, thirty-two failures of truck tires made of synthetic rubber with cotton cord occurred to only one failure of comparable synthetic rubber tires of thin-wall construction.

Munitions Plants

In addition to the new plants for production of synthetic rubber that United States Rubber constructed and operated for the government, the company was given contracts to operate six munitions plants. To administer the operations of these plants that were engaged in entirely new lines of production, four new divisions were organized, each under a general manager assisted by the necessary staff including factory managers, superintendents, and supervisory and technical personnel. Most of these staffs had to be drawn from the established organization, and the transfer and reshuffling of so many employees called for a high degree of administrative effort and know-how. Heading the newly created Munitions Division was John W. McGovern, former assistant general manager of the Tire Division.

In the late summer of 1941, the site of the Des Moines ordnance plant had been a cornfield; on Jan. 31, 1942 the plant started operations, and nine months later, Robert P. Patterson, Under-Secretary of War, notified the company that it had been awarded the Army-Navy Production ("E") Award for the plant's record in producing .30 and .50 caliber cartridges. The Des Moines plant was among the largest small-arms munitions plants in the country. Not only did the plant win a star on its "E" flag for continued excellence of performance, but its operations were said to have "saved the Federal Government, over original cost estimates, an amount equal to the whole cost of the Des Moines plant, and many millions of dollars to boot."[25]

When the production of civilian tires other than those required for essential truck or bus operation was curtailed, United States Rubber discontinued tire manufacture at its Eau Claire plant. The plant was sold to the government, machinery for making tires was replaced with ordnance equipment, and additional buildings were erected. Three months after construction was started, the Eau Claire Ordnance Plant was put into operation by United States Rubber on Aug. 17, 1942. Producing .30 caliber cartridges, Eau Claire became on June 17, 1943 the second ordnance plant operated by the company to receive the "E" award.

Three other ordnance plants, operated for the government by United States Rubber, were placed in production in 1942—Milwaukee Ord-

58. Manufacture of military items during World War II.

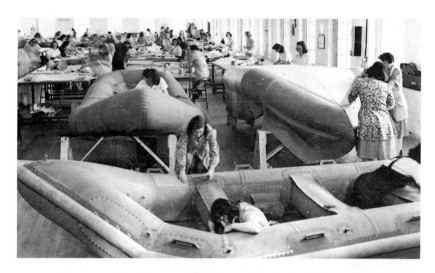

58a. Ten-man attack boats, Woonsocket, R.I.

58b. Rubber-coated barrage balloons, Naugatuck, Conn.

58c. "Victory grandmothers" stitching shearling (sheepskin linings) for aviators' boots, Mishawaka, Ind.

58d. Final inspection of .50-caliber ammunition, Des Moines Ordnance Works.

58e.   Army raincoats, made without natural rubber, Mishawaka.

nance on Aug. 19, Scioto Ordnance at Marion, Ohio on Nov. 16, and Charlotte (N.C.) Ordnance on Dec. 21. The contract to construct and operate the shell-loading plant at Charlotte had been awarded to United States Rubber by the Navy as late as August, 1942. Ernest G. Brown, who had been production manager of the Mechanical Goods, General Products, and Rubber Thread Divisions, was appointed general manager of the Shell Loading Division, which operated the Charlotte plant.

During 1942, the company was also given a contract for operation of a government-owned plant at Williamsport, Pa., known as the Pennsylvania Ordnance Works (POW), for production of trinitrotoluene (TNT). On May 1, 1942 John E. Caskey, who had been assistant general manager of the Naugatuck Chemical Division, was made general manager of the Explosives Division, in charge of operating POW. To alleviate a serious local housing shortage, 460 new dwelling units were constructed; other problems were also mastered, and POW was placed in production Feb. 24, 1943.

In Canada, the Dominion Rubber Company formed a subsidiary, Dominion Rubber Munitions, Ltd., which manufactured .50 caliber naval anti-aircraft ammunition at Cap de la Madeleine, Quebec. Three of Dominion's plants were later involved in the manufacture of ammunition: the

Papineau plant in Montreal, Dominion Tire in Kitchener, and the footwear plant at St. Jerome. Production included 20 millimeter shells for aircraft cannon and tracks for medium and heavy tanks. At first these tracks were made of rubber; when rubber could no longer be spared, they were made of steel. The St. Jerome plant also made fuel cells, and the Papineau factory produced storage tanks.

The first of the plants owned by United States Rubber to win the "E" award was Mishawaka, whose workers were honored in a letter from Secretary Patterson on Dec. 26, 1942. The basis for the recognition was the manufacture of several million raincoats without any rubber in the waterproofing, and with a rejection rate of only about 1%. The plant had also done an outstanding job in production of fuel cells, specialized military footwear, diving dresses, fire-fighting suits, parka suits for cold climate warfare, and other items.

Assault Wire

The story of the development and production of assault wire, one of United States Rubber's minor war products in terms of dollar volume, is an example of the length to which industry went to meet the requirements of the armed forces. In the early thirties, the Bristol, R.I., wire plant wished to create a thinner and better insulation for wire conductors of small diameter. At the suggestion of Elmer Roberts, Harold D. Rice, a chemist at the Bristol plant who was engaged in this development project, worked out a method of dipping wire in latex, then running the coated wire successively through a coagulant, a dryer, and a vulcanizer. By passing the wire several times through the dipping, coagulating, and drying stages, the desired thickness of latex compound could be applied. The result was a light flexible wire that was first used commercially for radio hookups.

In his application for a patent, Rice pointed out that insulation from normal latex contained from 11 to 12% of water soluble, nonrubber ingredients; in the new method, this percentage was reduced, by centrifuging the latex or by creaming it with certain agents, to as low as 2½ to 3%. By comparison, the best known types of dry crude rubber contained from 7 to 8% of nonrubber ingredients.

In 1936, the Signal Corps requested development of a front-line communication wire consisting of two insulated conductors twisted together and weighing not more than 30 pounds per mile. Other requirements included minimum breaking strength of 50 pounds per conductor and maximum loss in electrical transmission of 6 decibels per mile after immersion in water for 48 hours. United States Rubber developed such a wire, using fine steel strands twisted around copper for the conductors. When the defense program was accelerated in 1941, the company was asked to set up to produce thousands of miles of this wire. New equipment capable of producing this volume was designed and installed, and, by 1943, United States Rubber's production of assault wire "W130" was approximately sixteen times what it was at the beginning of the project. The company not only shared its know-how with two competitors so that they could assist in supplying the military requirements, but even maintained in these competitors' plants technical personnel who supervised the installation of the necessary equipment and instructed production workers.[26]

Ironically, the eminence of United States Rubber's manufacturing know-how and the high quality of its mechanical rubber goods operated to its disadvantage. On other occasions during World War II, when it was found that the total industry capacity was inadequate to meet wartime requirements, the government asked United States Rubber to share its formulas and processes with other companies. Many of these plants were relatively small at that time, but with the advantage of the knowledge supplied by United States Rubber—and often equipped with the most modern equipment installed in plants built during the war—these companies greatly expanded their production. After the war, they continued to supply a much larger percentage of the total market for mechanical goods than they had supplied before the war. Thus United States Rubber's contributions to the war effort sometimes resulted in loss of position in the postwar industry.[27]

Problems Met by Industrial Relations Department

Even this condensed summary of the company's activities during the first year of the war would not be complete without mention of the work done by the industrial relations departments at the various plants. Despite the fact that 5,029 employees had been inducted into military service by the end of 1942, the total number of employees in plants then stood at 51,803, with 28,881 more working in the eight plants operated for the government. The total of 80,684 employees was 63% higher than the average number employed in 1941. By 1943, production of war products boosted the number of employees to 89,000. This increase had been accomplished by attracting workers in every possible way: those on retirement, wives and sisters of men in the armed forces, unemployed members of rural families, and high school students and teachers who worked a "victory shift" after school hours. In some instances, employment offices were set up in nearby towns. Sometimes arrangements were made to operate special buses for workers who otherwise had no way to get to the plant.

Obviously, all of these arrangements would have been of little value without special efforts to maintain good working conditions and high morale; other employers were actively recruiting workers, and anyone dissatisfied with the United States Rubber Company did not need to expect much difficulty in finding other employment at as good or better hourly wages. The success in maintaining high rates of production during that difficult period is the best measure of the work of the industrial relations department under wartime conditions.

Another assignment handled by that department during the war was promotion of war bonds through payroll deductions. In a considerable number of the company's plants, 100% of the employees participated in this program; the average for the whole company at the end of 1942 was 98.97% of the employees with an average deduction of 8.3% of their wages or salaries.

Since the wartime production of many items ordinarily made for the civilian market was severely restricted, if not entirely discontinued, a number of the company's salesmen were transferred to the manufacturing organization. In the Footwear Division, about one-half of the sales force was given such assignments; their earnings were maintained at the individual salesman's previous level. They were advised to endeavor to learn whatever was required to be helpful in their temporary role as production men, and, to the credit of both the salesmen who were thus transferred and the manufacturing groups with which they were associated, it can be said that the net results were advantageous to all concerned. Salesmen gained a greater appreciation of manufacturing problems and, at the same time, lent valuable assistance to the production program.

Executives Loaned to Government

In addition to the large number of management and supervisory personnel who were transferred to the several plants operated by United States Rubber for the government during the war, more than fifty men holding responsible positions with the company were given leaves of absence for full- or part-time service with different governmental agencies. Among them were:

J. W. Bicknell, Managing Director, Plantations Division	Vice-President, Rubber Reserve Company
C. S. Ching, Director, Industrial and Public Relations	Member, War Labor Board
Walter Emery, Economist, Commercial Research Department	Member, War Production Board
W. A. Gibbons, Director, General Development	Member, American Rubber Mission to the Soviet Union
W. F. Lund, in charge of insurance	Organization of Naval Insurance
S. P. Thacher, Manager Field Engineering and Service, Tire Division	Chief of Rubber Section, Army and Navy Munitions Board
L. D. Tompkins, Vice-President, Director	Assistant Deputy Rubber Director
T. H. Young, Director of advertising	Member, Advertising Council advising War Production Board

Changing of the Guard

On Sept. 28, 1942, Herbert E. Smith succeeded F. B. Davis, Jr., as president of United States Rubber Company; Davis continued to serve as chairman of the board. During the last two years of Davis' presidency, the advantages of decentralized management had been strikingly demonstrated by the organization's swift response to wartime conditions and demands. The company had been faced with sudden curtailment of production of numerous items for civilian use, confronted with urgent demands for development of many new military items, and forced to enter fields of operation entirely foreign to its established business. Each challenging situation had been met successfully. Furthermore, the rapid creation of government-financed facilities for large-scale production of synthetic rubber would prove to be one of the most remarkable contributions of private industry to the winning of World War II. United States Rubber was leading the industry in this accomplishment.

Not surprisingly, the effect of all these shifts from normal peacetime production and activities to war products and services was a reduction in net sales in 1942. Even though shipments of war products during the first half of 1942 were three times larger than shipments in the corresponding 1941 period and continued at an even higher rate for the remainder of the year, they did not compensate for loss of sales of rubber goods for civilian consumption. Consequently, 1942 net sales (exclusive of value of production in plants operated for the government, and exclusive of fees received for their construction and operation) were approximately $24 million less than in 1941. Although net income, before adjustments and provisions for war losses and for income and excess profits taxes, was almost $1.5 million more in 1942 than in 1941, final net income of $8,381,000 for 1942 was almost 39% less than in 1941. Nevertheless, Davis and his staff could take some measure of satisfaction in the transformation that had occurred in the company's financial position since he first assumed office.

If the financial improvement between January, 1929 and December, 1942 does not appear too impressive today, it must be remembered that it was accomplished during years of severe depression. Furthermore, the company had struggled for several years to survive in the face of tremendous odds. That it did survive was due largely to the financial ability of William de Krafft, supported by the unflagging efforts of operating divisions and the auxiliary departments as they sought to curtail costs and increase sales and profits.

To recapitulate briefly, funded indebtedness as of Dec. 31, 1928, had exceeded $104,475,000 and comprised 46% of the company's capital structure. In addition, bank loans of $25,750,000 existing on that date more than offset the additional cash, $23,276,000 received Jan. 11, 1929 from sale of the new issue of 728,412 shares of common stock. In contrast, funded debt of $34,563,000 on Dec. 31, 1942 represented only 23.2% of the capital structure, and there were no outstanding bank loans or notes. The 1928 statement had shown the combined value of common stock and surplus to be $116,342,000, but included in assets were $58,925,000 of intangible assets, and also the cash receivable on Jan. 11, 1929 for the new stock issue. Without these two items, the worth of the common stock would have been only $34,141,000; there would not have been any surplus added in that figure. As of Dec. 31, 1942, the combined value of common stock, earned and capital surplus, was over $49,608,000, despite war losses and charges in 1942 against both earned and capital surplus totaling almost $18,700,000.

After the Japanese army overran Sumatra and the Malay Peninsula early in 1942, the company's investment in its rubber plantation subsidiaries had been written off with the exception of their London bank balance of $2,159,000. The charge against 1942 income, together with other foreign war losses in United States Rubber's export operations, amounted to $15,487,000. After provisions totaling $11,600,000 for federal and foreign income and excess profit taxes, together with a $40,000 deduction for earnings applicable to minority interests in subsidiaries, $8,381,000 remained to be added to earned surplus. After elimination of $2,347,000 due to removal of plantations and certain other foreign subsidiaries from the consolidated statements, and after payment of 4%

dividend on preferred stock, earned surplus as of Dec. 31, 1942 was $20,590,000; capital surplus was $11,627,000. Best of all, much dead-wood had been eliminated; United States Rubber was a vigorous, profit-able organization.

Davis continued as chairman of the board and as a member of the executive committee until Dec. 31, 1948. He also continued to serve as a member of the finance committee until it was eliminated on Oct. 9, 1957, when a newly organized executive committee, of which Davis became a member, was assigned the powers and duties of the former finance committee. On April 31, 1959, after thirty years of service, Davis resigned as a director and thus as a member of the executive committee. In recognition of his service, he was made a lifetime advisory director, a position he held until his death on Dec. 22, 1962.

Smith was the first president of United States Rubber to rise to that position from the ranks of the company. After leaving the University of California (class of 1911), he first went to work as a driller for a mining company; then on Aug. 1, 1913, he was employed as a salesman for the Gorham-Revere Rubber Company, a subsidiary of United States Rubber, in San Francisco. Six months later he was given sale of mechani-cal goods along the waterfront, and a little later sold the complete line of the Revere Rubber Company and United States Rubber in San Fran-cisco and an outlying territory. In 1915, he was transferred to Revere's New York City branch, and was appointed assistant manager of that branch in 1917. After the Mechanical Goods Division was formed in 1918, Smith was made assistant western sales manager of the division, and, in September of that year, manager of the division's New York branch. The next year, he became manager of the consolidated branch of United States Rubber in the city. Then in February, 1924, Smith was appointed general manager of the Export Company with the specific assignment of surveying the overseas organization and the value of over-seas inventories. The results of that survey and the record of Smith's advancement to a vice-presidency and the board of directors of United States Rubber have been covered in previous chapters.

Smith served as president and chairman of the executive committee until Jan. 1, 1949 when he succeeded Davis as chairman of the board and chief executive officer. Harry E. Humphreys, Jr., formerly a vice-president and chairman of the finance committee, then succeeded Smith as president. (The scope of the present volume does not extend beyond the first half-century of the corporate existence of the United States Rub-ber Company. Therefore, biographical information pertaining to the pres-

59. Herbert E. Smith (president, Sept. 28, 1942-Dec. 31, 1948), left,
and H. E. Humphreys, Jr. (president, Jan. 1, 1949-Oct. 9, 1957).

idents of the company, whose terms of office began after 1942, has
been omitted.)

SUMMARY

The previous half-century had been marked by momentous changes—
political, economic, industrial, and sociological. Many of the small enterprises that characterized the nineteenth century had been replaced by
large corporations. Invention and technical progress had greatly altered
both the economy of the nation and the lives and occupations of its
citizens. Shortly after the formation of the United States Rubber Company in 1892, a few horseless carriages appeared on the streets. Considered to be little more than a mechanical curiosity at that time, the
internal combustion motor revolutionized transportation and the living
habits of millions. Rubber tires, of small consequence in 1892, accounted
for about three-fourths of the country's annual consumption of rubber

just before World War II began; rubber footwear lost its earlier predominant role.

The organization and management of United States Rubber had been changed from the relatively loose control exercised over companies consolidated during the 1890's. Under the direction of F. B. Davis, Jr., trained in Du Pont management principles, the various divisions and auxiliary departments had been attuned by 1942 to the established objectives of the corporation, while division managers and heads of departments had broad decision-making powers and were held responsible for actual operations. The transition had not been always smooth; it had been influenced by events and by the management philosophies of successive presidents of the company. Fortunately for United States Rubber, the need for decentralized responsibility had been recognized at its most critical period; the strengths of the organization had been tapped; the groundwork had been laid for even greater expansion and diversification.

During its first fifty years, United States Rubber repeatedly demonstrated persistent vitality and resiliency under adverse circumstances. It had shown the ability to adapt to changing conditions both within and without its corporate body. This ability resulted from the combined resources, physical and otherwise, of the various units of the company, and of the talents, energies, and aspirations of their thousands of employees. Top executives of United States Rubber have recognized this fact; some have been heard to say, in effect, "In a pinch, what has saved our company from failure is the fund of experience, the loyalty and the ability of the employees, all the way down to those on the lowest rung of the ladder."[28]

Nevertheless, the future progress of the company still depended in large measure upon the skill of top management in drawing upon these resources and its ability to understand and to utilize their strengths; to correct and improve where needed; to recognize the most promising avenues for growth; and to direct effectively profitable and soundly conceived expansion in those fields.

Since 1942, United States Rubber has been served by four presidents: Herbert E. Smith (Sept. 28, 1942-Dec. 31, 1948), Harry E. Humphreys, Jr. (Jan. 1, 1949-Oct. 9, 1957), John W. McGovern (Oct. 9, 1957-Oct. 31, 1960), and George R. Vila (Nov. 1, 1960 to the present). During the same period, net sales rose to over $1 billion in 1962, declined to $980 million in 1963, and set a new record of $1,086,588 in 1964, 7.9% above the previous record set in 1962. This figure is

Having so many trademarks in so many countries

UniRoyal | **UniRoyal** | **UniRoyal**
U.S. RUBBER | DOMINION RUBBER | ENGLEBERT

UniRoyal | **UniRoyal** | **UniRoyal**
CROYDON | NORTH BRITISH RUBBER | SAMPER S.A.

used to be confusing.

Since The United States Rubber Company now has plants in 23 foreign countries, some of our trademarks have a decided local flavor.

In Canada, for instance, we're known as Dominion Rubber Ltd.

In Germany, France and Belgium, they call us Englebert S.A.

In Britain, our name is North British Rubber Co., Ltd.

Italy knows us as Rub-Co-Plast, S.p.A.

Other plants in Latin America, Australia and the Far East have their own variations.

So we needed a unifying corporate trademark. A name broad enough to cover a lot of ground, yet small enough to fit on a package, a letterhead or an advertisement. And one that was easy to say in any language.

A name like UniRoyal.

From now on, you'll be seeing our new trademark used with a lot of brands you're already familiar with. Names like U.S. Royal,® Keds,® Kedettes,® Vyrene,® Lastex,® Naugahyde,® Royalene,® Koylon,® Eskiloos,® Usflex,® and U. S. "Timing"® Belts.

UniRoyal doesn't replace any existing trademarks. It only identifies them. The way your last name identifies the family you belong to.

And what's a family without a family name? Especially one that's grown as large as ours.

United States Rubber Company, New York, N. Y.

60. Advertisement announcing new UniRoyal trademark (one of a series).

a gain of approximately 270% since 1942, and 245% more than 1941, the last year before wartime restrictions on the use of rubber became effective.

More significant, perhaps, than the gain in net sales has been the company's growing diversification and the broadened character of its international operations; by 1964 it was operating plants in twenty-two foreign countries and 20% or more of its sales dollars came from non-rubber products (see Chapter 2, p. 20 for details). The word "rubber" said Vila, was "no longer truly descriptive of the broad scope of the company's product diversification and manufacturing capabilities." Therefore, the advertising department was directed in 1962 to search for a new trademark that would tie together all the subsidiary companies around the globe and all their famous brands. It was specified that the new mark should not be restrictive nor imply any incorrect connotation; it should be brief and easy to pronounce in most languages. After an intensive two-year research program, during which several thousand names were reviewed and tested, the UniRoyal trademark was adopted. UniRoyal is a combination of Uni (from United States Rubber) and Royal (long used as part of the brand name of tires and a long list of other goods made by the company), while the rectangular blue background has long been associated with Keds and many other products of the company.

Considerable space was taken in trade papers and periodicals of general circulation to publicize the new mark and to explain the underlying reasons for its adoption. These advertisements and publicity releases stated it was not the company's intention that UniRoyal replace United States Rubber nor the names of its subsidiary companies. Instead, it would appear in connection with them as shown in Figure 60. The adoption of UniRoyal is significant evidence that the present management of the United States Rubber Company intends to keep the corporation's future progress unhampered by any artificial limitations stemming from its past history, while maintaining the good will earned during more than sixty years. All of its far-flung operations should benefit from this closer identification with the parent company and with its established standards of quality.

Commenting on the significance of the adoption of the UniRoyal trademark, an investment service wrote in April, 1965, "Today, this company is, in fact, a company in the truest sense of that word. The diversified operations of U.S. Rubber are at long last working together as a team."[29] The author does not concur in any implications that teamwork has been absent in the management or operations of United States Rubber in previous years, but unquestionably the new mark symbolizes and will stimulate an increased awareness of the community of interests of all segments of the company's world-wide activities.

[1] *GR-S* (government rubber-styrene) designated the synthetic produced in government-owned plants from butadiene and styrene.

[2] George B. Newitt, "History of the Fuel Cell Division, United States Rubber Company, 1940-1945," 1947, privately printed, United States Rubber Company, Mishawaka, p. 3. This entire section is based almost entirely on Newitt's history.

[3] United States Rubber Company, "The Story of United States Rubber Company," c. 1946, privately printed, New York, p. 35.

[4] Frank A. Howard, *Buna Rubber, The Birth of an Industry* (Princeton: D. Van Nostrand Co., Inc., 1947), p. 40.

[5] *Buna Rubber, The Birth of an Industry*, pp. 47-58, 70-157. By 1939, when plans for producing butyl rubber commercially were being made, butadiene as the comonomer was replaced with isoprene, and commercial production of butyl rubber since that time has been with isoprene.

[6] "History of the Fuel Cell Division," p. 55.

[7] H. A. Winkelmann, quoted in *The Vanderbilt Rubber Handbook* (9th ed.; New York: The Vanderbilt Company, 1948), p. 18.

[8] *Commodity Year Book—1941* (New York: Commodity Research Bureau, Inc., 1941), p. 463.

[9] U.S. Dept. of Commerce, *Industrial Reference Service, Part 10, "Rubber"* (Washington: U.S. Gov't Printing Office, April, 1941), p. 1.

[10] The OPM was absorbed later by the War Production Board.

[11] E. G. Holt, "A Survey of the Rubber Industry," in U. S. Dept. of Commerce, *Industrial Reference Service, Part 10, "Rubber"* (Washington: U.S. Gov't Printing Office, August, 1941), pp. 1-4.

[12] *Buna Rubber, The Birth of an Industry*, pp. 125-57.

[13] *The Vanderbilt Rubber Handbook*, p. 38. In more recent years, buna-S has come to be known as SBR (styrene butadiene rubber).

[14] Tires made with GR-S in January, 1942, were said to be comparable in performance to tires of 1914, but by January, 1943, they were said to be about 80% as good as most 1941 tires made of natural rubber. *US*, house organ of United States Rubber Company, II (August, 1943), p. 26.

[15] *US*, II (August, 1943), p. 26.

[16] *US*, II (August, 1943), pp. 13-27; also *The Story of United States Rubber Company*, privately printed, p. 10.

[17] *Report of the Rubber Survey Committee* (Washington: Gov't Printing Office, Sept. 10, 1942).

[18] A scrap rubber salvage campaign had been disappointing; it brought in only about 450,000 tons of miscellaneous scrap, far below previous estimates. *Report of the Rubber Survey Committee*, p. 59.

[19] The production of butadiene from alcohol was a temporary measure only; the permanent synthetic rubber industry was built on utilization of petroleum by-products (*Commodity Year Book—1948*, p. 404). Production of butadiene from alcohol tended to relieve the pressure on the petroleum industry, which was hard pressed in 1942 to increase production of high octane aviation gasoline.

[20] Charles Morrow Wilson, *Trees and Test Tubes* (New York: Henry Holt and Company, 1943), p. 124.

[21] *US*, II (August, 1943), pp. 13-16.

[22] Frederic J. Dewhurst and Associates, *America's Needs and Resources* (New York: The Twentieth Century Fund, 1947), p. 779. Illustrative of the difficulties faced by forecasters, a prediction made in the same work regarding future usage of the synthetic rubber plants lumped them together with plants for the production of aviation gasoline. The conclusion was that a "generous estimate would be that about 80% of these facilities will eventually find commercial use in peacetime" (p. 641). By 1955 consumption of synthetic rubber in this country had reached approximately 895,000 long tons, and four years later had exceeded one million long tons. See U.S. Dept. of Commerce, *Statistical Abstract of the United States, 1960* (Washington: U.S. Gov't Printing Office, 1960), p. 811.

[23] Leslie Roberts, "From Three Men," privately printed by the Dominion Rubber Company, Montreal, 1954, p. 31.

[24] "United States Rubber Declares Dividend on its Common Stock," *Rubber Age*, XLVIII (March, 1941), pp. 400-02. Also, "A Brief Story about United States Rubber Company," company archives, p. 6.

[25] *US* (December, 1943), p. 25.

[26] *US* (March, 1943), pp. 3-8; also (June, 1943), p. 12.

[27] H. W. Willard, interview, 1963.

[28] Fred S. Carpenter, letter to author, 1965.

[29] *The Value Line Investment Survey*, XX (New York: Arnhold Bernhard & Co., Inc., April, 1965), p. 147.

Appendixes

A

Supplementary Tables

Table A-1.   Average annual prices, Para rubber and all commodities, 1856-90 (averaged according to importance, certain expenditures considered uniform; 1860= 100).

	Para Rubber	All Commodities (weighted average)		Para Rubber	All Commodities (weighted average)
1856	90.9	108.5	1874	136.4	120.5
1857	65.5	109.6	1875	106.4	119.8
1858	58.2	109.1	1876	116.4	115.5
1859	86.4	102.0	1877	105.5	109.4
1860	100.0	100.0	1878	89.1	103.1
1861	100.0	95.9	1879	92.7	96.6
1862	87.3	102.8	1880	147.3	103.4
1863	159.1	122.1	1881	138.2	105.8
1864	145.5	149.4	1882	158.2	106.3
1865	218.2	190.7	1883	194.5	104.5
1866	181.8	160.2	1884	174.5	101.8
1867	118.2	145.2	1885	101.8	95.4
1868	122.7	150.7	1886	110.9	95.5
1869	149.1	135.9	1887	138.2	96.2
1870	181.8	130.4	1888	138.2	97.4
1871	181.8	124.8	1889	134.5	99.0
1872	131.8	122.2	1890	145.5	95.7
1873	134.5	119.9			

Source: "Wholesale Prices, Wages, and Transportation," *Reports of Committees of the Senate of the United States for the Second Session of the 52nd Congress, 1892-93*, III (Washington: U.S. Gov't Printing Office, 1893), pp. 9, 52.

TABLE A-2.   Average annual prices, Para rubber and all commodities, 1890-1926 (1913=100).

	Para Rubber	All Commodities *			Rubber Para	All Commodities *
1890	103.8	80.5		1908	107.9	90.1
1891	98.0	80.0		1909	183.5	96.9
1892	83.8	74.8		1910	236.3	100.9
1893	88.8	76.6		1911	137.6	93.0
1894	83.6	68.7		1912	130.3	99.1
1895	92.0	70.0		1913	100.0	100.0
1896	99.1	66.7		1914	76.3	98.1
1897	104.7	66.8		1915	69.0	100.8
1898	114.9	69.6		1916	82.9	126.8
1899	123.3	74.9		1917	80.3	177.2
1900	121.6	80.5		1918	68.0	194.3
1901	105.3	79.3		1919	59.8	206.4
1902	90.1	84.4		1920	41.2	226.2
1903	112.2	85.5		1921	22.5	146.9
1904	134.7	85.6		1922	22.6	148.8
1905	153.9	86.2		1923	30.8	153.7
1906	150.3	88.6		1924	26.2	149.7
1907	131.7	93.5		1925	70.5	158.7
				1926	47.1	151.0

*The number of commodities varied from 199 in 1890 to 404 in 1926.

SOURCE: *U.S. Dept. of Labor, Statistics Bulletin No. 440* (Washington: U.S. Gov't Printing Office, 1927), pp. 9, 212-13.

TABLE A-3.   Average annual wholesale prices, Para rubber, 1890-1930 (dollars per pound; landed New York).

1890	$0.838	1904	$1.088	1918	$.549
1891	.791	1905	1.243	1919	.483
1892	.676	1906	1.213	1920	.333
1893	.717	1907	1.063	1921	.182
1894	.674	1908	.817	1922	.183
1895	.743	1909	1.481	1923	.248
1896	.800	1910	1.908	1924	.212
1897	.845	1911	1.110	1925	.569
1898	.927	1912	1.052	1926	.380
1899	.995	1913	.807	1927	.268
1900	.982	1914	.616	1928	.186
1901	.850	1915	.557	1929	.164
1902	.727	1916	.669	1930	.144
1903	.905	1917	.648		

SOURCE: *Statistics Bulletin No. 440*, pp. 212-13; U.S. Dept. of Commerce, *Statistical Abstract of the United States* (Washington: U.S. Gov't Printing Office, 1931), p. 740.

TABLE A-4.   Annual high, low, and average wholesale spot prices, crude rubber No. 1, ribbed smoked sheet, 1906-42 (cents per pound; landed New York).

	High	*Low*	*Average*
1906	150	86	....
1907	138	93	....
1908	130	75	....
1909	208	128	....
1910	288*	141	206.60
1911	184	114	141.30
1912	140	108	121.60
1913	113	59	82.04
1914	93	56	65.33
1915	79	58½	65.85
1916	102	55	72.50
1917	90	52	72.23
1918	70	40	60.15
1919	57	38½	48.70
1920	56½	16	36.30
1921	21¼	11½	16.36
1922	28⅜	13⅝	17.50
1923	37⅛	24¾	29.45
1924	40⅛	17⅝	26.20
1925	121	34⅜	72.46
1926	88½	36¾	48.50
1927	41¾	33	37.72
1928	41¼	17	22.48
1929	26⅞	15½	20.55
1930	16½	7½	11.98
1931	8⅝	4¼	6.17
1932	4¾	2½	3.49
1933	9⅞	2⅞	5.96
1934	15⅞	8¾	12.92
1935	13¾	10½	12.37
1936	23	13½	16.41
1937	26⅞	14	19.39
1938	17 3/16	10¼	14.64
1939	24	14 15/16	17.57
1940	24	18¼	20.10
1941†	24⅞	19⅛	22.40
1942†	22½	22½	22.50

*In the annual report for fiscal year 1910-11, Colt stated that "fine Para" rubber sold as high as $3.00 a pound in July, 1910.

†Government fixed price, August, 1941 through December, 1946, 22½.

SOURCE: *Rubber Industry Facts, Statistical Appendix* (New York: Rubber Manufacturers Association, Inc., 1963).

TABLE A-5.   Financial data, United States Rubber Company, 1893-1901.

Year Ended March 31	Net Income (thousands)	Common Shares Outstanding, End of Fiscal Year	Earnings per Common Share Outstanding, End of Fiscal Year	Common Shares Outstanding (adjusted)*	Earnings per Common Share Outstanding (adjusted)*	Net Worth (thousands)	Ratio of Debt to Net Worth (%)
1893	$ 549.9†	139,848	$0.10	599,500	$.02	$27,387.5	3.4%
1894	1,267.7†	201,660	1.16	866,700	.27	39,813.4	2.0
1895	2,716.4	"	5.77	"	1.34	40,442.7	0.3
1896	1,085.8	"	(2.31)‡	"	(.54)	39,976.5	3.0
1897	1,635.5	"	.41	"	.10	39,656.6	3.6
1898	1,570.8	"	.09	"	.02	39,675.4	2.9
1899	2,596.6	236,660	3.02	1,017,100	.70	48,015.0	4.0
1900	2,837.9	"	4.03	"	.94	48,024.2	3.5
1901	(—101.9)	"	(3.41)§	"	(.79)	47,216.5	5.9

*Adjusted for subsequent stock splits and stock dividends.

†From other sources.

‡Regular dividends totaling $1,552,040 were paid on preferred stock, reducing surplus by $466,203.

§Dividends totaling $705,765 were paid on preferred stock from surplus.

In Chapter VII reference is made to a later court ruling that dividends on noncumulative preferred stock of a New Jersey corporation are payable out of net profits only and for only the years in which the net profits are actually earned. See pp. 288-89.

Prior to 1928 the reported assets included several million dollars of intangible assets, such as goodwill and patents. For this study no attempt has been made to determine the amount of intangible assets. Ratio of debt to net worth has been calculated on the basis of assets reported for years prior to 1928.

Source: Annual reports to stockholders.

TABLE A-6.   Motor vehicle factory sales, 1900-29.

	Passenger Cars	Motor Trucks and Buses	Total
1900	4,192	....	4,192
1901	7,000	....	7,000
1902	9,000	....	9,000
1903	11,235	....	11,235
1904	22,130	700	22,830
1905	24,250	750	25,000
1906	33,200	800	34,000
1907	43,000	1,000	44,000
1908	63,500	1,500	65,000
1909	123,990	3,297	127,287
1910	181,000	6,000	187,000
1911	199,319	10,681	210,000
1912	356,000	22,000	378,000
1913	461,500	23,500	485,000
1914	548,139	24,900	573,039
1915	895,930	74,000	969,930
1916	1,525,578	92,130	1,617,708
1917	1,745,792	128,157	1,873,949
1918	943,436	227,250	1,170,686
1919	1,651,625	224,731	1,876,356
1920	1,905,560	321,789	2,227,349
1921	1,468,067	148,052	1,616,119
1922	2,274,185	269,991	2,544,176
1923	3,624,717	409,295	4,034,012
1924	3,185,881	416,659	3,602,540
1925	3,735,171	530,659	4,265,830
1926	3,692,317	608,617	4,300,934
1927	2,936,533	464,793	3,401,326
1928	3,775,417	583,342	4,358,759
1929	4,455,178	881,909	5,337,087

SOURCE: U.S. Dept. of Commerce, *Historical Statistics of the United States, Colonial Times to 1957* (Washington: U.S. Gov't Printing Office, 1960), p. 462.

Table A-7.   Earnings per common share and net worth, United States Rubber Company, 1902-18.

Fiscal Year Ended March 31	Common Shares Outstanding, End of Fiscal Year	Earnings per Common Share Outstanding, End of Fiscal Year	Common Shares Outstanding (adjusted)*	Earnings per Common Share Outstanding (adjusted)*	Net Worth† (thousands)	Ratio of Debt to Net Worth (%)
1902	236,660	$ .51	1,017,100	$ .12	$54,173.0	35.0
1903	"	5.67	"	1.32	56,710.8	33.5
1904	"	3.05	"	.71	57,433.6	34.5
1905	"	7.94	"	1.85	59,313.5	42.4
1906	250,000	4.14	1,074,500	.96	82,810.4	31.1
1907	"	4.42	"	1.03	85,373.4	33.1
1908	"	.23	"	.05	85,547.7	26.7
1909	236,660	(1.46)	1,017,100	(.34)	83,867.5	26.2
1910	250,000	7.84	1,074,500	1.83	90,934.4	31.3
1911	"	2.20	"	.51	91,484.3	33.2
1912	"	6.31	"	1.47	96,181.2	40.1
1913	360,000	9.68	1,289,400	2.70	125,312.8	42.5

| Nine Months Ended 12/31/13 | 360,000 | 9.53 | 1,289,400 | 2.66 | 129,813.9 | 47.1 |

Calendar Year						
1914	"	8.39	"	2.34	130,746.8	42.8
1915	"	9.64	"	2.69	133,969.4	49.5
1916	"	15.12	"	4.22	140,736.5	53.5
1917	"	18.01	"	5.03	139,798.5	77.4
1918	"	38.51	"	10.75	153,661.3	62.1

*Adjusted for subsequent stock splits and stock dividends. Earnings have been adjusted, where possible, to conform to present accounting practice.

†Prior to 1928, assets included an undisclosed amount of intangible assets.

Source: Annual reports to stockholders.

TABLE A-8.   Financial data, United States Rubber Company, 1902-18.

Fiscal Year Ended March 31	Net Sales (thousands)	Net Income (thousands)	Net Income as Per Cent of Net Sales
1902	$25,436.2	$ 119.5	0.47
1903	28,276.6	1,342,4	4.75
1904	33,396.9	1,075.6	3.22
1905	32,931.2	3,761.9	11.42
1906	32,868.6	3,881.3	11.81
1907	39,715.7	4,590.4	11.56
1908	41,860.4	3,553.6	8.49
1909	31,889.4	3,152.8	9.89
1910	38,711.1	5,535.2	14.30
1911	40,888.7	4,349.8	10.64
1912	36,775.9	5,376.3	14.62
1913	91,782.9	7,729.5*	8.42*

Nine Months Ended 12/31/13	$87,349.7	$ 6,949.4	7.96

Calendar Year			
1914	$ 83,678.8	$ 7,805.1	9.33
1915	92,861.0	8,267.5	8.90
1916	126,759.1	10,279.0	8.11
1917	176,159.7	11,445.6	6.50
1918	215,398.4	18,824.9	8.74

*Before provision of $7 million "for depreciation," which has been considered more properly charged against surplus than against 1913 earnings. Otherwise, earnings have been adjusted, where possible, to conform to present accounting practice.

SOURCE: Annual reports to stockholders.

TABLE A-9.   Index of wholesale prices, tires and tubes, 1913-42 (1957-59=100).

1913	218.2	1923	115.3	1933	44.3
1914	182.2	1924	97.5	1934	47.3
1915	163.3	1925	103.8	1935	48.1
1916	168.9	1926	105.3	1936	49.6
1917	208.5	1927	78.9	1937	58.7
1918	241.4	1928	66.7	1938	60.7
1919	220.3	1929	57.4	1939	61.7
1920	244.8	1930	54.0	1940	54.3
1921	188.5	1931	48.4	1941	58.4
1922	121.5	1932	43.3	1942	70.8

SOURCE: U.S. Dept. of Labor, Bureau of Labor Statistics, various publications.

TABLE A-10.   Value of tire and tube production, 1900-37 (millions of dollars; destined for domestic consumption; current producers' prices).

Dollars (in millions)		Dollars (in millions)		Dollars (in millions)	
1900	$ 7.8	1916	$156.1	1927	$574.9
1905	9.3	1917	329.1	1928	551.0
1906	12.5	1918	491.3	1929	437.8
1907	15.6	1919	515.4	1930	336.9
1908	17.5		or 546.6*	1931	273.4
1909	23.4	1920	678.9	1932	194.5
1910	36.0	1921	323.5	1933	196.7
1911	45.5	1922	335.8	1934	....
1912	58.3	1923	348.3	1935	215.1
1913	86.6	1924	382.0	1936	....
1914	92.7	1925	555.1	1937	261.2
1915	104.9	1926	616.3		

*The estimate of $515.4 million for 1919 is comparable with the estimates for the preceding years; $546.4 million is the adjusted estimate, based in part on additional data available for 1919 and subsequent years.

SOURCE: U.S. Dept. of Commerce, *Historical Statistics of the United States, Colonial Times to 1957* (Washington: U.S. Gov't Printing Office, 1960), p. 420.

TABLE A-11.   Thirty-three years of tire prices, 1909-41 (list prices as of April).

	30" x 3½" (fabric)		30" x 3½" (fabric)	4.40 x 21
1909	$35.05	1926	$15.45	$18.55
1910	30.60	1927	9.95	12.90
1911	24.90	1928	8.70	12.90
1912	24.90	1929	7.45	9.90
1913	19.60	1930	6.75	8.25
1914	17.00	1931	6.05	7.05
1915	12.20	1932	5.45	6.35
1916	13.40	1933	....	5.65
1917	15.10	1934	....	8.15
1918	18.25	1935	....	8.60
1919	20.65	1936	....	8.60
1920	23.20	1937	....	10.05
1921	20.00	1938	....	10.55
1922	13.75	1939	....	9.65
1923	15.95	1940	....	8.70
1924	12.65	1941	....	9.05
1925	12.30			

SOURCE: Ralph C. Epstein, "Concentration and Price Trends in the Rubber Tire Industry, 1930-47," privately printed, 1949, p. 45.

TABLE A-12.   Financial data, United States Rubber Company, 1919-28.

	Net Sales (thousands)	Net Income* (thousands)	Net Income* as Per Cent of Net Sales	Net Worth (thousands)	Ratio of Debt to Net Worth (%)
1919	$225,589.5	$23,645.6	10.48	$207,063.2	45.9
1920	256,150.1	(18,011.5) †	(7.03)	179,349.6	90.2
1921	164,706.6	12,117.8	7.36	184,517.4	73.8
1922	168,786.4	7,569.4	4.48	186,566.8	68.0
1923	186,261.4	5,949.7	3.19	186,996.5	73.3
1924	172,214.4	7,447.7	4.32	189,235.4	69.5
1925	206,473.7	12,822.1†	6.21	196,817.2	76.9
1926	215,528.3	(5,258.8) †	(2.44)	186,349.7	80.4
1927	193,442.9	13,174.5	6.81	194,315.4	73.8
1928	193,480.1	(23,432.5) †	(12.11)	182,749.9	81.0

*Net income has been adjusted, where possible, to conform to current accounting practice.

†After writedown of inventories and purchase commitments: 1920, $39,859,000; 1925, $5,000,000; 1926, $17,400,000; 1928, $15,000,000. Income shown for 1928 is also after provision of $10 million for property adjustments and contingencies.

Prior to 1928, intangible assets were not segregated from tangible assets. Prior to July 1, 1938, consolidated balance sheets and income statements excluded U.S. Rubber Plantations, Inc., and the latter's subsidiaries. Dividends from the plantations company were included in consolidated income, and United States Rubber Company's investment, at cost, in the plantations was included in its assets.

SOURCE: Annual reports to stockholders.

TABLE A-13.   Earnings per common share, United States Rubber Company, 1919-28.

	Common Shares Outstanding, End of Fiscal Year	Earnings per Common Share Outstanding, End of Fiscal Year	Common Shares Outstanding (adjusted)*	Earnings per Common Share Outstanding (adjusted)*
1919	720,000	$25.84	2,578,800	$7.21
1920	810,000	(28.66) †	"	(9.00) †
1921	"	8.24	"	2.59
1922	"	2.53	"	.80
1923	"	.53	"	.17
1924	"	2.76	"	.87
1925	"	9.40†	"	2.95†
1926	"	(12.92) †	"	(4.06) †
1927	"	9.83	"	3.09
1928	"	(28.93) †	"	(9.09) †

*Number of shares adjusted for subsequent stock splits and stock dividends. Net income has been adjusted, where possible, to conform to current accounting practice.

†After writedown of inventories and purchase commitments: 1920, $39,859,000; 1925, $5,000,000; 1926, the adjusted number of common shares these writedowns were equivalent to: $15.45 per share in 1920; $1.94 per share in 1925; $6.75 per share in 1926; $5.82 per share in 1928. Also, earnings per common share in 1928 were after provision of $10 million for property adjustments and contingencies.

SOURCE: Annual reports to stockholders.

TABLE A-14.   Balance sheet items, 1928-42 (in thousands).

	Current Assets	Receivables (net)	Inventories (net)	Current Liabilities	Total Debt	Contingent or General Reserves	Other Reserves	Tangible Net Worth*
1928	$148,158	$43,912	$66,549	$43,161	$148,013	$1,299	$12,368	$118,796
1929	116,752	42,453	57,500	37,304	118,894	....	14,524	111,821
1930	84,148	31,171	44,050	11,729	107,020	....	6,971	94,731
1931	62,606	22,387	27,038	7,625	93,602	....	2,563	85,672
1932	48,228	15,937	19,800	15,743	85,109	....	2,698	75,604
1933	50,100	16,653	25,254	10,779	82,318	....	3,043	75,738
1934	57,744	17,212	29,298	14,178	83,452	2,107	1,271	75,083
1935	62,546	22,118	29,138	15,267	75,764	3,442	1,307	77,397
1936	80,647	27,271	40,406	23,693	77,243	4,309	1,301	88,458
1937	90,310	21,563	57,858	26,768	77,884	2,650	1,336	96,095
1938	89,940	23,050	50,167	23,262	70,081	2,908	1,566	94,735
1939	105,220	29,770	60,973	30,710	74,333	3,373	1,666	101,922
1940	121,108	36,109	64,454	38,563	80,030	3,609	2,097	106,329
1941	154,815	39,184	76,666	66,465	104,831	4,114	3,612	110,992
1942	138,671	45,547	78,128	35,512	94,039	4,464	2,245	113,396

*Reserves for contingencies or "General Reserves" were not segregated in annual reports for 1929 to 1933, inclusive. For comparative purposes, and in keeping with the practice of the company as indicated by its annual reports, "tangible net worth" shown here does not include amounts shown under "Contingent or General Reserves."

SOURCE: Annual reports to stockholders.

TABLE A-15. Operating statement data, 1928-42 (in thousands).

	Net Sales	Cost of Sales (other than depreciation) Plus S. and A.	Depreciation	Net Operating Profit or (Loss)	Interest Paid on Funded Indebtedness	Other Income (net)	Other Charges Against Earnings	Net Income or (Deficit)
1928	$193,480	$178,949	$5,153	$ 9,378	$6,098	$1,000	$27,713	$(23,433)
1929	192,962	178,576	6,643	7,743	5,918	....	6,502	(4,677)
1930	157,075	150,569	7,347	(841)	5,577	....	15,646	(22,064)
1931	114,132	108,608	9,673	(4,149)	4,893	2,034	2,465	(9,473)
1932	78,300	76,995	6,541	(5,236)	4,382	1,449	2,190	(10,358)
1933	88,327	77,941	6,463	3,923	3,846	996	1,680	(606)
1934	105,477	94,991	5,966	4,520	3,632	....	1,432	(544)
1935	127,794	109,938	5,582	12,274	3,460	500	5,783	3,531
1936	160,361	138,929	5,535	15,897	2,849	231	2,535	10,744
1937	186,253	166,885	5,636	13,732	2,574	607	6,904	4,861
1938	154,936	134,939	8,306	11,691	2,189	884	1,893	8,494
1939	195,311	171,600	8,190	15,521	1,681	960	4,581	10,219
1940	228,989	201,127	8,452	19,410	1,527	1,161	7,619	11,425
1941	315,345	271,939	8,650	34,757	1,450	1,453	21,096	13,663
1942	290,992*	249,918	7,695	33,379*	1,332	4,193	27,859†	8,318§

*Exclusive of $3,022,000 fixed fees received for constructing and operating plants for the government.

†Includes foreign war losses of $15,487,000.

§After charges of $15,487,000 against 1942 income for war losses. In addition, $2,347,000 was eliminated from earned surplus and $859,000 from capital surplus, due to removal of plantations and certain other foreign subsidiaries from consolidated statements.

Amounts shown as charges against earnings or as net income have been adjusted, where possible, to conform to current accounting practice.

Prior to 1936, selling and administrative expense was not shown separately from manufacturing costs, and therefore in this table has been combined with "cost of sales" for subsequent years. "Other charges" include adjustments, special provisions, and income, excise, and excess profits taxes.

SOURCE: Annual reports to stockholders.

Table A-16.   Rubber consumption in the United States by types, 1890-1942 (in long tons).

	Natural	Synthetic	Reclaimed
1890	13,500	....	....
1891	15,300	....	....
1892	14,700	....	....
1893	15,900	....	....
1894	13,900	....	....
1895	16,700	....	....
1896	13,700	....	....
1897	17,300	....	....
1898	18,600	....	....
1899	22,700	....	....
1900	20,308	....	....
1901	22,954	....	....
1902	21,244	....	....
1903	23,240	....	....
1904	26,089	....	....
1905	27,021	....	....
1906	28,640	....	....
1907	28,817	....	....
1908	32,403	....	....
1909	39,789	....	....
1910	42,210	....	....
1911	41,728	....	....
1912	55,937	....	....
1913	51,987	....	....
1914	62,265	....	....
1915	98,990	....	....
1916	117,611	....	....
1917	157,371	....	....
1918	160,000	....	....
1919	215,000	....	73,535
1920	206,000	....	75,297
1921	177,772	....	41,351
1922	301,499	....	54,458
1923	319,422	....	69,534
1924	328,769	....	76,072
1925	388,481	....	137,105
1926	366,149	....	164,500
1927	373,000	....	189,500
1928	437,012	....	223,000
1929	467,408	....	212,700
1930	375,735	*	153,500
1931	350,000	*	123,000
1932	332,000	*	77,500
1933	401,079	*	85,000
1934	453,223	*	100,855

TABLE A-16.   *Continued*

	Natural	Synthetic	Reclaimed
1935	491,544	*	120,565
1936	575,000	*	141,486
1937	543,600	*	162,000
1938	437,031	*	120,800
1939	592,000	1,750†	170,000
1940	648,500	2,560†	190,244
1941	775,000	6,259†	251,231
1942§	376,791	17,651	254,820‖

*Small unrecorded quantities were produced and used.
†Estimated.
§After Japanese occupation of the rubber-producing areas in the Far East, a little natural rubber found its way by devious means into this country, but the amounts were relatively small. In 1943, imports of natural rubber totaled 60,000 long tons, and this was possible only because the United States had sponsored expansion of rubber production in Latin America.
‖Accurate data prior to 1919 not found.

SOURCE: *Rubber Industry Facts, Statistical Appendix* (New York: Rubber Manufacturers Association, Inc., 1963), Tables 10 and 11.

TABLE A-17.   Significant financial ratios, 1928-42.*

	Current Assets/ Current Liabilities (times)	Receivables/ Net Sales	Inventories/ Net Sales	Net Operating Profit (or Loss)/ Net Sales	Net Income or (Loss)/ Net Sales	Net Income or (Loss)/ Tangible Net Worth	Tangible Net Worth/ Total Debt
1928	2.9	22.7%	34.4%	4.8%	(12.1)%	(19.7)%	80.3%
1929	3.1	22.0	29.8	4.0	(2.4)	(4.2)	94.1
1930	7.2	19.8	28.0	(0.5)	(14.0)	(23.3)	88.5
1931	8.2	19.6	23.7	(3.6)	(8.3)	(11.1)	91.5
1932	3.1	20.4	25.3	(6.7)	(13.2)	(13.7)	88.8
1933	4.6	18.8	28.6	4.4	(0.7)	(0.8)	92.0
1934	4.1	16.3	27.8	4.3	(0.5)	(0.7)	90.0
1935	4.1	17.3	22.8	9.6	2.8	4.6	102.2
1936	3.4	17.0	25.2	9.9	6.7	12.1	114.5
1937	3.4	11.6	31.1	7.4	2.6	5.1	123.4
1938	3.9	14.9	32.4	7.5	5.5	9.0	135.2
1939	3.4	15.2	31.2	7.9	5.2	10.0	137.1
1940	3.1	15.8	28.2	8.5	4.9	10.7	132.9
1941	2.3	12.4	24.3	11.0	4.3	12.3	105.9
1942	3.9	15.7	26.8	11.5	2.9	7.4	120.6

*All ratios based on amounts at end of current year. Net income has been adjusted, where possible, to conform to current accounting practice. Tangible net worth is exclusive of all reserves.
SOURCE: Annual reports to stockholders.

Table A-18.   Annual consumption of types of synthetic rubbers, 1941-46 (in thousands of long tons).

	GR-S	Neoprene	Butyl	Buna-N Types	Total Synthetic
1941	.1	4.5*	n.a	1.7*	6.3
1942	2.6	6.8	.02	8.2	17.7
1943	132.0	26.2	.3	12.4	170.9
1944	495.6	46.2	10.8	14.1	566.7
1945	600.1	42.4	43.0	8.0	693.6
1946	632.1	44.4	79.2	6.0	761.7

*Estimated.

Source: *The Vanderbilt Rubber Handbook* (New York: R. T. Vanderbilt Company, 1948), p. 53.

B

Partnership Agreement

Between Lewis Brothers, Naugatuck

Articles of agreement Between Milo Lewis, Thomas Lewis, Sam'l J. Lewis and Wm B. Lewis of Naugatuck—

1. In prosecuting all the varieties of business in which the above named parties may be engaged there shall be no separate or private interest whatever except the clothing for each oneself and family.

2. Each of the above named parties shall be under a bond of ten thousand dollars to redeem (?) to Milo Lewis or his heirs all the fast property and reconvey all the movable property received from him or that may be in their possession through the influence of business at the present or any future time by receiving from him or his executor or administrator the notes that they have given him for such property amounting to a little more than thirty thousand dollars—

3rd Each family shall be sustained from the results of the business in which they are respectively engaged and there shall be no separate account kept for such expenses except for clothing; and for that each one shall keep a particular account and charge himself with the expenses of the same for himself and family.

4th It shall be the duty of Milo & Wm B. Lewis to superintend and take care of the farming business of sd concern. It shall be the duty of Thomas Lewis to take the charge of the cotton Mill now owned by sd concern and it shall be the duty of Samuel J. Lewis to superintend the India rubber shoe business in which he is now engaged and each party shall pursue persevereingly [sic] and faithfully their duties in the several stations which they occupy.

5th All important transactions in which any one or all of the parties wish to engage in aside from their regular business shall be submitted to the Co and before engaged in shall receive the approbation of a majority of the Co—

6th All the results of the various branches of business in which the sd Lewises shall be engaged shall be appropriated to the payment of debts due from Milo or Thomas Lewis or be applied to increase business operations in the way and to the object that a Majority of the Co shall deem most conducive to the interest of the whole concern.

7th The business at the cotton mill shall be done in the name of Thomas Lewis at the shoe shop in the name of S. J. Lewis & Co on the farm in the name of Milo & William B. Lewis and Milo and William B. Lewis shall indorse for each of the other concerns as far as may be necessary—

NOTE: Other than for changes in archaic abbreviations, the above is believed to be a true copy of the original agreement (apparently undated and unsigned) written with pen and ink, now in the possession of United States Rubber Company.

C

Plan for Formation of United States Rubber

Company and Certificate of Organization

AGREEMENT DATED JAN. 27, 1892

(Exhibit A)

It is intended to form a company to be styled "The United States Rubber Corporation," or to be known by some other appropriate title, which company shall have power to acquire the various plants or interests therein now engaged in the manufacture of rubber boots or shoes within the United States.

The Company shall have the right to issue $25,000,000 8 per cent preferred stock; $25,000,000 common stock.

Preferred stock shall be issued in payment for each manufacturing property to an amount which at par shall represent:

A. The value of the plant, machinery, tools, and fixtures, by an appraisement to be made by Charles S. Smith, Henry W. Cannon, and Charles H. Dalton, they to employ such experts as they may select.

B. The value of all other assets, above liabilities, guaranteed by the manufacturer whose interest shall be acquired.

In case only a portion of the whole interest in any of said manufacturing properties be acquired, a pro rata amount of preferred stock, as above provided for, shall be issued therefor.

The common stock shall be issued, among other things, to represent the increased earning capacity by reason of the consolidation of the interests acquired, and shall be issued to an amount equal to the issue of preferred stock.

Provision shall be made by the United States Rubber Corporation that 5 per cent of the total capital stock of said corporation shall be delivered to Messrs. H. B. Hollins & Co., bankers, of the city of New York, in payment of the charges of lawyers, accountants, appraisers, experts, and services of bankers, and all other services attending the organization of said corporation; said payment of 5 per cent, however, to be made to Messrs. H. B. Hollins & Co. only whenever and as from time to time the stock of said corporation is issued, payable in common stock.

Additional common stock to the amount of $1,000,000 shall be issued full paid in consideration of the transfer of the properties or of interest therein to the consolidated company, whenever and as soon as the condition of "Addendum 1" shall have been complied with. The said $1,000,000 in common stock shall be deposited with the Central Trust Company of New York, and be by it delivered as directed by Messrs. H. B. Hollins & Co., bankers, upon payment by them to the consolidated company of a subscription of $1,000,000 of preferred stock at par, which payment Messrs. H. B. Hollins & Co., at the request of the proprietors of the several manufacturing interests which shall be acquired, have agreed to make, as soon as the conditions set forth in "Addendum 1," shall be fulfilled. The acceptance by said proprietors and said H. B.

Hollins & Co., of the plan herein, and in "Addendum 1," set forth shall be evidence of such request and agreement.

Addendum 1.

The general plan provided for in Exhibit A shall be operative and shall go into effect whenever there shall have been acquired, either after the ownership or majority interest in manufacturing properties, the value of whose assets, measured by the authorized issue of preferred and common stock at par, as set forth in Exhibit A, shall equal $15,000,000.

AGREEMENT DATED FEB. 1, 1892

This memorandum of agreement, made and entered into the first day of February 1892, between Messrs. H. B. Hollins & Company, Mr. Charles R. Flint, Mr. Joseph P. Earle and Mr. Richard C. Sibley.

Whereas, the parties hereto are interested in bringing about the consolidation into one parent or consolidated corporation interests in several companies now engaged in the manufacture of rubber boots and shoes throughout the United States; and

Whereas, It has been agreed between the parties hereto that a condition of the participation in said consolidation by each of said companies is that a certain commission shall be paid by such consolidated company to Messrs. H. B. Hollins & Company; and

Whereas, It has been agreed that each of the parties hereto shall participate in said commission to the extent and in the manner set forth in this agreement;

Now, in consideration of one dollar in hand paid by each party hereto to each of the others, the receipt whereof is hereby acknowledged, and in further consideration of the services in and about said consolidation heretofore contributed and hereafter to be contributed by each party hereto for the benefit of each of the other of said parties:

It is hereby agreed as follows:

First, Said commission, which is payable in the common stock of the consolidated company as shall be paid by said company to Messrs. H. B. Hollins & Company as above receipted, shall be divided as follows:

A. Mr. Flint shall receive of such stock at par $200,000; Messrs. H. B. Hollins & Company, $100,000; Mr. Earle, $100,000.

B. Such balance as shall remain shall be divided into four equal parts; one part shall belong to and be paid over to Mr. Flint; one part to Messrs. H. B. Hollins & Company and one part to Mr. Earle; and one part to Mr. Sibley.

(Signed) H.B.H. & Co., C.R.F.

Second, This agreement is in lieu of and is substituted for any other understanding as to the subject matter of this agreement whether written or oral, heretofore entered into between the parties hereto.

In witness whereof, the parties hereto have hereunto and unto three other originals hereof set their hands and seals the day and year first above written.

(Signed) H. B. Hollins & Co.
(Signed) Charles R. Flint
(Signed) Richard C. Sibley
(Signed) Joseph P. Earle

(Endorsed on back as follows) :

We, Joseph P. Earle and Charles R. Flint, for value received, have assigned, transferred, set forth. and by these presents do assign, transfer and set forth unto the New York Commercial Company, Limited, a corporation of the State of New York, all our right, title, interest in and to the within agreement, and in and to all our rights, interests and privileges thereunder.

New York, February 1, 1892.

(Signed) Henry Earle
Witness to signatures of Joseph P. Earle and Charles R. Flint. (Signed) Joseph P. Earle
(Signed) Charles R. Flint

CERTIFICATE OF ORGANIZATION

We, the undersigned, William Barbour, of Paterson, New Jersey, and William L. Trenholm, J. Edward Simmons, John P. Townsend, and John I. Waterbury, of New York City, New York, do hereby associate ourselves into a Company under and by virtue of the Provisions of an Act of the Legislature of the State of New Jersey entitled "An Act Concerning Corporations," approved April 7, 1875, and the several supplements thereto and acts amendatory thereof, for the purposes hereinafter mentioned, and we do hereby assume to and for said Company all the rights, powers and privileges granted to and conferred upon corporations by the laws of the said State of New Jersey, and do hereby certify and set forth as follows:

I. The name assumed to designate such Company and to be used in its business and dealings is United States Rubber Company.

II. The places in the State of New Jersey where the business of said Company is to be conducted are the City of New Brunswick in the County of Middlesex, and also those other cities, towns and villages in said State in which said Company may hereafter deem it expedient to conduct its business, and the City and County in which the principal part of the business of said Company within said State is to be transacted and conducted is the said City of New Brunswick in the County of Middlesex. The part of the business of the said Company to be carried on without the said State of New Jersey is as hereinafter stated. The City, County and State in which the principal office or place of business of the said Company out of the State of New Jersey is to be situated, is the City, County and State of New York, and the said Company also proposes to have a business office in the City of Boston, Massachusetts, and one in the City of Chicago, Illinois and carry on operations in all of the States and Territories of the United States and in foreign countries.

The objects for which the said Company is formed are the making, purchasing and selling rubber boots and shoes and all goods of which rubber is a component part, and the various materials entering into the manufacture of any and all such goods, and also the acquiring and disposing of rights to make and use any and all such goods and materials and the doing and transacting all acts, business and things incident to or relating to or convenient in carrying out its business as aforesaid which are authorized by law, including the purchasing stock of any company or companies owning, mining, manufacturing or producing materials or other property necessary for its business, or of any other company whose shares it may lawfully purchase and exercising with relation thereto all the rights, powers and privileges of individual owners of the shares of such stock.

The portion of said Company's business which is to be carried on out of the State of New Jersey is its financial business generally and as well such portion of its manufacturing business and the business of buying and selling as it may from time to time find convenient.

III. The total amount of the Capital Stock of said Company is $50,000,000. The number of shares into which the same is divided is 500,000 and the par value of each share is $100. The stock of the said Company is to be of two kinds, to wit, general stock and preferred stock. The amount of the preferred stock shall at no time exceed one half of the total outstanding capital stock of the Company. The holders of the preferred stock shall be entitled to receive semi-annually all net earnings of the Company determined and declared as dividends in each fiscal year up to but not exceeding 8 per cent per annum on all outstanding preferred stock before any dividend shall be set apart or paid on the general stock, but such dividends upon the preferred stock shall not be cumulative, and the preferred stock shall not be entitled to participate in any other or additional earnings or profits. In case of liquidation or dissolution of the Company the holders of preferred stock shall be entitled to receive cash to the amount of their preferred stock at par before any payment in liquidation is made upon the general stock, and shall not thereafter participate in any of the property of the Company or proceeds of liquidation. The amount of capital stock with which the said Company is to commence business is the sum of $100,000 divided into 1000 shares of the par value of $100 each, of which 500 shares are to be preferred and the remaining 500 shares general stock. Additional issues on account of the total authorized capital stock may be made from time to time, either in preferred or general stock, or both, in such sums and in such manner as the Board of Directors of the Company may determine, and in accordance with law and with this Certificate.

IV. The names and residences of the stockholders and the number of shares held by each are as follows:

		Number of Shares	
Names	*Residences*	General	Preferred
William Barbour	Paterson, N.J.	100	100
William L. Trenholm	New York City, N.Y.	100	100
J. Edward Simmons	" " " "	100	100
John P. Townsend	" " " "	100	100
John I. Waterbury	" " " "	100	100
	Total shares	500	500

V. The period at which the said Company shall commence shall be the 30th day of March 1892, and the said Company shall terminate on the 30th day of March 1942.

In witness whereof, we have hereunto affixed our hands and seals respectively this 29th day of March, in the year 1892.

W. Barbour	*(L.S.)*
W. L. Trenholm	*(L.S.)*
J. Edward Simmons	*(L.S.)*
John P. Townsend	*(L.S.)*
John I. Waterbury	*(L.S.)*

State of New York)
City and County of New York) ss.:

Be it remembered that on this 29th day of March 1892, before me, the subscriber, a Master in Chancery of the State of New Jersey personally appeared William Barbour, William L. Trenholm, J. Edward Simmons, John P. Townsend, and John I. Waterbury, who I am satisfied are the incorporators in the foregoing instrument named; and I having first made known to them the contents thereof, they did each acknowledge that they signed, sealed and delivered the same as their voluntary act and deed, and for the uses and purposes therein expressed.

In witness thereof, I have hereunto set my hand.

Randolph Parmly,
Master in Chancery of New Jersey.

NOTE: The above material is from *Report to the 57th Congress, 1901, of the Industrial Commission on Trusts and Industrial Combinations*, XIII (Washington: U.S. Gov't Printing Office, 1901).

Biographical Data, First Four Presidents

The following biographical sketches of the first four presidents of United States Rubber Company are taken almost entirely from the "First Section of History of United States Rubber Company" by Walter Emery, Commercial Development Department, United States Rubber Company, 1946.

WILLIAM L. TRENHOLM, president, April 4—Oct. 15, 1892.

Trenholm was born Feb. 3, 1836, in Charleston, S. C., the son of George A. Trenholm, a leading cotton merchant. He graduated from South Carolina College in 1855 and in 1856 married Kate Louise Macbeth of Charleston, by whom he had eight children. For several years he was in the Liverpool office of John Fraser & Company; his father was a member of this firm.

During the Civil War his father was Secretary of the Treasury of the Confederate states, and William served with the South Carolina troops, rising from first lieutenant to lieutenant colonel. In 1865 he became special aide to Governor Perry of South Carolina, in charge of relations between federal authorities and the citizens of the coastal counties. In 1868 he and his father formed the banking firm of George A. Trenholm and Son.

President Cleveland appointed him a member of the United States Civil Service Commission in November, 1885, and Comptroller of the Currency in 1886. He resigned that office on April 18, 1889 to become president of the American Surety Company, New York City, which, during the ten years of his presidency, became one of the city's leading financial institutions.

On April 4, 1892, at the first directors' meeting following filing of the Certificate of Organization of United States Rubber Company on March 30, 1892, he was elected president. He served until Oct. 15, 1892, and remained a director of the company until May 18, 1897.

He also was one of the organizers in 1889 and first vice-president of the State Trust Company of New York. From January, 1898 until his death on Jan. 11, 1901, he was president of the North America Trust Company. Trenholm was author of *The People's Money* (1890) and of several articles on banking, currency, and tariffs.

ROBERT D. EVANS, president Oct. 15, 1892-May 12, 1893; March 4, 1896-May 26, 1897.

Born in St. John, New Brunswick, Canada, in 1843, Evans graduated from English High School, Boston, and became a clerk for Hall Rubber Company. During the Civil War, he was wounded twice at the second battle of Bull Run. On Oct. 1, 1867 he married Marie Antoinette Hunt of Boston; there were no children.

After the Civil War he was a partner for a time with Charles M. Clapp, then operating the Aetna Mills at Jamaica Plain, Mass. Evans had exclusive rights to manufacture a wringer roll known as the Moulton, but when New York and Boston manufacturers brought suits against the firm for patent infringements, Clapp wished to discontinue manufacture and the partnership was dissolved. Evans, however, decided to continue manufacturing the rolls, started the Eagle Rubber Company, and successfully defended his rights.

In 1873 he organized the American Rubber Company as a jobbing concern to handle the products of the Eagle Rubber Company. The two companies were consolidated in 1877 as the American Rubber Company and established a factory at Cambridgeport, Mass., manufacturing rubber clothing, carriage cloth, rubber boots and shoes, and wringer rolls.

When the American Rubber Company was acquired by United States Rubber Company on April 7, 1892, Evans was elected a director of the latter. On Oct. 15, 1892, he became president of the company, serving until May 12, 1893, when he was succeeded by Joseph Banigan. Banigan resigned March 4, 1896 and Evans again was elected president. He remained in office until May 26, 1897, and continued on the board of directors until May 17, 1898. While serving in these capacities Evans also acted as director of purchases, giving particular attention to raw materials.

In 1899 Evans was one of the organizers of United States Mining Company, later becoming president of that firm. He also organized the Yuba Consolidated Gold Mine Company, and had interests in firms connected with the gathering of native rubber in South America and the planting of guayule in Mexico. He died July 6, 1909.

JOSEPH BANIGAN, president May 12, 1893-March 4, 1896.

Banigan was born in County Monaghan, Ireland, June 7, 1839. When he was 8 years old, his parents emigrated to America and settled in Providence. At 9, Joseph was an apprentice with the New England Screw Company; at 21 he was well established as a journeyman jeweler. That year he married Margaret Holt, daughter of John Holt, who later became superintendent and a director of the Woonsocket Rubber Company. Banigan had four children by his first wife. Several years after her death, he married Maria T. Conway of New York City.

Banigan was still in his twenties when he joined John Haskins, one of the pioneers in the rubber industry. He remained with that firm, later organized as Goodyear India Rubber Stopper Company, until 1866. Then, in partnership with Lyman A. and Simeon S. Cook, and with $10,000 borrowed capital, he began manufacturing wringer rolls and rubber blankets in a small plant in Woonsocket,

The Woonsocket Rubber Company was incorporated June 7, 1867, on his twenty-eighth birthday, with a capital of $100,000. In October, 1868, the plant made its first "ticket" of rubber footwear, which eventually would be the mill's only product. Banigan directed that all profits in excess of an annual cash dividend of 8 per cent should be issued as stock or devoted to expansion of the business. In 1882 accumulated profits paid for a new mill built at Millville, Mass. at a cost of $750,000, and, in 1884, for another new mill at Woonsocket, the "Alice" mill.

For several years during the eighties, Banigan was a large stockholder in the Goodyear Metallic Rubber Shoe Company. During that period, the Woonsocket

Rubber Company was the sole selling agent for G.M.R., and the latter company confined its production to rubber shoes.

When the United States Rubber Company was formed in 1892, Banigan said that the "rubber trust" did not include his company, and that it included only weaker manufacturers who had old-fashioned machines and appliances. But in 1893 United States Rubber acquired the total outstanding capital stock of the Woonsocket company in exchange for United States Rubber's common and preferred stock having a total par value of $9,227,800. (A total of $5,851,400 of preferred stock and an equal amount of common stock were issued by United States Rubber Company for the acquisition of all the capital stock of Woonsocket Rubber Company and the Marvel Rubber Company, Woonsocket, and for a deed to the property of the Lawrence Felting Company, Millville.)

Banigan, his son J. J. Banigan and Walter S. Ballou, an official of Woonsocket, were named to the board of directors of United States Rubber. Joseph Banigan was made president of the company on May 12, 1893, and was re-elected president and named general manager in April, 1894.

He was re-elected in April, 1895, but on June 19, 1895, the directors made the first vice-president, Robert D. Evans, general manager. Evidently there was dissension between Banigan and the other directors, for on March 4, 1896, he resigned from office and, for the second time, Evans became president. (Evans in his report to the stockholders on May 25, 1896, said "Mr. Banigan . . . voluntarily retired.") Possibly the opposition to Banigan was aggravated by his blunt statements in his annual reports that "There are too many factories for the production of rubber boots and shoes, and this will be particularly true when the improved methods are fully adopted," and his repeated recommendation that the company's output be concentrated in the factories of the larger companies in the United States Rubber System. He advocated operating at full capacity the plants of the Woonsocket Rubber Company, Goodyear Metallic Rubber Shoe Company, and L. Candee and Company; operating either the American Rubber Company or the National India Rubber Company, Goodyear Metallic Rubber Shoe Company, and L. Candee and stopping production at all the other factories. Since the twenty-five members of the board of directors included the principal stockholders or officers of the affected companies, it is not strange that they were antagonistic to his recommendations and voted to accept his resignation. His subsequent incorporation of the Joseph Banigan Rubber Company and its ultimate acquisition by United States Rubber have been previously related.

Banigan was active in the organization of the American Wringer Company, and was its president until his death in Providence on July 28, 1898. He also was president of the Providence Evening Telegram Company, Providence Building Company, a director of National Cash Register Company, Mosler Safe Company, Glenark Knitting Company, and of two banks in Providence. He is said to have been "the financial mainstay of the Mormon sugar beet industry, and to have made possible the erection of the Pioneer Electric Dam at Ogden, Utah."

He endowed a chair of political economy in the Catholic University School of Social Science and established two scholarships at Brown University. Pope Leo XIII made Banigan a Knight of the Order of St. Gregory the Great in recognition of his generosity to the Catholic church.

FREDERICK M. SHEPARD, president, May 26, 1897-May 23, 1901.

Shepard was born Sept. 24, 1827 in Norfolk, Conn. His father was a farmer, hotelkeeper, and postmaster. Information regarding his early years is scanty, but he appears to have moved first to Hartford and then to New York City, where in 1853 he became secretary-treasurer of the Union India Rubber Company. This company was formed five years before as a consolidation of interests of various licensees under Goodyear patents. These apparently did not include license to manufacture footwear, belting, or hose.

In 1854 he married Annie C. Rockwell; there were six children.

In 1857 he organized the Rubber Clothing Company, which at first operated principally as selling agent for the Beverly Rubber Company. Gradually he added other lines and entered the export trade. In 1872 the rubber business of H. G. Norton and Company was purchased. At about the same time the Goodyear Rubber Company, Middletown, Conn. was incorporated, with Shepard as president. (The corporation still operates a factory at Middletown.)

The Norton company was selling agent for National Rubber Company, Bristol, R. I., in which Shepard became a stockholder. For several years he had had no connection with the Union Rubber Company, but later bought an interest in it again and became its president in 1876. He also was a large stockholder in the Lambertville Rubber Company, Lambertville, N. J.

The National Rubber Company was reorganized by Samuel P. Colt in 1887 as the National India Rubber Company. In 1892 the company was acquired by United States Rubber, and on Oct. 15, 1892, Shepard became a director of United States Rubber, remaining on the board until his death on June 30, 1913. He served as president of the company from May 26, 1897 until May 23, 1901, when, at the age of 74, he declined re-election and was succeeded by Colt. It is interesting to note that he continued as president of Goodyear Rubber Company (Middletown) while he was president of United States Rubber.

After 1868 Shepard lived in East Orange, N. J., where he established the East Orange Safe Deposit and Trust Company, the East Orange National Bank, and the Orange Water Company. For many years he was a director of the Mutual Benefit Life Insurance Company, Newark. While serving on the advisory board of the Orange Memorial Hospital, he erected and equipped a pavillion for the treatment of tubercular diseases. He gave to Norfolk a public park, land for a fire department and a water system, and contributed to road and school improvements.

Shepard died June 30, 1913, in Norfolk.

E

Organization Charts

Sept. 1, 1902

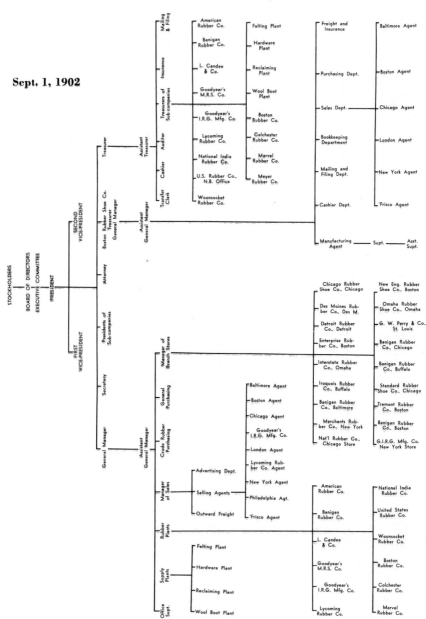

March, 1924

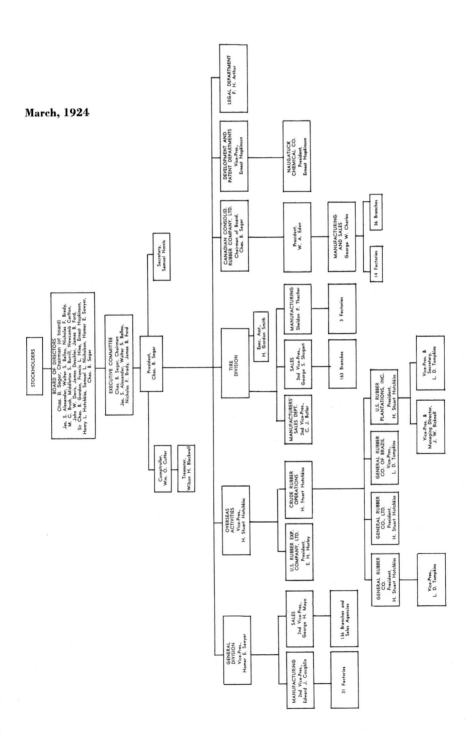

Sept. 1, 1928

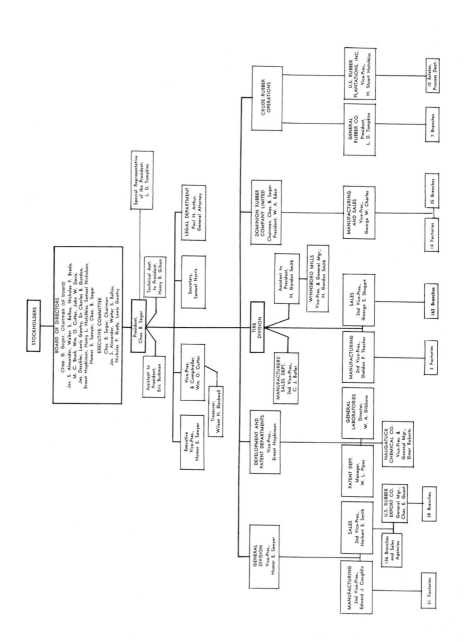

STOCKHOLDERS

BOARD OF DIRECTORS
Chas. B. Seger, Chairman (of board)
Jas. S. Alexander, Walter S. Ballou, Nicholas F. Brady,
M. C. Brush, Wm. O. Cutter, John W. Davis,
Jas. Deutscher, Lewis Gawtry, Sir Charles B. Gordon,
Ernest Hopkinson, Henry L. Hotchkiss, Samuel Nicholson,
Homer E. Sawyer, Chas. B. Seger

EXECUTIVE COMMITTEE
Chas. B. Seger, Chairman
Jas. S. Alexander, Walter S. Ballou,
Nicholas F. Brady, Lewis Gawtry

Special Representative
of the President,
L. D. Tompkins

President,
Chas. B. Seger

Technical Asst.
to President,
Henry R. Gilson

LEGAL DEPARTMENT
Paul H. Arthur,
General Attorney

Secretary,
Samuel Norris

Assistant to
President,
Eric Burkman

Vice-Pres.
& Comptroller,
Wm. O. Cutter

Treasurer,
Wilson H. Blackwell

Executive
Vice-Pres.,
Homer E. Sawyer

MANUFACTURERS'
SALES DEPT.
2nd Vice-Pres.,
C. J. Butler

CRUDE RUBBER
OPERATIONS

U.S. RUBBER
PLANTATIONS, INC.
Vice-Pres.,
H. Stuart Hotchkiss

10 Estates,
Process Dept.

GENERAL
RUBBER CO.
President,
L. D. Tompkins

7 Branches

DOMINION RUBBER
COMPANY LIMITED
Chairman, Chas. B. Seger
President, W. A. Eden

MANUFACTURING
AND SALES
Vice-Pres.,
George W. Charles

35 Branches

14 Factories

Assistant to
President,
H. Gordon Smith

WINNSBORO MILLS
Vice-Pres. & General Mgr.,
H. Gordon Smith

TIRE
DIVISION

SALES
2nd Vice-Pres.,
George S. Shugart

163 Branches

MANUFACTURING
2nd Vice-Pres.,
Sheldon P. Thacher

3 Factories

GENERAL
LABORATORIES
Director,
W. A. Gibbons

DEVELOPMENT AND
PATENT DEPARTMENTS
Vice-Pres.,
Ernest Hopkinson

PATENT DEPT.
Manager,
W. L. Pipes

NAUGATUCK
CHEMICAL CO.
Vice-Pres. &
General Mgr.,
Elmer Roberts

U.S. RUBBER
EXPORT CO.
General Mgr.,
Chas. E. Guest

38 Branches

GENERAL
DIVISION
Vice-Pres.,
Homer E. Sawyer

SALES
2nd Vice-Pres.,
Herbert E. Smith

136 Branches
and Sales
Agencies

MANUFACTURING
2nd Vice-Pres.,
Edward J. Coughlin

31 Factories

April 23, 1929

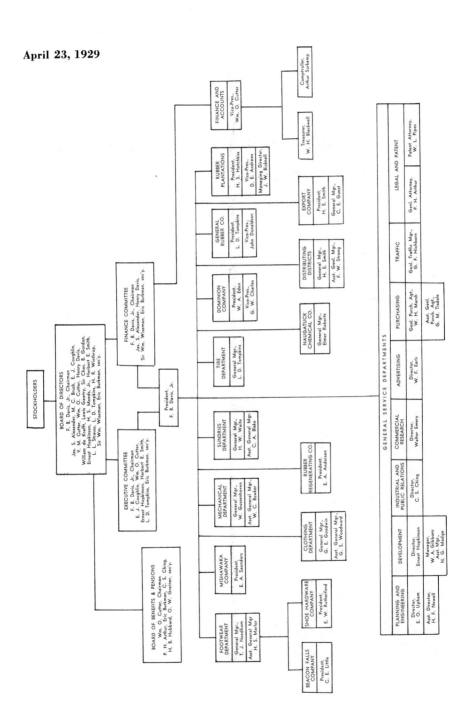

F

Major Subsidiary Companies, 1928

	Capital Stock	
	Authorized	*Issued*
American Rubber Company, Cambridge, Mass. (waterproof clothing, arctics, gum shoes, balloons)	$ 500,000	$ 500,000
Boston Rubber Shoe Company, Malden, Mass. (waterproof footwear, canvas shoes, soles and heels, lasts, carriage cloth)	1,000,000	1,000,000
Cady-Iverson Shoe Company (distributing)	200,000	189,100
Dolgeville Felt Shoe Company		
Preferred, $50 par	15,000	15,000
Common, $50 par	25,000	25,000
Dominion Rubber Company, Canada (footwear, tires, mechanical rubber goods, reclaimed)		
Preferred	3,000,000	3,000,000*
Common	3,000,000	3,000,000
Eureka Fire Hose Company, Jersey City, N. J. (cotton fire hose)	500,000	500,000
Fabric Fire Hose Company, Sandy Hook, Conn. (cotton fire hose)		
Preferred	50,000	50,000
Common	50,000	50,000
G and J Tire Company, Indianapolis (tubes, motorcycle tire casings, tire accessories)		
Preferred	1,000,000	
Common	1,000,000	1,000,000
General Rubber Company, New York City and overseas (procurement and sale of rubber)	10,000,000	10,000,000
Goodyear's India Rubber Glove Manufacturing Company, Naugatuck, Conn., $25 par (waterproof footwear, canvas shoes, drug sundries, hospital supplies)	500,000	500,000
Goodyear's India Rubber Selling Company, Naugatuck (distributing)	1,000	1,000
The Goodyear Metallic Rubber Shoe Company, Naugatuck, $25 par (waterproof footwear, canvas shoes)	50,000	50,000
H. B. Hanford Company (distributing)	60,000	60,000
The Hartford Rubber Works, Hartford, Conn. (tire casings)		
Preferred	1,000,000	500,000
Common	1,000,000	1,000,000

	Capital Stock	
	Authorized	*Issued*
Hubmark Rubber Company	1,000	1,000
Lycoming Rubber Company, Williamsport, Pa. (waterproof rubber footwear, canvas footwear)	500,000	400,000
McCord-Norton Shoe Company, Kansas City, Mo. (leather shoes)	2,000	2,000
William F. Mayo Company, Boston ("seconds" and "thirds," and job lots of footwear)	25,000	25,000
Mechanical Fabric Company, Providence (rubber thread, card cloth, coated and plied stockinet, rubber insulating tape)	1,000,000	150,000
The Mechanical Rubber Company, Cleveland and Chicago (molded specialties, jar rings, mats and matting, friction tape, hose, belting, packings, heels and soles, sundries, tubing)	1,400,000	1,400,000
Meyer Rubber Company, New Brunswick, N. J. (holding)	500,000	500,000
Mishawaka Rubber and Woolen Mfg. Co., Mishawaka, Ind., $50 par (BALL-BAND, waterproof footwear, canvas shoes, leather and woolen footwear)	700,000	700,000
Morgan and Wright, Detroit (tire casings)		
Preferred	3,000,000	3,000,000
Common	2,500,000	2,500,000
National India Rubber Company, Bristol, R. I. (KEDS, insulated wire and cable)		
Preferred	1,000,000	800,000
Common	2,500,000	2,500,000
Naugatuck Chemical Company, Naugatuck, $50 par (chemicals, labels)	250,000	250,000
New York Belting and Packing Company, Passaic (rubber hose, belting, rubber soles and heels, cotton hose, tubing, packings, molded specialties, sundries)	600,000	600,000
Revere Rubber Company, Chelsea, Mass. (rubber soles and heels, belting, rubber hose, packings, cotton hose, molded specialties, sundries)		
Preferred	3,000,000	500,000
Common	2,000,000	500,000
Rubber Regenerating Company, Mishawaka and Naugatuck (reclaimed rubber)	1,000,000	1,000,000
Rubber Regenerating Company, Ltd., Manchester, England (reclaimed rubber)	£150,000	£80,000
St. Paul Rubber Company, St. Paul (distributing)	25,000	25,000
The Shoe Hardware Company, Waterbury, Conn. (lasts, buckles)	100,000	100,000
United States Rubber, Inc. (incorporated in Delaware, 1928; holding)	25,000	25,000
United States Rubber Company, Utah (distributing)	25,000	25,000
United States Rubber Export Company, Ltd., New York City and overseas (export sales not including Canada)	100,000	25,000

	Capital Stock	
	Authorized	Issued
U. S. Tire Company, New York City (manufacture and sale of tires)	500,000	500,000
Winnsboro Mills, Winnsboro, N. C. (cotton tire cord, woven cotton fabrics)	2,000,000	2,000,000
Woonsocket Rubber Company, Woonsocket, R. I. (waterproof rubber footwear, canvas footwear)	1,500,000	500,000

*Of the preferred, 2,747,300 were owned by United States Rubber, and of the common, 2,799,800.

Many of the subsidiaries listed owned capital stocks of one or more other companies. For example, General Rubber Company owned the entire capital stock ($10 million) of United States Rubber Plantations, Inc., which owned the entire capital stocks of the subsidiaries—which in turn owned and operated the rubber plantations. Another subsidiary owned most of the capital stock of Beacon Falls Rubber Shoe Company, which in turn owned capital stock of other companies. Some subsidiaries also operated plants or owned the capital stock of distributing companies besides those listed here. Unted States Rubber Company also owned the entire capital stock of a number of subsidiaries that were inactive in 1928 and are not included in the foregoing list.

The company owned the leasehold and 20-story office building at Broadway and 58th Streets, New York City, in which its headquarters had been located since May, 1912. It also owned a modern laboratory building at Passaic, N.J., where the central development department and General Laboratories were located.

SOURCE: Listing Statement, A-8925, New York Stock Exchange, Dec. 1, 1928.

G

Letter from F. B. Davis, Jr. to

Stockholders and Employees

April 29, 1929

To Stockholders and Employees of the United States Rubber Company:

Since my election as President of the United States Rubber Company, I have given much careful thought, in collaboration with members of the organization, to those problems of the Company which appeared to require prompt attention, of which I conceive the problem of organization to be most urgent, lying as it does at the very foundation of all concerted action necessary to realize that large measure of success which I believe the Company can and ought to achieve.

It is gratifying to find in the personnel of the Company so much of capacity, intelligent ability, and loyalty to the principle of company success, that it has not been deemed necessary or desirable thus far to go outside of the company to fill any important position. We believe that with proper organization we have sufficient personnel within the Company to create within the old company a *new* company, imbued wih a new spirit, capable of bringing to successful fruition all those elements of fundamental advantage which the Company possesses.

It is the purpose of this letter to announce to you the plan of organization which has been decided upon.

Broadly, the new plan of organization involves changing the system of centralized control which has existed heretofore into one in which the Company's business is divided into separate departments or companies, each directed and operated by a General Manager—or a President in the case of a subsidiary operating under its own name—who will have control and absolute responsibility for all of the operations of his department. The departments are established along the lines of commodities or groups of commodities having common characteristics of manufacture or distribution, as follows:

Tire

Pneumatic Tires & Tubes; Solids & Cushion; Bicycle & Motorcycle Tires & Tubes; Airplane Tires & Tubes; Tire Accessories.

Footwear

Waterproof; Keds; House Slippers; Felt Goods; Leather Shoes.

Mechanical Goods

Belting; Hose & Packing; Moulded & Miscellaneous Goods; Wire & Tape; Mats & Matting; Interlocking Tiling; Jar Rings.

Sundries

Golf Balls; Thread; Card Cloth; Hard Rubber; Bathing Accessories; Druggists' Goods; Flooring; Soles & Heels.

Clothing

Waterproof Clothing; Naugahyde Specialties; Carriage & Auto Topping.

Rubber Regenerating Company

Reclaimed Rubber.

Naugatuck Chemical Company

Heavy Acids; Lotol (Latex composition); Accelerators; Anti Oxidants; other Chemicals.

Dominion Rubber Co., Ltd., Canada

Waterproof Footwear; Tennis Footwear; Felt Footwear; Mechanical Goods; Sundries; Tires & Tubes.

General Rubber Company

Sprayed Rubber; Liquid Latex; Crepe, Smoked Sheet and other market grades.

United States Rubber Plantations, Inc.

Ten Estates in British Malaya and Sumatra, D.E.I., comprising 135,100 acres owned, 88,500 acres planted, and 59,000 acres mature.

Distributing Districts

Warehouses located in principal cities of the United States.

United States Rubber Export Co., Ltd.

Branches and distributors located in all countries throughout the world.

The General Manager of each department will control all of its activities, including manufacturing, selling, accounting, and research and development, and will report to the President. Each General Manager is entitled to use all the general service departments of the Company, and in fact will be expected to avail himself of their help to the fullest extent. These general service departments are as follows:

Finance and Accounts

Planning and Engineering

Development

Industrial and Public Relations

Commercial Research

Advertising

Purchasing

Traffic

Legal and Patent

This type of organization is designed to give each General Manager the greatest freedom of action, and all the help which can be usefully availed of from each and every department and individual in the Company. Correspondingly, the General Manager will be held absolutely and solely responsible for the success of his department.

Representing the Board of Directors, and advising with the President in the general administration of all of the activities of the Company, are two committees, of Directors who, on account of special knowledge and experience, are best qualified namely, the Finance Committee and the Executive Committee.

The Finance Committee comprises the President and members of the Board to act in matters of corporate finance.

The Executive Committee is made up of those members of the organization who have heretofore been charged with the responsibility of some of the major activities of the Company as it has heretofore been organized. This Committee will hold regular meetings each week. Its function is to advise with the President in all of operations of the Company related to manufacturing, selling, and development and research, and to represent the Board of Directors in the supervision of the operations of the various departments. Each member is entitled to and should have full knowledge of the affairs of all departments, will receive copies of *all* reports from *all* the General Managers of the various departments, and is expected to enter into discussion and act in an advisory capacity with respect to all of the activities of the Company, whether or not such activities are those with which he has been directly connected in the past.

It is our purpose in the near future to have a plan providing for participation in the profits of the Company by those who, by industry and intelligent effort, or conspicuous ability, make outstanding contribution to the Company's success.

The Company possesses many special advantages in the rubber world, such as: the enormous good will attaching to its trade marks, many of which date back to the very beginning of the rubber industry; its strong position in the field of production and purchase of crude rubber, with branch crude rubber houses in all the rubber markets of the world; its rubber plantations, which are many times larger than those of any other American manufacturer, and in fact larger than those of any other single concern in the world; its position of leadership in the scientific production of crude rubber, which is recognized throughout the entire rubber producing world; the splendid personnel and efficient organization of its Development Department, which has to its credit practically all of the notable features of advance which have been made for a number of years past; for example, the production of the new latex sprayed rubber, web fabric, a special tire building process now utilized in the building of the majority of tires made throughout the world, the establishment of a new line of possibilities in the arts by the use of rubber in latex form, and the development of a new line of chemicals to be used as accelerators and anti-oxidants. To these special advantages should be added important ideas now in process of development in the General Laboratories.

With an organization operating as outlined above, giving proper value to the advantages which the Company possesses, and receiving the active, energetic support of stockholders and employees, the Company must realize the greatest measure of successful achievement.

Yours very truly,

(Signed) F. B. Davis, Jr., President.

H

Sales of United States Rubber Company

(in millions of dollars)

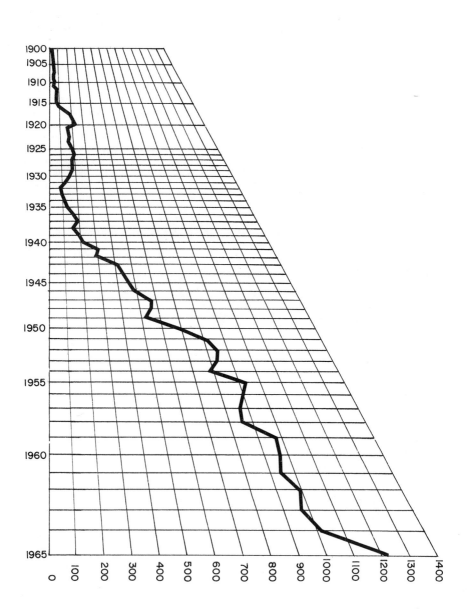

World War II Products

Airplane motor crankcases
Airplane seats
Airplane wing and tail sections
and subassemblies
Ammunition, .30 and .50 caliber
Antiaircraft shells, 40 mm.
Asbeston yarn, Asbeston fabrics, and
Asbeston fire-fighting suits
Assault wire
Aviators' winter flying shoes
Barrage balloons
Bogie wheels and rollers for tanks
and half-track vehicles
Bomb-loading equipment
Building wire for military structures
Bullet-sealing fuel cells and bladder-
type fuel cells
Bullet-sealing hose
Buna-S
C-102, a nonmetal substitute for
aluminum
Conductive sole rubber and leather
footwear for ordnance plants
Delousing bags
Demolition cable
Diving dresses
Ducts for warming airplane engines
Duffle socks
Electroformed intricate metal parts
Ferry tanks
Field telephone wire

Fittings for fuel cells
Frost covers for airplane wings
Fuel storage tanks and housings
Fuses and boosters
Inflatable boats, life rafts, and
pontons
Jettison tanks, auxiliary fuel cells for
airplanes, tanks, and other vehicles
Jungle boots
Jungle flotation bladders
Jungle food bags
Life preservers
Lifesaving suits
Machine tools for ammunition plants
Mustard gas latex gloves
Mukluks
Nonmetallic alcohol tanks
Parachute pack material
Parka suits
Powder bags for bullet loading
Shell-loading devices for 90 mm. and
17 mm. guns
Submarine jars
Tank treads, metal and rubber
Tourniquets
T.N.T.
Ustex yarns for parachute webs,
fire hose, and hydraulic hose
V-Boards and V-Board plastic cells
Water cells

NOTE: This list does not include tires and many other items related to peacetime production that were manufactured for the armed forces. Neither does it list those classed as essential for the economy or for the health and well-being of civilians. The list is chiefly intended to indicate the wide scope of the company's contribution to the war effort.

Flow of Materials Through
Intermediates to Finished Products, 1964

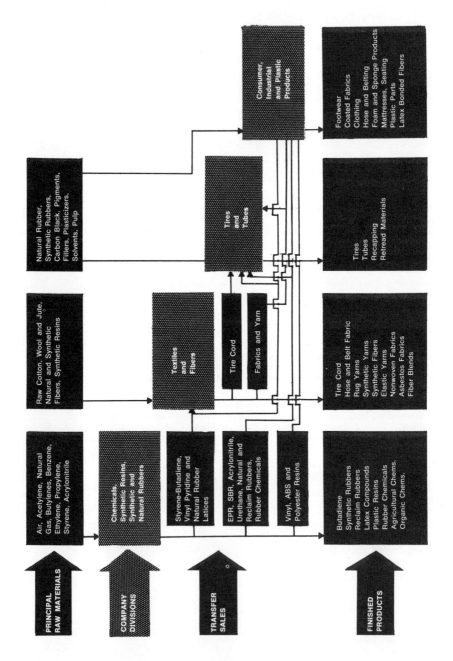

Bibliography

Bibliography

Books

ALDERFER, EVAN B., AND MICHL, H. E. *Economics of American Industry*. New York: McGraw-Hill Book Co., 1942.

ALLEN, HUGH. *The House of Goodyear*. Cleveland: The Corday and Gross Company, 1943.

ARNOLD, J. M. *Rubber*. Report of the Railroad Committee for the Study of Transportation. Unpublished. New York: American Association of Railroads, March 8, 1946.

Automobile Facts and Figures (1962 ed.). New York: Automobile Manufacturers Association, 1963.

BALL, JOHN M. *Reclaimed Rubber, The Story of an American Raw Material*. New York: Rubber Reclaimers Association, 1947.

BARKER, P. W. *Rubber: History, Production, and Manufacture*. U.S. Dept. of Commerce (Trade Promotion Series No. 209). Washington: Gov't Printing Office, 1940.

———. *Rubber Industry of the United States, 1839-1939*. U.S. Dept. of Commerce (Trade Promotion Series No. 197). Washington: Gov't Printing Office, 1939.

———. *Rubber: Some Facts on its History, Production, and Manufacture*. U.S. Dept. of Commerce. Washington: Gov't Printing Office, 1937.

BARUCH, BERNARD MANNES. *My Own Story*. New York: Henry Holt and Co., Inc., 1957.

BAUER, PETER T. *The Rubber Industry, a Study in Competition and Monopoly*. Cambridge: Harvard University Press, 1948.

Biennial Census of Manufactures, 1933, 1935, and 1937. U.S. Dept. of Commerce. Washington: Gov't Printing Office.

BOEKE, JULIUS H. *The Evolution of the Netherlands Indies Economy*. New York: Netherlands and Netherlands Indies Council, Institute of Pacific Relations, 1946.

BRADFORD, ERNEST S. "A Preliminary Report on the Golf Ball Market." Unpublished. New York: Feb. 6, 1917.

Brazil, 1939-1940, An Economic, Social and Geographic Survey. Quoted in *Industrial Reference Service, Part 10, Rubber and its Products* (No. 17). U.S. Dept. of Commerce. Washington: Gov't Printing Office, March, 1941.

Business Statistics (1959 biennial ed.). U.S. Dept. of Commerce, Washington: Gov't Printing Office, 1959.

CHANDLER, JR., ALFRED D. *Strategy and Structure, Chapters in the History of the Industrial Enterprise*. Cambridge: M.I.T. Press, 1962.

COLLIE, MURIEL F. *The Saga of the Abrasives Industry.* Greendale, Mass.; Grinding Wheel Institute and The Abrasive Grain Association, 1951.

COMMODITY YEAR BOOK, 1939. Also master ed., 1942, and 1948. New York: Commodity Research Bureau, Inc., 1939.

DEWHURST, J. FREDERIC, AND ASSOCIATES. *America's Needs and Resources.* New York: The Twentieth Century Fund, 1947.

DUCROS, SIR ARTHUR. *Wheels of Fortune.* London: Chapman and Hall, Ltd., 1938.

EDWARDS, CORWIN D. *The Price Discrimination Law, A Review of Experience.* Washington: The Brookings Institution, 1959.

EMMET, BORIS, AND JEUCK, JOHN E. *Catalogues and Counters.* Chicago: The University of Chicago Press, 1950.

EPSTEIN, RALPH C. *Concentration and Price Trends in the Rubber Tire Industry, 1930-1947.* Privately printed. 1949.

Federal Trade Commission Decisions, Findings, Orders and Stipulations, January 14, 1936 to July 9, 1936, XXII. Also *January 1, 1939 to May 31, 1939,* XXVII. Washington: Gov't Printing Office, 1939 and 1940.

FLINT, CHARLES R. *Memories of an Active Life.* New York: G. P. Putnam's Sons, 1923.

FLINT, CHARLES R., HILL, JAMES J., AND OTHERS in BRIDGE, JAMES H., ed. *The Trust: Its Book.* New York: Doubleday, Page and Company, 1902.

Foreign Commerce and Navigation of the United States, Calendar Year 1933. U.S. Dept. of Commerce. Washington: Gov't Printing Office, 1934.

GAFFEY, JOHN D. *The Productivity of Labor in the Rubber Tire Manufacturing Industry.* New York: Columbia University Press, 1940.

GOODYEAR, CHARLES. *Gum Elastic and Its Varieties.* New Haven: privately printed, 1853.

HAMILTON, WALTON, AND OTHERS. *Price and Price Policies.* New York: McGraw-Hill Book Company, 1938.

Historical Statistics of the United States, Colonial Times to 1957. U.S. Dept. of Commerce. Washington: Gov't Printing Office, 1960.

HOWARD, FRANK A. *Buna Rubber, The Birth of an Industry.* New York: D. Van Nostrand and Co., 1947.

ICKES, HARJLD L. *The Secret Diary of Harold L. Ickes, The First Thousand Days. 1933-1936.* New York: Simon and Schuster, 1954.

ILES, GEORGE in *Leading American Inventors.* New York: Henry Holt and Company, 1912.

Industrial Commission on Trusts and Industrial Consolidations, Report to 57th Congress, XIII. Washington: Gov't Printing Office, 1901.

LOWENTHAL, MAX. *The Investor Pays.* New York: Alfred A. Knopf, 1936.

McFADYEAN, SIR ANDREW. *The History of Rubber Regulation.* Edited for the International Rubber Regulation Committee. London: George Allen & Unwin, Ltd., 1944.

MEMMLER, D. K. (ed.) *The Science of Rubber.* Translated by R. F. Dunbrook and V. N. Morris. New York: Reinhold Publishing Corporation, 1934.

Moody's Manual of Investments, Industrial Securities, 1929. New York: Moody's Investors' Service, 1929.

NORTON, NANCY PAINE. "Industrial Pioneer: The Goodyear Metallic Rubber Shoe Company." Unpublished dissertation, Radcliffe College, 1950.

PARTON, JAMES in *Famous Americans of Recent Times.* Boston: Houghton, Mifflin and Company, 1867.

PEARCE, CHARLES ALBERT. *NRA Trade Practice Programs.* New York: Columbia University Press, 1939.

PELZER, KARL J. in PHILLIPS, TALBOT, ed. *South Asia in the World Today.* Chicago: University of Chicago Press, 1950.

PIERCE, FRANKLIN. *The Tariff and the Trusts.* New York: Macmillan Company, 1907.

Post-Trial Brief of the United States Rubber Company, Nov. 30, 1953, in the United States of America v. E. I. Du Pont de Nemours and Company, et al. in the U.S. District Court, Northern District of Illinois, Eastern Division. New York: privately printed, 1953.

Proceedings of the Second Pan-American Scientific Congress, Washington, D.C., 1915-1916. Washington: Gov't Printing Office, 1917.

Quarterly Financial Report for Manufacturing Corporations, Fourth Quarter, 1963. Federal Trade Commission. Washington: Gov't Printing Office, 1964.

REDMOND, GEORGE F. *Financial Giants of America,* II. Boston: The Stratford Company, 1922.

ROBERTS, HAROLD J. *The Rubber Workers.* New York: Harper and Brothers, 1944.

"Rubber," *Encyclopedia Britannica* (13th ed.), 1926.

Rubber Industry Facts, Statistical Appendix. New York: The Rubber Manufacturers Association, Inc., 1963.

"*The Rubber Industry in the U.S.A.*" Unpublished. New York: The Rubber Manufacturers Association, Inc., 1964.

Rubber Products Industry, A Statistical Compendium. New York: Industrial Conference Board, 1959.

Rubber Survey Committee, Report of, Sept. 10, 1942. Washington: Gov't Printing Office, n.d.

"Rubber, to Restrict the Use of." *Federal Register,* VI (Dec. 13, 1941); VII (Feb. 13, 1942); VII (April 4, 1942).

SINSABAUGH, CHRIS. *Who, Me? Forty Years of Automobile History.* Detroit: Arnold-Powers, Inc., 1940.

STERN, BORIS. *Labor Productivity in the Automobile Tire Industry.* U.S. Dept. of Labor Bulletin No. 585. Washington: Gov't Printing Office, July, 1933.

Statistical Abstract of the United States. U.S. Dept. of Commerce. Washington: Gov't Printing Office. Various issues.

Survey of Current Business, 1959 Statistical Supplement. U.S. Dept. of Commerce. Washington: Gov't Printing Office, 1959.

TOMPKINS, L. D. *Deposition, Transcript and Exhibits, United States v. Du Pont, General Motors, et al.* New York: privately printed, 1952.

TRACY, JOHN EVARTS. *Corporate Foreclosures, Receiverships and Reorganizations.* Chicago: Callaghan and Company, 1929.

The Vanderbilt Rubber Handbook (1948 ed.). New York: R. T. Vanderbilt Company, 1949.

VAN DER KROEF, JUSTUS M., in PHILLIPS, TALBOT (ed.). *South Asia in the World Today.* Chicago: University of Chicago Press, 1950.

WILSON, CHARLES MORROW. *Trees and Test Tubes.* New York: Henry Holt and Company, 1945.

Wholesale Prices, 1890-1926. U.S. Dept. of Labor (Bulletin No. 440). Washington: Gov't Printing Office, 1927.

"*Wholesale Prices, Wages, and Transportation,*" report by Mr. Aldrich, Committee on Finance, March 3, 1893, in *Reports of Committees of the Senate of the United States for the Second Session of the 52nd Congress, 1892-1893,* III Washington: Gov't Printing Office, 1893.

WOLF, HOWARD AND RALPH. *Rubber: A Story of Glory and Greed.* New York: Covici-Friede, 1936.

WOODRUFF, WILLIAM. *The Rise of the British Rubber Industry During the Nineteenth Century.* Liverpool: Liverpool University Press, 1958.

Periodicals and Newspapers

"*Annals of Rubber,*" reprinted from *India Rubber World*, 1936.

Bank and Quotation Record, V (Dec. 9, 1932), 93.

The Commercial and Financial Chronicle, CXXXVI (April 22, 1933), 2,812.

"The Dismissal Wage," *Factory and Industrial Management*, LXXIX (March, 1930), 536.

Dun's Review, XXXVII (Jan. 12, 1929), 26, and *Statistical Supplements*, I (February, 1937), 3.

Dun's Review and Modern Industry, LXXVII (February, 1961), 13.

The Financial Review, annual (1900, 1901, 1903, 1904).

Fuller, Warner. "The Background and Techniques of Equity and Bankruptcy Railroad Reorganizations—a Survey," *Law and Contemporary Problems*, VII (1940), 377-92.

Gibbons, Willis A. "The Rubber Industry, 1839-1939," *Industrial and Engineering Chemistry*, XXXI (October, 1939), 1,199 ff.

Hillman, Geoffrey T. " 'Two Way Stretch' Adamson," *Forbes* (April 15, 1934), 15.

Holt, E. G. "Some Fundamental Factors in the American Rubber Industry," *Survey of Current Business*, U.S. Dept. of Commerce (April, 1935).

———. "A Survey of the Rubber Industry," *Industrial Reference Service, Part 10, Rubber and Its Products*, U.S. Dept. of Commerce (August, 1941).

Hotchkiss, H. Stuart. "The Evolution of the World Rubber Situation," *Harvard Business Review*, II (January, 1924), 129-38.

Howe, Andrew M. "Don't be Afraid to Improve Your Trade-Mark," *Printer's Ink*, CL (March 27, 1930), 10-12.

India Rubber Journal, XCI (April 11, 1936), 430.

Jacobs, Nathan L. "The Interstate Commerce Commission and Interstate Railroad Reorganizations," *Harvard Law Review*, XLV (1931-1932), 865-89.

Keynes, J. M. "The Policy of Government Storage of Food Stuffs and Raw Materials," *The Economic Journal*, XLVIII (September, 1938), 450-51.

Reynolds, Lloyd G. "Competition in the Rubber Tire Industry," *American Economic Review*, XXVIII (September, 1938), 459-68.

Rubber, Industrial Reference Service, Part 10. U.S. Dept. of Commerce (1940), various issues.

"Rubber Plan Doesn't Stretch," *Business Week* (Feb. 23, 1935), 22.

"Rubber Scheme," *Business Week* (May 5, 1934), 22-23.

"Seger, Charles B." *Railway Age*, LXIV (March 22, 1918), 707.

Sutphen, VanTassel. Untitled article, *Harper's Weekly*, XLIII (April 8, 1899), 351-52.

"Textile Division, U.S. Rubber," reprint from *Textile Age* (November, 1942).

The New York Times. Numerous issues.

"U.S. Rubber, I, the Corporate State; II, Sumatra; III, Lastex," *Fortune*, IX (February, 1934), 52 ff.

"U.S. Rubber Moves Ahead," *Business Week* (Oct. 22, 1960), 100-111.

"United States Rubber Declares Dividend on its Common Stock," *Rubber Age*, XLVIII (March, 1941), 400-402.

Scottish Journal of Political Economy, II (February, 1955), 17-31.

William Woodruff. "An Inquiry Into the Origins of Invention and the Intercontinental Diffusion of Techniques of Production in the Rubber Industry," *The Economic Record* (Melbourne, 1962), 479-97.

Material from United States Rubber Company

A Brief History of the Organization of the United States Rubber Company. New York: privately printed, 1919.

EMERY, WALTER. "First Section of History of the United States Rubber Company." Unpublished. New York: 1946.

———. "History of Naugatuck Chemical Company," I. Unpublished. New York: 1946.

"Historical Highlights," New York: privately printed, n.d.

House Organ (later known as *Between US*). New York: privately printed company house organ, 1914-23.

"Minutes of the First Annual Sales Service Convention, Footwear Division, March 22-24, 1920." New York: privately printed, 1920.

NEWITT, GEORGE B. "History of the Fuel Cell Division, United States Rubber Company, 1940-1945." Unpublished. Mishawaka: 1947.

"Over 50 Years of Service through Creative Chemistry." New York: privately printed, ca. 1955.

"Report of Compliance of Respondent, Docket 3685, Federal Trade Commission." New York: privately printed, June 20, 1939.

Reports to Stockholders, Annual. New York: privately printed, 1893-1964.

The Ribbon and Seal. New York: privately printed house organ of United States Rubber Export Company, Ltd., 1922, 1923.

ROBERTS, LESLIE. "From Three Men." Montreal: privately printed by Dominion Rubber Company, Ltd., 1954.

Royal Dealer. New York: privately printed house organ of Tire Division, United States Rubber Company, June, 1963.

"Rubber from Forest to Foot." New York: privately printed supplement to *House Organ,* June, 1914.

SAWYER, HOMER E. *Histories of the United States Rubber Company and Some of the Subsidiary Companies.* New York: privately printed, 1915.

The Story of United States Rubber Company. New York: privately printed, 1946.

US. New York: privately printed company house organ, 1942, 1943.

"U.S." Rubber News. New York: privately printed company house organ, 1924-28.

NOTE: Additional information has been gained from applications filed by the company with the New York Stock Exchange for listing securities issued by the company. The author also has examined a body of papers connected with the operations of the company prior to 1943. This consisted of various memoranda, organization charts and notices, service records and other biographical information, notes of interviews, talks delivered to employees enrolled in training courses and to other groups, copies of correspondence, price lists, advertisements, and so on.

Other information, not otherwise available, has been gained from personal interviews and correspondence with many managerial personnel, including both active and retired executives of the company.

Index